WAR IN LATE ANTIQUITY

Ancient World at War

The books in this series are authoritative surveys of the relationship between warfare and the economy and culture of ancient Near Eastern and Mediterranean societies. The series explores the impact of military organization on social life and the place of war in the cultural and imaginative life of communities. It also considers the "face of battle," examining the experiences of combatants and civilians.

Published

War in Late Antiquity
A. D. Lee

War in the Hellenistic World
Angelos Chaniotis

War in Ancient Egypt
Anthony J. Spalinger

In Preparation

War in the Ancient Greek World
John Buckler

War in the Assyrian Empire
Mario Fales

War in the Roman Republic
John Serrati

War in the Ancient World
Philip de Souza

War in the Byzantine World
Frank Trombley

WAR IN LATE ANTIQUITY

A Social History

A. D. Lee

Blackwell Publishing

© 2007 by A. D. Lee

BLACKWELL PUBLISHING
350 Main Street, Malden, MA 02148-5020, USA
9600 Garsington Road, Oxford OX4 2DQ, UK
550 Swanston Street, Carlton, Victoria 3053, Australia

The right of A. D. Lee to be identified as the Author of this Work has been asserted in accordance with the UK Copyright, Designs, and Patents Act 1988.

All rights reserved. No part of this publication may be reproduced, stored in a retrieval system, or transmitted, in any form or by any means, electronic, mechanical, photocopying, recording or otherwise, except as permitted by the UK Copyright, Designs, and Patents Act 1988, without the prior permission of the publisher.

First published 2007 by Blackwell Publishing Ltd

1   2007

Library of Congress Cataloging-in-Publication Data

Lee, A. D.
 War in late antiquity : a social history / A. D. Lee.
   p. cm. — (Ancient world at war)
 Includes bibliographical references and index.
 ISBN 978-0-631-22925-4 (hardcover : alk. paper) — ISBN 978-0-631-22926-1 (pbk. : alk. paper) 1. Military art and science—Rome—History. 2. Rome—History, Military—30 B.C.-476 A.D. 3. War and society—Rome. I. Title.

U35.L44 2007
937'.08—dc22

2006036159

A catalogue record for this title is available from the British Library.

Set in 10/12pt Galliard
by SPi Publisher Services, Pondicherry, India
Printed and bound in Singapore
by COS Printers Pte Ltd

The publisher's policy is to use permanent paper from mills that operate a sustainable forestry policy, and which has been manufactured from pulp processed using acid-free and elementary chlorine-free practices. Furthermore, the publisher ensures that the text paper and cover board used have met acceptable environmental accreditation standards.

For further information on
Blackwell Publishing, visit our website:
www.blackwellpublishing.com

For James, Philip, and Naomi

CONTENTS

List of Figures ix
List of Maps x
List of Tables xi
Preface xii
Acknowledgments xv
Selected Roman Emperors during Late Antiquity xvi
Selected Persian Kings during Late Antiquity xviii
Table of Significant Events xix
Glossary xxi
List of Abbreviations xxiv

Introduction 1
  1. War and its Causes in Late Antiquity: An Overview 3
  2. The Evolution of the Late Roman Army: An Outline 9
  3. Ancient Sources for War and the Army in Late Antiquity: A Guide 14

1 Emperors and Warfare 21
  1.1. Changing Patterns of Imperial Involvement in Warfare 21
  1.2. The Unchanging Ideology of Victory 37

2 Military Loyalties and Civil War 51
  2.1. Retaining Soldiers' Loyalties 51
  2.2. Civil War and Military Unrest 66

3 The Infrastructure of War 74
  3.1. Manpower 74
  3.2. Supplying the Army 85
  3.3. Fortifications 98

4 The Economic Impact of War 101
  4.1. Economic Benefits of War 101
  4.2. Economic Costs of War 105

CONTENTS

5 The Experience of War — 123
   5.1. Soldiers — 125
   5.2. Urban Communities — 133
   5.3. Rural Communities — 138
   5.4. Women — 141

6 Soldiers and Society — 147
   6.1. Soldiers and their Families — 147
   6.2. Interaction between Military and Non-Military Elites — 153
   6.3. Military–Civilian Interaction at Non-Elite Levels — 163

7 Army, Warfare, and Religion — 176
   7.1. The Changing Religious Complexion of the Army — 176
   7.2. The Army and Religious Policy — 193
   7.3. A Christian Empire at War — 205

Notes — 212
Bibliography of Ancient Sources — 234
Bibliography of Modern Works — 240
Index of Ancient Sources — 263
General Index — 270

FIGURES

1.1.	Silver largesse plate of Valentinian I or II	43
1.2.	The Barberini ivory	44
1.3.	The victory column of Arcadius	46
1.4.	Gold *solidus* of the emperor Anastasius (491–518)	49
1.5.	Gold *solidus* of the emperor Valentinian III (425–55)	49
3.1.	Illustrations of the office of *magister officiorum* from the *Notitia Dignitatum*, showing the output of state arsenals (*fabricae*)	93
5.1.	Graffito from Dura-Europos depicting a town under siege	131
5.2.	Relief from the Arch of Constantine depicting the siege of Verona	132

MAPS

1. General map of the late Roman world   xxvi
2. State arsenals (*fabricae*)   91
3. The Balkans, Anatolia, and the *quaestura exercitus*   110
4. Egypt, Syria, Mesopotamia, and Persia   112

TABLES

1.1.	Emperors in Rome, 193–337	26
1.2.	Emperors in Rome and Constantinople, 337–95	31
2.1.	Expressions of esteem by emperors to troops (legal and documentary sources)	62
3.1.	Locations of arsenals (*fabricae*) by category of item produced	92
4.1.	Booty from Khusro's campaign in Syria, 540	103
4.2.	Subsidies paid by the empire to other states and peoples during late antiquity	121
6.1.	Correspondents with military officers of high rank: a summary	154
7.1.	Military intervention in church affairs during late antiquity	200

PREFACE

The military history of late antiquity has received significant attention in the last decade, notably in monographs by Hugh Elton, Geoffrey Greatrex, Martijn Nicasie, and John Haldon, as well as in important series of papers by scholars such as Peter Brennan, James Howard-Johnston, Philip Rance, Frank Trombley, Michael Whitby, and Constantine Zuckerman. The focus of much of this work, particularly the first three monographs, has been on strategy, tactics, and army structures – in other words, military history as usually understood. The monographs have also concentrated on discrete periods within late antiquity – so, Nicasie on the fourth century, Elton on the fourth and early fifth, and Greatrex on the early sixth. Haldon covers a more diverse range of subject matter, but since his primary concern is medieval Byzantine warfare, late antiquity receives attention only with respect to conditions in the later sixth and early seventh century.

While there are inevitably some points of overlap with elements of these studies (perhaps most obviously in Chapter 3), this book endeavors to follow a different overall trajectory. First, its concern is not with strategy, tactics, or campaigns *per se*, but rather with war in its wider social context, where "social" is interpreted in a very broad sense, as encompassing the political, economic, social, and religious dimensions of the late Roman empire – in other words, the ways in which warfare and the army impinged on "non-military" aspects of life. Secondly, it aims to deal with these topics across late antiquity as a whole, from the mid third to the early seventh century.

Needless to say, the volume's remit is potentially vast and I am conscious that there are subjects which might legitimately be included in a social history of war during late antiquity which do not feature here or have been dealt with more cursorily than they perhaps deserve. Moreover, the perspective adopted is primarily that of the empire, with only limited attention being given to the empire's neighbors, for whom the available sources are much more limited. The subjects which are treated here, however, are all ones which I consider to be of central importance to a rounded understanding of the wider impact of war and the Roman army in late antiquity, and I hope my discussion of them offers new insights not only into warfare and military institutions in this period, but also into many other aspects of the period, in ways which will be of interest to those who might not otherwise normally concern themselves with military history.

Numerous people have helped, in ways great and small, to bring this project to completion. Of fundamental importance has been the grant of a semester's leave by the School of Humanities at the University of Nottingham, and the provision of a second semester's leave through the Arts and Humanities Research Council's Study Leave scheme. I am particularly grateful to Peter Garnsey, Michael Whitby, and Peter Elford for their help in securing the latter, and to the AHRC for the funding which covered replacement teaching for a semester. My heartfelt thanks to John Drinkwater, who read a substantial number of draft chapters on which he offered invaluable detailed comment, as also to Mary McIntosh and David Noy for their helpful suggestions on drafts of the final chapter. I am also grateful to the two anonymous readers for Blackwell whose constructive feedback helped to improve the final text.

Early versions of sections of some chapters were presented as papers at two memorable conferences during 2005. My thanks to the audiences on both occasions for valuable feedback, and to the organizers for such enjoyable gatherings – Lukas de Blois and Elio Lo Cascio for the "Impact of the Roman Empire" workshop in Capri, and Ariel Lewin for the peripatetic "Late Roman Army in the Near East" conference at Potenza, Acerenza, and Matera. The University of Nottingham and the School of Humanities at Nottingham assisted with travel expenses for these two conferences respectively. The School of Humanities has also helped with the cost of some of the images. I am grateful as well to the audience at a departmental research seminar in Nottingham for helpful comments on a paper based on material from one chapter.

Numerous friends and colleagues have generously provided offprints or preprints of relevant articles, or help of other sorts, including Peter Brennan, Hugh Elton, Geoffrey Greatrex, Simon James, Noel Lenski, Ariel Lewin, Wolf Liebeschuetz, Katharina Lorenz, Andrew Poulter, Philip Rance, John Rich, Israel Shatzman, Ian Tompkins, Frank Trombley, Carrie Vout, Michael Whitby, Richard Winton, and David Woods. My thanks also to staff at the Hallward Library in Nottingham (especially Alison Stevens in Interlibrary Loans) and at the University Library and Classics Faculty Library in Cambridge. Not for the first time, my aunt Ruth provided valuable bibliographical help at an important stage. Finally, my thanks to Al Bertrand for inviting me to write this book and for his patient and calm support during the lengthy period of gestation, and to my copy-editor, Fiona Sewell, whose meticulous work has saved me from many inconsistencies and infelicities.

My wife Anna has once again borne with equanimity the stresses and strains which attend book production, particularly during the final lap, and I remain immensely grateful for her support and love. It would have been appropriate to dedicate this book to the memory of my father, who passed away during its writing, were it not for the fact that I have a long-standing commitment to my children which it is a pleasure to honor at last: thank you for the unique contribution which each one of you makes to our family, for your encouragement and patience during the writing process, and for helping me to keep late antiquity and academic life in proper perspective. This is not necessarily the particular subject on which I would have chosen to write a book for you, but you are old enough now to have some appreciation of the issues it raises, many of which remain relevant today.

ACKNOWLEDGMENTS

Acknowledgment is made to the following for permission to reprint substantial excerpts from translations:

Liverpool University Press, for excerpts from F. R. Trombley and J. W. Watt (trs.), *The Chronicle of Pseudo-Joshua the Stylite* (2000)

Harvard University Press for excerpts from the following volumes in the Loeb Classical Library:

> *Libanius: Selected Works*, vols. I–II (Loeb Classical Library 451–2), tr. A. F. Norman; Cambridge, Mass.: Harvard University Press, 1969–77
> *Libanius: Autobiography and Selected Letters*, vols. I–II (Loeb Classical Library 478–9), tr. A. F. Norman; Cambridge, Mass.: Harvard University Press, 1992
> *Procopius: History of the Wars*, vols. I–IV (Loeb Classical Library, 48, 81, 107, 173), tr. H. B. Dewing; Cambridge, Mass.: Harvard University Press, 1914–24
> *Procopius: De Aedificiis (On Buildings)* (Loeb Classical Library 343); trs. H. B. Dewing and G. Downey; Cambridge, Mass.: Harvard University Press, 1940

> All volumes copyright by the President and Fellows of Harvard College. The Loeb Classical Library® is a registered trademark of the President and Fellows of Harvard College.

Acknowledgment is made to the following for permission to reproduce illustrations: Musée d'art et d'histoire, Ville de Genève (Fig. 1.1); The Master and Fellows of Trinity College, Cambridge (Fig. 1.3); Dumbarton Oaks, Byzantine Collection, Washington, DC (Figs. 1.4, 1.5); the Société nationale des Antiquaires de France and the Département des Antiquités orientales du Musée du Louvre (Fig. 5.1); and Wayne Boucher (Fig. 5.2).

Every effort has been made to obtain permission for the use of copyright items. The author and publisher would be glad to hear from copyright holders not so acknowledged.

SELECTED ROMAN EMPERORS DURING LATE ANTIQUITY

This list presents the names and dates of emperors referred to in this volume from the early third to the early seventh century, apart from those whose only appearance is in Table 1.1, where their regnal years are specified anyway. The frequent overlapping of dates is due to the common late Roman practice of having co-emperors.

Septimius Severus	193–211
Caracalla	211–17
Macrinus	217–18
Severus Alexander	222–35
Maximinus	235–8
Gordian III	238–44
Philip	244–9
Decius	249–51
Valerian	253–60
Gallienus	253–68
Claudius II	268–70
Quintillus	270
Aurelian	270–5
Probus	276–82
Carus	282–3
Carinus	283–5
Numerian	283–4
Diocletian	284–305
Maximian	286–305
Constantius I	293–306
Galerius	293–311
Maxentius	306–12
Constantine I	306–37
Licinius	308–24
Constans	337–50

SELECTED ROMAN EMPERORS DURING LATE ANTIQUITY

Constantius II	337–61
Julian	361–3
Jovian	363–4
Valentinian I	364–75
Valens	364–78
Gratian	375–83
Valentinian II	375–92
Theodosius I	379–95
Arcadius	395–408
Honorius	395–423
Theodosius II	408–50
Constantius III	421
Valentinian III	425–55
Marcian	450–7
Avitus	455–6
Majorian	457–61
Leo I	457–74
Anthemius	467–72
Leo II	474
Julius Nepos	474–5
Zeno	474–91
Anastasius	491–518
Justin I	518–27
Justinian	527–65
Justin II	565–78
Tiberius II	578–82
Maurice	582–602
Phocas	602–10
Heraclius	610–41

SELECTED PERSIAN KINGS DURING LATE ANTIQUITY

Ardashir I	c.226–41
Shapur I	241–72
Narseh	293–302
Shapur II	309–79
Kavad	488–531
Khusro I	531–79
Khusro II	590–628

TABLE OF SIGNIFICANT EVENTS

c.226	Sasanian family overthrows Parthian Arsacid regime in Persia
249/50	Emperor Decius issues edict requiring sacrifice by all, thereby initiating first empire-wide persecution of Christians
260	Persian king Shapur I defeats and captures emperor Valerian in battle in northern Mesopotamia
299	Emperor Diocletian imposes humiliating peace settlement on Persia after Galerius' victory over Persian king Narseh the previous year
303	Emperor Diocletian initiates "Great Persecution" of Christians
312	Emperor Constantine defeats rival Maxentius outside Rome and begins supporting Christianity
324	Emperor Constantine defeats fellow-emperor Licinius and establishes new eastern capital of Constantinople at Byzantium
337	Persian king Shapur II embarks on first of three unsuccessful attempts to capture Roman frontier fortress of Nisibis (other attempts in 346 and 350)
351	Emperor Constantius II defeats western usurper Magnentius at Mursa
357	Junior emperor Julian defeats Alamannic confederation at Strasbourg
363	Emperor Julian invades Persia but dies of a wound during campaign; his successor Jovian surrenders Nisibis to Persia
376	Emperor Valens allows Goths to cross lower Danube and settle in Thrace
378	Goths inflict heavy defeat on major Roman army at Adrianople in Thrace
388	Emperor Theodosius I defeats western usurper Magnus Maximus
394	Emperor Theodosius I defeats western usurper Eugenius
406	Vandals and other Germanic tribes cross Rhine on New Year's Eve
429	Vandals cross from Spain to north Africa
439	Vandals capture Carthage
451	Roman general Aetius turns back Attila the Hun at battle of Chalons in Gaul

TABLE OF SIGNIFICANT EVENTS

468	Emperor Leo's expedition against Vandals is destroyed
476	Last western emperor (Romulus Augustulus) is deposed by Germanic general Odoacer
502	Persian king Kavad invades Roman territory in northern Mesopotamia where he besieges and eventually captures Amida (503)
505	Persian forces withdraw from northern Mesopotamia and emperor Anastasius has frontier fortress constructed at Dara
530	Roman general Belisarius defeats Persian army at Dara
531	Belisarius is defeated by Persian forces at Callinicum on Euphrates
533	Belisarius invades Vandal north Africa at Justinian's behest and completes overthrow of Vandal regime in following year
536	Belisarius invades Italian peninsula to reconquer it from Goths
540	Persian king Khusro I invades Syria, sacking many cities and extorting booty
541	Pandemic enters empire
552	Roman general Narses defeats Gothic king Totila at battle of Taginae in Italy, marking end of major hostilities in Gothic war
561/2	Emperor Justinian concludes 30-year peace agreement with Persia
572	Emperor Justin II abandons peace agreement with Persia and initiates abortive attempt to recapture Nisibis; campaign results in Persian capture of Dara
586	Roman victory against Persian forces at Solachon in northern Mesopotamia
590–1	Emperor Maurice helps to restore Khusro II to Persian throne
602	Military revolt on lower Danube results in overthrow of emperor Maurice and his replacement by army officer Phocas
604	Persian king Khusro II invades empire, making major territorial gains over following years
610	North African governor Heraclius overthrows Phocas
626	Joint Persian–Avar siege of Constantinople which eventually fails
628	Emperor Heraclius defeats Persian king Khusro II and captures Ctesiphon
636	Arab army defeats Roman army at River Yarmuk in Syria

GLOSSARY

adaeratio — commutation of a tax normally assessed and paid in kind to one paid in cash

annona — literally "the annual harvest"; used in a variety of senses: (1) the grain supply for the cities of Rome and Constantinople; (2) (especially when qualified with the adjective *militaris*) the collection and supply of grain to the army as part of the tax system established by Diocletian

Augustus — originally a key element in the name of the first Roman emperor (31 BC–AD 14), the term became a generic one for Roman emperors; during late antiquity it was not unusual for there to be two or more *Augusti* at the same time

Caesar — another common element in emperors' names during the Principate, it came in late antiquity to have the more precise meaning of junior emperor, as distinct from a senior emperor (Augustus)

comes rerum privatarum — "count of the privy purse"; a high-ranking financial official primarily responsible for managing the imperial estates, and the rents collected from them

comes sacrarum largitionum — literally "count of the sacred largesses"; a high-ranking financial official with oversight of matters relating to gold and silver – the mines that produced these metals, the mints that turned them into coinage, the taxes paid in them, and the payments in them to soldiers and bureaucrats

GLOSSARY

comitatenses	category of troops who "accompanied" the emperor, hence those in the mobile field armies, as distinct from the *limitanei*
comitatus	the emperor's retinue which, especially in the late third century, could include military units serving directly under the emperor's command
decennalia	celebration of the tenth anniversary of an emperor's accession to the throne
dux	senior officer in command of *limitanei* in a particular frontier province (or provinces)
exarch	literally "leader"; a position established in the late sixth century which combined civilian and military authority over the reconquered territories of Africa or Italy
fabricae	state arsenals for production of arms and armor
limitanei	category of troops stationed in frontier provinces (*limites*)
magister militum	literally "master of the soldiers"; the highest command in the late Roman army, though there were usually multiple *magistri* at any one time with oversight of different regions (often indicated by an additional phrase, e.g., *per Orientem* ("throughout the east"))
magister officiorum	literally "master of the offices"; a senior civilian palace official with oversight of the palace bureaucracy, the imperial communications network, and the state arsenals (*fabricae*)
nomismata	Greek term for *solidi*
Notitia Dignitatum	literally "register of dignities"; an administrative document recording the staff in the imperial bureaucracy and the military units under the command of different generals and officers
Principate	a modern term referring to the period of Roman history from the first emperor Augustus (31 BC–AD 14) to the early third century; the term derives from the Latin word *princeps* ("leading man"), the title which most emperors in this period preferred to use as a way of avoiding the flaunting of their power (in contrast to late Roman emperors who often

GLOSSARY

	used the undiluted title *dominus* ("master")); the Principate is often also referred to as "the Early Empire," in contrast to "the Late Empire" of the mid third to early seventh century
solidi (sing. *solidus*)	stable gold coin introduced by Constantine; 3 *solidi* is thought to have been enough for a man to survive on for a year; 72 *solidi* = 1 lb of gold
Tetrarchy	a modern term (literally "rule by four") referring to the arrangement put in place by the emperor Diocletian in 293 whereby he shared power with three colleagues, and by extension to the period from Diocletian's accession to the imperial throne in 284 until the final collapse of the last vestiges of the arrangement when Constantine established himself as sole ruler of the empire in 324
vicennalia	celebration of the twentieth anniversary of an emperor's accession to the throne

ABBREVIATIONS

AABS	Australian Association of Byzantine Studies
ACW	*Ancient Christian Writers*
AE	*L'Année épigraphique*
ANRW	*Aufstieg und Niedergang der römischen Welt*
AnTard	*Antiquité tardive*
BGU	*Berliner griechische Urkunden*
BMGS	*Byzantine and Modern Greek Studies*
CCSL	*Corpus Christianorum Series Latina* (Turnhout, 1953–)
CIL	*Corpus Inscriptionum Latinarum*
CPL	*Corpus Papyrorum Latinarum*, ed. R. Cavenaile (Wiesbaden, 1958)
CPR	*Corpus Papyrorum Raineri* (Vienna, 1895–)
CSEL	*Corpus Scriptorum Ecclesiasticorum Latinorum*
DOP	*Dumbarton Oaks Papers*
FoC	*Fathers of the Church*
fr.	fragment
GRBS	*Greek, Roman and Byzantine Studies*
HSCP	*Harvard Studies in Classical Philology*
HTR	*Harvard Theological Review*
IGR	*Inscriptiones Graecae ad res Romanas pertinentes,* eds. R. Cagnat et al. (Paris, 1911–27)
ILS	*Inscriptiones Latinae Selectae,* ed. H. Dessau (Berlin, 1892–1916)
JRA	*Journal of Roman Archaeology*
JRS	*Journal of Roman Studies*
JTS	*Journal of Theological Studies*
MGH	*Monumenta Germaniae Historica*
MGH.AA	*Monumenta Germaniae Historica (Auctores Antiquissimi)*
MSNAF	*Mémoires de la société nationale des antiquaires de France*
NPNCF	Nicene and Post-Nicene Church Fathers
P.	papyrus
P&P	*Past & Present*
PBSR	*Papers of the British School at Rome*
PG	*Patrologia Graeca*, ed. J. P. Migne (Paris, 1857–1912)

ABBREVIATIONS

PL	*Patrologia Latina*, ed. J. P. Migne (Paris, 1844–64)
PLRE	*Prosopography of the Later Roman Empire*, ed. J. Martindale (Cambridge, 1971–92)
PO	*Patrologia Orientalis* (Paris, 1903–)
PSI	*Papiri greci e latini (Pubblicazioni della Società italiana per la ricerca dei papyri greci e latini in Egitto)* (Florence, 1912–)
RAC	*Reallexikon für Antike und Christentum*
RE	*Realencyclopädie der klassischen Altertumswissenschaft*, eds. A. Pauly, G. Wissowa, and W. Kroll (Stuttgart, 1893–)
RH	*Revue historique*
RIC	*Roman Imperial Coinage* (London, 1923–94)
SC	*Sources chrétiennes* (Paris, 1941–)
SEG	*Supplementum Epigraphicum Graecum*
TTH	Translated Texts for Historians (Liverpool)
ZPE	*Zeitschrift für Papyrologie und Epigraphik*

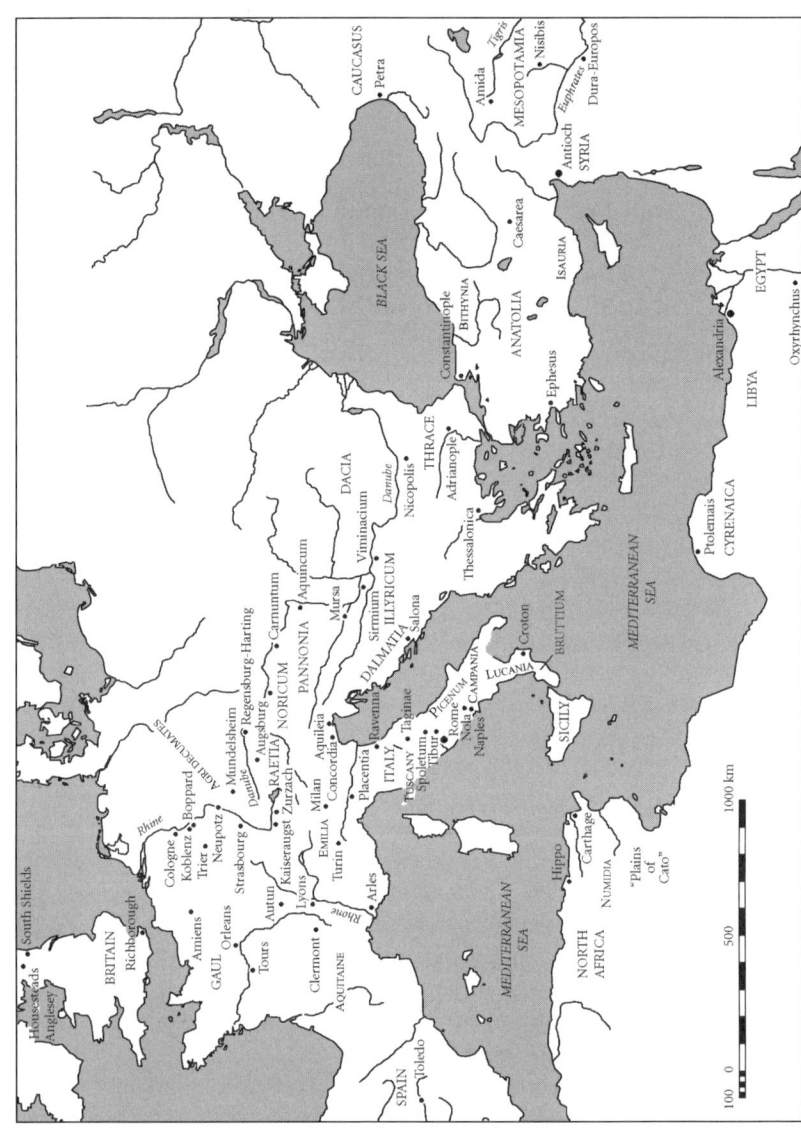

Map 1　General map of the late Roman world.

INTRODUCTION

War was a defining feature of Roman history during late antiquity. Intensive bouts of war framed the period – Persian and Germanic invasions in the mid third century, and Persian and Arab invasions in the early seventh[1] – while the regular incidence of war in the intervening centuries was also a significant characteristic of the period, particularly when compared with the centuries immediately preceding late antiquity. During the middle and late Republic (c.300–30 BC), there had rarely been a year in which the Roman state was not at war, either expanding territorial control in the Mediterranean or, in the first century BC, caught up in civil war. However, the tempo of war in Roman history was not constant. One feature which famously made Augustus' new monarchical system of government palatable to many in the empire was the cessation of civil war (Tacitus *Annals* 1.2), as monumentalized in his Altar of Peace. It was also the case that during the period from Augustus (31 BC–AD 14) to the early third century – the so-called Principate – the empire engaged in wars of expansion much less frequently than during the Republic, and external threats were limited. Moreover, while Augustus' new political arrangements did not manage to eliminate civil war completely, it became a rarer phenomenon during the first two centuries AD.

However, the incidence of war increased once again in the middle decades of the third century, and rarely relented thereafter during late antiquity. To the east, Sasanian Persia posed a much more serious military threat than the Parthian Arsacid regime had during the Principate, while a variety of Germanic and Asiatic peoples along the empire's northern frontier presented significant challenges. Some of the latter eventually occupied different parts of the western half of the empire during the fifth century and ended Roman political control in the western Mediterranean. Attempts to regain control of parts of the west, culminating in the campaigns initiated by the emperor Justinian in the mid sixth century, generated further warfare. Furthermore, internal rebellions and civil war once again became a more common phenomenon.

War was also a defining feature of late antiquity in so far as its renewed incidence contributed significantly to important changes in the empire's infrastructure. Not surprisingly, these changes included reorganization of the armed forces (outlined in the second section of this Introduction) and the underlying fiscal system (see Chapter 3.2.1 below). A further reflection of the more militarily oriented focus of government was the use of the term *militia* to refer not only to service in the army, but also to service in the civilian bureaucracy (a development which found physical expression in the military-style attire which late Roman bureaucrats wore: cf. Kelly 2004: 20–1). The greater incidence of war also affected the office of emperor, particularly during the first half of late antiquity since military competence now became an essential qualification for imperial office, resulting in the senatorial aristocracy losing the virtual monopoly on that position which they had held during the Principate (see Chapter 1.1.1 below).

As its subtitle is intended to indicate, however, this volume is not a history of war in the traditional sense. It does not devote space to such staples of the genre as campaigns, strategy, or tactics. Rather, its concern is to investigate war during late antiquity in the wider context of social history, where "social" is interpreted in very broad terms to encompass political, economic, social, and religious life – the interrelationships between war and these areas of life, and its impact on them. Such an approach necessarily gives considerable attention also to the "non-military" aspects of the institution most directly concerned with warfare – the late Roman army.

Chapter 1 starts at the top by focusing on the relationship between late Roman emperors and warfare, examining the factors which influenced the changing pattern of imperial involvement in war from the soldier emperors of the late third century to the palace-bound rulers of the fifth and sixth centuries, and the return to active participation in the early seventh. This chapter also considers the implications of these changing levels of participation for the legitimation of the emperor's position vis-à-vis the traditional ideology of military success.

Warfare during late antiquity was by no means always restricted to encounters with foreign enemies. Internal conflict between emperors and challengers and/or discontented troops was also a significant feature of the period. Chapter 2 investigates the strategies through which emperors sought to reinforce the loyalty of soldiers and minimize the scope for problems on this front, as well as examining the changing factors responsible for civil war and military unrest.

In Chapter 3, the focus shifts from the political sphere to that of the economic resources of the empire. It examines the infrastructure of war with reference to sources of military manpower, the use of the fiscal system to extract the money and supplies necessary for the maintenance of the army, the production of matériel, campaign logistics, and the economics of fortifications.

The economic theme continues in Chapter 4, albeit from a different angle – the economic benefits and costs of warfare. Significantly, much more can be said about the latter than the former, from a variety of perspectives – the costs of unsuccessful campaigns, the costs of being invaded, the costs of lost territory, and the costs of avoiding war.

Chapter 5 explores the human cost of conflict by investigating the experience of war in late antiquity from the bottom up – not just for combatants, but also for civilians in both urban and rural contexts, with specific attention to its impact on women.

Chapter 6 pursues the social thread initiated in the previous chapter by examining the theme of soldiers and society from a number of angles. Discussion of the family life of soldiers is followed by an investigation of relations between military and non-military at different levels of society.

Chapter 7 examines another important dimension of social history in the form of the army, warfare, and religion. A central issue here is the impact of Christianity on the ethos of the army, which entails discussion of Christian attitudes to war. The chapter also investigates the role of the army in the implementation of religious policy, and concludes with consideration of the impact of Christianity on the empire's reasons for waging war and effectiveness in doing so.

In view of the volume's deliberate avoidance of the more traditional aspects of military history, the remainder of this Introduction provides background detail on some of these aspects necessary for an understanding of what follows – specifically, an overview of the causes of war in late antiquity (which also serves as a guide to the major episodes of conflict), and an outline of the evolution of the Roman army during late antiquity. Finally, the most important ancient sources are introduced.

1. War and its Causes in Late Antiquity: An Overview

Investigation of the factors which precipitated war during late antiquity primarily entails consideration of the empire's relations with its neighbors to the east and the north. In order to keep it within reasonable bounds, however, this investigation avoids explicit discussion of a number of broader issues about which whole books could be and have been written, in particular the role of the barbarian invasions in the fall of the western half of the empire, and the debate about imperial "grand strategy" (both of which can, however, be pursued through the suggestions for further reading indicated at the end of the Introduction). It also privileges larger-scale conflicts at the expense of the "background noise" of low-level raiding and skirmishing which was the more typical experience for many of those living in frontier regions, since it is the former about which the ancient sources have far more to say. At the same time, it does draw attention to the various types of armed conflict generated within the empire.

The empire's most powerful enemy was Sasanian Persia, which controlled much of the region covered today by Iraq, Iran, and Afghanistan. Sasanian Persia had the resources and the organizational capability to present a serious challenge to the Roman empire (Lee 1993: 15–20; Howard-Johnston 1995). It controlled a very substantial territorial base, and its ability to develop and expand the Tigris–Euphrates irrigation network which it inherited from previous regimes is testimony to its capacity to tackle complex administrative tasks. There can be no doubt that the establishment of the Sasanian dynasty in place of the Parthian Arsacids in the mid 220s contributed to the greater frequency of war in this region during late antiquity. Successful leadership in external wars was an important ingredient in the legitimation of Persian kings and the maintenance of their internal position (Michael Whitby 1994), and while Persian infantry may not have been a match for Roman strength in this area of combat, this disadvantage was offset to a significant degree by Persian prowess on horseback. Moreover, the Persians proved competent in the important area of siege warfare.

None of this is to say that the Persians were always or primarily responsible for the initiation of war. It was more a case of a cycle of aggression and counter-aggression fueled by mutual suspicion (cf. Lee 1993: 20–5). Successive Roman campaigns down the Euphrates against the Parthian capital at Ctesiphon during the second century (which had helped to undermine confidence in the Arsacids and thereby contributed indirectly to their replacement by a more proactive regime) had instilled a mistrust of Roman intentions, and must have contributed to the new Persian government's willingness to invade Roman territory in the 230s and 250s. Roman invasions of Persian territory – such as those initiated by Gordian III and his advisers in the early 240s, Carus in the early 280s, and Galerius in the late 290s – were to a significant degree attempts to redress the balance.

Galerius' victory in 298 and the ensuing settlement of 299 established the parameters of relations for much of the fourth century. Judging by the actions of Shapur II during the 330s to 350s, the Persians were determined to undo the surrender of territory east of the Tigris which had been imposed upon them in the peace treaty, and to prevent a recurrence by forcing a Roman withdrawal from the northern Mesopotamian strong point of Nisibis. However, Shapur's three attempts to capture that city failed, and it was only the debacle of the emperor Julian's invasion of Persia in 363 which finally gave Shapur the opportunity to dictate terms. Significantly, however, he did not try to push the frontier any further west, despite previous Sasanian rhetoric about restoring the Achaemenid Persian empire of old (that is, the empire of Darius and Xerxes in the fifth century BC, which had included all of Anatolia). As for Julian's ill-fated expedition, it does not seem to have been his intention to bring additional tracts of Persian territory under direct Roman control, since he apparently intended to withdraw after one campaigning season (cf. Ammianus 23.2.5); rather, it was a case of a riposte to recent Persian pressure and possibly the placing of a Roman nominee on the Persian throne (cf. Libanius *Letters* 1402). It has also sometimes been seen as an attempt to solve domestic problems through foreign policy – in this case, the evident lack of progress in Julian's attempt to undo the consequences of Constantine's support for Christianity and revitalize traditional cults in the empire. It is likely that success in Persia would have restored the momentum of his religious policies within the Roman empire (cf. Browning 1975: 193). As with any military endeavor into Persia during the Roman period, too, one should not discount the baleful influence of the specter of Alexander the Great, luring individuals to try to emulate his example.[2]

Constantine's support for Christianity and – Julian's short reign aside – the progressive influence of that religion on the Roman state had other important implications for Roman–Persian conflict. Constantine's willingness to champion Christianity's cause prompted him in the late 320s to send Shapur II a letter containing a veiled threat against the Persian king, should he mistreat the Christians living within his kingdom, whose presence had been swelled by the prisoners of war carried off from eastern Roman cities by the Persians during the mid third century (Eusebius *Life of Constantine* 4.9–13). Constantine appears to have been preparing to make good that threat with a planned invasion of Persia in 337, only prevented by his death (Barnes 1985a). Subsequent emperors, however, were to justify the initiation of war against Persia by reference to the mistreatment of Christians living within Persian territory, as Theodosius II and Justin II did in 421 and 572 respectively (Socrates *Church History* 7.17 with Holum 1977; Evagrius *Church History* 5.7). The difficulty is to know to what extent religious concerns were a genuine motivation and to what extent they were a convenient pretext. As with other subjects in Roman history, trying to draw too sharp a distinction between religion and politics may risk imposing an anachronistic and false dichotomy, but it is also apparent that both Constantine and Theodosius II took their Christianity seriously enough for such concerns to constitute a genuine reason. At the same time, one can also identify plausible non-religious motivations, at least in the cases of Theodosius II and Justin II: neither had any military pedigree and so stood to benefit from military success, while Justin II was keen to free himself from the burden of annual payments to the Persians which he had inherited through Justinian's peace treaty of 561/2 (for further discussion of this issue, see Chapter 7.3.1, pp. 205–7).

More traditional concerns with booty and plunder seem to have been the primary motivation behind the Persian invasions of 502 and 540 initiated by kings Kavad and Khusro I respectively: the former was seeking redress for Roman unwillingness to contribute financially to the defense of the Caucasian passes against nomadic invaders from the north, while the latter took advantage of Roman preoccupations in the western Mediterranean to extract substantial sums of money from the cities of Syria through sacking them or threatening to do so (see Chapter 4.1 below). The final and most intense conflict between the two powers in the early seventh century, however, had very different origins. The Roman emperor Maurice had helped a young Khusro II regain his throne in 591 following a military coup; after the former was himself toppled and killed in a military coup in 602, Khusro invaded Roman territory. His formal justification was a desire to avenge the death of his mentor Maurice, but it is hard not to suspect that his real motivation was a concern to demonstrate to the Persian nobility that he was not beholden to the Romans. Against a background of internal turmoil within the Roman empire, Khusro's invasion achieved rapid and unprecedented success, with Persian forces occupying Egypt for the first time and advancing deep into Anatolia. This is unlikely to have been Khusro's aim at the outset, but one can well understand his ambitions expanding as his troops maintained their forward advance. By 626, Persian forces were besieging Constantinople, and Khusro must have believed that he was close to overthrowing the Roman empire. That hope was undone by the daring counter-strategy of the emperor Heraclius which resulted in the Persian capital of Ctesiphon, rather than Constantinople, being sacked within a few years (for the details see Howard-Johnston 1999; Kaegi 2003: 100–91). One might have anticipated that the ensuing dynastic upheaval in Persia would facilitate an end to any serious military problem in the region for the foreseeable future, but any such hopes soon evaporated in the face of the unexpected emergence of a new threat from Arab tribes, energized by the new religion of Islam, whose forces were able to take rapid advantage of the war-weariness of the two powers during the 630s to overthrow the Sasanian dynasty and dispossess the Roman empire of many of its most economically valuable provinces in the east, above all Egypt.

Whereas the advent of the Sasanian dynasty in Persia offers at least the start of an explanation as to why the empire's eastern frontier proved a war-prone zone during late antiquity, there is no such straightforward explanation with regard to the northern frontier and the peoples in the regions beyond the Rhine and the Danube. During the third and fourth centuries these were Germanic tribes, and the reason why they posed a more serious problem compared with their forebears during the Principate appears to be related to their coalescing into larger units, sometimes described in modern discussions as confederations. Just as Sasanian aggression in the mid third century can be linked indirectly to Roman aggression against the Parthian Arsacids in the second, so the greater threat posed by Germanic tribes in the third century can be attributed to the impact of earlier Roman diplomacy, trade, and culture on the tribes, which unintentionally facilitated more centralized political structures. However, weaknesses in military organization still usually left them at a disadvantage relative to Roman forces (Todd 1975: 179–80; Elton 1996: 45–88), and the prime objective of these tribal confederations during the third and much of the fourth century seems to have been acquisition of booty from Roman territory, rather than permanent settlement on Roman land. In the same way, Roman expeditions beyond the northern frontier in this period were generally intended to destabilize tribal structures and to serve as deterrents against further raiding, rather than to add new territory to the empire.[3]

It was only under the onslaught of the nomadic Huns from Central Asia in the later fourth century that one Gothic confederation, the Tervingi, requested, and was granted, imperial permission to settle within the empire. There were many precedents for such an arrangement, which need not have resulted in conflict, but in this case abuses by some of the Roman officials overseeing the settling of the Goths provoked a revolt among the latter and initiated half a decade of warfare during which the Romans suffered considerable losses, both in manpower and prestige. Thereafter Germanic incomers became increasingly keen to settle permanently on Roman territory and their leaders to extract honors and resources from the Roman state. Much of the warfare of the fifth century involved Roman attempts to contain these groups, while also fending off fresh threats to the northern frontier, particularly from the Huns, whose horsemanship and expertise in archery posed serious problems for the empire. Although the Hunnic threat was eventually seen off in the east, attempts at containment of Germanic peoples in the west mostly failed, and prime provinces were gradually removed from the imperial orbit until imperial authority in the west disappeared completely during the 470s.

It is worth pausing at this point to reflect on the contrasting fates of east and west during the fifth century. These were at least in part the result of diverging military capabilities, but these in turn, to an important degree, reflected differences in underlying infrastructures and circumstances. The eastern half of the empire was wealthier and more populous than the west, and importantly, its richest region – Egypt – was never exposed to serious external threat during these years. Moreover, the fifth century was the one century during late antiquity when the east's major enemy – Persia – was (with two minor exceptions) preoccupied elsewhere, allowing Constantinople to concentrate more of its military resources on the lower Danube. Although the east experienced periods of political instability and civil war, these came in the final decades of the century. In the west, on the other hand, the early decades of the fifth century featured a highly disruptive combination of civil war and foreign invasion, which initiated the process whereby the imperial court increasingly lost control of significant regions and their revenues. The most serious loss in this respect was the Vandal occupation of north Africa during the 430s – the wealthiest part of the west – which hamstrung the ability of western emperors to maintain the army at previous levels. Instead, generals found themselves having to come to arrangements with Germanic settlers whereby they provided troops in return for more land or other inducements, most notably in the coalition of disparate forces which the Roman commander Aetius assembled to meet Attila's thrust into Gaul in 451. This was therefore a significantly different army to that of the fourth century and that in the east in the fifth century.

INTRODUCTION

The importance of north Africa's wealth prompted a number of abortive imperial campaigns, initiated from Constantinople, to regain it from the Vandals during the fifth century. Despite this discouraging record, Justinian launched a fresh invasion in 533 which met with surprisingly rapid success, and prompted him to follow it up with an attempt to reclaim Italy from the Goths. It has sometimes been suggested that Justinian's initial decision to invade north Africa was actually an attempt to re-establish his credibility after the embarrassment of the so-called Nika riot the previous year, when he was almost driven from the imperial throne by the mob in Constantinople (cf. Averil Cameron 1993b: 108–9) – in other words, another example of emperors resorting to foreign adventures as a way of solving a domestic problem – although Justinian does seem to have had a larger vision for the restoration of Roman greatness from the outset of his reign (cf. Honoré 1978: 18–19). At any rate, it was only in these contexts that the Roman empire of late antiquity embarked on what might be described as expansionist wars, though since their objective was the recovery of what had, until comparatively recently, long been imperial territory, they were "expansionist" only in a rather restricted sense.

The campaign in Italy proceeded with considerable success until the early 540s when a nexus of circumstances – a more energetic Gothic king in Italy, renewed Persian aggression in the east, and the destabilizing impact of a Mediterranean-wide pandemic – combined to ensure that the war dragged on for another decade. At the same time, the rapid reconquest of Africa turned sour as indigenous Berber tribesmen proved increasingly troublesome with their persistent raiding. Little more than a decade had elapsed after the final termination of war in Italy in the early 550s before another Germanic people, the Lombards, invaded the peninsula and initiated a fresh bout of warfare, while the arrival of another nomadic people from Central Asia, the Avars, on the lower Danube frontier was the signal for further conflict there and in the northern Balkans, which was to last on and off until the 620s (including their co-operation with the Persians in the siege of Constantinople in 626). Problems in this region were compounded by the low-intensity warfare of Slavs who launched periodic small-scale raids into the Balkans.[4]

As if war with foreign states and peoples was not a regular enough occurrence during late antiquity, there were also plenty of instances of internal conflict (discussed in more detail in Chapter 2.2). After the almost endemic incidence of military rebellion and civil war during the middle decades of the third century, the more stable conditions of the fourth century still had their fair share of internal conflicts. Most of these were the result of individual ambition to gain or extend imperial power, and the understandable desire of an incumbent to suppress such attempts – so, for example, Constantine against Maxentius and Licinius in the early decades of the fourth century, Constantius II against Magnentius and Julian in the early

350s and 360s, Procopius and Valens in the mid 360s, and Theodosius I against Magnus Maximus and Eugenius in the late 380s and early 390s. The wild region of Isauria in south-eastern Anatolia, infamous for its brigandage, also required the commitment of significant military forces during the fourth century to contain outbreaks of conflict between highland raiders and settled communities (Matthews 1989: 355–67) – one example out of many illustrating the point that the army often played as important a role in maintaining internal order as it did in defending the empire's frontiers (a theme emphasized by Isaac 1992).

As already noted, the early decades of the fifth century in Britain and Gaul were characterized by considerable internal strife, arising from a combination of short-lived usurpers, the impact of foreign invaders, and the more mysterious phenomenon of the Bacaudae in western Gaul, who have been portrayed by some as peasant rebels, and by others as local notables showing too strong an inclination toward independence from the state.[5] In the east, the new century began with the abortive revolt by the Gothic general Gainas in 400, but thereafter internal conflict was less common until the later decades of the century when leading figures from Isauria became involved in imperial politics – involvement which generated civil war in the 480s (Zeno against Illus) and the 490s (Anastasius against Longinus).[6] The Samaritans, an offshoot of Judaism in Palestine, also initiated significant revolts against the imperial authorities in 484 and 529 (Isaac 1992: 89–90) – one instance of many from late antiquity of internal conflict with a religious dimension.[7] Mutiny by the army rank and file was another theme in these later centuries, as in north Africa following its reconquest from the Vandals, and Phocas' rebellion against Maurice in 602, precipitated by the unhappiness of soldiers being forced to winter north of the Danube. Finally, the category of internal armed conflict might even be extended to include urban rioting and its suppression by military force, with the most notorious example being the Nika riot in Constantinople in 532, which almost resulted in the overthrow of Justinian (Gregory 1983; Liebeschuetz 2001: 249–83).

The end of antiquity, signaled by the Arab invasions of the early seventh century, was not marked by any slackening in the tempo of warfare and armed conflict. If anything, that tempo increased and intensified through the seventh century. However, the Roman empire changed so significantly as a result of the Arab inroads – huge territorial losses demanded a radical rethinking of the empire's military infrastructure[8] – that as far as the "social" history of war is concerned, the early seventh century marks a major watershed.

2. The Evolution of the Late Roman Army: An Outline

The organizational development of the late Roman army is not a primary concern of this study, but some knowledge of its salient features will facilitate understanding of the subject matter of the chapters which follow.[9] Although their recognizable descendant, the Roman army during late antiquity was in many respects very different from the Roman forces which had conquered Gaul under the command of Julius Caesar in the first century BC and subdued the Jewish rebels in Jerusalem and Masada in the first century AD. The core of the army of the late Republic and Principate had been the citizen legions of 5,000–6,000 heavy infantry, supplemented by units of light infantry and cavalry recruited from provincials (the *auxilia*). During the Principate, there was an increasing trend toward the permanent stationing of units on the frontiers, with detachments (*vexillationes*) being withdrawn temporarily in the event of an expeditionary force being needed. By contrast, the army of the fourth century comprised a greater number of smaller units, with a typical unit size of 1,000 men or fewer; the role of cavalry had become more prominent; and regional field armies stationed away from the frontiers (whose troops were known as *comitatenses* because, initially at least, they accompanied the emperor on campaign) had become a permanent feature, alongside the other major category of soldier, usually referred to as *limitanei* – those based in the *limites* or frontier provinces.[10]

The larger number of smaller units gave greater scope for flexibility in deployment and supply, and for specialization of expertise (cf. Brennan 1980, 1998c), while the greater prominence of cavalry afforded increased tactical mobility – although the significance of this development ought not to be overemphasized at the expense of the role of infantry, which remained fundamental (cf. Michael Whitby 2004: 160–3). It is the emergence of the distinction between *comitatenses* and *limitanei*, however, which has occasioned the most significant debate. Some of this debate has concerned the identification of possible precursors of a strategic reserve in Septimius Severus' increasing the forces stationed in Italy at the start of the third century (E. Birley 1969) and Gallienus' concentration, albeit temporary, of a specialized cavalry force in northern Italy in the 260s (de Blois 1976: 26–30). However, the main focus has been the respective roles of Diocletian and Constantine in shaping the structure of the fourth-century army (see Nicasie 1998: 1–7 for a helpful summary of previous scholarship). This debate has partly been fueled by the famous but highly tendentious contrast drawn by the early sixth-century historian Zosimus (2.34) between a careful Diocletian who strengthened the empire's frontiers and an irresponsible Constantine who withdrew troops from the frontiers and based them in the empire's cities. Zosimus' antagonism toward Christianity and his determination to pin the blame for the empire's subsequent woes on Constantine undoubtedly influenced his assessment, which drew too sharp a contrast between the policies of the two emperors: significant armed forces accompanied Diocletian on his movements around the eastern Mediterranean and could be regarded as a type of mobile field army, while archaeological and epigraphic evidence shows that Constantine did not neglect the defense of the frontiers.

INTRODUCTION

As this suggests, the emergence of the main organizational features of the fourth-century army was an untidy process, and that sense of untidiness is reinforced by further details. For example, the title given to the commanders of the field armies – *magister* (plural *magistri*) – is associated with Constantine, but that given to those in charge of the forces in the frontier provinces – *dux* (plural *duces*) – is first attested during Diocletian's reign. Moreover, the term *limitanei* first occurs only in 363 (*Theodosian Code* 12.1.56), with the term *ripenses* (first featuring in a law of 325, *Theodosian Code* 7.20.4) its apparent precursor; but this latter term, meaning literally "those on (or defending) the riverbank," must have taken its origin from troops stationed along the Rhine or the Danube, rather than referring to all troops stationed in frontier provinces, with all that that implies about a more piecemeal approach to change. Even the term *comitatenses* is problematic. Although its first appearance in a legal text is in a law of Constantine's from 325 (*Theodosian Code* 7.20.4), the term also features in the epitaph of a cavalryman, Valerius Iuventinus, from Thyatira in Anatolia who had served for 20 years in a unit based at the town of Anchialus on the Black Sea coast of Thrace (*CIL* 3.405), with the Valerius element of his name anchoring him in the tetrarchic period. Location and time imply that he served in the forces of one of the eastern tetrarchs, most probably Galerius or Licinius, prior to Constantine's acquisition of the east in 324, and that one of these emperors is therefore likely to have had some role in the evolution of the *comitatenses*, which, as so often happens in the case of those who end up on the losing side, has been consigned to oblivion (see Brennan (forthcoming) for further discussion of some of these points).

Leaving aside the ultimately insoluble issue of responsibility for their creation, was the development of regional field armies detrimental to the military effectiveness of the empire, as Zosimus implies? His criticism is based on two points: first, that stationing troops in cities in the interior of the empire undermined their discipline; and second, that withdrawal of most of the troops from the frontiers left the inhabitants of those regions exposed to attack. The first criticism is a long-standing *topos* which is demonstrably false (Wheeler 1996), while the second minimizes the numbers and quality of the forces which remained in the frontier provinces. In fact, while clearly not without its risks, the development of field armies can be seen as a rational response to the problem of dealing simultaneously with serious threats on more than one frontier (cf. Crump 1975: 65; Tomlin 1987: 119–20), while the tendency in some modern scholarship to characterize the *limitanei* as second-rate troops is unjustified (Isaac 1992: 208–13).

On Constantine's death, his three sons took responsibility for different parts of the empire, which meant a formalization of the idea of regional field armies, and since the empire was only briefly united again under one emperor on two subsequent occasions – during the reign of Julian (November 361 to June 363) and in the final months of the reign of

INTRODUCTION

Theodosius I in 394–5 – multiple field armies remained a constant feature. Indeed, by the end of the fourth century, the *comitatenses* in the eastern half of the empire were organized into five armies: one each in Syria, Thrace, and Illyricum, and two on either side of the Bosporus near Constantinople – the so-called "praesental" armies, due to their proximity to the imperial court. This pattern remained virtually unchanged in the east through the fifth and sixth centuries, apart from Justinian creating an additional field army for Armenia, a region which assumed increasing importance as a field of operations in his period. This diffused pattern was not replicated in the west in the late fourth century, where the influence of the powerful general Stilicho ensured that military power was concentrated in his hands.

Another salient feature which has long attracted debate is the more noticeable presence of non-Romans in the empire's armed forces during late antiquity. This is an aspect of recruitment which will be discussed in more detail in Chapter 3 as part of a consideration of the "infrastructure of war." Leaving aside the difficulty of defining "non-Romans," suffice it to say for the moment that the Roman army had a long history of using and integrating non-Romans, and that the implication that its later "barbarization" somehow undermined its effectiveness is not supported by the martial prowess of the peoples from whom such recruits were generally drawn, nor is there strong evidence for a lack of discipline or loyalty on the part of those troops. The presence in the army of significant numbers of individuals recruited from outside the empire, as well as interaction with neighboring peoples, did, however, influence the evolution of late Roman arms and armor (Coulston 2002: 20–2).

One of the greatest obstacles to an accurate assessment of the performance of the late Roman army is the dearth of sources for the fifth century, the period when the empire confronted some of its most serious military challenges and – in the west – succumbed. It is difficult, however, to demonstrate conclusively that the empire experienced the setbacks it did in the later fourth and fifth centuries primarily because of deficiencies in the quality and training of troops (cf. Elton 1996: 265–8; Lee 1998: 232–7; Michael Whitby 2004); more plausible explanations can be found in poor generalship and, in the west, the increasing erosion of the government's tax base as it lost control of major regions, above all north Africa. As already noted in the previous section, this progressively limited the ability of fifth-century western emperors to fund the recruitment and payment of sufficient troops and meant a growing dependence on alliances with the leaders of Germanic settlers to make up the shortfall.

The army of the eastern half of the empire which continued into the sixth century shows evidence of both continuity and change. On the one hand, the broad distinction between *comitatenses* and *limitanei* remains, while on the other, the opening of Procopius' history presents cavalry, particularly mounted archers, as the pre-eminent type of unit in his day, suggesting that the balance between infantry and cavalry had now shifted decisively in favor of the latter. However, this shift ought not to be overemphasized: while cavalry had become an even more important component, not least because of the empire's encounters with mounted nomadic peoples such as the Huns during the fifth century, the detailed narrative of Procopius' own history shows that infantry units retained their fundamental importance, particularly in set-piece battles (cf. Rance 2005).

Two further features of the sixth-century army warrant mention, the first of which is the presence of units referred to as "federates." The name was not new, since it had been used in the fourth century to refer to units of troops provided by allied peoples for specific campaigns, and units of this type continued to feature, but the term also came to refer to a category of regular soldier. Although still predominantly recruited from among foreign peoples, they were distinct from the older type of federate in so far as they were in permanent employ and received regular pay (Jones 1964: 663–6; Scharf 2001). The second feature is another category of troops referred to as *bucellarii* – literally, "biscuit men," from the double-baked bread which soldiers took with them on campaign. This term can also be traced back to the late fourth century, when *bucellarii* appear as the private bodyguards of generals. By the sixth century, they seem to have grown in numbers and to have functioned much more like regular soldiers, while still retaining ties of personal loyalty to their commander. Although this ambiguous and distinctive aspect of their status might potentially have posed a problem for emperors vis-à-vis generals, this does not seem to have been the case, with *bucellarii* instead functioning as a type of elite troops who could be relied upon in difficult situations precisely because of their personal loyalty to a commander (Jones 1964: 666–7; Schmitt 1994; Michael Whitby 1995: 116–19).

Having emphasized the ways in which the late Roman army changed both in comparison with the army of the Principate and during late antiquity itself, it is worth drawing attention to at least one remarkable continuity in the army through late antiquity – the longevity of Latin as a significant language in military contexts.[11] This is unsurprising during the fourth century when there was a succession of emperors whose origins were in the Latin-speaking Balkans and when the same region was a major source of recruits. Where it becomes more intriguing is in the sixth century when the focal point of the empire had become the eastern Mediterranean, in which Greek was the lingua franca.[12] The presence in Constantinople of further emperors from the Latin-speaking parts of the Balkans during the first half of the sixth century – Anastasius, Justin I, and Justinian – ensured that Latin retained a degree of status and usage in government contexts, reflected also in the literary outputs of individuals such as Priscian and Corippus (cf. Dagron 1969). As far as the army is concerned, it would not be surprising to find a residue of Latin usage in an institution with a natural tendency toward traditionalism, and there is documentary evidence for the continued use of

INTRODUCTION

Latin in official military communications in Egypt in the early sixth century (*P. Rylands* 609 [505]). Moreover, the author of a military treatise, written in Greek toward the end of the sixth century, explained in the preface that

> we have paid no attention to the niceties of graceful writing or fine-sounding words. This is not something sacred we are doing. Our concern, rather, has been with practicality and brevity of expression. With this in mind, a good number of Latin terms and other expressions in ordinary military use have been employed to make it easier to understand the subject matter. (Ps.-Maurice *Strategy* preface (lines 27–31) [tr. Dennis])

These fifty or so Latin terms, comprising both words of command and technical military vocabulary for such things as maneuvers and ranks, were mostly transliterated into Greek script in the text, but this was presumably as a pronunciation guide for those whose first language was not Latin.[13] All this was a tangible (or rather, audible) legacy from a time when the Roman army had enjoyed unchallenged supremacy.

3. Ancient Sources for War and the Army in Late Antiquity: A Guide

Investigating war in its broader social context during late antiquity entails consideration of many subjects not usually regarded as falling within the purview of military history. As a result, this volume includes reference to a very wide range of ancient sources – too many and varied to warrant individual introduction at this point. Some are germane only to a particular chapter or section of a chapter, which will therefore be the appropriate point to provide such background as may be necessary. There are, however, some sources which feature more regularly and prominently, and which may usefully be introduced here at the outset.

Particularly important for much of what follows are the narrative histories written by Ammianus Marcellinus in the fourth century and Procopius in the sixth, the former written in Latin, the latter in Greek.[14] The surviving books of Ammianus' history provide a continuous and full account of the 25 years from 354 to 378 – years which encompassed such episodes as Julian's Persian campaign (363) and the defeat by the Goths at Adrianople (378). Procopius produced a detailed narrative of military affairs during the first 25 years of the reign of the emperor Justinian, from 527 to 552, including the reconquest of north Africa from the Vandals and the prolonged attempt to recapture Italy from the Goths. Both men wrote what is often referred to as "classicizing" history – that is, history which aspired to emulate the models of the classical past such as Thucydides. Politics and war had long been established as the primary focus of this genre, and Ammianus and Procopius were both well qualified to write about military matters. Ammianus had served as a junior officer in the mid fourth century and participated in Julian's invasion of

INTRODUCTION

Persia, providing himself with inside knowledge of the army as an institution and of the experience of a major campaign. Procopius had a civilian rather than a military background, and was probably a lawyer by training; however, he became secretary to one of the leading generals of the mid sixth century, Belisarius, in which capacity he was an eyewitness to many of the most famous military actions of the 530s and built up a network of contacts on whom to draw for knowledge of events during the 540s. The benefit of these men's experience of war was reduced to some extent by the conventions of the genre within which they wrote – their descriptions of battles could, for example, rely heavily on stereotypes – but they often wrote about particular episodes in such detail that they inevitably included much invaluable circumstantial matter. Procopius also wrote a laudatory account of Justinian's building program, which contains material of relevance to fortifications in the sixth century.

Ammianus and Procopius were by no means the only late Roman historians to focus on warfare, but of those known to have done so during late antiquity, they were the best qualified. The classicizing histories of Agathias and Theophylact Simocatta also survive in complete form from the second half of the sixth century, the former continuing Procopius' account during the mid 550s, the latter covering the reign of the emperor Maurice (582–602). Neither, however, had experience of military affairs comparable to that of Ammianus or Procopius, and it shows in their treatment of warfare and related subjects. Yet other late Roman classicizing historians have survived in the form of excerpts (often substantial) quoted by later writers or preserved in compilations (these are often referred to as "fragments," abbreviated to "fr." in source references). These include Priscus and Malchus from the mid fifth century, and Menander from the late sixth century, whose history was a conscious continuation of Procopius and Agathias down to 582 (and who was then continued by Theophylact). The more fragmentary state of their surviving texts makes it less easy to evaluate their competence as commentators on military matters, but none of them is known to have had such active engagement as Ammianus or Procopius.

A very different style of historical writing is represented by the *Chronicle* traditionally attributed to Joshua the Stylite. Written in Syriac, the Aramaic dialect widely used in Syria and Mesopotamia during late antiquity, it records events affecting the communities of northern Mesopotamia in the final years of the fifth century and the early years of the sixth, especially Edessa and Amida. Those years included the Persian invasion of 502 and the ensuing sieges of Amida, and the *Chronicle* reports in considerable detail on those events and the associated campaigns by Roman and Persian armies. It is a text with its own agenda, in so far as the author wrote from an explicitly Christian perspective and viewed the warfare of these years as God's judgment on the inhabitants of the region. On the other hand, its author was clearly a contemporary of the events described, he was not afraid to make comments critical of the Roman response to the Persian invasion, and he includes an enormous amount of circumstantial detail concerning the impact of warfare at the local level.

Military treatises were a very different genre from these various types of historical writing, with the potential to provide a different perspective on aspects of war. The earliest of those produced in the late Roman period was probably a work entitled *On Military Affairs* (*De Rebus Bellicis*), authorship unknown and intended recipient uncertain, though most plausibly the emperor Valens (364–78). It was perhaps as much a political pamphlet as a military treatise, since it presents proposals for the reform of the tax system. On the other hand, its overriding purpose is to improve the military efficiency and effectiveness of the empire (even including suggestions for labor-saving military hardware), and to that end it offers interesting comment on what its author perceived as current weaknesses. The other fourth-century text is likely to have been produced soon after, since it was probably addressed to the emperor Theodosius I (379–95). The *Epitome of Military Science* by Vegetius provides a systematic treatment of army organization, training, and tactics. As far as Vegetius was concerned, however, standards had deteriorated, and he spends much of his treatise advocating a return to practices of old – which sometimes makes it difficult to determine what current practices were. Despite this limitation, the treatise still sheds light on some aspects of fourth-century military organization and behavior. From the late sixth century comes another important work in this category, the treatise on *Strategy* attributed to the emperor Maurice. Written in Greek, not Latin (unlike the previous two works), it includes an intriguing section outlining the military practices of the empire's major enemies. It also provides invaluable insight into the assumptions underpinning the empire's military organization in that period. The concern with reform evident in all these texts reflects the military pressures with which the empire had to cope during late antiquity.

Collections of imperial laws also have much to offer, since these include legislation bearing on subjects as diverse as the privileges and behavior of soldiers, the fiscal system designed to support the army's operations, and measures to alleviate the impact of warfare. The first major extant collection was produced in 438 on the initiative of the emperor Theodosius II (408–50) and therefore took his name – the *Theodosian Code*. Book 7 of its 16 books is devoted to military affairs, but many of the other books also contain items of relevance to aspects of this study. In 529 the emperor Justinian (527–65) effectively updated the *Theodosian Code* by adding a selection of laws issued in the intervening century, and reordering the material into 12 books, with the title the *Justinianic Code*. A revised edition was published in 534, but there were no further attempts to update the *Code*, although Justinian's subsequent laws and some of those of his successors were eventually gathered into a collection referred to by modern scholars as the *Novels*, not because they are regarded as works of fiction, but because they were *leges novellae* – "new laws." Unlike the two codes, in which the texts of laws were heavily edited so as to reflect their essential core, the *Novels* generally retain the full texts, including the prefaces, which often indicate something of the circumstances which prompted a law to be issued.

A different, and unusual, type of official document is represented by a text known as the *Notitia Dignitatum* – the "register of dignities" – which lists the empire's senior civilian officials and their staffs, and the senior military officers and the units under their command. Divided into two parts – one for the eastern half of the empire, the other for the west – it is thought to reflect arrangements at the end of the fourth century in the east, and in the early fifth century in the west. Understanding the text presents numerous challenges and since it does not include details of contingents recruited from outside the empire, it cannot be regarded as providing a comprehensive overview of the forces at the disposal of the empire at that time. Nevertheless, although a set of lists may not sound particularly interesting, it reveals much about military organization and the history of army units.

Another valuable category of source material for the study of the late Roman army comprises original documents preserved on papyrus – ancient writing paper. These can only survive down the centuries where dry conditions prevail, and so have been found in substantial quantities only in parts of Egypt, although some have also turned up in other places in the Near East and even a small number, surprisingly, at Ravenna in Italy. They are chiefly of value in documenting aspects of the army's administrative infrastructure, although there are also important archives of letters and legal documents which shed light on the status and role of soldiers and veterans in their local communities. The editing and publication of papyri is an ongoing endeavor, and is one of the most important ways in which new evidence about the ancient world continues to be brought to light. Papyri are conventionally referred to by the abbreviation "*P.*" followed by a location – typically their place of origin or the city in one of whose libraries they can now be found – and then a number: for example, *P. Oxyrhynchus* 3265 (after the ancient Egyptian town of that name, which has proved to be one of the most productive sources of papyri), or *P. London* 1912 (now held in the British Library).

Inscriptions are another medium through which ancient texts are preserved in their original form, and since archaeological excavations regularly uncover new examples, they are another source of new data, albeit not as plentiful for the late Roman army as for that of the Principate. Perhaps the most valuable categories of inscription for the study of the late Roman army are soldiers' epitaphs, which can illuminate career progression and the movements of military units, and building inscriptions, of relevance to fortification policies and funding. The most commonly cited collections of inscriptions are the *Corpus Inscriptionum Latinarum* (*CIL*) and *Inscriptiones Latinae Selectae* (*ILS*), with *L'Année epigraphique* (*AE*) reporting new discoveries.

Finally, numismatic evidence – coins – is principally of value here for the subject of imperial ideology – that is, the images and slogans which emperors wanted to project to the empire's population at large concerning military success, or more specifically to the soldiers concerning the emperor's concern for their welfare. The authoritative guide to coinage for most of the late Roman period is the relevant volumes of the *Roman Imperial Coinage* (*RIC*), supplemented for the sixth century by the standard catalogue of early Byzantine coinage (Bellinger 1966).

Further Reading

General introductions to late antiquity

For any readers relatively unfamiliar with late antiquity, a succinct overview can be found in the final third of Cornell and Matthews 1981 (which, despite its title, comprises much more than maps), with fuller treatments in P. R. L. Brown 1971, Averil Cameron 1993a, 1993b, and Mitchell 2006. Potter 2004 includes a good survey of the first half of late antiquity.

Volumes XII to XIV of the new edition of the *Cambridge Ancient History* (Bowman et al. 2005; Averil Cameron and Garnsey 1998; Averil Cameron et al. 2000) are a valuable, more detailed reference resource, with both narrative and thematic chapters, as also is Jones 1964. Bowersock et al. 1999 contains a series of helpful essays on major themes, and encyclopedia-style articles on a wide range of important subjects.

War and its causes

For a succinct introduction to warfare in the Greco-Roman world which gives attention to the broader context and to late antiquity, see Sidebottom 2004. The best overview of war as a phenomenon in late antiquity is Shaw 1999. Sabin et al. (forthcoming) includes a substantial and wide-ranging set of chapters on warfare in late antiquity. For discussion of the salient features of the Sasanian Persian state, see Lee 1993: 15–20, Michael Whitby 1994, and Howard-Johnston 1995. The history of Roman–Persian warfare and relations can be followed via the ancient sources in two sequential documentary histories: Dodgeon and Lieu 1991 and Greatrex and Lieu 2002. For the emergence of Germanic tribal confederations, see the convenient overviews in Geary 1999: 110–11 and Halsall 2005: 45–8; for their military capabilities in the fourth century, the best discussion is Elton 1996: 45–8. For the impact of the Huns, see Heather 1995, and for Hunnic society and organization, Matthews 1989: 332–42.

For discussions of the barbarian invasions and the fall of the western half of the empire, see Halsall 2005, Heather 2005, and Ward-Perkins 2005, each of which contains further references to the vast literature on this subject. The issue of "grand strategy" was first injected into discussions of Roman

INTRODUCTION

military history by Luttwak 1976 (which in fact focuses primarily on the Principate and does not go beyond the early fourth century); good discussions include Mann 1979, Millar 1982, Isaac 1992: 372–418, Wheeler 1993, Whittaker 1994: 60–97, and Greatrex (forthcoming)). Another subject not discussed in the present volume – the evolution of military capabilities and organization in the successor kingdoms of the early medieval west – can be pursued in Bachrach 2001 and Halsall 2003.

The evolution of the late Roman army

The best overview of the development and character of the late Roman army remains Jones 1964: 607–86, even if some of his conclusions require modification on points of detail; for briefer overviews, see Demandt 1989: 355–72 and Zuckerman 2004; Tomlin 1987 provides a succinct survey down to the fifth century. The evolution of the army during late antiquity can also be followed through the relevant chapters in successive volumes of the new edition of the *Cambridge Ancient History*: Campbell 2005, Lee 1998, Michael Whitby 2000a. Michael Whitby 2004 also offers a wide-ranging discussion of many issues relating to the late Roman army, with particular attention to the third and fourth centuries. For more detailed treatments of the fourth-century army, see Elton 1996 and Nicasie 1998, and for the sixth-century army, Haldon 1999 and Syvänne 2004. Southern and Dixon 1996 is useful on archaeological evidence for the army. There has been a valuable survey of recent work on late Roman military history in a series of review articles in the French journal *Antiquité tardive*: Carrié and Janniard 2000, Janniard 2001, and Carrié 2002.

Ancient sources for war and the army in late antiquity

The remainder of what follows focuses on guidance about sources, though not details of editions and translations of "literary" and legal sources, which can be found in the bibliography of ancient sources at the end of this volume.

For Ammianus and Procopius, the most detailed studies are Matthews 1989 and Averil Cameron 1985 respectively (although the latter is less interested in military aspects). Barnes 1998 is the most important contribution to the study of Ammianus since Matthews, while Greatrex 2003 offers a helpful critical survey of more recent work on Procopius. Crump 1975 offers focused discussion of Ammianus as a military historian, as does Rance 2005 for Procopius. For evaluations of Agathias and Theophylact, see Averil Cameron 1970 and Michael Whitby 1988 respectively. For Priscus and Malchus, see Blockley 1981, and for Menander, Blockley 1985a. Michael Whitby 1992a is a valuable discussion of Agathias, Menander, and Theophylact. For the context and authorship of the *Chronicle* attributed to Joshua the Stylite, see Trombley and Watt 2000: xi–li.

INTRODUCTION

For the *De Rebus Bellicis*, see Thompson 1952a and Hassall 1979, and for Vegetius, Milner 1996: xiii–xli. Philip Rance's forthcoming translation of and commentary on the treatise on *Strategy* attributed to Maurice promises to illuminate not just that text, but sixth-century warfare more generally. Note also two further military treatises in Greek, not referred to in the text above: the anonymous treatise *On Strategy*, sometimes attributed to Syrianus and sometimes dated to the sixth century (edition and translation in Dennis 1985, discussion of date with references to previous literature in Cosentino 2000), and Urbicius *Invention* (*Epitedeuma*) from the reign of Anastasius (491–518) (edition, translation, and discussion in Greatrex et al. 2005).

The best study of the *Theodosian Code* is Matthews 2000. Honoré 1978 includes much of value on the background to the production of the *Justinianic Code*, but this later code, and Justinian's *Novels*, have yet to receive the same attention which the *Theodosian Code* has attracted in recent years (for an overview of which see Lee 2002b).

There are valuable discussions of aspects of the *Notitia Dignitatum* in Goodburn and Bartholomew 1976, and Brennan 1996, 1998b; for a convenient summary of the issues relating to the dating of the document, see Kelly 1998: 163–5. Peter Brennan is producing a translation of and commentary on the *Notitia* which will mark a major advance in understanding of this deceptively straightforward text.

Although the following volumes devote only limited attention to late antiquity, they offer more general guides to the potential value of papyri, inscriptions, and coins, respectively, as evidence for the ancient world, as well as the principal methodological issues they raise: Bagnall 1995, Bodel 2001, and Howgego 1995.

1

EMPERORS AND WARFARE

Rulership in antiquity often relied on military success for legitimation, and late antiquity was no exception. What is particularly interesting about late antiquity, however, is that, despite the pressing military circumstances in which the empire often found itself, a significant number of Roman emperors in this period did not involve themselves directly in warfare, instead delegating command to their generals. This phenomenon of non-campaigning emperors raises important questions which are considered both in this chapter and, to some extent, in the next.

The first half of this chapter traces the changing patterns of imperial involvement in warfare, investigating the factors which appear to have influenced the decisions of emperors and/or their advisers as to the wisdom or otherwise of direct participation in campaigning. The second half of the chapter addresses the issue of military success, and the ways in which emperors endeavored to communicate an ideology of victory to the inhabitants of the empire even when the emperor himself could not claim credit, or when there was little to claim credit for.

1.1. Changing Patterns of Imperial Involvement in Warfare

Broadly speaking, late antiquity falls into two halves with respect to imperial involvement in warfare. During the third and fourth centuries, nearly all emperors took an active role in campaigning, whereas during the fifth and sixth centuries this became the exception rather than the rule. It was only in the early seventh century that the pattern came full circle with the resumption of active campaigning by the emperor Heraclius.

Since the level of imperial involvement which characterized the second half of the third century represented something of a contrast with the Principate, the first part of this section examines the factors and circumstances which brought about this change. The second part focuses on the fourth century, during which there can be observed growing tensions between the claims of military experience and ties of heredity in determining occupation of the imperial throne. The third part investigates the range of possible reasons for the major shift at the end of the fourth century, and on through the fifth and sixth centuries, whereby it became very rare for emperors to undertake campaigning in person, even when they had military experience.

1.1.1. The later third century: the advent of soldier emperors

> How pampered by good luck in administering the state and obtaining praise were those emperors who, while spending their days at Rome, had triumphs and victory titles of nations conquered by their generals accrue to them. Thus when Fronto...was praising the emperor Antoninus [138–61] for having brought the war in Britain to completion, although he remained behind in the city [of Rome] in the palace itself, and had delegated command of the war to others, he averred that the emperor deserved the glory of its whole launching and course, as if he had actually presided at the helm of a warship. But you, invincible Caesar, were the commander-in-chief of that whole expedition of yours, both of the actual sailing and the fighting itself, not only by right of your imperial authority but by your personal participation, and by the example of your firm resolve were its instigator and driving force. (*Latin Panegyrics* 8(5).14.1–3 [trs. Nixon and Rodgers, with revisions])

This passage occurs in a panegyric delivered before the emperor Constantius I at Trier in 297 or 298, following his recovery of Britain from usurpers (Nixon and Rodgers 1994: 105). While this circumstance explains the choice of Britain as the point of comparison, the specific contrast between Constantius and the second-century emperor Antoninus Pius undoubtedly oversimplifies matters somewhat. First, Antoninus was one of the few emperors from the period of the Principate not to have engaged actively in military campaigning of any sort either prior to or after becoming emperor, and so cannot be regarded as typical in this respect. Second, "the panegyrist inflates the role of Constantius in the expedition, not surprisingly, and obscures that of the praetorian prefect Asclepiodotus, who is not so much as mentioned by name or even title. Yet it is clear from later sources that Asclepiodotus was generally credited with the victory" (Nixon and Rodgers 1994: 133 n.52).

Despite these qualifications, however, the passage does encapsulate a fundamental contrast with regard to the military involvement of emperors during the Principate, on the one hand, and during the late third century, on the other. For although it is possible to cite the counter-example of Trajan as an emperor during the Principate who was very much "hands on" when it came to campaigning, and although Constantius may not have been quite as closely involved in the campaigning in this instance as his panegyrist implies, it is undeniable that emperors during the Principate did not for the most part spend the bulk of their time campaigning and did regularly spend much of their time in Rome, whereas those of the late third century devoted much of their time to active involvement in warfare, which significantly restricted the opportunities of most incumbents to be in Rome for any length of time.

This important change, one of the defining features of the transition from the Principate to late antiquity, was the result of the altered circumstances of the empire. During the Principate, military initiative lay largely with the empire and warfare was usually the result of the emperor and his advisers deciding to embark on an offensive campaign to expand the imperial domain; unwanted campaigns were for the most part the result of revolt by discontented provincials within the empire, notably the Jews. An exception to this was the Marcomannic war of Marcus Aurelius, toward the end of the second century, which might be regarded as heralding third-century developments – namely, the emergence of militarily stronger neighbors to the north of the empire, such as the Goths and the Alamanni, but also to the east, in the form of the Sasanians, who overthrew the Parthian Arsacid regime in the mid 220s. These exogenous changes had the effect of removing the military initiative from the empire to a significant degree, so that warfare during the third century, and especially the second half of the century, was predominantly defensive in nature.

In these often desperate circumstances it was no longer realistic to rely on emperors drawn from a social group whose military competence was not assured – namely, the senatorial aristocracy. Until 235, all emperors were, with one minor exception, senators by background,[1] and while some of these had undoubtedly demonstrated military proficiency (most notably Trajan, but one might also include here Tiberius (prior to his accession), Vespasian, Titus, and Septimius Severus), there could be no assurance that this would invariably be the case:

> Despite the increased number of military commands available to senators [during the Principate],...the emperor could not count on finding men of significant military experience for the major consular provinces and...there was no deliberate attempt to ensure regular military experience of commanding troops...The Romans had no military academy, no formal process for educating officers in ordnance, tactics, and strategy, and no systematic means for testing the quality of aspirants to top commands...The length of time spent in commanding an army of several legions and *auxilia* was normally too limited to allow the development of a military hierarchy or specialized high command which could have provided a fund of military experience...Few emperors had much, if any, military experience before they assumed the purple. (Campbell 1987: 22)

Against this background, the overthrow of the unlucky young emperor Severus Alexander in 235 by the short-lived Maximinus acquires a greater significance than one might otherwise have expected. While the manner of Severus' death – brutally murdered by his own troops – can be seen, with hindsight, as an important precedent for the coming decades, it is the difference in the social background and military experience of the two men which is of importance. Alexander was of senatorial status and, still only in his early twenties in 235, he had had little time to gain much personal knowledge of the army or of warfare, whereas the surviving evidence about Maximinus, unsatisfactory though it is, indicates a man who had acquired equestrian status (i.e., the status below that of senator) through a long military career (Syme 1971: 179–93; Drinkwater 2005: 28–30).

The accession of Maximinus did not mark an absolute rupture in the pattern of imperial office holding, for there were subsequent emperors of senatorial status – most prominently, Gordian III (238–44), Decius (249–51), Valerian (253–60), and Gallienus (253–68). Over the course of the third century, however, there was a gradual but inexorable shift of power into the hands of those of equestrian status. For some of these, access to power came through their holding of the office of praetorian prefect, long the acme of an equestrian career: the prime examples are Philip (244–9) and Carus (282–3), who (following Macrinus' example in 217) used the praetorian prefecture as a stepping stone to imperial power, but one should not overlook Timesitheus and Aper, whose tenure of the office allowed them to exercise a predominant influence during the reigns of Gordian and Numerian (283–4), even if they did not manage to become emperor themselves.

Yet this was not the most significant development. Praetorian prefects becoming emperor was a novelty, but the post had long lent itself to the exercise of significant political influence, stretching all the way back to Sejanus in the reign of Tiberius. What was strikingly new was the pattern foreshadowed by Maximinus and firmly established after the death of Gallienus in 268 by a succession of emperors – Claudius (268–70), Aurelian (270–5), Probus (276–82), and Diocletian (284–305). Once again, paucity of detail and a pejorative attitude toward emperors of non-senatorial origin mean that the meager surviving ancient sources for these decades are unsatisfactory as evidence for the careers of these men (Michael Whitby 2004: 179–80); nevertheless, there is no doubt about their military background, confirmed by their common Balkan origin (the major recruiting ground for the army in this period), and it looks like they were individuals who achieved equestrian status by promotion through the ranks to positions of command in the army (Syme 1971: 208–12; Potter 2004: 263–80; Drinkwater 2005: 48–58) – a reflection of a more general trend whereby equestrians increasingly dominated military commands at the expense of senators during the mid to late third century (Christol 1999: 625–7). It is unlikely that this important development was the result of a specific law of the emperor Gallienus, as one fourth-century writer claimed (Aurelius Victor *On the Caesars* 33.34, with Potter 2004: 640 n.188 for details of modern discussions). Rather, this development should be seen as recognition that, in the increasingly dire circumstances in which the empire found itself in the 260s, military competence was the fundamental desideratum for military commands – and, by logical extension, for the commander-in-chief. In this respect, then, the warfare of the mid third century had a significant impact on the political character of the Roman empire.

That impact, however, extended beyond affecting the type of man who held imperial office, significant though that change was; it also had a profound influence on his style of rule. Given the background of these soldier emperors and the severe problems which they confronted, it is unsurprising to find them closely involved in military campaigning and warfare. One important consequence of this close involvement is epitomized by the contrast in the opening passage between Antoninus, permanently resident in Rome, and Constantius, based in Trier and active on the northern perimeter of the empire. Although emperors during the Principate were often mobile and saw many parts of the empire – most famously, Hadrian – they invariably spent significant portions of their reign in Rome or its environs.[2] From the 230s onward, on the other hand, it became much rarer for emperors to spend much time in Rome, or in some cases even to visit the city (Table 1.1). During the period 193–235 (42 years), emperors spent about 22 years in Rome (52 percent). During the period 235–337 (102 years), emperors spent about 38 years in Rome (37 percent), with only 15 of these years falling during the 53 years of the Tetrarchy and Constantine (28 percent). The reduced proportion of time spent in Rome between 235 and 337 is even more significant when it is remembered that at a number of times in this period (especially during the Tetrarchy) there were multiple emperors.

Leaving aside those whose reigns were so short that they did not spend much time anywhere, this change was partly because emperors were heavily involved in military affairs along the empire's frontiers, and partly because, in a period when soldiers had become accustomed to making and unmaking emperors with alarming regularity, it was vital to maintain close contact with the troops; in the case of those emperors of non-senatorial origin, it may also betray a reluctance to deal at first hand with a disdainful senate. Certainly, this trend can only have served to diminish further the corporate ability of the senate to influence imperial politics. When an imperial visit to Rome did take place, it was usually occasioned by a ritual of importance, such as taking up the consulship, the staging of a triumph, or celebration of a major imperial anniversary – events which offered Balkan soldier emperors valuable symbolic opportunities to legitimate their positions and affirm their Roman identity.

As the city of Rome became increasingly less frequented by emperors during the second half of the third century, so other cities acquired greater prominence as emperors spent more time in bases closer to the frontiers. The Persian threat to the east meant that Antioch assumed even more importance than it had in the past, while the problems affecting the northern frontiers led emperors to make regular use of such cities as Sirmium, Serdica, Milan, and Trier, particularly after Diocletian developed a pattern of government where he shared power with three colleagues (Millar 1977: 40–53).

Table 1.1 Emperors in Rome, 193–337

Emperor	Reign	No. of years in Rome	Dates in Rome	Occasion
Septimius Severus	193–211	1	193	Accession
		1	196–7	
		6	202–8	
Caracalla	211–17	1	211–12	Accession
Macrinus	217–18	0		
Elagabalus	218–22	3	219–22	
Severus Alexander	222–35	9	222–31	
		1	233–4	
Maximinus	235–8	0		
Gordian III	238–44	4	238–42	Accession
Philip	244–9	1	244–5	Accession
		2	247–9	Millennial celebrations
Decius	249–51	1	249–50	Accession
Trebonianus Gallus	251–3	2	251–3	Accession
Valerian	253–60	1	253–4	Accession
Gallienus	253–68	1	253–4	Accession
		4	263–7	
Claudius II	268–70	1	268–9	Accession
Aurelian	270–5	1	270–1	Accession
		1	274	Triumph
Probus	276–82	2	280–2	Triumph
Carus	282–3	1	282–3	Accession
Numerian	283–4	0		
Carinus	283–5	1	284	
Diocletian	284–305	1	303	*Vicennalia*
Maximian	·286–305	1	293	
		1	299	Triumph
		1	303–4	*Vicennalia*
Constantius I	293–306	1	295	
Galerius	293–311	1	307	
Severus	305–7	0		
Maximinus Daia	305–13	0		
Maxentius	306–12	6	306–12	Rome his capital
Constantine I	306–37	1	312–13	Defeating Maxentius
		1	315	Decennalia
		1	326	Vicennalia
Licinius	308–24	0		

Note: In some cases, the occasion for an emperor's visit is not known, or in cases when he spent a substantial amount of time there, the reasons cannot be summarized succinctly. Only emperors who ruled for longer than 12 months are included.

Sources: Bowman et al. (2005: Appendix II (Imperial movements, AD 193–337)); Barnes (1982).

At the same time, the emergence of the so-called Tetrarchy coincides with some improvement in the surviving evidence, which provides a clearer picture of the extent to which, despite the emergence of these imperial bases, emperors were still having to maintain a highly mobile existence as they moved around the empire in order to tackle different crises. So, for example, Diocletian's legal pronouncements, which usually preserve both the place and date of issue, allow us to track his movements during the course of the year 290 (Barnes 1982: 51–2). At the start of that year, he was wintering in Sirmium following a campaign against the Sarmatians on the lower Danube; during the spring, he traveled eastward, reaching Antioch in early May, from where he embarked on a short campaign against Arab tribesmen before returning to Sirmium, where he spent much of the second half of the year prior to journeying to Milan for a "summit meeting" with his fellow-emperor Maximian – a round trip in excess of 3,000 miles. It was exertions of this sort which gradually restored a degree of stability to the empire's frontiers. With that stability, however, there also came renewed pressure to take into account considerations other than military experience in the selection of emperors.

1.1.2. The fourth century: military experience vs heredity

Meanwhile when [the emperor] Valentinian was assailed by a serious illness [at Amiens in August 367] and was close to death, the Gauls who were attending the emperor held a clandestine meeting at which it was proposed that Rusticus Julianus, then master of the records (*magister memoriae*), should be made emperor...They were opposed by some with higher concerns who championed Severus, then commander of the infantry (*magister peditum*), as a suitable man for this rank...But while these plans were being formulated in vain, the emperor recovered thanks to various remedies. As he reflected on his narrow escape from death, Valentinian decided to bestow the imperial insignia on his son Gratian, who was now approaching adulthood. And when everything was ready and the soldiers had been induced to grant their approval, Gratian arrived and the emperor advanced into the parade ground (*campus*) and mounted the tribunal. Surrounded by a splendid body of high-ranking officials, he took the boy by the hand, led him into their midst, and commended the future emperor to the army with a formal speech. (Ammianus 27.6.1–5)

During the Principate, hereditary succession had been the key determinant in access to imperial power, even when, as in the second century, it had involved emperors without sons adopting suitable successors; competition based on military power, as in 69 and 193, had been the exception. Even if its influence continued to be felt – as, for example, in Gallienus' proclaiming successive sons as Caesars, in the troops' elevation of Claudius II's brother Quintillus to the purple following the former's death in 270, and in Carus' naming his sons Carinus and Numerian as Caesars soon after his accession in 282 – the dynastic principle had had to bow increasingly to the claims of military competence. The climax of this countervailing tendency was Diocletian's experiment in sharing power between four emperors chosen for their military competence and without reference to blood.[3]

This arrangement proved its value in the short term in so far as it broke the cycle of usurpation which had plagued the empire during the mid third century. Diocletian's attempt to establish it as a long-term mechanism for the transmission of imperial power failed, however, in the face of a resurgence of the dynastic principle. Diocletian himself had a daughter but no son (which may have been an important factor in his willingness to embark on his experiment in the first place), but two of his chosen colleagues did have able and ambitious sons – Maxentius and Constantine – who expected their opportunity to follow in their fathers' footsteps. The tetrarchic system duly unraveled over the course of the opening decades of the fourth century until, by 324, one of those sons, Constantine, had emerged as sole ruler of the empire.

Thereafter, throughout the remainder of the fourth century, there is an interesting tension between the competing claims of military competence and blood ties, as reflected in the passage at the start of this section. Between 337 and 363 imperial power passed to Constantine's sons and nephews. However, the death of the last of these, Julian, in the midst of a military crisis, presented senior army officers with the opportunity to select a new emperor without the need to take account of dynastic considerations. The immediate circumstances – the army was trying to extricate itself from Persian territory – were not conducive to lengthy deliberation but the man finally agreed upon, Jovian, came from a very similar background to emperors of the late third century: he was a middle-ranking officer from the Balkans (Lenski 2002a: 16). Although Jovian himself had not necessarily had much opportunity until then to demonstrate prowess in command, he is likely to have benefited from his close association with men who had, namely his father Varronian and his father-in-law Lucillianus – both men with reputations for military competence in senior posts during the 350s (Lenski 2000: 506–8).

Although he had an infant son, Varronian, whom he no doubt intended to proclaim as Caesar, Jovian died after a reign of little more than seven months, and the youth of his son and the fact that he had not formally been proclaimed meant that there was a second opportunity to select a new emperor without reference to dynastic considerations, this time in somewhat less pressured circumstances. Although there was more civilian involvement in this decision, the main candidates discussed were mostly men "with qualifications remarkably similar to those of Jovian" (Lenski 2002a: 20), including the eventual successor, Valentinian, another middle-ranking officer of Balkan origin – all of which no doubt reflected a consciousness of the need for appropriate experience in the aftermath of the failure of Julian's Persian expedition. The surviving sources have little to say about the specific details of Valentinian's military record, but they do indicate that he was "a man with considerable military experience" (Lenski 2002a: 21). As with Jovian, the military record of Valentinian's father Gratian may also have been a factor of importance. Interestingly, when Valentinian consulted his senior officers about his intention to appoint an imperial colleague, one of them is said to have replied, "If you love your relatives, most excellent emperor, you have a brother; if it is the state that you love, seek out another man to clothe with the purple" (Ammianus 26.4.1), the most obvious interpretation being that Valentinian's brother Valens lacked the requisite military record (cf. Lenski 2002a: 51–2).

Valentinian, however, ignored this advice and soon after appointed his brother Valens as co-emperor, a reassertion of the dynastic principle further reinforced by his elevation of his son Gratian in 367, as related in the excerpt at the head of this section. Another reflection of the power of blood ties at this time was the usurpation attempt launched by Procopius against Valens in 365. Although ultimately unsuccessful, Procopius initially enjoyed considerable support largely because he was able to present himself as a relative of the former emperor Julian, an evident advantage on which he tried to capitalize further by parading before his troops the wife and daughter of Julian's cousin and predecessor Constantius II, whose presence is said to have "excited his men to fight more resolutely" (Ammianus 26.9.3, with further discussion in Lenski 2002a: 97–101).

When military disaster supervened once again to eliminate Valens at the battle of Adrianople in 378, Gratian, now the senior emperor (although only 19 years of age), faced a dilemma. Under normal circumstances, dynastic considerations would have dictated his younger brother and co-emperor, Valentinian II, taking over Valens' role as emperor of the eastern half of the empire. However, Gratian and his advisers appreciated that the crisis in the Balkans consequent upon the Gothic victory at Adrianople required the attentions of a man with more military experience than Gratian himself had, let alone his seven-year-old brother. Hence the choice of Theodosius, whose father had been a successful general under Valentinian I and who had himself already demonstrated comparable competence as a commander on the lower Danube in recent years (Ammianus 29.6.15; cf. Matthews 1975: 91–8 and Leppin 2003: 29–34). Although Theodosius may not, in the event, have been able to expel the Goths from the empire, that had more to do with temporary manpower shortages than generalship, and he did contain the problem in the early 380s, as well as dealing effectively with two western usurpers (Magnus Maximus and Eugenius) in the late 380s and early 390s.

As will be apparent from the foregoing overview, the reassertion of the dynastic principle had mixed results in terms of the military record of the empire in the fourth century, notably the defeats and deaths of Julian and Valens (neither of whom had the sort of military experience which Theodosius did). On the other hand, however much ancient commentators may have criticized him (e.g., Eutropius 10.10.1; Ammianus 21.16.15; Libanius *Orations* 18.205–7), Constantius II did demonstrate considerable military sense in his conduct of affairs on the eastern frontier and more generally (Blockley 1989), perhaps reflecting the fruits of his father's efforts to train him in warfare (Julian *Orations* 1.9a–13b). Similarly, when presenting the eight-year-old Gratian to the troops at Amiens in 367, Valentinian was quick to acknowledge that Gratian did not yet have the requisite military training and experience to be emperor, but assured them that he had the aptitude and commitment to acquire them with time (cf. Rufinus *Church History* 11.13). This awareness of the need for such a background reflects the fact that, even if military experience was again having to compete more strongly against the claims of blood ties when it came to their selection, emperors during this period continued to be actively involved with the army and in campaigning, as is clear from narrative accounts of the period, particularly the detailed history of Ammianus Marcellinus (cf. Matthews 1989: 283). As with third-century emperors, this is corroborated by the relative rarity with which fourth-century emperors visited Rome and, in the case of emperors based in the east, Constantinople (Table 1.2). Although the latter city was consecrated by Constantine in 330, Theodosius I (379–95) was the first emperor to spend any substantial periods of time there (seven years in total), thereby setting "a fourth-century record for sustained imperial immobility" (McLynn 2004: 261) – a record, however, which, interestingly, also earned him criticism in some quarters (Zosimus 4.33, 50).

The only real exception to this general pattern of active campaigning prior to 395 was Valentinian II, who was a minor for most of his reign and, once a young adult, apparently faced the powerful opposition of the general Arbogast to any attempt on his part to gain military experience.[4] While the exception to the rule for the period before 395, however, the experience of the young Valentinian proved to be an ominous precedent for developments after Theodosius' death in 395.

1.1.3. The fifth and sixth centuries: non-campaigning emperors

So long as it was the case that emperors went out to wars in person, the [praetorian] prefecture had a certain power and influence, if not as great as it had been, greater, nonetheless, than all the other magistracies. But from the time when Theodosius I, making provision for the indolent dispositions of his own sons, put a curb on valour by legislation, prohibiting, through them, a Roman emperor from going forth to the wars – from then on matters concerning wars became the field of the generals. (John the Lydian *On the Magistracies of the Roman State* 2.11.3–4 [tr. Carney, with revisions]; cf. 3.41.3)[5]

Table 1.2 Emperors in Rome and Constantinople, 337–95

		Rome				Constantinople	
Emperor	Reign	No. of periods	Date	Occasion	No. of periods	Date	Occasion
Constantine II	337–40	0			0		
Constans	337–50	1?	340?		0		
Constantius II	337–61	1	357	Vicennalia and triumph	5	May 337	Constantine's funeral
						Sep. 337	
						Early 342	Expulsion of bishop Paul
						Oct. 343 (or 349)	
						Winter 359	
Julian	361–3	0			1	Dec. 361– May 362	
Jovian	363–4	0			0		
Valentinian I	364–75	0			1	364	Accession of Valens
Valens	364–78	0			3	Dec. 364– Aug. 365	Accession and consulship
						370–1	Famine
						May 378	En route to deal with Goths
Gratian	375–83	1	May 376		1	Oct. 378	After battle of Adrianople
Valentinian II	375–92	1	388	During Theodosius' campaign vs Maximus	0		
Theodosius I	379–95	2	June– Aug. 389	After defeat of Maximus	2	380–7	
			Oct. 394– Jan. 395	After defeat of Eugenius		391–4	

Sources: Seeck (1919); Dagron (1974: 79–85); Barnes (1993: Appendix 9); Barnes (1998: Appendix 10).

As this excerpt from a sixth-century commentator indicates, albeit in a somewhat muddled manner, the death of Theodosius I in 395 marked a critical juncture, a fundamental reversal, with regard to imperial involvement in warfare. For more than two centuries thereafter, until the reign of Heraclius in the early seventh century, it was extremely rare for the emperor to lead the army or to campaign in person. The reasons for this are to be sought elsewhere than in John the Lydian's fanciful claim about legislation by Theodosius I. In the context of the years immediately after Theodosius' death, this change comes as no real surprise. At the time of their father's demise, Arcadius and Honorius, who succeeded to the throne in the eastern and western halves of the empire, were about 17 and 11 years old respectively (it is not possible to be more precise about Arcadius' age since his date of birth is known only approximately). There was clearly no immediate prospect of the younger of the two taking an active military role; Arcadius might perhaps have begun to do so, had he had the ability and determination of an Alexander – but it is apparent that he did not. Upon his death in 408 at the age of 31, he was succeeded by his son Theodosius II, who was then seven years old – so perpetuating the pattern in the eastern half of the empire.

In the west, the dominant force at Honorius' court until 408 was the general Stilicho. Although not an outsider – he was linked by marriage to the imperial family well before Honorius' accession – it was in his interests to ensure that any nascent military ambitions on the part of the emperor were not encouraged. A militarily active Honorius might have become more independent, or if he had died on campaign, Stilicho's own position might well have become tenuous. At the same time, Stilicho's publicist, the poet Claudian, sought to assuage any concerns about Honorius' lack of military experience in a series of panegyrics delivered in the early years of his reign. In that of 396, when Honorius was 11 years old, Claudian emphasized his familiarity with military camps and weapons from an early age, Theodosius' measures to ensure that Honorius received an appropriately rigorous training, and Honorius' keenness to accompany his father on the campaign against Eugenius in 394 (not, however, permitted) (*Panegyric on the Third Consulate of Honorius* 22–62). Two years later, Claudian was emphasizing Honorius' military pedigree with reference to the achievements of his father and grandfather, and even hinting at a possible association with Trajan, who had also originated from Spain (*Panegyric on the Fourth Consulate of Honorius* 18ff.); he refers to the role of the army in Honorius' formal elevation as emperor (169ff.); he imagines Theodosius' advice to his son about the conduct of war, including encouragement to participate in the soldiers' work since "with you as their comrade, they will press on the more readily" (320ff.); he reiterates Honorius' supposed desire to participate in the expedition of 394 – "Do you think me still a child? . . . Give me arms now. Why is my age an objection?" – and Theodosius' response – that he is too young, but has great military successes in store if he gives himself to training in war (352ff.); and he concludes by crediting Honorius with one of his father's earlier victories because Honorius was holding the consulship at the time, and by asserting that "once the author of your father's victories, now you will be the author of your own...A time will come when you, victor beyond the Rhine estuary, and Arcadius, laden with the spoils of captive Babylon, will inscribe your shared year with a greater consulship" (638ff. [tr. Barr]).

By the time of Stilicho's fall in 408, Honorius was nearly 24 years old, at which point he could have begun to assume the more active military role which Claudian had purported to predict. That he did not do so could reflect understandable trepidation at the particularly severe problems Italy faced at that time, in the form of Alaric and the Goths, but what little is known about his character indicates that, despite Claudian's rhetoric, Honorius was an individual ill-suited to military endeavor. According to one anecdote, he (then resident in Ravenna) was more preoccupied with the well-being of his pet chickens than that of Rome at the time of the Gothic sack of the city in 410 (Procopius *Wars* 3.2.25–6).

Following his death in 423, Honorius' eventual successor (after a short period of political turmoil) was Valentinian III, who came to the throne in 425 aged six. Like Honorius, he too was dominated for much of his reign by a powerful general in the person of Aetius, who no doubt will have discouraged any military interests in the emperor. In the west, at any rate, a combination of accession to the throne at a young age and the presence of dominant generals at court seems to have ensured that for the half century following Theodosius' death, no western emperor was involved in military campaigning.[6]

As for the eastern half of the empire, the youth of emperors was also a factor, though dominant generals were less so, since in the east civilian bureaucrats managed to maintain control vis-à-vis the military in a way which did not happen in the west (which is not to say that there were not occasional scares, as in the Gainas episode in 400, on which see Liebeschuetz 1991: 104–25; Alan Cameron and Long 1993: 161–75, 201–11). This divergence can be accounted for, at least in part, by reference to the differing military structures in east and west: in the latter, Stilicho had created a centralized command structure, whereas in the former military power was more dispersed (Jones 1964: 609–10; Lee 2000b: 60). Like Honorius, too, Theodosius II – who ruled the east for most of the first half of the fifth century (408–50) – does not seem to have had any inclination to undertake military activities once he reached adulthood, preferring to focus his attention on scholarly pursuits and personal piety and rarely venturing beyond the confines of Constantinople (cf. Lee 2000b: 34–6).[7]

The phenomenon of non-campaigning emperors did not escape contemporary criticism, most explicitly in Synesius' tract *On Kingship* (*Peri basileias/ De regno*), written in 398 (but unlikely to have been delivered in this format before Arcadius: Liebeschuetz 1991: 106; Alan Cameron and Long 1993: 127–42). As part of his veiled attack on the palace eunuch Eutropius, whose excessive influence over Arcadius he deplored, Synesius urged the emperor to involve himself actively with his soldiers:

> Now my speech must go on to lead the emperor from out his palace, and, after his friends, to hand him over to his soldiers, second friends these; and further to make him descend to the plain and inspect his men, their arms, and their horses. There he will ride with the cavalry, charge with the infantry, arm himself heavily with the hoplites, manoeuvre with the targeteers, and hurl the javelin with the light-armed troops, enticing every man to living comradeship by association in their operations; so that not merely in semblance shall he call them fellow-soldiers. They will come to know him when he addresses them on the field... This custom is capable of bringing goodwill towards him in that the spectacle of a ruler is not a rare one to his soldiers...
>
> The king will benefit from this close intercourse, not only because the army will surround him as one unified organism, but also because many of the incidents on these occasions are, some of them, an exercise in warlike affairs, and at the same time will be initiations, and preparations of a kind, for the functions of command and awaken his ambition for great and serious tasks. It is no small advantage in active service that he can address by name, a general, a commander of a unit, the commander of a squadron or a brigade, or a standard-bearer, as the case may be; that he can call up and exhort any of the veterans from his knowledge of them... Who would not be lavish with his blood when the king has praised him? This benefit then will come to you from frequent contact with your troops... The king is a craftsman of wars, just as a cobbler is a craftsman of shoes. The latter is laughable when he does not know the tools of his craft; how then shall a king understand how to use his tools, namely soldiers, when he does not know these tools? (*On Kingship* 13–14 [tr. Fitzgerald]).

Half a century later, the Gallic aristocrat Sidonius Apollinaris lamented the consequences of non-campaigning emperors: "Since that time [the reign of Theodosius I], much has been lost, for with the emperor, whoever he be, closely confined (*principe clauso*), it has been the constant lot of the distant parts of this wretched world to be laid waste" (Sidonius *Poems* 5.358ff.). Intriguingly, the historian Sulpicius Alexander, probably writing early in the fifth century, referred to Valentinian II in remarkably similar phraseology as being "shut in the palace in Vienne" (*clauso apud Viennam palatii aedibus principe Valentiniano*) (preserved in Gregory of Tours *History of the Franks* 2.9, with discussion in Stroheker 1970).

The expression of such reservations, however, had no noticeable impact on the behavior of emperors during the first half of the fifth century. Moreover, once a pattern of emperors not campaigning had become established over the half century following 395, there was always a likelihood that sheer inertia would ensure that the pattern persisted. That it did so in the fifth-century east is nonetheless somewhat surprising, given that those who succeeded Theodosius II down to the end of the century – Marcian (450–7), Leo (457–74), and Zeno (474–91) – were all men with military experience prior to coming to the throne. Perhaps one should distinguish between the first two and Zeno, insofar as it looks like Marcian and Leo had only reached the middling ranks of the officer class (the tribunate – i.e., commanding a unit) and so may not have felt competent to command armies.[8] Moreover, both faced the problem of powerful generals, in the form of Flavius Zeno (not to be confused with the later emperor) and Aspar, who presumably did all they could to ensure that these emperors did not undertake military campaigning themselves. Age may also have been a consideration: Marcian was born in 392, so was approaching 60 when he acceded to the throne, while Leo was probably born in 401, so would have been only a few years younger than Marcian when he became emperor in 457. Zeno, on the other hand, was an experienced soldier (cf. *Anonymous Valesianus* 9.39) who had held a number of senior commands prior to becoming emperor in 474 when in his mid to late 40s. Once emperor, however, he did not engage in any campaigning himself: he expressed his intention to lead an army against the Goths in Thrace in 478, but then apparently changed his mind (Malchus fr.18.3), and campaigns against various internal challengers to his position seem to have been entrusted to others on his behalf.

This apparent reluctance on the part of men with military experience to engage in campaigning once they became emperor, particularly in the face of significant military challenges, is perhaps explicable in terms of certain traumatic fourth-century events – specifically, the deaths of Julian and Valens in battle in 363 and 378. As previously noted, both events created constitutional crises over the succession, with attendant instability: the fall-out from Julian's death was arguably felt for some years afterward, until the end of Procopius' revolt in 367, while Valens' demise at Adrianople precipitated a major problem in containing the Goths, which was not achieved until 382– and even that settlement did not represent a definitive solution. It may be that fifth-century emperors in the east and their advisers were influenced by the memory of these events (cf. Kaegi 1981: 21–3; McCormick 1986: 47; Michael Whitby 1992b: 302–3).[9]

In the west, on the other hand, some emperors in the decades after the death of Valentinian III in 455 were more militarily active, though necessarily on a limited scale, given the parlous state of imperial finances in that half of the empire. Avitus (455–6) had served under Aetius during the 430s, rising to the rank of *magister* in Gaul, in which capacity he saw active service against the Huns and Visigoths, and his brief reign came to an end as a result of defeat in battle, albeit by the generals Majorian and Ricimer rather than a foreign invader. After a brief hiatus, Majorian emerged as Avitus' successor, campaigned in Gaul, and attempted unsuccessfully to mount an invasion of Vandal north Africa (a setback which resulted in his elimination by Ricimer in

461). Anthemius (467–72) had a distinguished military record in the east prior to his accession, but although he was involved in preparations for campaigns against the Vandals and Visigoths, he seems to have delegated campaign leadership to others (specifically Marcellinus and his own son Anthemiolus), rather than being involved personally. Finally, Julius Nepos (474–5) was another individual with a military background who, with the support of the eastern emperor Leo, fought his way to the throne in the west in 474, though his hold on power proved too brief for him to take any military initiatives. As will be apparent, then, although a number of the final emperors in the west had the experience and inclination to engage in active campaigning, the severity of the west's problems prevented them from achieving the sort of success which might otherwise have helped to stabilize their regimes.

Returning to the east in the period after the demise of the west, Zeno's successor in 491 was Anastasius, a man with no military background whose age at accession (about 61) precluded him from acquiring one. Unusually, the widowed empress, Ariadne, had been allowed to nominate her late husband's successor, perhaps because she was the last descendant of the emperor Leo. Why she chose Anastasius is not entirely clear, but given her husband's trials and tribulations it is perhaps less surprising that she opted for an individual from a non-military background.[10] At any rate, he proved a good choice in so far as he managed to restore stability to the empire's affairs over the ensuing decades. His successor, Justin I, did have a military background and had recently been involved in the successful repulse of the attempted seizure of power by the *magister* Vitalian (Greatrex 1996: 135–6), though his position as commander of the palace guard also played a crucial part in his gaining the throne on Anastasius' death in 518; however, since he was already in his mid to late sixties, he did not lead Roman forces in person. Nor did his adopted son and successor Justinian (527–65), who is not known to have had any significant military experience despite his holding the (presumably honorific) post of praesental *magister* for seven years or so before his accession. His successor, Justin II (565–78), had a background in the imperial bureaucracy and so continued the sixth-century pattern of non-campaigning emperors.

Tiberius II (578–82) and Maurice (582–602) both had military experience prior to their accession, even if they had begun their careers as bureaucrats (cf. Menander fr.23,2: "[Maurice] had not been trained in war and conflict" at the time he was appointed *magister* of the east), but once elevated to the throne, they left campaigning to subordinates, apart from three occasions, in 584, 592, and 598, when Maurice briefly led troops short distances from Constantinople into Thrace (Theophylact Simocatta 1.7.2, 5.16.1–6.3.8, 7.15.7, with Michael Whitby 1988: 143, 156–8, 163); interestingly, on the second occasion, he did so in the face of concerted opposition from courtiers apparently concerned for his safety (Theophylact

Simocatta 5.16.2–4). Phocas (602–10), the usurper who overthrew Maurice, had a military background as a relatively junior officer, but also appears to have directed campaigns from Constantinople rather than taking an active role himself. It was not until the reign of Heraclius (610–41) that there was a genuine return to the campaigning emperors of the third and fourth centuries. This partly reflects the context of his accession – he led forces from north Africa to overthrow Phocas – but above all the circumstances which he inherited – a major war on two fronts against Persia and the Avars, against whom the empire had already lost substantial ground by 610, which meant that a man of his experience could not sit in Constantinople leaving others to get their hands dirty. Perhaps the Phocas episode had made him and his advisers realize that, whatever the risks on the battlefield, it was not an option to distance himself from the army and risk another usurper emerging from that quarter.

1.2. The Unchanging Ideology of Victory

Military success had always been a fundamental ingredient in political power at Rome. This tradition did not lose any of its force during the Principate, the important difference being that the emperor necessarily monopolized military glory (cf. Gagé 1933). Although military success was in short supply during the middle decades of the third century, it remained important to maintain the ideology of victory, and this continued to be the case throughout late antiquity, even when the empire suffered severe setbacks. Although the habit of emperors not campaigning in person meant that the imperial office was better protected from any adverse effects arising from military defeat, one might have expected that it would make it difficult for emperors to maintain an aura of military invincibility. It is clear, however, that this was not the case. From the Principate, emperors were able to claim the credit and the glory for the successes of subordinates (Gagé 1933: 6–8; Kent 1994: 46–7), and late Roman emperors had an impressive array of media at their disposal through which their subjects could be made aware of military successes, whether gained by the emperor's own endeavor or that of others.

1.2.1. Verbal media

By frequent repetition of empty praise and a vain parade of facts which were obvious, some of Constantius' courtiers inflated his natural self-conceit after their usual manner, ascribing to his lucky star any success in any corner of the world. This big talk by his toadies encouraged him to set forth in the edicts which he published then and later a number of arrogant lies; though he had not been present himself at an action, he often declared that he alone had fought and conquered and inclined a merciful ear to the entreaties of native kings. If, for example, while he was in Italy, one of his generals distinguished himself against the Persians, no mention would be made of him in a very long bulletin, but letters wreathed in laurel would be sent to extract money from the provinces, in which Constantius informed them with odious self-praise that he had fought in the front rank. Statements by him are still extant in the imperial records which show his vainglorious habit of praising himself to the sky. When this battle was fought near Strasbourg, from which he was forty days' march away, his account of the action stated that he had drawn up the order of battle, taken his place by the standards, put the barbarians to flight, and had [the Alamannic ruler] Chnodomar brought before him. Disgraceful to relate, he said nothing of the glorious exploits of Julian. (Ammianus 16.12.68–70 [tr. Hamilton])

Perhaps the most immediate way in which campaigning emperors were able to communicate military success to a wide audience was through the dispatch of victory reports to be posted and read out in the major cities of the empire. In one of his sermons, John Chrysostom made reference to the absolute silence which prevailed in the theater when imperial letters of this sort were read out (*Homily on Matthew* 19.9 (*PG* 57.285)). Circumstantial allusions to the practice survive in a range of different sources. A church council at Serdica in 343 was interrupted by the arrival of a victory report (*epinikia*) over the Persians from Constantius (Athanasius *History of the Arians* 16.2); Symmachus reported to a friend his having read out in the senate in Rome a letter with news of imperial victories in 379 (*Letter* 1.95.2; cf. *Consular Lists of Constantinople s.a.* 379); the ability of an Egyptian holy man to foretell the future was confirmed when, soon after, "there arrived in Alexandria the letter of victory (*epinikia*) of the pious emperor Theodosius announcing the destruction of the tyrant Eugenius [in 394]" (*History of the Monks* 1.64); and in a wry inversion of normal practice, one Christian ostentatiously tore down a copy of Diocletian's first persecution edict in Nicomedia, "declaring mockingly that victories over Goths and Sarmatians were being proclaimed" (Lactantius *On the Deaths of the Persecutors* 13.2).[11]

The excerpt at the head of this section concerning the aftermath of Julian's victory at Strasbourg in 357 provides further valuable evidence on the subject of victory reports. Despite Ammianus' trenchant criticisms, Constantius was fully justified in claiming the credit for a success achieved under his auspices, even if he showed less magnanimity than Theodosius I in acknowledging the role of his general (cf. Symmachus *Memoranda* 47.2). As Ammianus' comments indicate, these reports could be very detailed and they were intended to enhance the reputation of the emperor.[12] The tradition of emperors claiming credit for victories gained by their subordinates also provided scope for non-campaigning emperors to accrue vicarious military prestige in this way, as when Theodosius II led an impromptu celebratory march through the streets of Constantinople on the arrival of news of Aspar's suppression of the usurper John in Italy (Socrates *Church History* 7.23), and Maurice instigated chariot-racing on receipt of victory reports over the Persians from Heraclius senior in 589 (Theophylact Simocatta 3.6.5).

The only surviving text of a victory report derives from the early seventh century, when Heraclius seems to have sent back regular reports of his progress (Theophanes *Chronicle* pp. 313–14). The final one, announcing his defeat of Khusro in 628, is preserved in a chronicle (cf. Howard-Johnston 1994: 70–2):

> In the 18th year of the reign of Heraclius...on the 15th of the month May...in the most holy Great Church [Hagia Sophia] were read out dispatches which had been sent from the eastern regions by Heraclius, our most pious emperor, which announced the fall of Khusro and the proclamation of Siroe as the Persian king. They were as follows: "Let all the earth raise a cry to God; serve the Lord in gladness, enter into his presence in exultation, and recognise that God is Lord indeed...And let all we Christians, praising and glorifying, give thanks to the one God, rejoicing with great joy in his holy name. For fallen is the arrogant Khusro, opponent of God..." (*Easter Chronicle* pp. 727–8 [trs. Whitby and Whitby])

The text continues at considerable length, but it is in some respects atypical, in so far as its overtly Christian emphasis shifts the focus away from the emperor's achievements to the divine aid which he credits with his success. This partly reflects the way in which religious devotion had increasingly been harnessed by the state during the second half of the sixth century (Averil Cameron 1979) and partly the way in which the long war against Persia in the early seventh century had developed into a quasi-religious conflict (cf. Howard-Johnston 1999: 39–40).

The fact that victory reports were read out meant that they were in principle accessible to a wide audience, unlike other verbal media which required varying degrees of literacy. At the simplest level, there were the various imperial titles employed in inscriptions and laws which were generally on public display and which conveyed information about the emperor's military successes, whether at the generalized level of *victor* and *triumphator*, or at the specific level of success against a particular people, as in *Alamannicus* or *Gothicus* – victor over the Alamanni and over the Goths respectively. Knowledge of the use of such titles by particular emperors is obviously dependent on the random survival of sources. Analysis of the surviving evidence (as tabulated by Rösch 1978, especially in the tables after p. 172) indicates employment of the title *victor* by nearly all late Roman emperors. *Triumphator* seems to have become less popular as the fourth century progressed, but then is used consistently from the end of the fourth century onward, and it is tempting to see a possible correlation between its revival and the advent of non-campaigning emperors keen to insist on their military credentials. For titles which refer to foreign peoples, it is less easy to discern any clear patterns beyond their striking and significant efflorescence under Justinian and his successors, as in the following formula used in the preambles to a number of Justinian's laws: *Imperator Caesar Flavius Iustinianus*

Alamannicus Gothicus Francicus Germanicus Anticus Alanicus Vandalicus Africanus pius felix inclitus victor ac triumphator semper Augustus (Rösch 1978: 167).[13]

At the other end of the spectrum in terms of demands on educational attainment lay the use of rhetoric, poetry, and other literary genres to celebrate military success. The audience capable of appreciating such work was naturally a very small proportion of the empire's population, but it was important since it included those who held positions of power and influence at court. More often than not, the existence of such works is known only through chance references to them rather than through their survival. Hence, Faltonia Betitia Proba, the wife of a prefect of the city of Rome and better known as the author of a Christian poem based on Virgil, also wrote a poem about Constantius II's defeat of the usurper Magnentius (*PLRE* I.732; Clark and Hatch 1981: 98); one of Julian's bodyguards is reported to have celebrated his deeds in epic verse (Socrates *Church History* 3.21; cf. Viljamaa 1968: 27); when a student in Constantinople, a lawyer named Eusebius witnessed the revolt of Gainas, whose suppression he commemorated in a poem in four books in heroic meter (Socrates *Church History* 6.6.36); the empress Eudocia, among others, produced poems in honor of Roman military success against Persia in the early 420s (Socrates *Church History* 7.21.7–10); the defeat of the Isaurians by Anastasius' generals in the 490s prompted a six-book epic by Christodorus, while Anastasius' Persian war of a decade later resulted in a poem by Colluthus (*Suidas, s.v.* Christodorus, Colluthus); and John the Lydian, a middle-grade bureaucrat in the early sixth century, recorded that he wrote an account of the Persian wars of Justinian's early years (John the Lydian *On the Magistracies of the Roman State* 3.28). In this last case, John is explicit that Justinian commissioned the work, and this may have been the case with some of the other items noted above. Alternatively, ambitious individuals may have produced the work on their own initiative in the hope of winning imperial favor and patronage (cf. the reasons given by Menander (fr.1) for writing his history during the reign of Maurice).

None of these works has survived, but others have, to provide some idea of their typical content. Papyrus fragments preserve small portions of an epic poem probably written to honor the military achievements of the Tetrarchs (cf. Barnes 1976: 183; for alternative possible contexts, see Viljamaa 1968: 65–6):

> Just as Zeus goes from Crete above Othrys and Apollo leaves sea-girt Delos for Pangaeus, and as they don their arms the noisy throng of Giants is set to trembling, in such fashion the elder lord [Diocletian] with his army of Ausonians reached the Orient in the company of the younger king [Galerius]. They had the likeness of the blessed gods, one in strength matched Zeus on high and the other the fair-haired Apollo... (*P. Strasbourg* 480 [tr. Dodgeon in Dodgeon and Lieu 1991: 125])

In the early fifth century, Cyrus of Panopolis wrote a short encomium of Theodosius II in which he likened him to a range of Homeric heroes, including Achilles (*Greek Anthology* 15.9). Another, even more fragmentary, papyrus preserves a hexameter encomium which may well relate to Zeno's suppression of the revolt of Illus in the 480s (MacCail 1978). Although the panegyrics of Priscian and Procopius for Anastasius focused mainly on the emperor's non-military achievements, they gave some attention to the Isaurian war and how "the army of the invincible emperor, favored in arms, and its generals, no less powerful in their loyalty than in their courage, brought utter ruin on those they killed and put to flight" (Priscian *Panegyric* 63–5; cf. Procopius of Gaza *Panegyric* 7–10, *Greek Anthology* 9.656). An anonymous epigram looked forward to the Persians, Saracens, and Huns being defeated by Anastasius, "whom time brought into the world to outshine even Trajan" (*Greek Anthology* 9.210).

The introduction to Agathias' collection of epigrams also celebrated Justinian's military prowess (cf. Viljamaa 1968: 60–2):

> Let no barbarian, freeing himself from the yoke-strap that passes under his neck, dare to fix his gaze on our king, the mighty warrior; nor let any weak Persian woman raise her veil and look straight at him, but, kneeling on the ground and bending the proud arch of her neck, let her come uncalled and submit to Roman justice... Go now, thou Roman traveller, unescorted over the whole continent and leap in triumph... You will be amid the possessions of our wise king, whichever way you progress, since he has encompassed the world in his dominion. (*Greek Anthology* 4.3, lines 47–52, 77–8, 93–6 [tr. Paton])

Writing as he was for a newly enthroned emperor who had no military experience, Corippus might have been excused for the omission of any military references in his panegyric for Justin II, but he managed to use his description of Justin's accession attire adeptly to sidestep this seemingly insurmountable obstacle:

> He put on his royal limbs the red thongs... with which the victorious Roman emperor tramples conquered kings and tames barbarian necks. Only emperors, under whose feet is the blood of kings, can adopt this attire... The robe, which was adorned with tawny gold and outdid the sun as the emperor stretched out his right hand, covered the imperial shoulders in glowing purple. A golden brooch fastened the joins with its curving bite, and from the ends of chains hung jewels which the fortunate victory in the Gothic war produced and which Ravenna, loyal to our rulers, brought back, and which Belisarius carried from the Vandal court. The indications of your triumphs, pious Justinian, will remain while Justin is safe and rules the world. (Corippus *In Praise of Justin II* 2.105–27 [tr. Cameron])

The most detailed surviving examples of such literature, however, comprise the poetry of George of Pisidia celebrating the achievements of

Heraclius in the early seventh century, notably his *On the Persian Expedition* (early 620s) and *Heraclias* (late 620s) – both probably commissioned by Heraclius (Mary Whitby 1998b: 250–1). These poems are "chiefly concerned with the emperor as military leader" (Mary Whitby 1998b: 263) – hardly surprising, given the novelty of an emperor leading the army in person once again, and the successes which he achieved – but with a distinctively Christian emphasis which was novel (Mary Whitby 1994) (cf. above p. 39).

1.2.2. Visual media

> To these portraits [imperial statues and pictures] one emperor likes to add this representation, another that: some add depictions of the most famous cities offering them gifts, others, victories holding garlands over their heads; some, their officials doing homage to them, and decorated with the insignia of their office; others, hunting scenes and feats of archery; and yet others, barbarians overcome, and trampled under foot, or being slaughtered in various ways. (Gregory of Nazianzus *Orations* 4.80)

A range of artistic representations associating the emperor with victory has survived from late antiquity, together with descriptions of others no longer extant. As with the literary works just discussed, some of these artworks must have had a relatively restricted audience, but an audience which emperors nevertheless needed to impress and cultivate. This category of artwork includes:

1. plates made of precious metal, such as the silver dish from Kerch depicting a mounted emperor in military attire (probably Constantius II) and the silver *largitio* (largesse) plate of Valentinian I or II (Fig. 1.1),[14] likewise in military costume and flanked by soldiers (Leader-Newby 2004: 22–4), as well as the gold tableware which Justinian had inscribed with scenes of his triumphs (described by Corippus *In Praise of Justin II* 3.120–5);
2. the fine detail on imperial vestments, showing "barbarian phalanxes bending their necks, slaughtered kings and subject peoples in order... and Justinian himself... as victor in the midst of his court, trampling on the bold neck of the Vandal king" (Corippus *In Praise of Justin II* 1.275–87);
3. ivory carvings (typically exchanged as gifts among the aristocracy) such as the famous Probus diptych, depicting Honorius in military gear with a standard bearing the acclamation "May you always conquer in the name of Christ" (Kiilerich 1993: 65–8), and the so-called Barberini ivory, with a mounted emperor of the late fifth or sixth century triumphing over foreign enemies (Fig. 1.2); and

EMPERORS AND WARFARE

4   mosaics in the imperial palace like that on the ceiling of the vestibule known as the Bronze Gate, described by Procopius (cf. Michael Whitby 2000d: 64–5):

> On either side [of the mosaic] is war and battle, and many cities are being captured, some in Italy, some in Libya [i.e., north Africa]; and the emperor Justinian is winning victories through his general Belisarius, and the general is returning to the emperor, with his whole army intact, and he gives him spoils, both kings and kingdoms and all things that are most prized among men. In the centre stand the emperor and the empress Theodora, both seeming to rejoice and to celebrate victories over both the king of the Vandals and the king of the Goths, who approach them as prisoners of war to be led into bondage. Around them stands the Roman senate, all in festal mood. This spirit is

Figure 1.1   Silver largesse plate of Valentinian I or II.
This silver plate was discovered near Geneva in the eighteenth century, and is one of a number of silver plates from the fourth century depicting an emperor, probably given as gifts or rewards to leading courtiers. Although quite worn, the details on this particular example are still clear enough. The writing around the upper rim refers to the largesse of the emperor Valentinian, the central figure in military attire with a standard. The presence of soldiers emphasizes the military context, while in his right hand the emperor holds a globe surmounted by a winged victory offering him a victory wreath; at his feet are symbolic weapons of the defeated. For further discussion of this plate and the wider artistic context, see Leader-Newby 2004: 11–59. (Image © Musée d'art et d'histoire, Ville de Genève, inv. no. C 1241 (photographer: J. M. Yersin).)

Figure 1.2 The Barberini ivory.
Ivory was a valued artistic medium in late antiquity, most commonly used for consular diptychs – that is, hinged leaves of carved ivory depicting the consul and given as a celebratory gift to friends. This famous ivory (34 × 26 cm) seems to have served a somewhat different purpose, although it is unclear whether it was part of a diptych or a stand-alone item. It shows a victorious emperor in military dress on his charger, accompanied by a winged Victory and being presented by a military officer on the left with a statuette of victory, while conquered peoples present tribute in the lower register (where another winged Victory is also present), and Christ bestows his blessing from above. The identity of the emperor is not completely certain, but there are good reasons for thinking that it is Justinian (see Cutler 1991). The blank plaque on the right may originally have contained a civilian figure to balance the military figure on the left. The piece takes it name from the cardinal who owned it in the seventeenth century. (Image © Département des Objets d'art, Louvre, Paris (OA. 9063))

expressed by the cubes of the mosaic, which by their colours depict exultation on their very countenances. So they rejoice and smile as they bestow on the emperor honours equal to those of God, because of the magnitude of his achievements. (Procopius *Buildings* 1.10.16–19 [trs. Dewing and Downey])

There was of course also a range of artwork accessible to the wider public. Again, some of these items have survived, while others are known only through literary descriptions or the drawings of early modern travelers. They include:

1 triumphal arches, of which those of Galerius in Thessalonica and of Constantine in Rome survive (Kleiner 1992: 418–25, 444–55), while that of Diocletian in Rome (the so-called "Arcus Novus") is known only from some of its reliefs (Kleiner 1992: 409–13),[15] and that of Honorius in Rome from an inscription recording success against the Goths in the early years of the fifth century (*ILS* 798);
2 victory columns, of which Theodosius' (commemorating the defeat of Goths in 386) is known primarily from literary sources and fragments (Kiilerich 1993: 51–5; Sodini 1994: 48–55), and Arcadius' (celebrating the suppression of Gainas in 400) is known mainly from detailed drawings made before its demolition in the early eighteenth century (Fig. 1.3; Liebeschuetz 1991: 120–1, 273–8; Kiilerich 1993: 55–64; Sodini 1994: 56–66);[16]
3 equestrian statues, all known examples of which were in Constantinople – that of Constantine (Socrates *Church History* 1.16; cf. Bassett 2004: 242–4), those of Theodosius I and of Marcian (both recorded in poems preserved in the *Greek Anthology* 16.65, 9.802; cf. Bassett 2004: 208–11 on the former), and that of Justinian (Mango 1993), of which Procopius provides a detailed description (cf. Michael Whitby 2000d: 65–6):

And on the summit of the column stands a gigantic bronze horse, facing toward the east, a very noteworthy sight. He seems about to advance, and to be splendidly pressing forward...Upon this horse is mounted a colossal bronze figure of the emperor. And the figure is habited like Achilles, that is, the costume he wears is known by that name. He wears half-boots and his legs are not covered by greaves. Also he wears a breastplate in the heroic fashion, and a helmet covers his head and gives the impression that it moves up and down, and a dazzling light flashes forth from it...And he looks toward the rising sun, directing his course, I suppose, against the Persians. And in his left hand he holds a globe, by which the sculptor signifies that the whole earth and sea are subject to him, yet he has neither sword nor spear nor any other weapon, but a cross stands upon the globe which he carries, the emblem by which alone he has obtained both his empire and his victory in war. And stretching forth his right hand toward the rising sun and spreading out his

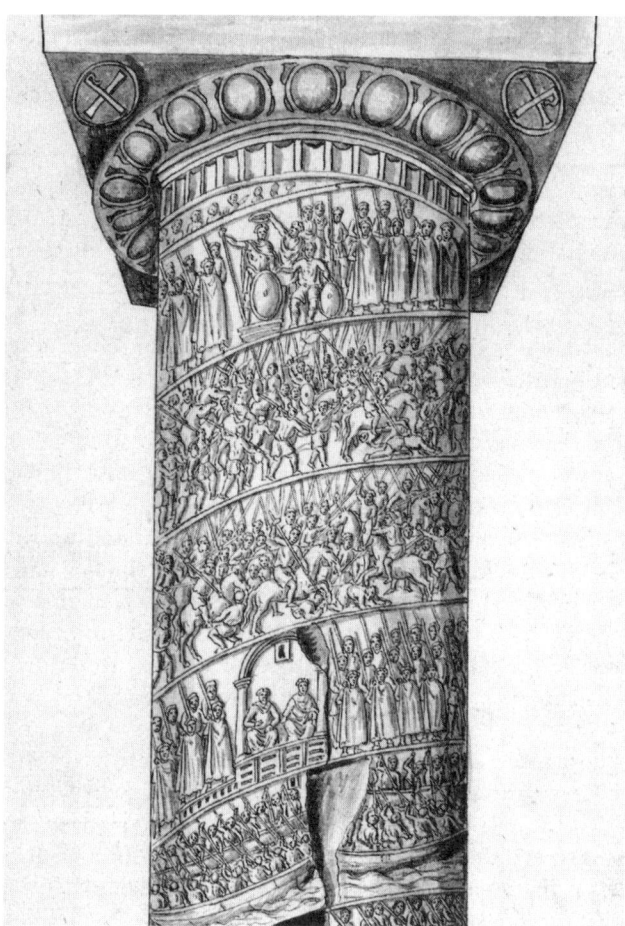

Figure 1.3   The victory column of Arcadius.
In 400, a rebellion by a Roman general, the Goth Gainas, which had threatened Constantinople itself was defeated. This victory was celebrated by the erection of a historiated (spiral) column, modeled on those of Trajan and Marcus Aurelius in Rome, in which reliefs depicted the sequence of events. The column itself has not survived, but a sixteenth-century German traveler made detailed drawings of the column when it still stood in Constantinople, and copies of these drawings are preserved in the Freshfield folder in the library of Trinity College, Cambridge. This particular part of one of the drawings, showing the upper spirals on the south side of the column, depicts two stages in the defeat of the rebellion – waterborne conflict on the Bosporus, and a land battle. The emperor Arcadius, who did not participate in the fighting, is shown twice: in the second lowest spiral, he is seen seated with another figure who is thought to be his brother Honorius, emperor in the west, symbolizing imperial solidarity, while in the top spiral, Arcadius is being crowned with a victory wreath after the successful outcome of the conflict (or alternatively, he is the seated figure looking on while a statue of perhaps his father Theodosius I is crowned). For further discussion of the episode and the column, see Liebeschuetz 1991: 111–26, 273–8. (Image reproduced by permission of the Master and Fellows of Trinity College, Cambridge.)

fingers, he commands the barbarians in that quarter to remain at home and to advance no further. (Procopius *Buildings* 1.2 [trs. Dewing and Downey])[17]

4   imperial portraits and icons, whether in the form of busts or paintings, were widely distributed in the cities of the empire (Ando 2000: 228–53), and could often include reference to military success, as the passage at the start of this section indicates. Consider also the following excerpt from one of his sermons in which John Chrysostom cast around for an appropriate analogy to explain the idea of the Old Testament as a foreshadowing of the truth fully revealed in the New:

> Come, let us direct our thoughts to the images that painters depict. You have often seen an imperial image covered with blue colour [i.e., the background wash]. Then the painter draws white lines, delineating an emperor, an imperial throne, horses standing nearby, bodyguards, and enemies lying below in chains. But while you watch these things being roughly sketched, you do not know the whole picture, but neither are you completely in the dark, for you are aware, however indistinctly, that it is a man and a horse being drawn. You do not know the identity of the emperor and the enemy with absolute certainty until the application of the colours reveals the truth and makes the appearance certain. (*Sermon on the words of Paul, "We do not want you to be ignorant,"* PG 51.247)

One such painting, depicting Roman emperors on golden thrones with Huns lying dead at their feet, could be seen in fifth-century Milan – that is, until Attila captured the city and ordered the scene to be repainted so that it showed Attila on a throne with emperors pouring sacks of gold at his feet (Priscus fr.22.3). Likewise, it was common practice during games in the circus at fourth-century Rome to display paintings showing the bravery of the emperor or the strength of the soldiers (Eunapius fr.68).[18] Nor should one forget depictions of Victory personified, such as are known from provincial cities like Ephesus (Roueché 2002). Even if these did not always have an explicit link with an emperor, they must nonetheless have served to reinforce the general ideology of victory.

Another, less permanent visual medium was victory ceremonial. Such occasions were necessarily ephemeral, but the opportunity they provided for a degree of active participation on the part of at least some of the emperor's subjects served to enhance their impact significantly. The central ritual was the military triumph, with its traditions stretching back centuries into the Republican period of Roman history, a ritual which evolved and changed during late antiquity, particularly under the joint impact of the increasing marginalization of the city of Rome and of the influence of Christianity (full discussion in McCormick 1986: 11–130). Other events might also be staged in celebration of military success, such as the "[annual] circus games [i.e., chariot races] staged [in Rome] for the victory [of Constantius II in 344] over the inhabitants of Adiabenica [a region of

Mesopotamia]" (*Calendar of Polemius Silvius*, January 31). It has been observed, interestingly, that the frequency of such occasions seems to have increased when the empire was struggling militarily (McCormick 1986: 43–4).

The major limitation inherent in these different visual media was that they were located and took place in the major cities, which meant that many inhabitants of the empire would still never have seen or experienced them. There was, however, one visual medium which could be relied upon to achieve wide circulation in the provinces – coinage – and emperors were clearly aware of its potential as a means of advertisement. Coins had the additional advantage that they combined visual messages with succinct slogans (traditionally referred to as the "legend," in the root sense of the word, viz. that which is available for reading). Importantly, these slogans would have been comprehensible to those with otherwise limited literacy. Perusal of the relevant indices of *Roman Imperial Coinage* leaves no doubt that victory was consistently the most common theme among the range of slogans used from the third to the fifth century, a pattern which the standard catalogue on early Byzantine coinage (Bellinger 1966) confirms as continuing through the sixth century.

Coins also communicated the military prowess of emperors through a range of images. The obverse side of the coin, which usually bore a bust of the emperor, almost invariably portrayed him in military gear of some sort. So, for example, in the early fourth century the emperor was shown wearing a military cloak (*paludamentum*) and breastplate "with a laurel wreath on his head emphasizing the triumph and perpetual success constantly associated with him" (Bruun 1966: 36). This remained broadly typical throughout the fourth century, until a major change occurred in the eastern half of the empire soon after the death of Theodosius I, when the angle of the bust moved from side on to facing, and the laurel wreath was replaced with "a crested, diademed helmet. In the right hand and carried over the shoulder behind the head is a spear, and in front of the left shoulder a shield which usually carries the motif of a horseman riding to the right over an enemy and striking him with a spear" (Kent 1994: 47)(Fig. 1.4 (left)). It is tempting to see this more pronounced military emphasis, which remained standard in the east into the sixth century, as an attempt to compensate for the lack of direct military involvement on the part of Arcadius and his successors, although there was no comparable move in the west.[19]

The reverse sides of coins offered more scope for variation, but a figure personifying Victory is a common feature throughout the fourth century and beyond, while the emperor treading on an enemy captive also occurs (Fig. 1.5 (right)). Some novelties were introduced in the fifth century, notably the advent in the east of Victory holding a long jeweled cross from the 420s onward (Fig.1.4 (right)), and in the west at about the same time, the emperor placing his foot on the head of a human-headed serpent,

Figure 1.4 Gold *solidus* of the emperor Anastasius (491–518).
The obverse side (on the left) of this coin shows the emperor in a typical representation from the eastern half of the empire during the fifth century, in military attire (crested helmet, breastplate, spear, shield), with the shield depicting a rider trampling on an enemy – all this, despite the fact that emperors in this period rarely if ever actually participated in military campaigning themselves. The reverse side (on the right) shows another typical image from fifth-century coins: a winged Victory holding a jewel-studded cross – an interesting fusion of artistic motifs from Classical and Christian traditions. The visual message is reinforced by the slogan *Victoria*. (Image reproduced by permission of Dumbarton Oaks, Byzantine Collection, Washington, DC.)

Figure 1.5 Gold *solidus* of the emperor Valentinian III (425–55).
The reverse side (on the right) of this coin shows a motif in common use by western emperors during the first quarter of the fifth century: the emperor in military attire holding an army standard in one hand and, in the other, a globe surmounted by a winged Victory proffering a victory wreath, while he treads on a prostrate captive; the slogan is again *Victoria*. (Image reproduced by permission of Dumbarton Oaks, Byzantine Collection, Washington, DC.)

representing a defeated usurper (Kent 1994: 55–6). It is worth emphasizing that the theme of victory features as regularly on issues of bronze coinage as on gold *solidi*, since rural inhabitants were more likely to encounter smaller-denomination coins.

Further Reading

There is no detailed analysis of **imperial involvement in warfare** during late antiquity, although Kaegi 1981: 20–5 and Michael Whitby 2004: 179–86, 2005: 367–77, have some useful comments; for imperial involvement in campaigning during the Principate, see Campbell 1984: 59–69.

On the theme of **victory** in late Roman art, Grabar 1936: 125–62 remains valuable, as do Gagé 1933 and Straub 1939 on victory as an element of imperial ideology. Ferris 2000 includes discussion of representations of the empire's enemies in late Roman art. On victory ceremonial in late antiquity, the relevant sections of McCormick 1986 are fundamental.

2

MILITARY LOYALTIES AND CIVIL WAR

The common association of late antiquity with barbarian invasions means that the form of war which most readily comes to mind in the context of this period is external conflict with neighboring states and peoples. However, late antiquity also witnessed a recrudescence of civil war with a regularity unknown since the late Republican period. A high incidence of civil war particularly characterized the mid third century, forcefully reminding subsequent emperors of the need to work hard at retaining the loyalty of troops. The first part of this chapter examines the varied strategies emperors used to reinforce ties of loyalty and so reduce the risk of military challenges and internal conflict. Needless to say, those strategies were not always effective, and the second part of the chapter investigates episodes of civil war and military unrest with a view to identifying the factors responsible, the changing patterns of incidence over the course of late antiquity, and the strategies employed by emperors to deal with ambitious generals.

2.1. Retaining Soldiers' Loyalties

A range of factors had the potential to influence the loyalties of soldiers. Perhaps the most obvious was military success, and so the range of media through which victory (or failing that, the appearance thereof) was communicated to the inhabitants of the empire (as discussed in the second part of the previous chapter) was also of particular significance for the emperor's relations with the army. However, there were other strategies for reinforcing loyalty, ranging from rituals of initiation to material incentives and symbolic gestures of identification, each of which will be discussed in this section. As in the previous chapter, an essential element throughout is the changing pattern of imperial involvement in warfare, since non-participation in campaigning by the overwhelming majority of emperors from the end of the fourth century onward removed them from regular direct contact with their troops.

2.1.1. Rituals of initiation

> They swear by God, Christ and the Holy Spirit, and by the Majesty of the Emperor which second to God is to be loved and worshipped by the human race. For since the Emperor has received the name of Augustus, faithful devotion should be given, unceasing homage paid him as if to a present and corporeal deity. For it is God whom a private citizen or a soldier serves, when he faithfully loves him who reigns by God's authority. The soldiers swear that they will strenuously do all that the Emperor may command, will never desert the service, nor refuse to die for the Roman state. (Vegetius *Epitome of Military Science* 2.5 [tr. Milner])

Although the idea of loyalty to the emperor was inculcated in soldiers in a variety of ways, rituals of initiation offered particularly important opportunities in this respect. One obvious instance of such initiation was when a soldier was first enrolled in the army; another – perhaps less immediately obvious – was when a new emperor came to the throne. It is clear that the potential of both occasions was appreciated in late antiquity.

With regard to the enrollment of a soldier, the key element from the perspective of the issue of loyalty was the oath which he was required to swear. There is perhaps a temptation to minimize the significance of this formal aspect of a soldier's induction, but such a view has been firmly rebutted in the context of modern armies:

> It is easy to regard the military oath as a meaningless charade which has little practical value. To do so is, however, to underestimate the importance of the first ritual in a ritualistic profession. The impact of the oath upon German officers and soldiers was recognised by Hitler, who, after the death of Hindenburg in 1934, had the impersonal oath of the Weimar Republic replaced by one in which the soldier swore personal allegiance to the *Führer* himself. Telford Taylor wrote that the oath "constantly emerged as a seemingly insurmountable obstacle to any decisive opposition to Hitler within the officers' corps"...Deserters [from the *Wehrmacht*] often sought to appease their consciences by claiming that they had signed their oaths in pencil, or that the sergeant who administered the oath had his back turned. Such elaborate excuses would not have been needed had the oath not possessed considerable moral authority. (Holmes 1985: 32–3)

That the Roman military oath had religious associations is apparent from its Latin designation, *sacramentum*, as also from the fact that early Christian writers sometimes used the swearing of the military oath as an analogy for baptism (cf., e.g., Michaelides 1970: 41–71). Something of its "moral authority" is reflected in a late fourth-century letter preserved on papyrus, in which a recent recruit comments that "for the sake of my oath I cannot leave my post" (*P. London* 3.982 with Rea 1997b: 190). Obviously the military oath was not a late Roman innovation (see Campbell 1984: 19–32 for its role during the Principate). Nevertheless, it is apparent from the extract at the head of this section that its content was modified during the fourth century in a way which reflected the influence of Christianity, and that modification served to strengthen the force of the oath through emphasis on divine sanction for the emperor's position. Unfortunately, it is difficult to trace any further developments in its format after the fourth century – precisely the period when the non-involvement of emperors in campaigning meant that it became even more important.[1]

By contrast, much more detail is known about the formalities relating to the initiation of a new emperor throughout late antiquity, and there is no doubt that the accession of emperors provided an important opportunity to strengthen ties between emperor and army. There was some precedent for the army playing a part in accessions during the Principate, notably in the civil wars of 68–9 and the early 190s, but the senate continued to have an essential role (Campbell 1984: 374–82). As the third century progressed, however, the army's involvement became increasingly prominent. "Maximinus was the first to come to power [in 235] solely as the choice of the soldiers" (Eutropius 9.1); "during the same period [238] in Africa the soldiers appointed as Augustus Gordian's son, Gordian [III]"; "[in 252] the soldiers bestowed the empire on Licinius Valerianus" (Aurelius Victor *On the Caesars* 27.1, 32.1); "Claudius succeeded Gallienus [in 268] after being chosen by the soldiers"; "after him Quintillus, the brother of Claudius, was elected emperor [in 270] through the agreement of the soldiers"; "the victorious army on its way back from Persia [in 284], since it had lost Carus, the Augustus,...made Diocletian emperor" (Eutropius 9.11, 12, 19). Reflecting on this trend, one commentator writing in the mid fourth century observed, with obvious regret, that "the power of the military increased and the right of appointing the emperor was seized from the senate down to our own times" (Aurelius Victor *On the Caesars* 37.5).

Although the advent of Diocletian as emperor in 284 marked the initiation of an intriguing experiment in the distribution of imperial power, in which his own wishes were clearly of paramount importance, he seems to have ensured that the army was seen to play an important formal role in the confirmation of new members of the Tetrarchy, if the events of 305 are a fair guide: the proclamation of the two new junior emperors ("Caesars") who were to join the imperial college upon the retirements of Diocletian and Maximian took place in the presence of troops, with representatives apparently having been summoned from various units (Lactantius *On the Deaths of the Persecutors* 19.1–3).[2] This was a pattern which, in broad terms, continued throughout the fourth century. Admittedly, circumstances dictated the prominence of the army in many cases. So, for example, army units played an important role in the acclamations of Constantine in 306 (Lactantius *On the Deaths of the Persecutors* 24.8; Eusebius *Life of Constantine* 1.22.1) and Julian in 360 (Ammianus 20.4), since both men were challenging incumbent emperors and it would hardly have been realistic to do so without strong military support. Likewise, a number of fourth-century emperors were proclaimed Augustus in the context of a military campaign – Jovian in 363 and Theodosius I in 379 (Ammianus 25.5; *Latin Panegyrics* 2.31.2) – so that the involvement of troops in the proclamation was only to be expected.[3]

This makes the remaining cases where sufficient detail survives all the more suggestive. The accessions of Valentinian I and Valens, both in 364, and the proclamations of Julian as Caesar (junior emperor) in 355, and of Gratian, Arcadius, and Honorius as *Augusti*, in 367, 383, and 393 respectively, did not take place during military campaigns or as the first step in an attempted usurpation, so attendant circumstances did not demand the presence of the army.[4] Nevertheless, Valentinian's accession at Nicaea involved his appearing in appropriate regalia on a tribunal before an assembly of troops whom he then addressed – and if the content of the speech reported by the historian Ammianus Marcellinus bears any relationship to what he actually said,[5] then Valentinian emphasized that he owed his elevation to the will of the army (even if Ammianus' account of the preliminaries shows that the selection of Valentinian was in fact the result of discussions between senior military and civilian figures: Ammianus 26.2; cf. Philostorgius *Church History* 8.8). Julian's elevation as Caesar occurred in Milan, "on a high platform surrounded by eagles and standards in the presence of all the troops that were available" (Ammianus 15.8.4), with Constantius' appealing to the troops for their endorsement. Gratian's proclamation as Augustus at Amiens also took place with military units in attendance, again with much emphasis on their approval, according to Ammianus (27.6). Much less is known about the accessions of Valens, Arcadius, and Honorius, but all three have in common the fact they took place at the Hebdomon, "the seventh milestone" southwest of Constantinople (*Easter Chronicle* pp. 556, 562–3; Marcellinus *Chronicle* 393). The Hebdomon was the location of an army barracks and military parade ground (Janin 1964: 446–9), so the accession of these individuals must have been staged there, rather than in the city itself, in order to facilitate the formal involvement and symbolic assent of representative units of the army.

The army's endorsement of the accession of the emperor acquired even greater significance once emperors ceased to campaign. Apart from anything else, it provided a rare opportunity for at least part of the army to see and perhaps hear their nominal commander-in-chief. It is not therefore surprising to find that the formal accessions of Theodosius II (402),[6] Marcian (450), and Leo (457) all took place at the Hebdomon (*Easter Chronicle* pp. 568, 590; Constantine Porphyrogenitus *Book of Ceremonies* 1.91 [p. 410]). While knowledge of the first two occasions is limited to brief chronicle entries, the third is preserved in considerable detail in a source which appears to be based on an eyewitness account without literary embellishment,[7] and since only short excerpts of this text have previously been translated by others, a more extensive quotation is presented here:

> When Marcian of blessed memory had passed away and the senate's choice had fallen on Leo of blessed memory, everyone proceeded to the parade ground (*Kampos*, i.e., Hebdomon) – officials, palace guards (*scholai*), and soldiers, and Anatolius the patriarch of Constantinople (Martialis was the *magister*).[8] When the *labara*[9] and the military standards had been laid on the ground, everyone began to cry out: "Hear us, o God, we call upon you. Listen to us, o God: to Leo, life. Hear us, o God: Leo shall rule. O benevolent God, the public asks for Leo as emperor, the army asks for Leo as emperor, the laws await Leo, the palace awaits Leo. These are the prayers of the palace, these are the petitions of the army camp; these are the prayers of the senate, these are the prayers of the people; the world awaits Leo, the army awaits Leo. Let Leo, the adornment of all, come. Leo, the blessing of all, shall rule. Hear us, o God, we call upon you."
>
> Immediately Leo, count and tribune of the Mattiarii, was brought forth, and when he had ascended the tribunal, Busalgus the drill-master (*campidoctor*) placed the torque [a twisted gold band] on his head, and another torque was placed on his right arm by Olympius, likewise a drill-master. Immediately the *labara* were raised, and everyone cried out: "Leo, Augustus, you are victorious, you are pious, you are worthy of reverence! God has given you, God will keep you. Worshipping Christ, you will always be victorious. Leo shall rule for many years. God will protect the Christian empire." Immediately he was surrounded on the tribunal by the locked shields of the imperial guards (*candidati*) and after donning the imperial robe and putting on the diadem, he appeared thus to the people. Immediately he received the homage of all the officials in order of precedence. He took up a shield and a lance, and everyone acclaimed him as follows: "Powerful, victorious, worthy of reverence, fortunate, fortunate! You shall reign for many years, Leo, Augustus. God will protect this empire; God will protect this Christian empire," and more in a similar vein.
>
> Then Leo addressed them through the official responsible for imperial correspondence (*libellarius*) as follows: "The emperor Caesar Leo, victorious, ever worthy of reverence [says]: Almighty God and your judgment, very valiant fellow-soldiers, have chosen me to be emperor of the Roman state." Everyone cried out: "Leo, Augustus, you are victorious: he who has chosen you will guard you. God will preserve his own chosen one. God will protect his holy empire. [He is] holy and powerful!" The response of the emperor, Caesar Augustus: "You shall have me to exercise authority and rule as a fellow-soldier in your toils, which I learned to bear when still a fellow-soldier with you." Everyone shouted: "Good fortune! The army [accepts] you as emperor, o victorious one! The army [accepts] you as emperor, o fortunate one! We all desire you [as emperor]!" The emperor [replied]: "I have decided what donatives I ought to give to the troops." Everyone cried out: "[You are] worthy of reverence and powerful and most wise." The emperor [replied]: "For the inauguration of my holy and fortunate rule, I will give five *nomismata* [gold coins] and a pound of silver to each shield." Everyone shouted: "Worthy of

reverence and generous! From you come honors, from you come riches. May your reign be fortunate for us and a golden age!" The emperor Caesar Augustus [said]: "May God be with you." And he proceeded into the city, and the rest took place as prescribed. (Constantine Porphyrogenitus *Book of Ceremonies* 1.91 [pp. 410–12])

As the final sentence of the passage indicates, this was not the end of the event, and in fact the chapter continues with a description of the procession into the city, including visits to the imperial palace and the church of Hagia Sophia. Clearly, the advent of emperors who spent most of their time in the capital allowed scope for the evolution of more complex ceremonial rituals which gave an increasing role to Christianity in particular. Nevertheless, at this point in time, at any rate, the military dimension remained pre-eminent (even if there continued to be a token acknowledgment of the role of the senate at the start): the soldiers present are identified as a distinct group at the outset, symbolic actions are performed with the military standards, it is military officers who crown Leo with torques, Leo takes up military equipment before he speaks, he addresses himself explicitly to the troops present, his "fellow-soldiers," it is their acknowledgment of his right to rule which appears to be of critical importance, and it is they who benefit from the donative.

The proclamation of Leo's immediate (and short-lived) successor, his six-year-old grandson Leo II, witnessed a shift in location, from the Hebdomon to the hippodrome, inside the city and adjacent to the palace (Constantine Porphyrogenitus *Book of Ceremonies* 1.94 [pp. 431–2]). This shift in location appears to have been unplanned, since Leo seems to have elevated his grandson in response to impromptu demands from the hippodrome audience, who were perhaps worried that the ailing emperor might otherwise be succeeded by Leo's unpopular son-in-law Zeno (cf. Candidus fr.1); even so, at least one military element continued – the issuing of a donative (*Book of Ceremonies* 1.94 [p. 432]). Zeno's proclamation the following year (about which no other details are known) also took place in the hippodrome, and although the usurper Basiliscus reverted to the Hebdomon when he seized power in 475 (Theophanes *Chronicle* p. 121), no further imperial accession was to take place at the military parade ground.[10] Nevertheless, other military elements continued to feature. The accession of Anastasius in 491 had a number of elements in common with Leo's – the standards were laid on the ground, Anastasius was crowned with a torque by a drill-master, and a donative was promised to the troops; he was also raised on a shield, something which did not happen to Leo, but for which there were fourth-century precedents (Constantine Porphyrogenitus *Book of Ceremonies* 1.92 [p. 423]). Similarly in 518, Justin I was lifted on a shield, was crowned with a torque by a drill-master (after which the standards were raised from the ground), received a lance and shield, and promised the customary donative to the soldiers (*Book of Ceremonies* 1.93 [p. 429]). Much less detail is preserved concerning Justinian's accession, though it is said to have followed the same pattern as his adoptive father's, except that Justin's illness meant that it took place within the palace rather than in the hippodrome (*Book of Ceremonies* 1.95 [pp. 432–3]). The detailed, if more literary, account of the elevation of Justin II in 565 provided by the poet Corippus confirms important continuities with reference to the placing of a torque by a drill-master (during which the latter says, significantly, "I confer on you the position of emperor") and the raising on a shield, though surprisingly there is no mention of donatives for the troops (Corippus *In Praise of Justin II* 2.129–40). Little detail is known about the remaining two sixth-century accessions (those of Tiberius II and Maurice), although Tiberius did issue the standard accession donative to troops,[11] which also makes it likely that Justin had in fact done so (cf. Jones 1964: 624).

Having focused on continuities in the military dimension, it must be acknowledged that important changes in the ceremonial rituals can also be observed across the course of the fifth and sixth centuries. In particular, besides the relocation from the Hebdomon to the hippodrome and/or the palace, the patriarch took an increasingly important role in affairs, reflecting the growing importance of Christianity in legitimating imperial rule. However, the fact that military elements remained in place despite such changes occurring suggests that their continuing presence was not simply a matter of inertia, but rather reflected conscious recognition on the part of emperors and their advisers of the importance of these symbolic gestures in retaining the loyalty of the army.

2.1.2. *Material incentives*

And on 29th July [511] the emperor assembled all the commanders of the forces and all the officers of the scholarians [the imperial guard] and the patricians, and he said to them, "According to my regular custom I wish to give a donative." For so it had been his practice to give it once every five years ever since he became emperor, at the same time requiring oaths from all the Romans to the effect that they would not act treacherously against the empire. But on this occasion he required them to take the oath in the following manner: a copy of the gospel being placed for them, they went in and received the five *denarii* [i.e., *solidi*] each, and they swore as follows: "By this law of God and by the words which are written in it, we will contend with all our might for the true faith and for the empire, and we will not act treacherously either against the truth or the emperor." In this manner, indeed, he required them to take the oath, because he heard that Macedonius [patriarch of Constantinople] was trying to raise a rebellion against him. On 30th July the emperor gave a largesse to the whole army. (Ps.-Zachariah *Church History* 7.8 [trs. Hamilton and Brooks])

The military-oriented rituals in the accession ceremonials of emperors were bound to have their greatest impact on those troops physically present, but one aspect – the accession donative – had a much wider impact. Other types of donative (about which more will be said below) were certainly distributed to troops throughout the empire (*P. Beatty Panopolis* 2.161–4 [298]; *P. Oxyrhynchus* 4367 [325/37]; Procopius *Secret History* 24.27–8), so it is inconceivable that this was not also the practice with the accession donative. The impact of the accession donative was of course enhanced by the fact that it represented a genuine material benefit for soldiers. Although calculating the value of ancient coins to contemporaries is notoriously difficult, some sense of the significance of the accession donative may be gained from the knowledge that one *solidus* would buy about 1,000 lb of bread, and that "a poor man might survive on less than 3 *solidi* p.a." (Davis 2000: 137). In other words, the sum of five *solidi* and one pound of silver (equivalent to about another five *solidi*) was a generous bonus.

Another type of donative closely related to the accession donative was that distributed to troops in celebration of the five-yearly anniversary of the emperor's accession. There was a tradition of emperors giving donatives to the troops during the Principate, though not, it seems, on any sort of regular cycle (Campbell 1984: 186–98; Bastien 1988: 11–16), so that the more consistent evidence for quinquennial donatives in late antiquity may reflect, if not an innovation, then a conscious regularization of this practice by late Roman emperors. The evidence for the quinquennial donative comprises literary references relating to the fourth, fifth, and sixth centuries;[12] attempts to correlate actual issues of coins with these occasions (Bastien 1988: 53–128) are more problematic (Burnett 1989; King 1990). The sum involved was apparently about half the value of the accession donative, so another useful supplement to a soldier's income, particularly in periods when the existence of multiple emperors with different accession years might mean such donatives were paid more frequently than every five years (cf. Jones 1964: 624). Even when there was only one emperor ruling, the opening anecdote about Anastasius shows that the quinquennial donative was still regarded as being sufficiently attractive to reinforce loyalty to the emperor. This makes Procopius' claim that Justinian effectively abolished the quinquennial donative somewhat surprising:

> There was a law that once in every five years the emperor should bestow on every soldier a fixed sum of gold; and every fifth year they sent to all parts of the empire and presented each soldier with five gold coins. It was quite impossible even to invent an excuse for evading this duty. Yet from the day that this man took over the running of the state he has never done anything of the kind or shown any intention of doing it, although no fewer than thirty-two years have already gone by, so that this custom has been forgotten by most people. (Procopius *Secret History* 24.27–9 [tr. Williamson, with revisions])

While it is unlikely that Procopius' claim is completely false, some of his other bald statements in the *Secret History* about Justinian's policies vis-à-vis the army are open to question, notably his assertion that Justinian abolished the *limitanei* (*Secret History* 24.12–14, with discussion in Jones 1964: 661–3, Isaac 1992: 210–11, Michael Whitby 2005: 361–2). While he undoubtedly experienced problems with maintaining army pay later in his reign (cf. Chapter 2.2, p. 72 below), "it is hardly credible that the armies would have made no protest and would have fought as well as they did, if they had suffered such a cut, and it seems likely that Procopius either exaggerated delays in the payment of the donative, or misrepresented a measure whereby the donative was consolidated with the annual *annona*" (Jones 1964: 284–5).

Other types of donative also receive occasional mention – for the emperor's birthday (*P. Beatty Panopolis* 2.161–4; *P. Oxyrhynchus* 561) and for the anniversaries of the foundations of Rome and Constantinople (Sozomen *Church History* 5.17.8) – but it is not known how consistently these were issued (full details in Bastien 1988: 17–27). However, donatives were by no means the only material benefits which soldiers received (that is, over and above their normal pay). Soldiers also received a variety of tax privileges in the fourth century. Perhaps the most interesting example of these is the record of those granted by Licinius in 311 and preserved on a bronze tablet found in Thrace:

> Since in all matters we desire that provision shall always be made for the advantage and profit of our soldiers on account of their loyalty and labours, in this matter also, dearest Dalmatius, we believe that we must exercise our forethought in making arrangements to provide for our said soldiers. Wherefore, in consideration of our said soldiers' labours, which they undergo through continual expeditions for the State's maintenance and benefit, we believe that we must make arrangements with foresight, not only that during their period of military service they may delight in the enjoyment of the rewards that we have provided suitable to their labours, but also that after military service they may obtain a quiet repose and suitable freedom from care. Therefore we believe that we must bring to the attention of your Devotion that our said soldiers during their term of military service in accordance with our statute shall be exempted, indeed, to the extent of 5 tax units (*capita*) from the property tax and from the customary charges of payments in kind; and that, when these same men secure honourable discharges after the completion of the full legal period of service, they shall have the same exemptions. But those men, indeed, who in like manner receive honourable discharges, although after twenty years of service, shall be exempted from charges in kind to the extent of 2 tax units, that is, one for each man and also one for his wife ... The said soldiers shall receive the rewards that they deserve from us, rewards earned through their military service, and that they may enjoy forever the eternal benefits of our said indulgence and that the eternal provision of our ordinance may steadfastly

> endure, it is our will that the text of this our indulgence shall be inscribed on tablets of bronze and shall be dedicated among the standards in each camp. (*AE* 1937.232 [trs. Johnson et al.])

The interest of this example resides not just in the substantive privileges granted and the differentiation between those who completed a full term of service (probably 24 years) and those who completed 20 years, but also in the language in which their grant is couched and the steps taken to advertise them throughout the army (cf. Corcoran 1996: 145–8).

Licinius was not unique in his use of such privileges as a way of strengthening the loyalty of troops to himself. Constantine also granted extensive tax privileges to his soldiers when they retired, as recorded in an unusual law preserved in the *Theodosian Code* – unusual because it takes the form of a dialogue between the emperor and some veterans (cf. Corcoran 1996: 257–9):

> When he had entered the imperial headquarters of the army and had been saluted by the military prefects and tribunes and by the most eminent men [viz., the praetorian prefects], the acclamation arose: "Augustus Constantine! The gods preserve you for us! Your salvation is our salvation. In truth we speak, on our oath we speak."
>
> The assembled veterans cried out: "Constantine Augustus! To what purpose have we been made veterans if we have no special grant of imperial privileges?"
>
> Constantine Augustus replied: "It is my duty to increase the happiness of my fellow veterans more and more, rather than to diminish it."
>
> Victorinus, a veteran, then said: "We pray that you do not allow us to be compelled by law to perform compulsory public services and to bear grievous burdens in all places."
>
> Constantine Augustus replied: "Indicate more plainly. What are the compulsory public services especially that most persistently oppress you?"
>
> All the veterans said: "Surely, you yourself fully understand."
>
> Constantine Augustus then proclaimed: "Be it known that it has just now been conceded to all veterans by my munificence that no one of them shall be compelled by law to the performance of a compulsory municipal service, or to service on public works, or to any tax payment imposed by magistrates, or to any imposts. In whatever public markets they may engage in business they shall not be compelled to pay the market taxes . . . By this same edict we have also prohibited our treasury from disturbing anyone at all of these veterans, but they shall be allowed to buy and sell, so that their special legal privileges may be cited in court with full force, under the protection of the repose and peace of our generation, and their old age shall enjoy to the full their leisure after their labours." (*Theodosian Code* 7.20.2.1–6 [320] [tr. Pharr with revisions])

Subsequent emperors confirmed these privileges during the fourth century (*Theodosian Code* 7.20.6 [342], 9 [366]), while the inclusion of Constantine's exchange with the veterans in 320 in the *Justinianic Code* (12.46.1) implies that these privileges remained in force through to the sixth century.

2.1.3. Symbolic gestures of identification

> Do not be surprised, I pray, if, after your having undertaken the hard work of long marches and the accumulation of such an abundance of supplies, when my confidence in you was leading me forward and we were approaching barbarian territory, I seem suddenly to change my plan and turn to a more peaceful course of action... I will explain briefly, my loyal fellow-soldiers (*commilitones mei fidissimi*), why I wished you all to assemble here; lend a favorable ear to my brief explanation... The kings and peoples of the Alamanni, fearing the extent of glory you have attained (news of which has spread to the inhabitants of the most distant parts), have asked, through these spokesmen whom you see with bowed heads, for forgiveness for their past offences and for peace. As someone who is careful, not one to rush into things, and mindful of what is advantageous, I think there are many reasons for granting this, if I have your agreement. (Ammianus 14.10.11–14)

Emperors and their advisers were also attuned to the value of symbolic gestures designed to reinforce soldiers' sense of affinity with the reigning emperor. One area where there was scope for this was emperors' use of language of identification. The best-known example of this was an emperor referring to the troops as his "fellow-soldiers" (*commilitones*), as represented in the extract above from a speech placed by Ammianus in the mouth of Constantius II during campaigning on the northern frontier in 354, when he faced the delicate task of persuading his troops to acquiesce to a peace settlement with the enemy instead of embarking on an offensive with its prospects of booty and bloodletting (cf. also Symmachus *Orations* 1.19 for a speech, placed in the mouth of Valentinian I, which begins with *fidissimi commilitones*). The use of this expression had a long-established pedigree. Even if its use during the Julio-Claudian dynasty appears to have been limited, it came to the fore during the civil war of 68–9 and thereafter remained in regular use during the Principate (Campbell 1984: 32–8). However, the language of identification encompassed a range of other phrases, from "our soldiers" and "our army," to the more explicitly flattering "our very valiant troops" (see Table 2.1 for references and variations from late antiquity). Emperors in the third and fourth centuries could, of course, continue to use the term *commilitones* with justification, because for the most part they did undertake the rigors of campaigning alongside their troops. After 395, however, it was difficult for non-campaigning emperors to use this terminology without the risk of reminding troops that they were no longer active participants in warfare.[13] At the same time, it became even more important that soldiers maintained some sense of identification with their emperor. So although the term *commilitones* may have dropped out of use, other related phraseology continued to be employed after 395. Indeed, it appears to have been used with greater frequency, if the legal sources are any sort of guide.

Table 2.1 Expressions of esteem by emperors to troops (legal and documentary sources)

Expression	Period	References	Total
milites nostri, "our soldiers"	Pre-395	*AE* 1937.232 (311), *CJ* 6.21.3 (254), 8.50.12 (293), 7.64.9 (284/305), *CTh* 7.4.1 (325), 7.4.6 (360)	6
	Post-395	*CTh* 7.4.22 (396), 7.1.18 (400), *NTh* 4.3 (438), *CJ* 4.65.31 (457/74), 12.35.18.1, 6 (492), 1.17.1 (530), 1.27.2.11 (534), *NJ* 130.8–9 (545)	8
noster exercitus, "our army"	Pre-395	*CTh* 11.7.3 (320)	1
	Post-395	*NTh* 6.1 (438), *CJ* 1.27.1.43 (534), *NJ* 130.6–7 (545)	3
commilitones nostri, "our fellow-soldiers"	Pre-395		0
	Post-395	*ZPE* 61 (1985) 274 (395/423), *De Caer.* 1.91 (474)	2
devotissimi milites, "very loyal soldiers"	Pre-395	*CJ* 10.26.2 (364)	1
	Post-395	*CTh* 7.5.2 (404), 16.10.19 (408), 7.8.13 (422), *CJ* 12.35.18.3–4 (492), 12.37.17.1 (491/518), 1.27.2.4 (534)	6
devotissimus exercitus, "very loyal army"	Pre-395		0
	Post-395	*CJ* 4.40.4 (410/13)	1
fortissimi milites nostri, "our very valiant soldiers"	Pre-395		0
	Post-395	*CTh* 7.6.4 (396)	1

fortissimi milites, "very valiant soldiers"	Pre-395		0
	Post-395	*CTh* 7.6.5 (423), *CJ* 12.50.22 (457/74), 12.35.18.3–4 (492), 12.37.17 (491/518)	4
fortissimi ac devotissimi milites, "very valiant and loyal soldiers"	Pre-395	*CTh* 7.4.17 (377)	1
	Post-395		0
fortissimus exercitus, "very brave army"	Pre-395		0
	Post-395	*NMaj* 1.1 (458)	1
dicatissimi milites, "very dedicated soldiers"	Pre-395		0
	Post-395	*CJ* 12.35.18 (492)	1
milites nobilissimi, "very noble soldiers"	Pre-395		0
	Post-395	*SEG* 9.356 (501)	1
Overall totals	Pre-395		9
	Post-395		28

Note: Expressions are broadly grouped in order of ascending complexity. Where a text was written in Greek, the relevant phrase has been noted above under the appropriate Latin equivalent. *CJ* = *Justinianic Code*; *CTh* = *Theodosian Code*; *De Caer.* = Constantine Porphyrogenitus *Book of Ceremonies*; *NJ* = Justinian *Novels*; *NMaj* = Majorian *Novels*; *NTh* = Theodosius II *Novels*.

The point of tracking these phrases in legal sources is that literary sources, such as historical narratives like that of Ammianus, were influenced by canons of usage from previous centuries and by conventions about the presentation of speeches, so that the extract at the head of this section, for example, is less a verbatim report of what Constantius actually said to his troops and more Ammianus' view of how he believed an emperor ought to express himself in such a situation. Legal sources, on the other hand, are closer to documentary evidence. Rhetoric undoubtedly also influenced their formulation, but the fact remains that these were official documents disseminated throughout the empire (cf. Matthews 2000: 181–99), which therefore provide a more accurate guide as to the language which emperors and their advisers used when communicating with troops (among others). Furthermore, the chronological spread of legal sources gives reasonably equal weight to the period before and the period after 395. Although the final data set remains quite small, even when supplemented with examples from documentary evidence (e.g., inscriptions), it is nevertheless of some significance that the use of the language of identification with troops seems to be more frequent after 395.

Another way of trying to enhance soldiers' sense of loyalty to the reigning emperor was through giving units names which included that of the emperor. Although there was some precedent for this during the first two centuries AD, it nevertheless remained relatively uncommon until Caracalla, in the early third century, included his family name (Antoninus) in the titles of all army units, thereby establishing a more definite trend (even if no subsequent emperor went to quite the same lengths as he did) (Campbell 1984: 88–93; cf. Fitz 1983: 228, listing 227 occurrences of the epithet *Antoniniana* in inscriptions). A number of Caracalla's successors during the first half of the third century also seem to have been quite generous in honoring units with their name; thereafter, examples tail off dramatically, but this has more to do with the general decline in the erection of inscriptions in the mid to late third century, and there are still epigraphic examples of at least one unit bearing an emperor's name for most of the emperors who managed to retain power for any length of time in this period (Fitz 1983: 228).

For the period from the late third to the early fifth century, the *Notitia Dignitatum* provides numerous examples of units named after emperors from the Tetrarchy (sometimes using Diocletian's terminology of identification with Jupiter and Hercules), and the families of Constantine, Valentinian, and Theodosius. From the 420s through to the end of the sixth century, the evidence is once again more scattered, but there are a large number of units bearing Justinian's name: *Numidae Justiniani* (*P. Cairo* 67321), *equites Perso-Justiniani* (*ILS* 2810), *Primes Felices Justiniani* (*CIL* 8.9248), *Justiniani Vandali* (Procopius *Wars* 4.14.17), *Bis Electi Iustiniani* and *Scythae Justiniani* (*P. Freer* 08.45 c–d [Gascou 1989]), *Libyes Justiniani* and *Paraetonitae Justiniani* (Justinian *Edict* 13.18), as well as a couple named after

Tiberius (Theophanes p. 251 (*Tiberiani*); T. S. Brown 1984: 281, *s.v.* Vitalis 4, an officer in the unit of the second *Tiberiaci*). Although the scattered nature of the evidence makes it impossible to discern any clear pattern vis-à-vis before and after 395, the appearance in the *Notitia Dignitatum* of half a dozen units named after Arcadius and more than 20 after Honorius, and Justinian's evident concern to name units after himself, are noteworthy in the context of non-campaigning emperors.

One important limitation on the value of special unit titles has been noted with reference to the Principate: "once special legionary titles had been bestowed, they tended to remain under succeeding emperors. They became a mark of honour to a legion and lost any particular connotations of association with an individual emperor" (Campbell 1984: 93). This limitation would have been offset to some extent in periods when sons succeeded fathers as emperor and would stand to gain some benefit from that association. Nevertheless, it remains a limitation compared with other forms of symbolic gesture.

Potentially the most effective medium through which to make symbolic gestures was coinage, since these had the widest distribution of any medium, while the survival of Roman coins in large quantities means that generalizations based on this evidence generally have a greater claim to credence.[14] Of particular relevance here are some of the slogans which featured on the reverse side of coins. The slogans of most direct relevance are *fides exercitus* ("the loyalty of the army") and *fides militum* ("the loyalty of the soldiers"). Investigation of the relevant indices of *Roman Imperial Coinage* (*RIC*) reveals only a small number of issues of coins bearing *fides exercitus* in the first and second centuries, the earliest examples occurring, interestingly, in the context of the civil war of 68–9 (*RIC* I.190–1, 224, 229–31, II.67). There are further instances during the reigns of Antoninus Pius and Commodus (*RIC* III.141, 143–4 (Antoninus); 378, 380, 382, 420 (Commodus)), of whom neither engaged in active campaigning; both therefore had greater need to create some sort of rapport with the army.[15] The slogan, or similar ones, next occur in the context of civil war again in the 190s (*RIC* IV.25–6 (Pescennius Niger), 47 (*fides legionum*: Clodius Albinus), 180 (*fides legionum*: Septimius Severus, 193)), while Caracalla's use of it on one issue early in his reign has been interpreted as "an appeal to the troops after the murder of [his brother and co-emperor] Geta" (*RIC* IV.87). As the third century progressed, *fides militum* in particular features with increasing frequency, particular in the third quarter of the century (*RIC* V), reflecting the uncertainty of the times and the attempts of successive emperors to retain the loyalty of the troops. With the emergence of the Tetrarchy and an increasing degree of political stability, the theme of the loyalty of the troops is gradually superseded by *virtus militum*, "the bravery of the troops," which remains popular throughout the fourth century, supplemented under Constantine by *gloria exercitus*, "the glory of the army." During the fifth century, the priority appears to have become the theme of *victoria* (Kent 1994: 54–5; cf. Chapter 1.2, pp. 48–50 above).

2.2. Civil War and Military Unrest

> Although he suffered grievous defeats in foreign wars, Constantius prided himself on his success in civil conflicts, and bathed in the blood which poured in a fearful stream from the internal wounds of the state. (Ammianus Marcellinus 21.16.15 [tr. Hamilton])

Although the distinction between civil war and foreign war seems straightforward enough, civil war is a term which nevertheless presents some definitional challenges. Those challenges can be illustrated by considering three episodes out of a number from late antiquity, each of which has a good claim to be classified as civil war:

1   In 324, Constantine, then emperor of the western half of the empire, invaded the territory of his fellow-emperor and erstwhile ally Licinius, who controlled the east. Since both men had previously co-operated and acknowledged one another as legitimate co-emperors, it was not a case of one challenging the other for the position of emperor, but rather of Constantine's unwillingness to continue sharing power.
2   In 351, Constantius II advanced westward to defeat Magnentius, an army officer who had, the previous year, overthrown and killed Constantius' brother Constans, ruler of the west.
3   In 537, the general Germanus defeated Roman troops in north Africa who had, the previous year, tried to take control of the region in their own interests, as a result of discontent with various aspects of central government policy.

Since all three episodes involved Roman forces fighting against Roman forces, they can legitimately be described as instances of civil war, but clearly there are some important differences between them. It could be argued that the first episode is rather atypical in so far as it involved two emperors of equal status fighting one another. This cannot be paralleled from the period of the Principate, with the only other comparable examples being Licinius' campaign against his fellow-tetrarch Maximinus Daia in 313, an earlier confrontation between Constantine and Licinius in 316–17, and the conflict between Constantine's two sons, Constantine II and Constans, in 340.[16] The second and third episodes are more common scenarios – the outcomes of what can be described as, respectively, usurpation and military mutiny. Both of these terms are, of course, heavily value-laden, reflecting the perspective of the established regime. Those doing the "usurping" and the "mutinying" would presumably have described their actions in rather different terms – perhaps as defending certain interests against tyranny or mistreatment. From the perspective of agency, however, what broadly distinguishes these two scenarios is that civil war arising from usurpation predominantly develops from the ambitions of an individual, who manages to win the support of troops to his cause (or sometimes from a dissatisfied officer corps in search of a viable leader, as in the case of Magnentius), whereas civil war arising from mutiny predominantly emerges out of fundamental discontent among the rank and file, which eventually finds leadership through which to channel that discontent.[17]

It is not always easy to tease out which of these two factors was more important in a specific situation, a problem which particularly besets analysis of the mid third century. Civil war was a regular feature of these years, but the deficiencies of the surviving sources make it very difficult to determine whether individual ambition or group discontent played the more important role in precipitating any particular episode. Thereafter, however, a broad pattern is easier to discern. During the fourth and fifth century, civil war was usually the result of usurpation, whereas in the sixth and early seventh century discontent among the rank and file played the more significant role.

In analyzing the usurpations of the fourth and fifth century for the existence of any common factors, there is little point in dwelling on the motives of the lead individuals, since in most cases insufficient is known about them to be able to comment meaningfully on motivation, beyond unhelpful generalizations about ambition and the like.[18] It is more fruitful to consider the factors which may have influenced troops to support the usurper in question and may explain their willingness to engage in war against fellow Roman forces. One factor which played a part in a number of usurpations from these centuries was the evident importance of blood ties with a recent emperor in inducing soldiers to lend their support. The loyalty of troops in Britain to the memory of his recently deceased father Constantius (one of the original tetrarchs) must have been a significant factor in their endorsement of Constantine's proclamation at York in 306. Although Magnentius is the name most readily associated with usurpation in 350, two other individuals – Nepotianus and Vetranio – also seized the opportunity to make a play for power, and of these the former was able to claim blood ties with Constantine (Zosimus 2.43.2), while the latter had the backing of Constantina, sister of the emperor Constantius II (Philostorgius *Church History* 3.22 with Drinkwater 2000: 153). As nephew of Constantine and cousin of Constantius II, Julian was, of course, very definitely a member of the imperial family. Procopius was able to build up military support for his attempt to replace Valens in 365 by appealing to his relationship with Julian and the Constantinian dynasty, as reflected in both the presence of Constantius' widow Faustina in his entourage and the coinage Procopius issued, and corroborated by the links which certain units and commanders who supported the usurpation had with the Constantinian dynasty

(Lenski 2002a: 98–101). Magnus Maximus, who overthrew Gratian in 383, seems to have been related to Theodosius (*PLRE* I.588). Although he had no claim of any sort to the throne, the usurper Constantine III (407–11) apparently gained support in part on the basis of his name (Orosius 7.40.4). Both Basiliscus and Marcian, who initiated revolts against Zeno in the 470s, had family ties to Zeno's predecessor Leo, the former as brother-in-law through marriage to Leo's sister Verina, and the latter through marriage to Leo's daughter Leontia. Zeno himself was married to another of Leo's daughters, Ariadne, but Marcian claimed to have a better right to the throne than Zeno because, although his wife Leontia was younger than Ariadne, Leontia had the distinction of having been born "in the purple" – that is, after Leo had become emperor (*PLRE* II.717). Marcian was also the grandson of Marcian, Leo's predecessor as emperor.

Although apparently not enough to prompt open mutiny, disgruntlement with the reigning emperor also sometimes played a part in making troops susceptible to the initiatives of ambitious generals. According to one source (Eutropius 10.9), Constans had become "unpopular with the soldiers"; the reason is unclear – one suggestion is resentment at the long period Constans spent in the Balkans, which "may have suggested that he favoured the Danubian forces over the Gallic" (Potter 2004: 471) – but that unpopularity must have aided Magnentius in his plotting (cf. Drinkwater 2000). Julian's Germanic troops in Gaul in 360 were notoriously unhappy about Constantius' request that a significant proportion of their number be transferred to the eastern frontier, since they had enlisted on the understanding that they would not have to serve east of the Alps (Ammianus 20.4.4; cf. Chapter 6.1. p. 151 below).[19] One factor which seems to have assisted Magnus Maximus in his overthrow of Gratian was the latter's alienation of some of his troops through favoritism toward a group of barbarian Alan recruits (Zosimus 4.35.2–3). Valentinian II's youth and lack of military experience may well have encouraged western troops to view the militarily competent Arbogast in a favorable light.[20] Zeno's unpopularity as an Isaurian, an ethnic group viewed by many as outsiders, no doubt played a part in the support which Basiliscus and Marcian were able to rally to their causes.

Various pre-emptive strategies were available to counteract the possibility of a prominent general capitalizing on his popularity with the troops to launch a bid for the throne. Although it may at first sight seem counterintuitive, one strategy was to remove any obvious cause for resentment or disgruntlement on the part of a general by ensuring that his military achievements received due recognition. During the Republican period of Roman history, the ultimate way of honoring a general had been the award of a ceremonial triumph through the streets of the capital, but Augustus had very quickly closed this avenue to anyone other than the emperor, presumably because fearful that it could become the basis for a challenge to his position.

This policy was adhered to by his successors throughout the Principate and late antiquity, with only one partial exception. In 535, Justinian sanctioned the holding of a triumph in Constantinople to celebrate the reconquest of north Africa from the Vandals, in which the successful general in this instance, Belisarius, was permitted to play a leading role in the occasion (cf. Chapter 4.1, p. 103 below). This willingness to revert, at least partially, to Republican tradition was presumably in part a reflection of Justinian's excitement about what was, after all, an extraordinary success, as well as his more general desire to promote the idea of a restoration of Roman greatness. However, he did not permit the holding of a triumph without some important changes to Republican tradition designed to ensure that the emperor was not overshadowed: Belisarius had to proceed on foot, rather than in a chariot, and when he reached the hippodrome, he had to prostrate himself before Justinian, just as the defeated Vandal king Gelimer did (Procopius *Wars* 4.9.1–12 with McCormick 1986: 125–9).

Together with this ceremonial occasion, Belisarius was also honored by the award of a consulship, which was a common method in late antiquity of acknowledging a successful general's exploits. The consulship was the ideal solution in this situation because the office retained great prestige, but no real powers, while it also served to integrate commanders into the civilian sphere. So, for example, the generals who helped Theodosius I overcome Magnus Maximus in 388 – Promotus and Timasius – held the consulships for 389 (*PLRE* I.750, 914); Flavius Zeno, the powerful general from the 440s (not the man who became emperor), held the consulship in 448 as a reward for his defense of Constantinople against the Huns the previous year (*PLRE* II.1199); and the two generals most responsible for success in the Isaurian war of the 490s, John the Scythian and John Gibbus, were honored with the consulship in 498 (*PLRE* II.602, 618). Belisarius' consulship in 535 proved in fact to be the last occasion on which this office was used to reward a general, and it is very likely that Belisarius' behavior during 535 contributed to Justinian's decision to discontinue the practice: Procopius reports the popularity which Belisarius enjoyed in Constantinople and elsewhere during that year, not least because of his generous distribution of largesse to the crowds from the wealth he had acquired from the Vandal booty (*Wars* 4.9.15–16, 5.5.18–19). Soon after, Justinian introduced a ban on the distribution of gold by anyone holding the consulship other than the emperor (*Novels* 105 [337]), and a few years after that, the office simply ceased to be held by anyone other than the emperor (Alan Cameron and Schauer 1982). It seems that Justinian may have decided that even allowing a successful general to hold the honorific office of consul for a year was courting danger.

Another strategy for dealing with potential threats from generals may have been to repost an individual perceived as posing a potential threat to a command from which it would be more difficult to initiate a challenge. This is what happened to the general Sebastianus in 375, when he was "sent to a distant post... because he was popular with the troops and so was particularly to be feared" (Ammianus 30.10.3), albeit on the initiative of another general (Merobaudes) rather than an emperor; however, Merobaudes' motive was not to seize power himself, but rather to facilitate the accession of Valentinian II following the death of Valentinian I.[21] While Justinian's reposting of Belisarius from Italy to the Persian frontier in 541 was in part dictated by military necessity, it was a convenient way of neutralizing what Justinian must have perceived as a growing threat, given the stories which were emanating from Italy about Belisarius having been offered the Gothic throne there (Procopius *Wars* 6.29.18–28, 6.30.1–2; cf. Justinian's much less public celebration of Belisarius' capture of Ravenna in 540: Procopius *Wars* 7.1.3–6).

The ultimate solution to the problem of a politically ambitious general was of course elimination. The clearest examples of this occurred in the sixth century. The first instance was that of Vitalian, a general who had shown his willingness to intervene in politics when he initiated civil war against Anastasius in 513, at least partly because of doctrinal differences; although eventually defeated in 515, he escaped and lay low, outliving the emperor (Evagrius *Church History* 3.43). Anastasius' successor, Justin, was in agreement with Vitalian on these religious issues and initially treated Vitalian favorably, bestowing high office and honors on him, including the consulship in 520. However, in that same year, Vitalian was murdered in the palace in Constantinople, with the sources almost unanimously attributing his death to Justin's ambitious nephew Justinian (*PLRE* II.1176). The other sixth-century case was Justin, the son of Justinian's cousin Germanus. A capable general, he was an obvious candidate to succeed Justinian after the latter died in 565 without any male offspring and without nominating an heir. However, he was absent from the capital at the crucial time, serving on the Danube frontier, which gave Justinian's nephew Justin, a palace official, a free hand to orchestrate his own succession. The new emperor soon recalled the other Justin to Constantinople, where, before long, the former began accusing the latter of plotting against him, resulting in his exile to Alexandria and eventual murder (*PLRE* III.753–4).

Moving back in time, there are the famous fifth-century cases of the murders of the eminent generals Stilicho, Aetius, and Aspar, the first done away with at the instigation of the emperor Honorius, the second killed in person by the emperor Valentinian III in 454, and the third eliminated on the initiative of the emperor Leo in 471. These instances are, however, somewhat different to those of Vitalian and Justin insofar as Stilicho, Aetius, and Aspar were not just politically ambitious, but had effectively been exercising political power in one half of the empire for a number of years prior to their deaths. Their deaths, then, were not cases of the elimination of potential political threats, but rather reassertions of imperial power against ambitious individuals who had achieved political dominance without recourse to civil war.[22] More akin to the examples of Vitalian and Justin is that of Marcellinus, a powerful general in Dalmatia in the 460s who was murdered in 468, though at whose instigation is unclear (cf. McGeorge 2002: 58–60). Zeno's apparent attempt to have Illus murdered in 477 (*PLRE* II.587) probably warrants inclusion here also, although this particular case is complicated by their common Isaurian background.

From the fourth century, there are some analogous cases. Theodosius, the father of the subsequent emperor Theodosius I, had had a successful military career during the reign of Valentinian I, but around the time of the latter's death in 375 he was executed in Carthage in mysterious circumstances. The most plausible explanation is a pre-emptive move by supporters of Valentinian's young sons, Gratian and Valentinian, to ensure that Theodosius did not take advantage of the situation to seize power himself (Matthews 1975: 64). The other instance is that of Silvanus in 355, though this is a little different, in so far as he had apparently gone as far as having himself proclaimed emperor.[23] Although the sources for this episode are much more plentiful compared with those for Theodosius senior, they remain problematic in many respects (Hunt 1999). The outcome, however, was the dispatch by Constantius II of a secret mission to eliminate Silvanus, as described by the historian Ammianus Marcellinus, one of the participants (Ammianus 15.5).

A striking characteristic of the sixth century is the rarity of civil war arising from the ambitions of a general, compared with earlier centuries of late antiquity. The only instance is Vitalian's attempt to overthrow Anastasius in 513–15, and this case is unusual, insofar as Vitalian does seem to have been genuinely motivated by disagreement with Anastasius over doctrinal matters (cf. Lee 2000b: 56–7). A survey of the holders of high military office during the sixth century reveals an interesting feature which surely helps to explain the scarcity of usurpations. A significant number of sixth-century generals were closely related to the reigning emperor, which in turn implies a conscious policy on the part of emperors with a view to minimizing threats from this quarter. Anastasius' two nephews Hypatius and Pompeius both held commands during his reign, as did another relative Ioannes and a relative of Anastasius' wife Ariadne by the name of Diogenianus (*PLRE* II: Hypatius 6, Pompeius 2, Ioannes 60, Diogenianus 4). Under Justin I, his two nephews Justinian and Germanus held posts as generals, even if the former's is likely to have been more honorific than practical in nature (*PLRE* II: Iustinianus 7, Germanus 4). During Justinian's reign, Germanus, his cousin, continued to hold important commands until his death in 550, as did other relatives: Justin (not the future emperor) and Ioannes, as well as the empress Theodora's brother-in-law Sittas (*PLRE* II: Germanus 4, *PLRE* III: Iustinus 4, Ioannes 46, Sittas 1). Two of Justin II's generals – Marcian and Justinian – were relatives of the emperor (*PLRE* 3: Marcianus 7, Iustinianus 3), while Maurice was married to one of Tiberius II's daughters (*PLRE* III: Mauricius 4). After Maurice himself succeeded Tiberius, he appointed his brother Peter and brother-in-law Philippicus to important commands

(*PLRE* III: Petrus 55, Philippicus 3). It is perhaps significant in this respect that when the troops mutinied in 602, they had to turn to a junior officer for leadership, in the person of the centurion Phocas.

While attempted usurpations were rare in the sixth century, however, mutinies by the rank and file became more frequent. Some of the troops involved in the reconquest of north Africa from the Vandals in the 530s, who subsequently remained there as a garrison, became disaffected with the authorities in Constantinople. The first major mutiny arose in 536 because of soldiers' liaisons with Vandal women, as a result of which they resisted the government's plans to make all previously Vandal-owned land into state property; this issue became entangled also with the government's ban on forms of worship associated with Arianism, the version of Christianity to which the Vandals had been converted (Procopius *Wars* 4.14). In 538 there was another short-lived bout of disturbance in the north African garrison because of delays in the receipt of pay (Procopius *Wars* 4.18). The garrison at Beroea surrendered to the Persians in 540 because of disgruntlement at their not having been paid, and there was also a danger of mutiny in Italy in 545 because of delays in pay (Procopius *Wars* 2.7.37, 7.12.7–8). Problems over pay resulted in further difficulties on the eastern frontier when 15,000 troops refused to participate in a campaign in Armenia in 579 until the emperor sent money (John of Ephesus *Church History* 6.28). In 588 a major mutiny broke out at Monocarton, an army base in northern Mesopotamia, after the emperor Maurice ordered a reduction of a quarter in soldiers' pay and rations (Theophylact Simocatta 3.1–2). Despite its serious nature, this mutiny did not result in civil war, primarily because of the mediation efforts of bishop Gregory of Antioch (Evagrius *Church History* 6.12). No such solution appears to have been available in 602, however, when troops on the lower Danube refused to obey the emperor Maurice's order that they spend the winter north of the Danube, instead choosing Phocas as their leader and marching on Constantinople to overthrow the emperor (Kaegi 1981: 101–19; Michael Whitby 1988: 24–7, 165–9).[24]

Perhaps unsurprisingly, much of this unrest was associated with conditions of service, and particularly delays in pay. This problem had occasionally arisen in earlier centuries at a localized level, as when an officer investigated claims at Oxyrhynchus in 360 that some military recruits had not received the money due to them (*P. Oxyrhnychus* 1103), while an otherwise mysterious episode of mutiny occurred in the 470s as a result of soldiers being deprived of their pay (Malchus fr.27). However, these sorts of difficulties do appear to have become more common in the sixth century, perhaps because of the greater use of expeditionary forces by Justinian (with attendant problems in communications) and perhaps because his ambitious plans placed an unaccustomed strain on the empire's finances.

Finally, there is the question of the impact of civil war on the empire. A negative (if also tendentious) view is evoked by one fourth-century commentator in the extract at the head of this section, while another famously observed of the battle of Mursa in 351, at which Constantius II defeated Magnentius, that "great resources were used up in that battle, sufficient for any foreign wars, which could have won many triumphs and brought peace" (Eutropius 10.12). It has also been suggested by a modern commentator that it was the usurpation of Magnus Maximus in the 380s which sealed the fate of the western half of the empire:

> After Maximus, no significant western emperor (we may exclude some shadowy and short-lived usurpers) ever went north of Lyons. The defeat of Maximus' western army by the eastern troops of Theodosius I, especially when coupled with the even bloodier slaughter of western regiments, again by Theodosius' men, during the usurpation of Eugenius in 394, was catastrophic for the defence of the region. (Halsall 2005: 48)

It has also been argued, however, that civil war and usurpation in the fourth century should not be seen in an unremittingly negative light: "Battles were lost and won by timely acts of betrayal. This kind of disloyalty helped to save the lives of soldiers, and the economy however achieved should be set against the unthinking assumption that Rome ruined herself by civil wars" (Wardman 1984: 232; cf. Drinkwater 2005: 63 on the third century). While undoubtedly true, this observation does not diminish the deleterious consequences of those occasions when the fighting went ahead. A broader chronological perspective over late antiquity as a whole also tends to reinforce the sense that civil war was fundamentally detrimental to the interests of the empire. The string of usurpers in the early fifth-century west was an unwelcome distraction from the urgent task of countering the dislocation caused by Goths, Vandals, and others in Gaul and Spain. The mutinies in sixth-century north Africa which came so soon after the reconquest did not facilitate the stabilization of imperial rule there and encouraged the disruptive raiding activities of the indigenous Berber tribesmen. And the revolt which resulted in the overthrow of Maurice's regime by Phocas in 602 unleashed a catastrophic chain of events which severely weakened the empire and left it vulnerable to the Arab invasions of the 630s.

Further Reading

The emperor's **strategies for retaining soldiers' loyalty** during late antiquity have not previously received detailed attention, but for differing perspectives on this subject during the Principate, see Campbell 1984 and Stäcker 2003. On late Roman accession ceremonies in general, see MacCormack 1981: 161–266.

For different aspects of **civil war and military unrest** in late antiquity, see Kaegi 1981: 1–137, Wardman 1984, Paschoud and Szidat 1997 (with Drinkwater 1998), and Drinkwater 2000.

3

THE INFRASTRUCTURE OF WAR

War had wide-ranging economic ramifications in late antiquity. Some of those ramifications arose from the impact of warfare on regions which experienced invasion and from the gains and losses which resulted from military campaigns – subjects which will be considered in the next chapter. The essential prerequisite for such military activity, however, was of course the existence of an army. Like the Roman army during the Principate, the late Roman army was a standing force, and maintaining that institution incurred substantial economic costs even before it was set in motion. This chapter investigates the nature of those costs. First, there is the question of manpower: how big was the army in this period relative to the population of the empire, and what were the main sources and mechanisms for gaining recruits? Secondly, how was the army paid, fed, clothed, and equipped, how much of a burden on the empire's economy did this impose, and what additional strains resulted from organizing the logistic support of campaigns? Thirdly, who paid for the physical infrastructure of fortifications which became such an important part of the landscape of the empire during late antiquity, and how much of a burden did they represent?

3.1. Manpower

3.1.1. *Making up the numbers: army size and its implications*

For war we need hands, not a list of names. (Synesius Letters 78)

Any discussion of the manpower needs of the late Roman military establishment must begin with the vexed question of the size of the army.[1] There are two kinds of ancient evidence of potential relevance – on the one hand, statements about army size in literary sources, and on the other, the data about army units contained in the *Notitia Dignitatum*, which offer the prospect of arriving at a figure through calculations. Most of the statements in literary sources relate to the late third or fourth century.

1 Despite his being a contemporary, the evidence of the Christian scholar Lactantius (*On the Deaths of the Persecutors* 7.2), to the effect that the size of the army quadrupled during the Tetrarchy, carries little specific credence (as distinct from the general idea that the army had grown bigger) because, first, it forms part of a patent polemic against the persecuting emperor Diocletian in which it suits Lactantius' purposes to exaggerate the burdens which Diocletian imposed upon the empire; secondly, it seems so obviously a simplistic calculation based on the existence of an imperial college of four emperors; and thirdly, a sudden increase on this scale would have been utterly impractical.

2 The statement of the sixth-century historian Agathias (5.13.7) – that under "earlier emperors" the army totaled 645,000 men – is also problematic because of the statement's polemical context (Agathias' criticism of Justinian for allowing troop numbers to run down drastically might have tempted him to inflate the pre-Justinianic figure) and because the reference to "earlier emperors" is too vague to pin the figure down chronologically (although most scholars opt for the united empire of the fourth century, since such a large figure is inconceivable if it referred to the eastern half of the empire only); on the other hand, it is a more precise figure than Lactantius' and one, moreover, which is not so high as to be in the realms of fantasy.

3 The sixth-century bureaucrat John the Lydian gives a very precise figure of 389,704 soldiers and 45,562 naval personnel (so a total of 435,266) during the reign of Diocletian (*On the Months* 1.27); even though he was writing well after the late third century and it is unclear what point in Diocletian's reign he is referring to, and even though he demonstrates naivety elsewhere when dealing with figures,[2] a number of considerations – his position as a bureaucrat with access to government papers, the very precision of the figures, and the fact that they are of a plausible order of magnitude – has prompted some scholars to give his statement serious consideration.

4 Finally, yet another sixth-century writer, the historian Zosimus (2.15.1–2), states that in 312 the two contenders for power in the west – Maxentius and Constantine – had forces of 188,000 and 98,000 respectively (so a total of 286,000 men for half the empire). Although Zosimus may well have drawn on a fourth-century source for these figures, whose reasonable degree of specificity lends them some plausibility, Zosimus' figures have also been impugned with considerable force as being unrealistically high for campaign armies of the period (Nicasie 1998: 202–7); on the other hand, it has also been suggested that these figures could reflect a temporary expansion in the number of troops during a period of civil war, analogous to the situation in the years of the Second Triumvirate at the end of the Republic (Carrié 1999: 637).

As already noted, the other important source for this question is the *Notitia Dignitatum*, whose official status and detail offer the prospect of cutting through the thicket of problems presented by the literary sources outlined above. The procedure is, in theory, straightforward: add up the numbers of all the different categories of military units listed in the *Notitia*, multiply those totals by the standard number of men in each category of unit, and add those totals together to reveal the number of men in the army as a whole. This relatively simple exercise is, however, beset with problems, some more serious than others. While the text of the *Notitia* for the eastern half of the empire probably reflects the state of the army before the end of the fourth century, the western half of the document continued to be revised into the fifth century, perhaps until the 420s (cf. Kelly 1998: 163–5 for a summary of the dating problems). It does not, therefore, represent a snapshot of the army at any one point in time, nor is it complete: the page for the forces in Libya (i.e., the region immediately west of Egypt) is missing, and the tiny number of units listed for Gaul must reflect the heavy losses of troops during conflict in the early fifth century (Jones 1964: 680).

The most serious problem, however, is uncertainty about the size of units. All the available evidence points to the fourth-century army comprising a larger number of smaller units, but determining precise numbers for the size of units is very difficult (cf. Coello 1996; Tomlin 2000: 169–73). One eminent scholar of this subject, A. H. M. Jones, used figures in literary sources and papyri to produce a set of unit sizes which, when combined with the evidence of the *Notitia*, gave a grand total of about 600,000 men in the army at the end of the fourth century, a figure whose proximity to Agathias' 645,000 seemed to enhance its credibility (Jones 1964: 680–4).

All subsequent discussions have necessarily taken Jones's calculations as the fundamental point of departure. Unsurprisingly, few scholars have been prepared to accept Jones's conclusions without some modifications, but for some this has been a question of only minor adjustments which have left them with a very similar outcome (Treadgold 1995: 49; Nicasie 1998: 76). Others have had more serious reservations about some of Jones's assumptions, such as the size of certain categories of unit, and have argued for figures somewhere between 400,000 and 500,000 (MacMullen 1980: 457–8; Lee 1998: 219–20; Carrié 1999: 636–8; Potter 2004: 126, 457). One particular feature which has prompted lower estimates has been the relatively small size of campaign armies in the fourth century – typically 15,000–30,000 troops, with Julian's Persian expedition of 65,000 being by far the largest army (cf. MacMullen 1980: 459–60; Lee 1998: 219–20); it is worth noting, however, that plausible arguments have recently been adduced to account for this apparent discrepancy.[3] Overall, it is clear that, unless new evidence (which would almost certainly have to be epigraphic or papyrological) were to shed significant fresh light on the subject, future discussions of this subject are unlikely to produce a more conclusive approximation. For the purposes of considering some of the wider implications of army size, the important point is to work with an estimate which is of the right order of magnitude, and a compromise of 500,000 is probably appropriate, even if such a compromise remains less satisfactory for some issues.[4]

As for the period after the fourth century, the only figure for the army is Agathias' claim (5.13.7) that Justinian had allowed the army to dwindle to only 150,000 men. This was, of course, the army for the eastern half of the empire, but even so, this is a significant reduction – so significant that scholars have generally accepted that Agathias must have omitted *limitanei* and be referring only to field army units (Jones 1964: 684; Treadgold 1995: 59–64), and it has been suggested that *limitanei* were likely to be comparable in number and therefore a total of about 300,000 is the right sort of order of magnitude for the army in the sixth century (Haldon 1999: 99–101).

The significance of these estimates depends on the context in which they are placed. One such context is army size as a proportion of the empire's total population. Yet again, there is scope for debate about the latter figure. One recent considered opinion has put the population of the empire in the mid second century at about 60 million inhabitants, although it is also acknowledged that the Antonine plague is likely to have reduced this by perhaps 10 percent by the end of the second century (Frier 2000: 813–16). Given the further reports of plague during the third century, an estimate of about 50 million for the early fourth century seems plausible, although the archaeological evidence for rural expansion from the fourth century onward, especially in the eastern Mediterranan (see Banaji 2001: 6–22 for a convenient summary), implies demographic growth over time in the rural population from which recruits were typically drawn. An army of about 500,000 men would therefore amount to no more than 1 percent of the empire's population – a very modest proportion (and this is before taking into account use of any manpower from outside the empire).

However, matters cannot be left there without consideration of further, more specific parameters. The army was, of course, drawn only from the male population (it was, literally, a case of manpower), which immediately halves the population pool and doubles the percentage, and it drew more particularly on males aged between about 20 and 45 years of age, which reduces the pool even further. How much further depends on assumptions about mortality rates, concerning which scholars disagree. One attempt at the calculations, using a slightly larger population for the empire (54 million) and a slightly smaller size for the army (445,000), with three demographic scenarios ranging from the conservative to the optimistic, produced an annual requirement to maintain the army of between about 27,000 and 45,000 men, which in turn represented between one man in about 19 and one in 23 from the male population aged between 20 and 45 (Carrié 1986:

470–8).[5] Similarly sanguine estimates have been suggested for the sixth century (Michael Whitby 1995: 83–4).

In principle, figures of this order of magnitude ought not to have imposed an excessive burden on the empire's eligible manpower (Carrié 1986: 474). However, this presupposes broad stability in the empire's circumstances – a stability which might be upset by a crisis of one sort or another. One such crisis situation was major military defeat which entailed significant loss of manpower, such as seems to have happened as a result of the battle of Mursa between Constantius II and the usurper Magnentius in 351, during Julian's Persian expedition in 363, and in the defeat at Adrianople in 378. Although no ancient source offers any figures for Mursa, one contemporary noted with frustration, as has been seen, that "great resources were used up in that battle, sufficient for any foreign wars" (Eutropius 10.12); it has been estimated that of the 65,000 troops Julian assembled in 363, 15,000 perished in Persia (Hoffmann 1969–70: I.306–8); and two-thirds of the army which faced the Goths at Adrianople died in battle (Ammianus 31.13.18) – that is, at least 10,000 men (Heather 1991: 147) and possibly as many as 26,000 (Hoffmann 1969–70: I.444; Lenski 2002a: 339). The need to replace 10,000–20,000 men quickly meant that annual recruiting requirements suddenly jumped by perhaps 50 percent or more, which could understandably impose at least a temporary strain upon manpower resources – of which there are clear signs in the sources (Tomlin 1972: 264–5; Lenski 2004: 101–3). Similarly, the pandemic of the 540s must have caused at least short-term recruitment difficulties, even if the mortality rate remains open to debate, as also the relative incidence of the disease as between urban and rural areas (Michael Whitby 1995: 102; Hordern 2005), while significant setbacks on the eastern frontier in the early 570s required a major recruitment drive on the part of Tiberius (Michael Whitby 1995: 89–90, 108).

It is worth adding that when such significant and sudden losses of manpower occurred, it was not just a matter of making up the numbers. In addition to the quantitative aspect, there was also the qualitative dimension – the loss of soldiers whose training and experience could not be replaced quickly. A number of episodes illustrate the importance of the qualitative dimension. At the battle of Callinicum in 531, a whole unit of Lycaonians (from a region of Anatolia) was slaughtered by the Persians because they were "thoroughly inexperienced...since they had only recently left off farming and entered into the perils of warfare" (Procopius *Wars* 1.18.38–40). Fifteen years later (in the immediate aftermath of the pandemic), Belisarius complained to Justinian that although he had managed to recruit a small number of soldiers in the Balkans for his campaign in Italy, they were "completely unpracticed in fighting" (Procopius *Wars* 7.12.4),[6] while in 587 another general with an army of 10,000 men found that he could only use 6,000 of them to confront the Avars because the remainder were considered unsuitable for combat (Theophylact Simocatta 2.10.8–9), probably due to inexperience (Michael Whitby 1988: 148). Indeed, the mid fourth-century author of a pamphlet proposing various reforms included, alongside various far-fetched ideas, a sensible suggestion to meet precisely this sort of problem:

> Because the service is frequently depleted by military disaster or boredom with the duties of camp life, so cutting the full strength, losses due to these causes are to be made good by a remedy of this kind, namely, that divisions of a hundred and fifty younger men, in addition to those who are listed on the pay-rolls, should be kept ready for action, trained in the use of weapons, and paid (as being recruits) at a lower rate, to be drafted into the place of those who have been lost if events should make this necessary. Given provisions of this kind, the full strength of the army will be maintained intact, and a supply of excellently-trained recruits will be at hand in good time against losses. (*On Military Affairs* 5.7–8 [tr. Ireland])

The response to this proposal is not known, but there is nothing to suggest anything like it was ever implemented.

3.1.2. Sources and mechanisms of recruitment

> Flavius Constantinius Theophanes, count, man of distinguished rank, count of the very loyal household troops and of the military administration of the Thebaid frontier to Flavius . . . Theodotus, very loyal tribune stationed at Hermopolis. Since I shall be taking steps in accord with the sacred order of our lord Anastasius – very devout, conqueror, ever Augustus – whereby young men of strong physique are to be attached to units to bring them up to strength, this order of mine hereby instructs Heracleon, son of Constantinius, a native of the city of Hermopolis, to serve in the unit at present entrusted to your care. If he is of military family, is neither of curial nor praesidial rank, and is not . . . [of] weak physique and is not enrolled on the census list, see to it that his name is entered on the register of the said unit, taking care that he is supplied from the Ides of . . . in the year of the consulate of the very distinguished Sabinianus and Theodorus [505] with the provisions together with the rest . . . and that he applies himself to his military duties – the above provided that he is known to have completed his eighteenth year. (*P. Rylands* 609 [tr. Roberts, with revisions])

This official document from the early sixth century provides one perspective on military recruitment in late antiquity, one which emphasizes some of the important practical criteria in determining eligibility for service – the physical parameters of age and fitness, and the relevance of social background – as well as drawing attention to the administrative infrastructure underpinning the process, reflected here in the reference to the unit register.[7] It is, however, a somewhat sanitized bureaucratic perspective which offers no hint of the potential for the use of compulsion, force, and even violence in the recruitment process. These are features which emerge anecdotally from other sources: the circumstantial detail in a biography of Pachomius, founder of communal monasticism in Egypt, that, as a young man conscripted into the army in the early fourth century, he and his companions were placed in prison each night as they were transported northward along the Nile valley (*Life of St Pachomius (Bohairic)* 7–8); the assumption in a sermon that it was normal for soldiers conducting recruiting levies to behave violently toward the peasants they were drafting (Gregory of Nyssa *Homily on the Forty Martyrs*, *PG* 46.784bc); the reference in a law to new recruits being tattooed as a way of identifying deserters (*Theodosian Code* 10.22.4 [398] with further discussion in Zuckerman 1995: 184–6); the report in a chronicle that the emperor Valens passed a law requiring monks to serve in the army and stipulating that those who refused were to be "beaten to death with cudgels" (Jerome *Chronicle s.a.* 375, with discussion in Lenski 2004).

It ought to occasion little surprise that compulsion and even violence should have a place in replenishing an institution whose very existence and ethos revolved around the use of force. It is certainly a feature which directs attention to one of the main issues for investigation with regard to maintaining the army's personnel, namely the extent to which the army relied on conscripts as opposed to volunteers from among the empire's population. While the examples referred to in the preceding paragraph show that conscription sometimes played a part, there remains the question of whether it was only invoked in times of crisis or had more general application. The other major issue to be considered is the extent to which the empire supplemented its military manpower from peoples living outside the empire. This is of course potentially related to the question of conscripts and volunteers, since a trend toward greater use of foreigners might imply a shortfall of internal recruits, though that shortfall, if the case, could in turn be due to unattractive conditions of service as much as a demographic downturn.[8]

While there continues to be debate about the role of conscription during the Principate (cf. Michael Whitby 1995: 65–6), there is in fact little doubt that Diocletian and his fourth- and fifth-century successors relied on conscription as a major source of recruits. Writing with reference to modern military systems, one sociologist has observed that "students of conscription find it most politically realistic to analyse conscription as a form of taxation" (Enloe 1980: 50). In the late Roman context, conscription literally was a form of taxation. Landowners were required to provide either suitable individuals (the number was proportional to the amount of land),[9] or money in lieu – the tax known as the *aurum tironicum* (literally "recruiting gold," on which see Delmaire 1989: 321–9) – though it was the government which decided which of these options applied in individual provinces year by year (Jones 1964: 615–16; Michael Whitby 1995: 65–6). As has often been noted, one of the factors said to have persuaded the emperor Valens to allow the Goths entry to the empire in 376 was their potential value as a source of military manpower; gold could then be levied from the provinces instead of men, to the benefit of imperial finances (Ammianus 31.4.4 with discussion in Lenski 2002a: 318–19). There has been more scope for debate about whether conscription continued in the sixth century, since those who have argued for a move to reliance on volunteers (Jones 1964: 668–70; Haldon 1979: 20–1) have relied primarily on silences in the sixth-century legal sources compared with fourth-century laws. As has been observed, however, those silences could reflect the government taking the status quo for granted rather than a change in the system, while there is other non-legal evidence which could point to at least some reliance on conscription (Michael Whitby 1995: 75–83).[10]

A more specific form of conscription used in the fourth century and probably introduced by Diocletian was hereditary service – the requirement that the sons of soldiers also join the army (Jones 1964: 615).[11] Valens re-emphasized the importance of this source (Lenski 2002a: 309–10), a law of 394 refers to children being inscribed on the registers of their father's unit (*Theodosian Code* 7.1.14; cf. 7.1.5, 8), and Gregory of Nazianzus is found writing to a general in the 380s requesting that an acquaintance who was the son of a soldier be released from the obligation to serve in the army in order to enter the church (*Letters* 225). Although there are hints that the practice may have lapsed by the mid fifth century – the future emperor Marcian had to make a conscious decision to enlist, even though he was the son of a soldier (Evagrius *Church History* 2.1), while the future holy man Saba was apparently under no obligation to serve despite his father being a soldier (Cyril of Scythopolis *Life of St Saba* 1, 9) – it is probably unwise to place too much weight on these anecdotes: Evagrius refers to Marcian's eagerness to follow in his father's footsteps, so it is possible that his enthusiasm pre-empted the inevitable, while Saba was brought up in Cappadocia, a long way from Egypt, where his father served. The evidence for the sixth century is ambiguous in the same way as for conscription more generally, but can be interpreted in a way which is consistent with ongoing hereditary obligation (Michael Whitby 1995: 79–81).

Another more specific form of conscription related to enemy prisoners settled on Roman territory. There was a long tradition of emperors allowing defeated peoples to take up residence within the empire,[12] and although their providing recruits for the army is not usually specified in the relevant sources, it is plausible that this should have been one of the considerations in imperial thinking. There is one particular category from late antiquity where a requirement of military service can be asserted with some confidence – that of *laeti* – even if the name is of obscure origin (and therefore not easy to translate) and the evidence concerning them is limited.[13] One important item is a law which places *laeti* in a list alongside the sons of veterans and expresses concern about the possibility of their avoiding the military levy (*dilectus*) (*Theodosian Code* 7.20.12 [400]). Ammianus' history includes a number of references to *laeti* as a category of soldier, including at one point the gloss that they are "the sons of barbarians born on this side of the Rhine" (20.8.13, 21.13.16).[14] The *Notitia Dignitatum* offers further confirmation with its listing, in a military context, of 12 prefects in charge of *laeti* at locations across Gaul, sometimes with an additional tribal designation, such as Franks or Sueves (*West* 42.33–44). The same chapter of the *Notitia* continues with a list of 23 prefects in charge of Sarmatian tribesmen (*Sarmatae gentiles*) at 17 locations in Italy and six in Gaul, implying that these too were barbarian prisoners settled on Roman land with an obligation to provide recruits for the army – a deduction corroborated by the law noted above, which includes Sarmatians alongside *laeti* and the sons of veterans. The last known reference to *laeti* occurs in a (textually problematic) law of 465 (Severus *Novel* 2), and since the locations of laetic and related lands referred to in the *Notitia* are all in the western provinces, it may be that this specific type of arrangement lapsed with the end of imperial rule in the west in the mid fifth century, even if the broader principle of redeploying defeated enemies in military service for the empire continued (e.g., Procopius *Wars* 1.15.25, 4.14.17).[15]

As already noted, an alternative way of approaching the question of the relative importance of volunteers and conscripts is to consider whether army service is likely to have been viewed as an attractive option. The following letter from the early fifth century reflects how there were invariably two sides to this question:

> Harsh rumors have been troubling me, bringing deplorable news. Some people are saying that you have gone mad and have taken leave of your senses, since you wish your son, to whom God has given the capacity for a complete education, to enter into arms and military service, which is a cheap and despicable game of death. Unless you *have* taken complete leave of your senses, step back from this dubious decision. Do not extinguish the light which his enthusiasm causes to burn brightly, but allow him to persevere in his studies. But grant *that* honor, or rather that punishment, to others, to those vagabonds to whom common ignorance is agreeable. (Isidore of Pelusium *Letters* 1.390 (*PG* 78.401))

Isidore clearly regarded soldiers and military service with disdain and the army as no place for anyone with real talent or a desire for social advancement, yet the young man's father must have viewed it as a suitable avenue of employment for his son. This difference of opinion is mirrored in the larger considerations which the issue entailed. On the one hand, it is generally thought that the value of soldiers' remuneration during late antiquity was inferior to that during the Principate (Jones 1964: 623–30), and references to desertion, to the branding of recruits with tattoos, to attempts to use influential acquaintances to help avoid the draft,[16] and to the willingness of potential recruits to mutilate one of their own digits as a way of rendering themselves ineligible for military service have been seen as indicative of the unpopularity of military service – and hence the need for conscription.[17]

On the other hand, it has also been observed that there were genuine material benefits to be gained from military service, such as enlistment bonuses (e.g., *P. London* 3.982 with Rea 1997b: 191), the regular donatives discussed in Chapter 2, pp. 58–9, and exemption from the poll tax, that the references in legal texts to desertion usually relate to new recruits as opposed to soldiers who had acclimatized to army life, and that the government remained strict about the exclusion from military service of certain categories of individual – an approach they could hardly have afforded to take had there been regular shortages of troops.[18] These details imply that, under normal circumstances, reasonable numbers of volunteers are usually likely to have been forthcoming to supplement those recruited through conscription of one sort or another.

One feature of recruitment policies within the empire which warrants special comment is the evident interest of the imperial authorities in drawing on the manpower of groups perceived as having particularly martial qualities. One of the most interesting examples of this is the use of Isaurians – a case which conforms closely to the characteristics of what has been described by a sociologist of modern military systems as "the Ghurka syndrome" (Enloe 1980: 23–49).[19] This analysis, based on the study of various "martial races" in more recent periods of history, such as Ghurkas, Cossacks, Kurds, and Scots, has identified various common features in such peoples. They have been "geographically distinct," living in regions which were "typically remote, often mountainous," "near historic invasion routes," and have "fought quite successfully against absorption into the expanded state (nation-state, empire or colony), skilfully using their knowledge of their rugged terrains to resist otherwise superior military opponents," as a result of which they have "won begrudging respect from their encroaching enemies," who in due course have sought to harness their fighting abilities to the service of the state, albeit with potential risks apropos their reliability and loyalty (Enloe 1980: 26–7). This description could easily have been written about the Isaurians in late antiquity. Isauria was a mountainous region in the southeastern corner of Anatolia, adjacent to the major military route between the Anatolian plateau and northern Mesopotamia; it was notorious for banditry and the difficulties the Roman authorities had in imposing central authority there; and it became a source of valuable recruits for the army, with some individuals rising to high command and one – Zeno – becoming emperor in the later fifth century. Even then, the region remained problematic with regard to its allegiance to Constantinople.[20]

This interest in recruits from "martial races" also extended beyond the empire's boundaries, raising a subject which has generated much debate about the so-called "barbarization" of the late Roman army and the possible contribution of such a development to the apparent military weakness of the empire during late antiquity.[21] That the late Roman army employed foreign recruits is not in doubt. The institution of *laeti* and related units derived from barbarians settled within the empire shows that there was a willingness to use soldiers of foreign extraction, while there were precedents from the second century for the empire requiring defeated enemies to provide troops – a practice which late Roman emperors regularly followed (Nicasie 1998: 87–8), and with good reason. Many of the empire's neighbors had strong martial traditions which made their young men excellent fighters, while removal of significant numbers of warriors in this way reduced the potential for further trouble on that particular frontier.

Two features of the late Roman army have particularly contributed to the impression that the army came to be dominated by foreigners. The first is the number of units with titles which include the name of a foreign people. Consider, for example, the entries in the *Notitia Dignitatum* (*East* 28, 31) for the garrison in Egypt at the end of the fourth century, which include the 8th Squadron of Vandals, the 7th Squadron of Sarmatians, the 4th Cohort of Juthungi, the 1st Squadron of Abasgi (a tribe from the Caucasus), an unnumbered squadron of Germani, the 1st Squadron of Franks, the 1st Squadron of Quadi, the 11th cohort of Chamavi, the 9th Cohort of Tzani (another Caucasian people), the 9th Cohort of Alamanni, and the 7th Cohort of Franks. While there is little doubt that these units originally comprised individuals from the foreign people in question, the units were almost certainly formed during the final decades of the third century and thereafter replenished themselves from the local community where they ended up being stationed. By the end of the fourth century, therefore, the soldiers of the 8th Squadron of Vandals will for some considerable time have been Vandals in name only, but Egyptian provincials in origin (Carrié 1986: 476; Bagnall and Palme 1996).

The second feature which has encouraged the idea of growing foreign dominance is the incidence of individuals with foreign names in positions of command in the army. It is certainly a striking feature of the military history of late antiquity to encounter very un-Roman-sounding names in charge of the defense of the empire, but it is a phenomenon which needs to be kept in perspective. In the first place, ethnic identity has too many potential ingredients to be accommodated within a simple binary contrast between Roman and non-Roman. Consider, for example, the well-known case of Stilicho, whose father was a Vandal but whose mother was Roman (*PLRE* I.853), and who almost certainly lived all his life within the empire; or the less well-known case of Petrus, born in Persian Arzanene, captured while still a boy by the future emperor Justin I during the war with Persia in 502–5, and educated in the Roman empire (*PLRE* II.870). Both men have a stronger claim to be classified as Roman than non-Roman, but their histories illustrate the complexities that such cases can involve – and for many of those who held high command in the army, the surviving sources do not provide this sort of detail about their backgrounds.[22] Secondly, after making due allowance for the gaps in the evidence, recent statistical analyses of the data for the fourth and fifth centuries have concluded that the number of foreigners holding positions of command in the Roman army remained less than a third and did not increase over time (Elton 1996: 145–52, 272–7; Nicasie 1998: 100–3 [based on the work (in Dutch) of Teitler]). These analyses do not extend beyond the end of the western empire in 476, so it is worth adding that investigation of the relevant data for *magistri militum* from the eastern empire, during the period from 476 to 641 in the *Prosopography of the Later Roman Empire* (*PLRE*), indicates that the proportion of foreigners declined somewhat (about 20 percent of the total).[23]

This section has focused on manpower, but given that a substantial proportion of the late Roman army comprised cavalry, it is appropriate to conclude with a brief comment about horsepower – how suitable cavalry mounts were obtained. This was more straightforward than manpower because the issue of volunteers and conscripts was not relevant, although problems could still arise with regard to the quality of horses. It is apparent from incidental remarks in literary sources that there were imperial estates which played a role as stud farms, though the significance of this contribution cannot be estimated (references in Elton 1996: 116). The legal sources, especially the *Theodosian Code*, indicate that horses could be levied directly from landowners as a form of taxation in kind, or they could be compulsorily purchased by the government with the proceeds of specially designated money taxes (Delmaire 1989: 314–21; Hyland 1990: 83–6, including a helpful table setting out the relevant data from the *Theodosian Code*).

3.2. Supplying the Army

3.2.1. Food and money

[From the head official of the district of Panopolis in Egypt] to the town council: Letters have just arrived from Aurelius Isidorus, procurator of the Lower Thebaid, in which he gives orders concerning both the preparation of the same *annona* of the most noble soldiers who are expected to arrive here with our ruler Diocletian, the invincible senior emperor, and also the provisions. Accordingly, enclosing a copy of what has been written concerning these same provisions, I am obliged to order you to take measures for these provisions, and to select receivers and overseers for each staging post and each kind of provision, and report to me; and also to appoint for the provisions capable men who are able to execute the duty (*leitourgia*) entrusted to them. (*P. Beatty Panopolis* 1.221–4 (398) [tr. Skeat, with revisions])

During the Principate soldiers were paid in money, after deductions at source for the cost of clothing, equipment, and food. In the fourth century, by contrast, soldiers received the bulk of their income in kind – principally grain, but also meat, oil, and wine (with equipment and clothing also supplied by the state, as outlined in the next section of this chapter). This is one of the distinctive features of the supply arrangements of the late Roman army, at least in the fourth century – the way in which the tax system was geared to provide consumables direct to the troops. This system was known as the *annona* (literally "the annual harvest"), though since this term was also used with reference to the arrangements for supplying grain to the populations of Rome and (from 330 onward) Constantinople, the army's *annona* was sometimes referred to more specifically as the *annona militaris*.

The origins of the *annona militaris* have been the subject of some debate, principally because the third century is significantly less well documented than the fourth. On one influential view, the *annona militaris* was introduced during the mid third century as a way of obviating the effects of inflationary pressures on the value of soldiers' pay (Van Berchem 1937). Others, however, have demurred (e.g., Rickman 1971: 278–83; Carrié 1977: 379–80; Mitchell 1993: 1.232, 1.252–3; Rathbone 1996: 338), and it has recently been demonstrated in detail that, prior to Diocletian at the end of the third century, the *annona* referred only to the special requisitioning of supplies for armies on campaign, and not to any more generalized system for supplying the army as a whole (Mitthof 2001: 37–81).

It was, then, Diocletian's reshaping of the empire's fiscal system which established the *annona militaris* as the basis for army supply until the sixth century. The official with ultimate oversight of the system was the praetorian prefect, a senior post which, from 312 onward, was purely civilian in remit.[24] As indicated in the opening document, however, the real burden of collecting the foodstuffs stipulated by the praetorian prefect and his subordinates fell on the members of the empire's numerous town councils (*curiae*), the so-called *curiales* or decurions who effectively constituted the local elites of communities throughout the provinces. Members of the curial class were periodically assigned to undertake official duties for fixed periods (known as liturgies), among which was responsibility for collecting produce from the local peasantry (making up any shortfall out of their own resources) and ensuring its transportation to local granaries or direct to any locally stationed military units (see Mitthof 2001: 83–258 for detailed discussion of the mechanics based primarily on the papyrological evidence from Egypt).

Since the major grain-producing region of the empire – Egypt and north Africa – lay considerable distances away from the regions where the major concentrations of troops were – the provinces adjacent to and behind the eastern and northern frontiers – there will also necessarily have been some longer-distance transport of foodstuffs. Legal sources provide some indication of the arrangements, which relied on the imperial network of roads, staging posts, and wagons (Jones 1964: 458–60), with literary and archaeological evidence also offering insights: Ammianus refers to grain being transported to the Rhine frontier from Aquitaine and Britain in the mid fourth century (17.8.1, 18.2.3)²⁵, while the distribution of a particular category of late Roman pottery container (for oil) in the Aegean and in military contexts along the lower Danube has been plausibly linked to the functioning of the *annona militaris* over longer distances (Karagiorgou 2001). Recent excavations at the sites of fifth-century forts on and near the lower Danube (Iatrus and Gradishte [Dichin] respectively) have also uncovered structures with raised floors and the remains of considerable quantities of burnt grain and quern stones for grinding, which have been interpreted as military granaries, with the size of structures suggesting the possibility that the forts served as supply bases.²⁶

A subsidiary issue which warrants comment at this point is ownership of land by soldiers. There are a number of laws from the fifth and sixth century which refer to ownership of land, not by retired soldiers, but by those serving in frontier provinces, that is *limitanei* (Theodosius II *Novels* 24.4 [443]; *Justinianic Code* 1.27.2.8 [534]), suggesting that at least some categories of soldier might increasingly have been expected to be self-sufficient to some degree. Such a possibility can be countenanced, provided it does not entail any assumptions about the *limitanei* becoming a part-time militia and deteriorating in quality. It will have been possible for the soldiers to benefit from the land without being distracted by having to undertake the farming themselves, which could be delegated to family members, tenants, or slaves (Michael Whitby 1995: 110–16; Brennan 1998a: 199–200).

An important development from the late fourth century onward was a trend toward commuting the *annona* taxes assessed in kind into payments in cash (more specifically gold coin) – a practice known as *adaeratio*. There were obvious benefits to the state from such a development: gold coin was easier to move around the empire than wagons of grain, and it allowed the state to accumulate financial reserves in the imperial treasury. At the same time there are aspects of *adaeratio* which remain puzzling. The legal evidence indicates a fairly comprehensive shift to payment in cash in the western half of the empire by the middle of the fifth century, whereas in the east "the process was more gradual and less complete" (Jones 1964: 460). Such a pattern is surprising when the west was less monetized than the east (for possible solutions to this conundrum, see Barnish et al. 2000: 195). There is also the question of how peasants in some of the more remote parts of the empire obtained the gold coin needed to pay their commuted taxes (for discussion of this problem, see Wickham 2005: 74–5). As far as supplying the army was concerned, however, the most important consequence of the shift toward *adaeratio* was increased use of the compulsory purchase of foodstuffs at fixed prices (the technical terms for which were *coemptio* in Latin and *synone* in Greek) (Barnish et al. 2000: 196–7; Wickham 2005: 75–6) – a practice which necessarily favored the interests of the state over those of peasants.

As noted in the previous chapter (pp. 58–9), regular donatives were an important additional source of income for soldiers, and these were always paid in bullion or coin. Donatives were funded through a separate set of taxes, oversight of which was the responsibility of a financial official known as the count of the sacred largesses (*comes sacrarum largitionum*). Liability for these taxes fell on certain designated groups who could be expected to have ready access to gold and silver: the senatorial aristocracy, the curial elite (i.e., members of city councils), and urban craftsmen and merchants. When a new emperor came to the throne or celebrated the quinquennial anniversary of his accession, the senatorial aristocracy were expected to pay a tax euphemistically labeled the *aurum oblaticium* (literally "freely offered gold"), while the curial elite paid a parallel tax called the *aurum coronarium* ("garland-like gold") (Jones 1964: 430–1; Delmaire 1989: 387–409). From the reign of Constantine in the early fourth century until the reign of Anastasius at the end of the fifth, urban tradesmen were required to pay a five-yearly tax which went by the name *collatio lustralis* ("the five-yearly collection") in the west and *chrysargyron* ("the gold and silver [tax]") in the east (Jones 1964: 431–2; Delmaire 1989: 354–74). Ancient sources provide a few data on the amounts levied through these different taxes, on the basis of which the following conclusions have been drawn concerning their relative impact on the three social categories involved:

> What is significant about the figures for the *aurum coronarium* and the *collatio lustralis* is that an admittedly small number of nevertheless perhaps relatively, and often absolutely, wealthy *curiales* were expected to produce appreciably less than an admittedly much larger number of relatively, and often absolutely, poor artisans, merchants and members of the professions. What is significant about those for the *aurum oblaticium* is that, while they are huge in comparison with the others, the sums involved are nevertheless minute in comparison with those for senatorial revenues and fortunes. Even the larger of the two [216,000 *solidi* in 578] amounts to less than the annual cash revenue of a single major Roman senatorial household. (Hendy 1985: 175–6)

In light of this, it is not surprising that Anastasius' decision to abolish the *collatio lustralis* in 498 received such a rapturous welcome throughout the cities of the eastern Mediterranean (e.g., Ps.-Joshua Stylites *Chronicle* 31).[27]

As far as the larger picture is concerned, some inhabitants of the Roman empire in late antiquity had little doubt that the army was the major consumer of imperial resources and represented a heavy economic burden. Authors of military treatises had occasion to comment on this. So, from the fourth century: "Let me turn to the vast expenditure on the army, which must be cut down in a not dissimilar fashion: because of this expenditure, the whole system of tax-collection is in trouble" (*On Military Affairs* 5.1 [tr. Ireland]); and from the sixth (probably): "the financial system was set up to take care of matters of public importance that arise on occasion … But it is principally concerned with paying the soldiers. Each year most of the public revenues are spent for this purpose" (*On Strategy* 2.4 [tr. Dennis]). If one suspects an element of rhetoric or tendentiousness in these claims, then there is the reported comment of a senior financial official in the mid fourth century to the effect that "the resources of the empire are denuded to supply them [the soldiers] with pay" (Ammianus 20.11.5). And there is a range of other, more circumstantial evidence: an exiled bishop in the mid fourth century is said to have returned his exile "allowance" of 1,000 *solidi* to the emperor on the grounds that the emperor had greater need of the money to pay his troops (Theodoret *Church History* 2.13); the anti-Christian emperor Julian justified the confiscation of church funds from one city with reference to army expenses (*Letters* 115 (Bidez)); while in the early fifth century, another emperor justified the confiscation of temple treasures on the same grounds (*Theodosian Code* 16.10.19 [407]).

An understandable desire to test this impressionistic evidence against such data as survive has prompted various attempts to calculate the overall cost of the army as a proportion of the empire's tax revenues. Even assuming a reasonable number of relevant data were available (which is not the case), it is a difficult calculation because of the sheer range of factors involved in the equation, not to mention the need to accommodate change over time. One attempt (based on one approximate point in time – the mid sixth century – and one major administrative part of the empire – the eastern prefecture) concluded that the army accounted for about one third of the budget (Hendy 1985: 172).[28] Another attempt (based on calculations at five points during the fourth to sixth centuries) produced proportions of two-thirds or higher (Treadgold 1995: 198). While there can be no doubt that the army was the single largest item of imperial expenditure, this latter estimate does seem rather high, particularly since it leaves so little to cover the costs of the imperial bureaucracy and of the grain supply to Rome and Constantinople, and at least partly for this reason, a third recent, self-confessed "guesstimate" opts for army costs of "at most...half of the budget...around [the year] 400," while "a third to a half of the revenues of the empire seems a fair guess for the cost of the army around 550."[29]

3.2.2. Matériel

> Flavius Calladinus, a veteran, served (*militavit*) in the arsenal for arrow production (*fabrica sagittaria*); he lived for about eighty years, and provided for this sarcophagus from his own funds. (*CIL* 5.8742 [Concordia, northern Italy, late fourth century])

Any army will be severely handicapped in its effectiveness if there is no system in place for the supply of weapons and armor. During the Principate, this need was met primarily through workshops within legionary camps, although in the eastern provinces particularly, where legions were often based in cities, there may have been some reliance on private manufacture

(Bishop and Coulston 1993: 183–6). In parallel with the development of the *annona*, late antiquity saw the establishment of a centrally organized infrastructure of state arsenals or *fabricae* responsible for production of weapons and armor, like the one in which Flavius Calladinus worked. It is highly likely that Diocletian was also responsible for this development. He is certainly credited with the construction of *fabricae* at Nicomedia, Antioch, Edessa, and Damascus (Lactantius *On the Deaths of the Persecutors* 7.8–10; Malalas *Chronicle* pp. 307–8), while the geographical distribution of *fabricae* at the end of the fourth century – recorded in the *Notitia Dignitatum* (*East* 11.18–39, *West* 9.16–38) and confirmed by surviving references in literary sources and inscriptions (James 1988: 257–61; Delmaire 1995: 87) – "betrays deliberate planning" which "depends on a map of the provinces as it was reorganized by Diocletian ... and relates to the dioceses which were a tetrarchic innovation" (James 1988: 263, 265).

A striking feature of the data about the *fabricae* preserved in the *Notitia Dignitatum* is their specification of the type of item produced at each location.[30] Tabulation of this data reveals some interesting patterns (Table 3.1). The most common item was shields, manufactured in at least 17 locations, followed by *arma* in at least 10 places. How best to translate *arma* is a moot point, but there is much to be said for the view that it included both armor and weapons, rather than just the former; armor and swords were produced separately at a small number of locations in the west, but the three places making swords can hardly have been responsible for the whole empire's needs (cf. James 1988: 261). There were, on the other hand, smaller numbers of *fabricae* which specialized in items with more specific applications, such as the armor for heavy cavalry and catapults used in siege warfare.[31]

The locations of the different *fabricae* can be explained with reference to a number of factors (cf. James 1988: 263, 267–9). Relative proximity to the military units they supplied was obviously important, and is reflected in the presence of *fabricae* in the northern and eastern provinces where the greatest threats to imperial security were expected.[32] This requirement had, however, to accommodate the need to guard against capture by the enemy, so that almost all *fabricae* were positioned a good distance away from the frontiers, though on good lines of communication; the only *fabricae* found on the frontier itself – on the Danube at Ratiaria, Aquincum, Carnuntum, and Lauriacum – specialized in the production of shields, which, in the event of their falling into enemy hands, could only have been used to inflict damage on Roman soldiers and civilians with the greatest difficulty. Access to the relevant raw materials, especially iron, was another important consideration in choice of site.[33]

The practical functioning of *fabricae* would no doubt be illuminated by the discovery of the archaeological remains of an actual establishment, but they have proved difficult to identify on the ground; the most promising

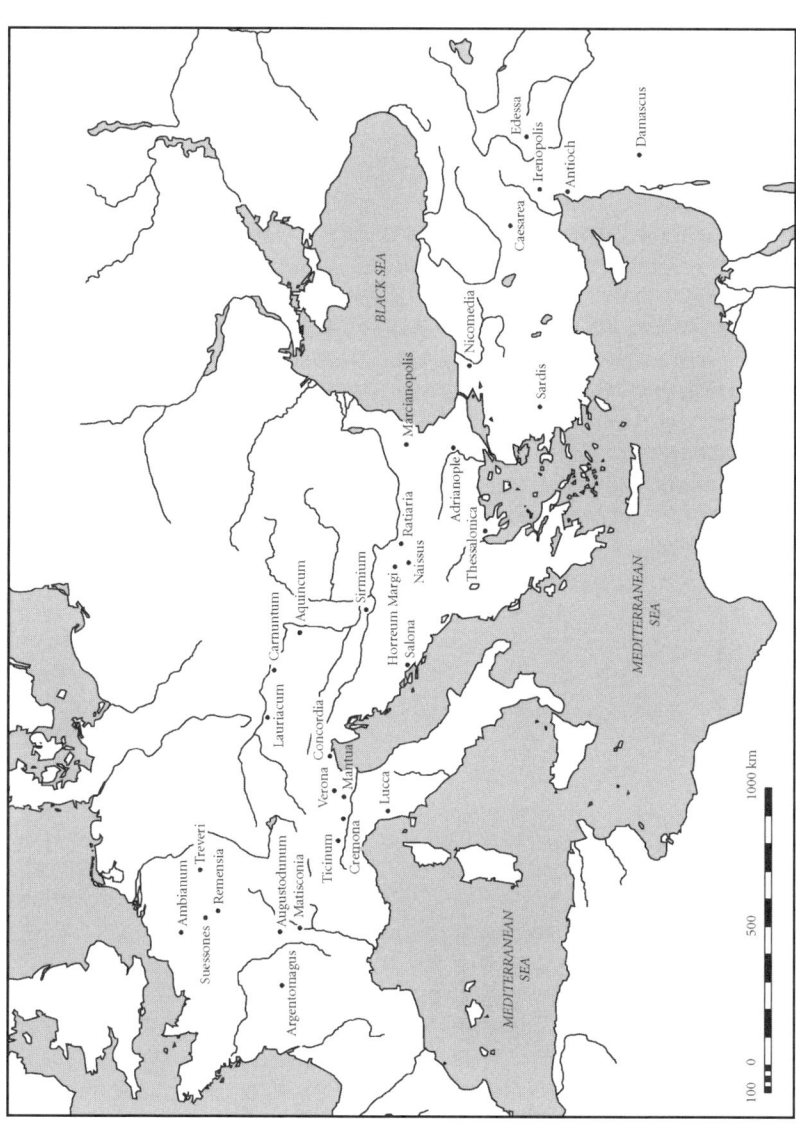

Map 2 State arsenals (*fabricae*).

Table 3.1 Locations of arsenals (*fabricae*) by category of item produced

Shields (*fabricae scutariae*)	Weapons and armor (*fabricae armorum*)	Armor (*fabricae loricariae*)	Swords (*fabricae spathariae*)	Spears (*fabricae hastariae*)	Cavalry armor (*fabricae clibanariae*)	Military saddles (*fabricae scordiscorum*)	Arrows (*fabricae sagittariae*)	Bows (*fabricae arcuariae*)	Catapults (*fabricae ballistariae*)
East:									
Damascus	Damascus								
Antioch	Antioch			Irenopolis (Maras)	Antioch				
Edessa (Urfa)	Nicomedia				Caesarea (in Cappadocia)				
Nicomedia	Sardis				Nicomedia				
Sardis	Adrianople								
Adrianople	Marcianopolis								
Marcianopolis	?Thessalonica								
Horreum Margi (Cuprija)	?Naissus (Nis)								
?Ratiaria (Achar)									
West:									
Sirmium (Mitrovica)	Sirmium	Mantua	Lucca		Augustodunum	Sirmium	Concordia	Ticinum	Augustodunum Treveri
Aquincum (Budapest)	Salona	Augustodunum	Remensia (Reims)				Matisconia (Maçon)		
Carnuntum (Petronell)	Verona		Ambianum						
Lauriacum (Lorch)									
Verona	Argentomagus (Argenton)								
Cremona									
Augustodunum (Autun)									
Treveri (Trier)									
Ambianum (Amiens)									

Note: Arsenals are listed following the pattern of the *Notitia Dignitatum*, which moves broadly from east to west.
Source: *Notitia Dignitatum, East* 11.18–31, *West* 9.16–38, with emendations suggested by James (1988: 324).

possibility to date was found in the 1970s at Amiens (known site of a *fabrica*), where archaeologists found workshops with metal slag in a fourth-century context (Bayard and Piton 1979: 162–5). A different type of archaeological evidence has been more fruitful for this subject, namely helmets. Although not named explicitly as a category of production in the *Notitia*, helmets were presumably subsumed under the heading of armor; they certainly feature in the illustrations which accompany the relevant entries in the *Notitia* (Fig. 3.1). Study of surviving helmets has shown that there was a significant change in their design in the late third century, with a shift to a simpler format which lent itself to mass production, albeit at the expense of quality and craftsmanship (James 1988: 271–3, 331 (fig. 10)).

The establishment of the *fabricae* was significant not just because it reflected a greater degree of central planning and control, but also because it effectively removed the production of weapons and armor from the immediate context of the army and therefore served to reduce the risk of usurpation. The entries in the *Notitia Dignitatum* indicate that the *fabricae*

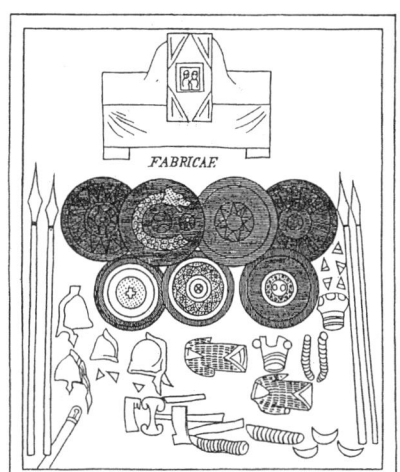 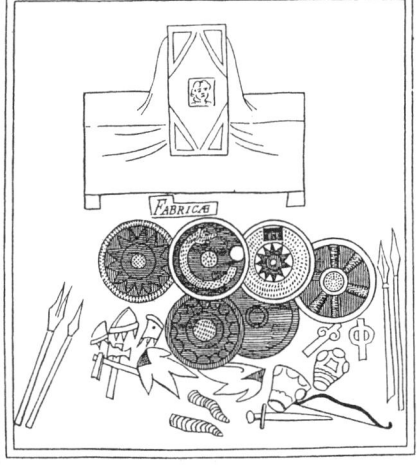

Figure 3.1 Illustrations of the office of *magister officiorum* from the *Notitia Dignitatum*, showing the output of state arsenals (*fabricae*).

The *Notitia Dignitatum* ("register of dignities") listed the senior civil and military posts in the late Roman empire, together with appropriate illustrations. These line drawings reproduce the illustrations accompanying the office of *magister officiorum* ("master of the offices") for the eastern (right) and western (left) halves of the empire. The *magister* was a civilian official, but his responsibilities included oversight of the state arsenals (*fabricae*), reflected here in the assortment of arms and armor on display. (Reproduced from O. Seeck's 1876 edition of the *Notitia Dignitatum*.)

came under the authority of the master of the offices (*magister officiorum*) (cf. Fig. 3.1). Although some of the master's heterogeneous range of responsibilities entailed military elements (cf. Delmaire 1995: 85–6), he was a predominantly civilian official whose close proximity to the emperor allowed the latter to maintain a closer eye on him than was usually possible with military commanders.[34] Given their integral importance to the empire's military effort, it is not surprising to find that workers in the *fabricae* were classified as performing a form of military service (*militia*). Like that of soldiers, too, their work was treated as a hereditary obligation (James 1988: 275–80), although this probably had as much to do with ensuring a steady supply of skilled workers in an environment which must have favored practical apprenticeship.[35]

Appropriate clothing was another requirement of soldiers, and the *Notitia* also includes references to a range of establishments associated in some way with the production of cloth or clothing for official purposes of some sort. These establishments, which are referred to by various terms (*gynaecea* [woolen mills], *linyfia*, *linea vestis* [linen mills], and *bafia* [dyeworks]), appear as part of the responsibilities of two financial officials, the *comes sacrarum largitionum* and the count of the privy purse (*comes rerum privatarum*) (*Notitia*, West 11, East 13.14, 16–17, 20). Although it has been suggested that these establishments were intended, at least in part, to produce high-quality vestments for civilian officials at the imperial court (Jones 1964: 836–7), their geographical distribution, as indicated in the *Notitia*, has also been linked to the disposition of military forces (Wild 1976: 53–4). If so, they presumably supplemented military clothing acquired through the tax known as the *vestis militaris*.

The *vestis militaris* emerged in the late third century as a replacement for the system which had prevailed during the Principate, whereby military clothing was acquired through weavers selling their product direct to agents of the central government. By the end of the third century, responsibility for supplying the clothing had shifted to communities. No doubt weavers were still doing the actual work, but it was communities who now bore the financial burden, which was calibrated to the units of taxation introduced by Diocletian; it has been estimated, for example, that Egypt had to provide about 9,000 items of clothing per annum (Sheridan 1998: 88). Perhaps the new system was designed to circumvent the problems of inflationary pressures (Sheridan 1998: 86). One peculiarity of the system was that while the surviving documentation for the *vestis militaris* uses the language of actual pieces of clothing, the tax was levied in cash rather than in kind: "Perhaps the government chose to use clothing vocabulary to remind taxpayers where their money was going" (Sheridan 1998: 73). The principal laws relating to the *vestis militaris* were retained in the *Justinianic Code*, implying that the tax continued to be levied into the sixth century (Delmaire 1989: 344).

3.2.3. Campaign logistics

> The outcome of war depends largely on provisions, and it is inevitable that those who lack them will be beaten by their enemy. For bravery cannot dwell together with hunger, because nature will not allow anyone to starve and to be brave at the same time. (Procopius *Wars* 8.23.15–16 [tr. Dewing])

The Roman army in late antiquity was a standing army, and the preceding two sections have focused on the infrastructure which supported that army whether the empire was at war or not. In the event of a major campaign, however, further measures had to be undertaken to facilitate the sustenance of a concentration of troops away from their usual bases. There is a range of anecdotal evidence concerning what this entailed, such as the following description of campaign preparations in the later fifth century:

> Zeno speedily summoned all the legions, both those stationed near to the Black Sea and those throughout Asia and the eastern districts. A large force assembled from all quarters; baggage wagons were prepared, cattle and grain were purchased, and all things of use to an army were made ready. (Malchus fr.18,1 [tr. Blockley]; cf. Julian *Orations* 1.21b–d)

Some sources refer to the stockpiling of food at points along the anticipated route of advance: so, for example, Constantius II had three million measures of grain made ready in Raetia (modern Switzerland) in preparation for his planned counter-thrust against Julian following the latter's proclamation as rival emperor in 360 (Julian *Letter to the Athenians* 286b);[36] Julian in turn had stores of food made ready in northern Mesopotamia for his advance into Persia (Ammianus 23.3.6); and supplies for Valens' campaign against the Goths in 367 were "conveyed...on a large fleet of transports through the Black Sea to the mouths of the Danube, and thence by means of river boats [were] stored...in the towns along the river to facilitate the supply of the army" (Zosimus 4.10.4 [tr. Ridley]). Other sources refer to the movement of supplies from one part of the empire to another in preparation for a campaign: so, for example, there are a number of third-century inscriptions from the region of Pisidia in southern Turkey which allude to the role of leading citizens in organizing the shipping of supplies to Syria in readiness for military campaigns (Bean and Mitford 1970: 38–45; Mitthof 2001: 73–4; Elton 2005); a mid fourth-century text refers to Egypt playing a role in the provision of food for "the emperor's army and the Persian war" (*Description of the Whole World* 36), while the temporary famine around Antioch resulting from the influx of troops prior to Julian's campaign in 363 was partially alleviated by Egyptian grain (Julian *Beardhater* 369b); and in the early sixth century, supplies again had to be imported from Egypt to meet the needs of the substantial numbers of troops campaigning in northern Mesopotamia in the aftermath of Kavad's invasion of 502 (Ps.-Joshua Stylites *Chronicle* 70).

These glimpses provide some sense of the logistical challenge which campaigns presented to the imperial authorities. The extent of that challenge has been fleshed out by careful investigation of the parameters of feeding an army on the move (Haldon 1999: 139–89, 281–92, Haldon 2005). The starting point is calculations of daily grain rations, how much bread and longer-lasting double-baked "biscuit" (*bucellatum*) this is likely to have provided (the latter also being significantly lighter in weight), and the fodder requirements of different types of animal (horse, donkey, mule, pack-pony, and ox). It is estimated that an army of 10,000, for example, comprising 6,000 infantry, 4,000 cavalry, and 1,000 remounts, would have needed at least 24,000 kg (23.5 tons) of foodstuffs per day (Haldon 2005: 91). This line of enquiry can be pursued further in a variety of directions – by consideration of cereal yields in order to estimate the acreage needed to support an army of a given size which was living off the land; and by calculation of the carrying capacity of different types of pack-animal, and of the additional food requirements which the presence of those animals would entail. For the earlier example of an army of 10,000, "an expedition of up to twenty days away from supply depots or foraging opportunities is logistically quite feasible, provided that 8,500–9,500 mules or pack-animals were available" (Haldon 2005: 98). Of course, a supply train of that size would necessarily slow down the speed of progress, but that problem could be reduced if the soldiers themselves carried a substantial proportion of their rations, as a number of sources suggest was common practice in late antiquity (Ammianus 17.8.2, 17.9.2; *Historia Augusta, Life of Severus Alexander* 47.1).

In principle, armies significantly larger than 10,000 faced very serious logistical difficulties, which was no doubt an important factor in limiting the typical size of expeditionary forces during late antiquity (cf. the data tabulated by Nicasie 1998: 204–5). If one considers the particular circumstances of the largest known forces from late antiquity, it is possible to see how these potential logistical problems must in practice have been less severe than might have been expected on the basis of army size alone. Julian's army of 65,000 for the invasion of Persia in 363 (Zosimus 3.10.2), the largest known force from the fourth century, was able to take advantage of water transport down the Euphrates, which must have eased supply constraints significantly. Similarly, Leo's Vandal expedition of 468 was seaborne. In the case of the largest known army from the sixth century – that of 52,000 deployed by Anastasius against Kavad's in 502 (Ps.-Joshua Stylites *Chronicle* 54) – it was based in one region within Roman territory, so that, although it still presented challenges with regard to supply, these cannot have been nearly as great as for a force of comparable size on the move in enemy territory.

Oversight of military logistical organization was clearly a significant responsibility. During the second century it appears to have fallen to individuals bearing the title *praepositus copiarum* ("prefect of supplies") or a variation on that; toward the end of that century and into the first half of the third, the title became *praepositus annonae* (Mitthof 2001: 68–70), although an official in Valerian's Persian expedition in 259/60 is described as the "count of the treasury and in charge of grain provisions" (*komēs tōn thēsaurōn kai ephestōs tē agora tou sitou*: *PLRE* I.528 [Fulvius Macrianus 2]). From the fourth century onward, the office of praetorian prefect seems to have included responsibility in this area: Constantius II's prefect Vulcacius Rufinus was blamed for the delay in the arrival of supplies for a campaign against the Alamanni in 354 (Ammianus 14.10.3–4); when he was junior emperor in Gaul during the later 350s, Julian's prefect Florentius is found concerning himself with such matters on a number of occasions (Ammianus 18.2.4, 20.4.6, 20.8.20; Julian *Letter to the Athenians* 280a); and Valens' supply arrangements for his Gothic campaign in 367, alluded to earlier, were organized by his praetorian prefect Auxonius (Zosimus 4.10.4).

There was a move toward specialization of responsibility during the fifth century when a deputy praetorian prefect was appointed to oversee provisioning for the Vandal expedition of 441 (*Justinianic Code* 12.8.2.4)[37] – a development for which there is further evidence from the sixth century. Two individuals – Apion and Calliopius – were successively appointed as deputy praetorian prefects between 503 and 505 with specific responsibility for overseeing the provision of food for the forces sent to repulse Kavad's invasion of northern Mesopotamia (Ps.-Joshua Stylites *Chronicle* 54, 70, 77). An official sent to northern Mesopotamia in 531 to prepare granaries in all the cities on account of the war then underway with Persia (Malalas *Chronicle* p. 467) looks very much like another case of a deputy praetorian prefect (cf. also *PLRE* II.674 (Leontius 27) for another possibility). Although the praetorian prefect John the Cappadocian organized the initial supplies for the Vandal expedition before it left Constantinople in 533, a former praetorian prefect, Archelaus, accompanied the expedition with the title of "deputy praetorian prefect in charge of supplies" (Procopius *Wars* 3.15.13). During the Gothic war in Italy a number of individuals were appointed as praetorian prefects of Italy, with the task of facilitating the supply of Roman forces campaigning there (Procopius *Wars* 7.6.9 (Maximinus); Agathias 1.18.1–2 (Antiochus)); perhaps the change from appointing a deputy was regarded as appropriate here when Roman forces had already recovered substantial parts of the peninsula. At any rate, a subsequent law of Justinian's made specific provision for the post of deputy praetorian prefect on the eastern frontier in the event of expeditionary forces there requiring supplies (*Novels* 134.1 (556)).

It is hardly surprising to find indications in the sources that the supply requirements of expeditions imposed additional burdens on the empire's inhabitants. This included the imposition of supplementary levies (e.g., MacMullen 1976: 104, 257 n. 22; Hendy 1985: 221–4; Lenski 2002a: 129; Wipszycka 1969; MacCoull 1994), while for those who happened to live in the region where the campaigning was taking place, there was usually the additional burden of troops helping themselves to local produce (e.g., Procopius *Wars* 7.1.8–10, where Belisarius' exemplary treatment of peasants implies that the norm was otherwise).

3.3. Fortifications

> From this point we must proceed to the defences with which Justinian surrounded the farthest limits of Roman territory. Here indeed my narrative will be constrained to halt painfully and to labour with an impossible subject. For it is not the pyramids which we are about to describe – those celebrated monuments of the rulers of Egypt, on which labour was expended for a useless show – but rather all the fortifications whereby this emperor preserved the empire, walling it about and frustrating the attacks of the barbarians on the Romans. (Procopius *Buildings* 2.1.2–3 [tr. Dewing and Downey])

The construction of buildings had always been an important way for emperors to express their power and their aspirations, as indeed for most rulers before and since, and emperors during late antiquity were no different. What was different, however, was their priorities, as Procopius implies above: while there remained scope for impressive civil and religious architecture, the empire's circumstances meant that more mundane considerations of defense acquired increasing precedence. Procopius' *Buildings* presents the most detailed description of imperial building activity during late antiquity, and four of its six books are devoted to a description (and sometimes, a mere listing) of the fortifications for which Justinian claimed credit, whether by way of construction or restoration.[38] From the perspective of the infrastructure of war, the central question is how the erection and repair of military installations and city walls were funded.[39]

Military installations are the more straightforward category. Since they were integral to the army's performance of its responsibilities, their construction will typically have relied on the labor of soldiers who presumably were authorized to requisition whatever materials were necessary from the surrounding district. This is certainly the image presented by Ammianus in his description of the emperor Valentinian's program of building forts and towers along the Rhine frontier in the 370s, where it is soldiers who are stripped to the waist carrying earth and almost submerged in water securing the foundations of a river-side fortress (28.2.1–8).[40] On the other hand, the construction of the frontier fortress at Dara in 506 entailed the use of stonemasons from all over the region, paid from imperial funds (Ps.-Joshua Stylites *Chronicle* 90; Ps.-Zachariah *Church History* 7.6). No doubt the use of skilled craftsmen in this context was due to the fact that the Persians were adept at siege warfare, and so forts in the region needed to be constructed to a high standard if they were to offer effective resistance.

THE INFRASTRUCTURE OF WAR

City walls present more of a problem. Emperors sometimes did provide funding to assist with the construction of defenses for cities and towns, as inscriptions confirm, such as the following from the town of Adraha, situated between Bostra and the Sea of Galilee in the north of the province of Arabia:

> Good fortune! For the safety and the victory of our lord emperor Gallienus Augustus, this wall was erected thanks to the gift of the emperor and the foresight of the very powerful Statilius Ammianus, performing the function of governor, under the direction of Isidore, equerry (*strator*), and the conduct of Verus, architect, under the supervision of Magnus, son of Bassus, and by the exertions of Aelius, son of Bassus, of Zenodorus, son of Taurinus, and of Sabinus, son of Germanus, in the year 158 [=263/4]. (*IGR* 1287)

Literary sources also provide information on the subject, such as the panegyrist who, in appealing to Constantine in 310 for financial help for the Gallic city of Autun, referred to the emperor's generous help to Trier with the rebuilding of its "entire circuit of walls" (*Latin Panegyrics* 6.22.4). Some of the most specific detail about imperial assistance with the construction of city walls is preserved in the *Chronicle* attributed to Joshua Stylites, in the context of rebuilding after the war with Persia in 502–5. The emperor Anastasius is reported to have given the governor of Osrhoene, Eulogius, 200 lb of gold (= 1,440 *solidi*) for the expenses of rebuilding the entire outer wall of Edessa, though the value of this figure in relation to the costs of city walls is diminished by the fact that the money was also used for the reconstruction of two aqueducts, a public bath, and his own headquarters (Ps.-Joshua Stylites *Chronicle* 87). Around the same time, Anastasius also gave an unspecified amount of money toward the construction of a wall for the city of Birta, near the Euphrates crossing at Zeugma (Ps.-Joshua Stylites *Chronicle* 91).[41]

Despite the concrete language used by the sources, it is unlikely that imperial funding involved "the sending out of so many bags of actual cash" from the imperial capital to the relevant location, but rather "the juggling of taxes" (MacMullen 1959: 210). In other words, emperors would fund projects by remitting a proportion of revenues owed to the imperial treasury from a locality and redirecting those monies to the costs of the relevant construction work there, although very occasionally the funds might fortuitously appear from an unexpected source: when the Roman general Solomon defeated the Berber leader Iaudas in 539, he captured a very substantial quantity of money, "by means of which Solomon surrounded many of the cities of Africa with walls" (Procopius *Wars* 4.20.28–9).

There was, however, no universal policy of emperors paying for the construction of city walls, and in many cases the burden must have fallen on the inhabitants of the city or town themselves, with members of the local elite having to stump up money and ordinary inhabitants having to supply labor (although by the sixth century, there is increasing evidence for the use of paid labor).[42] The great difficulty is knowing how common this scenario was, as against one involving imperial subventions (which may of course have been only partial anyway). But whichever way the work was financed, it must have represented a significant economic burden on the empire's resources, albeit not a recurrent one except in the long term or if a city or town experienced severe damage to its defenses as a result of siege. One counter-balancing consideration may, however, be seen in the dip which has been observed in the frequency of imperial patronage of civilian building projects from the late second century until the early fourth century (Mitchell 1987: 365). Although that dip can be seen as reflecting a range of pressures on imperial finances, it may at least partly have been due to a reordering of priorities in imperial building projects – in other words, some of the funds spent on fortifications in the early part of late antiquity was presumably money which would in the past have gone toward non-military construction, so that at least some of the spending on fortifications did not represent an additional burden on the imperial budget.

Further Reading

For discussions of the **size of the late Roman army**, see Jones 1964: 679–86; Luttwak 1976: 188–90; MacMullen 1980; Treadgold 1995: 43–64; Nicasie 1998: 74–6, 202–7; Carrié 1999: 636–9; Potter 2004: 455–9; Michael Whitby 2004: 159–60.

The best discussions of **recruitment** in late antiquity are Jones 1964: 614–23, 668–79; Michael Whitby 1995 (much broader in coverage than its title indicates); and Brennan 1998a (whose title provides no clue as to its focus on recruitment); with Haldon 1979: 20–39, Elton 1996: 128–54, and Nicasie 1998: 83–96 providing valuable treatments of more specific aspects.

The best overviews of the **late Roman taxation system** in relation to the army are Jones 1964: 430–2, 458–61, 626–30, 671–4; Hendy 1989: 15–21; and Wickham 2005: 62–80; with detailed discussion of the *annona militaris* in Mitthof 2001 and of the taxes in gold in Delmaire 1989: 354–74, 387–409.

With regard to the provision of **matériel**, by far the best discussion of late Roman *fabricae* is James 1988. For imperial textile establishments, see Wild 1976 and Delmaire 1989: 443–55, and for the *vestis militaris*, Delmaire 1989: 332–45 and Sheridan 1998.

The **logistics** of campaigns are discussed in Haldon 1999: 139–89, 281–92, and 2005, and in Elton 2005, with the background from earlier centuries of Roman history discussed in Erdkamp 1998 and Roth 1999. The specific question of officials with logistical responsibilities is addressed by Jones 1964: 627–8, 673–4; Kaegi 1982: 98–113; Scharf 1991.

Discussions of the funding and construction of **fortifications** in late antiquity include MacMullen 1959 (which begins with the Principate); Jones 1964: 461–2, 736–7; Johnson 1983: 59–66 (third- and fourth-century west); and Pringle 1981: 89–94 (sixth-century Africa).

4

THE ECONOMIC IMPACT OF WAR

The previous chapter has focused on the infrastructure of war – manpower, supplies, matériel, and fortifications. These were all facets with economic implications, and so might be considered as part of the economic impact of war, if one interprets "war" in its broadest sense. This chapter discusses the economic impact of war in a more restricted sense, with reference to the economic consequences of campaigns and fighting (though inevitably it is not always possible to maintain a clear-cut distinction between this and matters of infrastructure). It will do so within a simple cost–benefit framework – that is, by trying to assess the economic benefits of war in late antiquity, and then comparing those benefits with the costs incurred by war. In the absence of statistical data, such an exercise can only operate in terms of approximations and estimates, but it does offer the possibility of clarifying the parameters of the subject.

4.1. Economic Benefits of War

Belisarius displayed the spoils and slaves from the war in the midst of the city and led a procession which the Romans call a "triumph," not, however, in the traditional manner, but going on foot from his own house to the hippodrome...And there was booty: first of all, whatever articles are usually set aside for royal use – thrones of gold and carriages in which it is customary for the king's consort to ride, and much jewellery made of precious stones, and golden drinking cups, and all the other things which are useful for the royal table. And there was also silver weighing many thousands of talents and all the royal treasure amounting to an enormous sum (for Geiseric had plundered the Palatine in Rome [in 455]...), and among these were the treasures of the Jews which Titus, the son of Vespasian, together with certain others, had brought to Rome after the capture of Jerusalem...And there were slaves in the triumph, among them Gelimer himself...and all of his family and as many of the Vandals as were very tall and good-looking. (Procopius *Wars* 4.9.3–10 [tr. Dewing])

The history of war-making during the Republican period of Roman history showed that a successful war could be profitable. Of course the level of profitability depended on the assets which the losing side had hitherto controlled, which will in turn have varied depending on such factors as their natural resources and level of economic development. The most direct and immediate way of exploiting a defeated enemy was through capturing booty, which in antiquity might take both material and human form. A longer-term method was to occupy that enemy's land and tax it, though that might also entail additional costs depending on how large a garrison was needed to maintain control of that territory.

With regard to booty, the Persians demonstrated that war in late antiquity could be profitable. Shapur I, Shapur II, and Khusro I in particular captured large numbers of Roman prisoners during their campaigns in the mid third, mid fourth, and mid sixth centuries, and deported them back to Persian territory, where they were put to a variety of constructive uses (see further Chapter 5, pp. 136–7 below). Khusro also accumulated substantial quantities of gold and silver from the cities of Syria during 540, when he sacked some and extorted money from others eager to avoid the same fate (Table 4.1). The specified amounts of gold and silver which he acquired were equivalent to nearly 70,000 *solidi*;[1] if one adds a notional amount for the unspecified quantities of booty, particularly that from the major city of Antioch, which were said to be enormous (Procopius *Wars* 2.9.15), then an overall figure of about 100,000 *solidi* seems a plausible estimate. This was a substantial windfall for Khusro, as well as a significant loss of resources for the Roman state (even if one from which it could be expected to recover in due course). Of analogous interest, albeit on a rather smaller scale, is the insight into the quantities of booty that could be carried off by Germanic raiders in the mid third century provided by the discovery in the early 1980s of a very substantial deposit of Roman metalware encased in the gravel beds of the upper Rhine. Comprising coins, weapons, metal tableware, mirrors, tools, and many other categories of item, and weighing more than 700 kg (1,500 lb) in total, the find has been interpreted as the contents of perhaps three or four Germanic wagons which met with disaster while recrossing the Rhine en route home after an otherwise successful plundering expedition in northern Gaul (Künzl 1993 [the definitive catalogue with superb color illustrations; I.319–20 for the number of wagons]; Callu 1995; Todd 1996).

There were occasions when the Romans also managed to acquire booty on a significant scale. They captured the baggage train of a Persian king complete with his treasure a number of times: in 298, when Galerius defeated Narseh and, in addition to capturing his wives, also secured "a very great quantity of treasure" (Eutropius 9.25); and in 576, when Khusro's baggage train fell into Roman hands during campaigning in Armenia, including gold and silver furniture, a golden carriage adorned with precious stones and pearls, valuable clothing, and the king's personal fire altar (John of Ephesus

Table 4.1 Booty from Khusro's campaign in Syria, 540

City	Sacked?	Booty seized or extorted	Reference in Procopius *Wars*
Sura	Yes	200 lb gold for ransom of prisoners	2.5.29
Hierapolis	No	2,000 lb silver	2.6.24
Beroea	Yes	2,000 lb silver	2.7.5–6
Antioch	Yes	Large quantities of gold, silver, marble from main church	2.9.14–16
Apamea	No	Whatever gold and silver could be found	2.11.24
Chalcis	No	200 lb gold	2.12.2
Edessa	No	200 lb gold	2.12.34
Dara	No	1,000 lb silver	2.13.28
Total gold		600 lb	
Total silver		5,000 lb	

Church History 6.8; Sebeos 8). The king's need for a reasonable degree of mobility must, however, have limited the volume of valuables obtained by the Romans on these occasions. The only really substantial quantities of material booty acquired by the empire during late antiquity were the contents of the Vandal treasury captured by Belisarius in 533/4, which, as Procopius noted, included booty from Vandal raids on Rome and Italy in the fifth century, which in turn included booty from as far back as the Roman sack of Jerusalem in 70 (*Wars* 4.3.25–7, 4.9.4–5), and those of the Gothic treasury in Ravenna also captured by Belisarius in 540 – "a notable sight" (Procopius *Wars* 6.29.37, 7.1.1–3).[2]

While it is apparent that these acquisitions were impressive, however, there is insufficient detail to estimate their contribution to the imperial budget. Indeed, the fact that booty from the Roman sack of Jerusalem in the first century was still identifiable in the sixth is a salutary warning, implying as it does that ancient bullion could sometimes be "thesaurized" for long periods – that is, instead of being melted down, minted, and put into circulation, it could sit idle in the imperial treasury, where it was effectively economically neutral. Moreover, even when put into circulation, its impact might not necessarily have been benign insofar as it could have caused price inflation.[3]

The one form of booty which the Romans did consistently acquire throughout late antiquity was prisoners, sometimes as a result of Roman aggression, as in Belisarius' successful campaign against the Vandals (Procopius *Wars* 4.3.24), or from the defeat and capture of invaders, as in Stilicho's overpowering of Radagaisus' forces in Italy in 406, when, it is said, the numbers captured depressed the price of slaves markedly (Orosius 7.37). A certain number of prisoners will typically have been distributed among the troops as booty (e.g., Malchus fr.20 [lines 252–3]), either to be their slaves or for them to sell on, but prisoners were also put to uses which were economically beneficial to the state. Stilicho enrolled 12,000 of the best of Radagaisus' forces into the army (Zosimus 5.26.5; Olympiodorus fr.9), and Justinian kept some captured Persian and Vandal soldiers as military units who were sent to serve in areas of the empire distant from their homeland, where their loyalties were unlikely to be divided (Procopius *Wars* 2.19.25 [with Hoffmann 1961/2], 4.14.17).[4] Other prisoners were settled on arable land and allowed to farm it, in due course providing tax income for the state and/or recruits for the army (see above, Chapter 3.1.2, pp. 81–2).

As for the empire acquiring new revenue-generating territory, this was not a common occurrence during late antiquity. Diocletian and Galerius added the five Transtigritane satrapies to the empire as a result of the peace settlement with Persia in 299, but most of these lands remained in Roman hands for little more than half a century, and even during this time, they were adversely affected by regular Persian inroads after the death of Constantine. Although Julian's objectives remain open to debate, one contemporary claimed that, had his expedition been successful, "we expected the whole Persian empire to form part of that of Rome, to be subject to our laws, receive its governors from us and pay us its tribute" (Libanius *Orations* 18.282; but cf. Introduction 1, p. 4 above). In the event, the only emperor to achieve really substantial additions to the empire's territory was Justinian, whose defeat of the Vandals and Goths returned north Africa and Italy to imperial control, after a gap of a century in the case of the former and about seventy years in the case of the latter. However, the recovery of these regions proved to be something of a mixed blessing. In north Africa, ongoing difficulties with the indigenous Berber tribesmen required the commitment of substantial military forces, while the length of the war in Italy had done much economic damage to the peninsula, from which it had virtually no time to recuperate before the arrival of the Lombards and the renewal of conflict for the rest of the century (see further below, Chapter 4.2.2, p. 116). A variety of figures relevant to the sixth-century imperial budget has survived, and the following pessimistic conclusion has been drawn from them:

> The financial position of the prefectures of Africa, Italy and Illyricum, *vis à vis* that of the East, was almost absurdly weak. The budget of Africa alone amounted to barely a tenth of that of the east... and the budgets of Africa, Italy and Illyricum combined amounted to barely a quarter of that of the east. In the long term (that is not forgetting the acquisition of the immediate contents of the Vandal and Ostrogothic treasuries), and as a source of surplus revenue, Justinian's reconquest was a dead loss. (Hendy 1985: 171)

This conclusion is probably too bleak, since others (using different evidence) have detected signs of moderate prosperity in north Africa in the later decades of the sixth century (e.g., Mattingly and Hitchener 1995: 213;

Wickham 2005: 20–1, 92, 124). However, even if "dead loss" is too extreme an assessment, it is also apparent that the recovery of north Africa did not benefit the imperial economy to the extent that one might have assumed it would on the basis of the region's importance in earlier centuries.

4.2. Economic Costs of War

Whereas the benefits of war could for the most part accrue only when the empire took the initiative in launching an expedition against an adjacent state or people, the economic costs of war could be felt whether the initiative lay with the empire or with its enemies. When the empire undertook a campaign, there was always the possibility of defeat, and defeat could be costly. When the empire's enemies managed to gain permanent control of any substantial part of the empire's territory, the loss of that territory was very definitely costly for the empire. But even if an enemy incursion did not have as its object permanent occupation of imperial territory or if imperial forces managed to expel the invaders, the resulting fighting could still have a detrimental economic impact for the empire, or at least for the region affected by the conflict.

4.2.1. The costs of defeat

> Because Leo embarked upon ten thousand warships called *liburnae* a host such as time for all its length had never yet wondered at, he brought the [praetorian] prefecture to uttermost penury, by putting it under strain and compelling it to meet the expenses of four hundred thousand fighting men engaged upon a campaign to be fought overseas... There was expended upon that ill-fated war... sixty-five thousand pounds of gold and seven hundred thousand of silver; and of horses, weapons and men as many as you might well estimate to have died across the time known to man. After all this, the entire state suffered shipwreck. For since the money in the treasury, and the emperor's private resources, was not enough to meet requirements, the entire reserves of the campaign forces were destroyed in the failures of the war. Not to make a long story of it, as a result of this dreadful debacle the treasury was no longer able to meet the demands it had to meet. (John the Lydian *On the Magistracies of the Roman State* 3.43–4 [tr. Carney, with revisions])

The previous section has considered the potential benefits to be derived from a successful war. Defeat in a campaign, on the other hand, could entail a double cost – the loss of potential gains *and* the waste of the resources expended on mounting the expedition. The most catastrophic financial setback experienced by the late Roman state as a result of military defeat in a single campaign was the emperor Leo's abortive expedition to regain control of north Africa from the Vandals in 468. Had the expedition been successful, then the economic benefits to the empire of regaining control of such a wealthy region would have been substantial, and might have reversed the downward spiral of the west (at this stage, the region had only been under Vandal rule for about thirty years, whereas by the time of its eventual recovery in 533, nearly a century had elapsed, with much greater damage to fiscal and economic infrastructure). Failure, however, had serious costs. Although there is a strong element of hyperbole in John the Lydian's observations, and his figures for the number of ships and soldiers are impossibly inflated, the amount he gives for the gold and silver expended is broadly in accord with the amounts given by other sources, equivalent to more than seven million *solidi* – "a sum that probably exceeded a whole year's revenue," whose loss created "a state of virtual bankruptcy" (Hendy 1985: 221–3).

There can be no doubting the psychological blow of this failure or the fiscal problems which resulted. At the same time, however, some important qualifications need to be registered. First, the failure did not hamstring the empire's finances permanently; recovery took time, but had certainly been achieved by the end of the fifth century (when Anastasius' budget began to show a surplus), if not sooner. Secondly, the Vandal expedition of 468 was probably an unusually expensive operation partly because of its scale and partly because of being seaborne. It failed primarily because the Vandals managed to destroy the Roman fleet, and the loss of so many ships must have been a major component in the financial losses incurred. Other late Roman military expeditions involving shipping of one sort or another are known – Constantius' reconquest of Britain from Allectus in the late third century; Julian's Persian expedition, which used water transport down the Euphrates; and Belisarius' invasion of Africa in 533. However, none of these was on a scale comparable to 468: the first only entailed crossing the Channel, which could be done with boats smaller in size and number; the second involved river-borne vessels which, while large in number, cannot have involved anything like the cost of seagoing ships; while the third was a much smaller expedition than Leo's, no doubt as a concession to the praetorian prefect John the Cappadocian, who famously opposed the expedition because of its likely cost and the still potent memory of the failure of 468 (Procopius *Wars* 3.10.1–18). Generally, however, land-based campaigns were much more common in late antiquity, and although their conduct involved significant outlay on beasts of burden and other transport such as wagons, this cannot have entailed anything like the expenses of a major seaborne expedition, and so any failures were correspondingly less catastrophic financially (as distinct from losses of manpower).

4.2.2. *The costs of being invaded*

See how death suddenly bore down on the whole world and the force of war struck so many people. The rough terrain of thick forest and high mountain, strong rivers with their fast currents, forts protected by their positions and cities by their walls, places made inaccessible by the sea, harsh locations in the wilderness, caves and caverns beneath gloomy cliffs – none of these was able to provide a refuge from the hands of the barbarians... Those not overcome by force succumbed to hunger. The unfortunate mother fell with her child and husband, the master submitted to servitude along with his slaves. Some lay as food for dogs, and blazing houses snatched life from many and provided their funeral pyre. Throughout settlements and estates, throughout fields and crossroads and every district, on every road this way and that, there was death, sorrow, destruction, burning, lamentation. All Gaul smoked like one great funeral pyre. (Orientius *The Admonition* 2.165–84)

This famous evocation of the travails of Gaul in the early fifth century is one of a number of laments on the impact of invasion during late antiquity (cf. Courcelle 1964: 79–101). However, while such laments may provide some insight into the psychological impact of invasion and their human cost (cf. Chapter 5 below), they often occur in self-consciously literary works – in this particular case, a poem heavily influenced by a reading of Ovid (Roberts 2002: 410–12) – and are necessarily impressionistic and generalizing. It is archaeological evidence which has the potential to offer a much better guide to the economic impact of invasion on the ground. A comprehensive survey of all the regions of the empire affected by war and invasion during late antiquity is beyond the scope of this study. Instead, this section offers four case studies of war-affected regions – two from the eastern half of the empire, two from the west – in an effort to do at least some justice to regional variation and diachronic change.

Of course, archaeological evidence presents methodological issues as much as literary sources do, and it is worth flagging up some of these at the outset. Identification of the impact of invasion in the archaeological record relies to a significant degree on signs of the abandonment or destruction of sites, but war need not be the only explanation for such features. Destruction can also be the result of natural catastrophes such as earthquakes – quite common in some of the empire's eastern provinces – and of the activities of others, such as the imperial army itself (Wightman 1985: 220), while the abandonment of sites can also be due to the reorganization of land into larger holdings (Wightman 1985: 245; Van Ossel and Ouzoulias 2000: 138) or to exogenous factors such as long-term climate change (Liebeschuetz 2001: 409–10; Chavarría and Lewit 2004: 21, 34–5) and disease – particularly relevant to the sixth century, which saw the outbreak of a pandemic in the 540s which then recurred at relatively frequent intervals into the seventh century.[5] The surviving remains do not always make it possible to differentiate between competing explanations, and reoccupation may not be visible if based on simple timber structures.

A. *Thrace and the lower Danube*

The apparently well-traveled author of a survey of the Roman world in the middle of the fourth century gave a positive assessment of the economic position of Thrace at that time, commenting in particular on the wealth of its agricultural produce and its plentiful manpower (*Description of the Whole World* 50). If this brief comment was in fact based on genuine knowledge of conditions – and there are "signs of modest prosperity" in the archaeological remains of larger fourth-century villas – then it implies that there had been a significant degree of recovery from the deleterious effects of Gothic attacks during the mid third century, which are the most likely cause of the destruction of many, though not all, rural villas in the region (Poulter 2004: 231; cf. Mulvin 2004: 378). This was the period during which the province of Dacia, north of the lower Danube, was effectively abandoned. While the loss of this province is indicative of the severity of the problems which the empire faced from Gothic tribes, the existence of Dacia until at least the middle of the century must also have served to mitigate the full effects of these incursions on regions south of the lower Danube.

Any renewed prosperity in the fourth century, however, proved relatively short-lived, as the region soon experienced the first of a series of major upheavals resulting from the intervention of successive peoples from north of the lower Danube.[6] In 376 the emperor Valens allowed the Goths to enter the region, and their presence precipitated a number of periods of intense conflict over the following two and half decades (Heather 1991: 142–56, 193–208). A generation later, the Huns increasingly encroached as Attila expanded his empire during the 430s and 440s (Michael Whitby 2000c: 704–12). The dissolution of his empire following his death in 453 brought further upheaval to Thrace, as subject peoples, notably further groups of Goths, established themselves there and engaged in warfare among themselves and against the imperial authorities during the 470s and 480s (Heather 1991: 240–308). After these Goths had finally been steered westward, the Bulgars (probably a Turkic people) became problematic in the final years of the fifth century and the early sixth century (Stein 1949–59: II.89–90), with difficulties for the region compounded by Anastasius' conflict in 513–15 with Vitalian, who was based in eastern Thrace (Stein 1949–59: II.177–85). In the mid to late sixth century, Slavs and Avars posed increasingly serious problems in the region, culminating in the Avar siege of Constantinople in 626 (Michael Whitby 1988: 69–89, 169–91; Curta 2001: 74–119).

As one would have expected, the regular periodic incidence of warfare in the region was very disruptive to economic life, as reflected in both written and material evidence. Destruction of villas in Thrace receives specific mention in the context of the Gothic revolt which culminated in Adrianople in 378 (Ammianus 31.5.8), and a series of laws during the 380s and early 390s refers to difficulties in finding enough town councilors (*decuriones*) for urban communities in Thrace (*Theodosian Code* 12.1.96 [383], 1.32.5 [386], 12.1.124 [392]) – a sure sign of an economic downturn in agriculture, since the elites of cities and towns derived most of their wealth from the countryside. Theodosius' abolition of the poll tax for peasants in Thrace

(*Justinianic Code* 11.52.1 [393]) presumably also reflects the economic tribulations of the region. Consistent with this is a growing body of archaeological data pointing toward the abandonment of rural villas in the north Bulgarian plain, owned by these local elites, most likely in the last quarter of the fourth century (Poulter 2002: 252–7, 2004: 242–4). With the advent of the Huns, even the security of major cities came under threat, with many being captured and destroyed (Michael Whitby 1988: 67), corroborated by excavations at Nicopolis which show the site to have been destroyed and abandoned toward the middle of the fifth century (Poulter 1995: 34–5). Although efforts were made to re-establish urban communities in the second half of the fifth century – Nicopolis, for example, was rebuilt, albeit on a much reduced scale (Poulter 1995: 35–44) – it should come as no great surprise to find that a law of Anastasius dealing with the levying of taxes justified the diocese of Thrace being treated differently "on account of the peasantry being diminished in number by barbarian inroads and the taxes in kind not being sufficient for the soldiers stationed there" (*Justinianic Code* 10.27.2.10 [491/505]).

Justinian made serious efforts to re-establish well-defended centers in the region (Michael Whitby 1988: 69–80; Curta 2001: 150–69), but his creation of the *quaestura exercitus* ("the quaestorship of the army") in 536 is a sure indication that Thrace's economic difficulties had not been resolved. The relevant law is preserved only in a later summary (*Novel* 41), which by itself is somewhat cryptic: it "gave to him a staff modeled on that of the praetorian prefect... It also specified how the supplies of both the field army (*comitatenses*) and the troops stationed in frontier provinces (*limitanei*) should be distributed, and it also placed five provinces under his authority, namely Scythia, Moesia, Caria, all the islands of the Cyclades, and the whole of Cyprus." Further evidence, however, helps to make sense of this arrangement. Another law (*Novel* 50) alludes to the *quaestor* being based at Odessus on the Black Sea coast, implying that the focus of his concerns was the two Thracian provinces, Scythia and Moesia, while the administrative history by the sixth-century bureaucrat John the Lydian (*On the Magistracies* 2.28–9) gives the *quaestor* the alternative title of "prefect of Scythia," since the provinces in question had been removed from the remit of the praetorian prefect, the official who oversaw the fiscal arrangements so crucial to the supply of the army. John also adds the helpful comment that Cyprus, Caria, and the Cyclades "were almost the most prosperous [provinces] of all." Piecing all this together, it becomes clear that the underlying *raison d'être* for the new post was solving the logistical needs of the military units stationed on the lower Danube by transferring resources from Caria, Cyprus, and the Cyclades, all of which were easily accessible by sea (cf. Stein 1949–59: II.474–5; Torbatov 1997; with Curta 2001: 184–5 for corroborative evidence from seals). The broader implication is that the agricultural productivity of Thrace itself remained in a depressed state.

Map 3 The Balkans, Anatolia, and the *quaestura exercitus*.
Underlined provinces (e.g. SCYTHIA) are those which formed the *quaestura exercitus*.

While the *quaestura* seems to have worked effectively – the post was still in existence in the 570s (*PLRE* III: Ioannes 91, Iulianus 20) – there was unlikely to be any improvement in Thrace's own economic performance so long as Justinian's preoccupation with the war in Italy and with renewed war with Persia during the 540s and early 550s left the region exposed to enemy inroads, with all their attendant instability (see the helpful tabulation of data on raiding activity in the Balkans between 493 and 626 in Curta 2001: 116–17). When Kotrigur Huns invaded in the late 550s, they are said to have found the lands south of the lower Danube deserted (Agathias 5.11.6). There was some respite during the 560s – there are no reports of raiding activity in the Balkans during this decade – but hardly long enough to make a difference to the region's economy before renewed war with Persia in the 570s and 580s prompted incursions into Thrace from across the lower Danube – the period which witnessed, for example, the final destruction of Nicopolis (Poulter 1995: 44–5). Peace with Persia in the 590s meant that Thrace received greater attention and imperial resources, until Phocas' revolt in 602 initiated a fresh bout of chaotic conditions, from which the region was not to recover for a long time.

B. Northern Mesopotamia and Syria

Northern Mesopotamia and Syria were another part of the empire which was exposed to significant periods of warfare during late antiquity, largely because of its proximity to Sasanian Persia. Viewing the period as a whole, however, the impact of war here was less unremitting than in Thrace and the lower Danube.

If the triumphal rhetoric of Shapur I's inscribed celebration of his military successes against the Romans is taken at face value, then Syria suffered significantly at Persian hands in the mid 250s, with 37 cities and towns and their surrounding territories being devastated; the fact that the focus of Persian plundering during Shapur's invasion in 260 was on communities further west into Cappadocia and Cilicia may perhaps mean that a thorough job had been done in Syria a few years earlier (although it is also possible that Shapur was making a political point about his ability to advance beyond Antioch).[7] Given the extent of Persian inroads and the apparent ease with which they were made, it is a reasonable assumption that the number of prisoners deported to Persia was large enough to have a noticeable impact on manpower and economic productivity in Syria and northern Mesopotamia, at least in the short term, and archaeological evidence from the most thoroughly investigated part of the region – the famous limestone massif to the east of Antioch – supports the idea that the mid third century witnessed a period, albeit brief, of economic stagnation (Tate 1992: 275–301, Tate 1996).

The first half or so of the fourth century saw further warfare between the two empires, but a phase in which the wider effects may well have been more

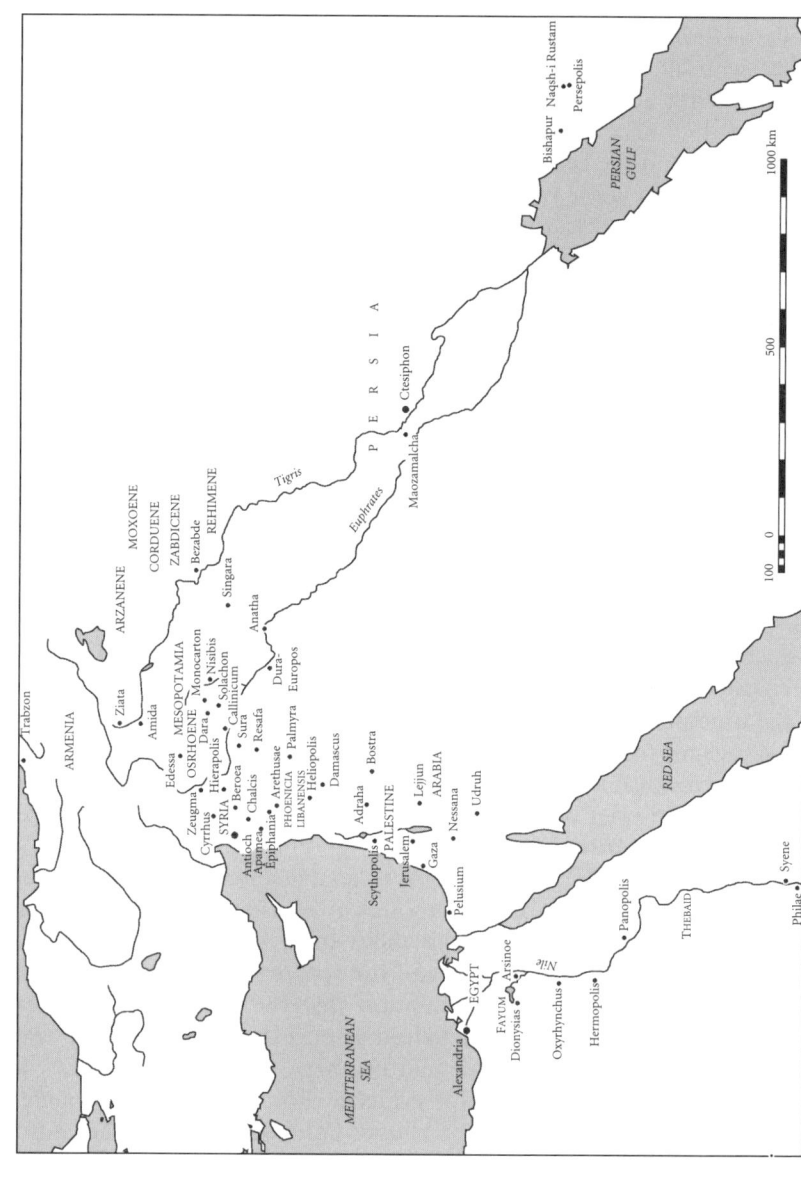

Map 4 Egypt, Syria, Mesopotamia, and Persia.

limited, both because there was a stronger element of stalemate and because much of the fighting focused on sieges of strong points. While care should be taken not to underestimate the potential for a long siege to result in significant negative economic consequences for the surrounding countryside, as the attackers drain more and more resources from the neighborhood, this also served to localize the adverse impact, particularly if the siege was unsuccessful, as was often the case in this period. In the period from 365 to 375 the focus of conflict moved northward into Armenia. At any rate, the fourth century saw the beginning of an upswing in rural prosperity, not only on the limestone massif (Tate 1992: 303–32), but also in other localities – surveys in the hinterlands of Beroea and of Edessa both point to improving economic conditions (Matthers 1981: 439–71; Marfoe et al. 1986: 38–46; Duncan-Jones 2004: 38–9). The fact that this developing prosperity continued on an enhanced scale as the fifth century progressed was no doubt due, at least in part, to the fact that relations between the two empires were quiescent for the most part, preoccupied as they both were with threats from Asiatic nomads along their northern frontiers.

It was not until the sixth century that the impact of war again made itself felt in this region in a way which had a significant long-term impact on its economic well-being. The conflict of 502–5 involved extended occupation of parts of northern Mesopotamia by large armies, and so it should perhaps occasion no surprise to find Anastasius having to remit taxes completely from the provinces of Mesopotamia and Osrhoene for a number of years (Trombley and Watt 2000: 83 n.401, 117 n.544). Fresh investment in church adornment has been seen as one indication of a return to relative normality by 509 (Trombley and Watt 2000: li), although replacement of demographic losses – a figure of about 100,000 killed or captured has been suggested (Trombley 1997: 168 n.56) – would have taken longer.

Conflict was renewed briefly in the late 520s and early 530s, but for the most part it involved less economically damaging pitched battles. The Persian invasion of 540, on the other hand, was an event on a scale comparable to Shapur's campaigns of the mid third century. Antioch was sacked and much of its population deported, and other communities had to buy off the Persians with substantial amounts of money and precious metal goods (cf. Table 4.1 and p. 102 above). This blow seems to be reflected in the communities on the limestone massif, where this period marks the end of economic expansion, not because of the direct impact of warfare, but because of the damage to the urban markets from which these communities had derived much of their prosperity (Tate 1992: 335–42; Foss 1995: 218–23). The epigraphic record on both the massif and the plains to the west around Antioch and Apamea also seems to corroborate a scenario involving demographic decline, at least over the next decade (Trombley 1997: 182). The Persian invasion of 573, during which Apamea was sacked, and the intermittent warfare over the next two decades renewed the pressure on the economy. Symptomatic of these conditions is the specific mention of Mesopotamia and the adjacent region of Osrhoene in a law of Tiberius II granting significant tax concessions throughout the empire: in these two provinces, taxes in kind were to be maintained at normal levels because of military needs (*Novel* 163 (575), preserved in Justinian's *Novels*). There was a decade's respite during the 590s, but this was followed by further war, culminating in the Persian occupation of Syria from 611 until the mid 620s. Although more recent work on the limestone massif has shown that this did not mark the dramatic caesura in the life of these communities that was once thought, it nevertheless meant a further contraction of the economy.

However, assigning full responsibility for these developments to the impact of war is complicated by the fact that in the year after the sack of Antioch in 540, the pandemic arrived in the eastern provinces of the empire, and was to recur periodically into the seventh century, so that the indicators of economic and demographic downturn noted above could owe as much, if not more, to the impact of disease. That impact will not have been uniform, insofar as the disease is likely to have spread more rapidly among the populations of urban centers than those living in the more dispersed settlement patterns of the countryside, but since the economic well-being of the countryside depended to a significant degree on urban consumers, those peasants who did not succumb will still have felt the effects indirectly. As far as Antioch is concerned, too, the city suffered a horrendous sequence of earthquakes during the sixth century – in 526, 528, 531/4, 551, 557, 577, and 588 (Downey 1961: 520–71) – which created a further drain on its resources, with subsidiary effects for the regional economy (cf. Foss 1997: 189–237).

C. *Northern Gaul*

A number of considerations have suggested that the inhabitants of northern Gaul experienced dire difficulties during the mid to late third century: the empire's abandonment of the so-called *Agri Decumates* – the wedge of territory formed by the upper Rhine and upper Danube (the modern-day Black Forest) – implied that Germanic tribes posed an increasingly potent threat; the brief emergence in the 260s of a breakaway "Gallic empire" (for which see Drinkwater 1987) appeared to be a further sign, at least in part, of the empire's struggling to cope with frontier difficulties; and archaeological evidence for the construction of fortifications around many towns in the second half of the third century (Wightman 1985: 221–7) seemed to offer further confirmation of the insecurity of the times. Given all this, it is not perhaps surprising that older scholarship tended to see the mid third century as a period of major devastation for both urban and rural communities in northern Gaul, apparently corroborated by destruction layers at numerous sites.

However, progress in the extent and sophistication of archaeological investigation in recent decades, coupled with a willingness to question previous assumptions, has modified the older picture in important ways.

It has been recognized that the abandonment of the *Agri Decumates* can be explained with reference to considerations other than Germanic tribes overwhelming Roman defenses in the region – for example, the need of the Gallic emperor Postumus for additional troops against Gallienus (Drinkwater 1987: 110, 226–7; Witschel 2004: 270). Furthermore, foreign invaders may not have been the only cause of destruction – "another possible culprit is the central imperial army, whether engaged in quelling resistance [from supporters of the breakaway Gallic emperors] or indulging itself in looting" (Wightman 1985: 220) – and the pattern of devastation and abandonment in the countryside is more varied and complex than previously appreciated (Wightman 1985: 243–50; Van Ossel and Ouzoulias 2000; Louis 2004), while there are also indicators of the existence of continued wealth in some localities: "The number and quality of tombs of the 3rd and 4th c. found in the region of Cologne attest to the vigor of rural society in this part of the Rhineland" (Van Ossel and Ouzoulias 2000: 154).

There was a strong degree of continuity in the maintenance of Gallo-Roman villas across most of northern Gaul during the first half of the fourth century, a period during which the Rhine frontier was generally stable. The impact of the destruction associated with the usurpation of Magnentius in the early 350s can be pinpointed quite precisely in some locations, thanks to numismatic evidence,[8] and fewer villas have been identified from the second half of the fourth century, except in the vicinity of Trier, whose favored status as an imperial center during the reigns of Valentinian I and Gratian provided economic stimulus to the locality – an illustration of the fact that the impact of war was not always negative. With the invasion of the Germanic Vandals, Alans, and Sueves in the early fifth century, it is unsurprising that the traditional villa effectively disappeared as a feature of the countryside in northern Gaul during the first half of the fifth century (Van Ossel and Ouzoulias 2000: 138, 143), while Trier itself was sacked (four times, according to one fifth-century source) – a fate shared by many other urban communities in the region (Wightman 1985: 300–11). All this suggests that economic conditions in northern Gaul will not have been as prosperous in the fifth century as previously, at least partly as a result of the impact of invasion and war. On the other hand, new forms of settlement emerged in due course (Percival 1992; Louis 2004), and some of those who survived may eventually have benefited from population decrease, greater availability of land, and relief from taxation and rents. What was bad for landlords will not necessarily have been bad for peasants.[9]

D. Italy

Although Italy's geographical position meant that it was less exposed to frontier incursions during the mid third century than were provinces adjacent to the Rhine and Danube, Germanic invasions did sometimes penetrate northern Italy – consider, for example, the recently discovered Augsburg inscription recording the rescue of large numbers of Italian prisoners from Juthungian raiders returning home in 260 (*AE* 1993.1231). It was incursions of this sort which prompted Aurelian to embark on the formidable project of providing the city of Rome itself with substantial new fortifications (Watson 1999: 143–52). However, while the sense of insecurity engendered cannot have been good for the economic outlook, this must be counterbalanced by recognition of the economic stimulus created by the decision of emperors to increase public provision of food in Rome, notably Aurelian's addition of pork and wine (Barnish 1987; Witschel 2004: 264). This is a trend which is likely to have continued during the fourth century, since the diversion of Egyptian grain from Rome to Constantinople would have prompted renewed emphasis on the cultivation of cereals in Italy, a development further intensified in the fifth century after the Vandal occupation of north Africa and the loss of grain exports from that quarter (Noyé 1994: 700). On the other hand, the Gothic invasion of Italy in the early fifth century, and Vandal raiding of coastal regions, especially in 440 and 455, must have had adverse effects on the prosperity of some areas, given the willingness of the government to remit taxes (or part thereof) on account of "enemy incursions" – all of central and southern Italy in 413; Campania, Picenum, and Tuscany in 418; and Sicily in 440 (*Theodosian Code* 11.28.7, 12; Valentinian III *Novels* 1.2). The stability of Gothic rule in the late fifth and early sixth century appears to have encouraged economic prosperity in many parts of the peninsula, if the correspondence of Cassiodorus is a fair guide (*Miscellanies* 8.31, 33), whereas the letters of the popes Pelagius I (556–61), Pelagius II (579–90), and Gregory I (590–604) reflect despair at the devastation resulting from nearly two decades of war between Justinian's forces and the Goths, and from the endemic conflict between Roman and Lombard forces from the 570s onward (T. S. Brown 1984: 6, 40).

The steady accumulation of archaeological data in recent decades has highlighted the need to avoid blanket generalizations about the impact of war on the peninsula during late antiquity (Christie 1996; Francovich 2002: 144–58; Arthur 2004). Different regions were exposed to the impact of war to varying degrees, while of course factors other than war also influenced economic life. The villa at S. Giovanni di Ruoti in Lucania is one particularly well-investigated example of a rural site which has corroborated some of the trends noted above, while also showing the dangers of oversimplifying developments (Barnish 1987; Small and Buck 1994). The original villa had in fact been abandoned in the early third century, well before the troubled times of the middle of the century. It was rebuilt in the early fourth century, with the high incidence of pig bones found at the site suggesting that it was one of the suppliers that benefited from imperial pork provision at Rome. In the early fifth century, when other parts of the peninsula were experiencing renewed insecurity, the villa was enlarged. Further enlargement in the late fifth century coincided with the advent of Gothic rule, while its final destruction probably occurred at some point during the 530s or 540s, the period of the Gothic war. Further south in Bruttium, on the other hand, away from the main focal points of that war, communities appear not to have been affected so adversely (Noyé 1994: 722).

The fighting in sixth-century Italy involved much blockading and besieging of cities and towns, with the potential for serious damage to the urban infrastructure. Although Rome was in many respects an exceptional case, it is difficult not to see some connection between the evident deterioration of Rome during the sixth century (Krautheimer 1980: 64–5) and the numerous sieges which the city underwent at Gothic and Lombard hands. Likewise, excavations at Milan suggest a deterioration of life in the sixth century (Liebeschuetz 2001: 371–2). Naples, on the other hand, seems to have enjoyed a relative degree of prosperity in the second half of the sixth century, despite experiencing some of the impact of war, perhaps capitalizing on the woes of other communities in Campania (cf. Arthur 2002). As with northern Mesopotamia and Syria, however, there is once again the problem here of separating out the effects of war from the influence of other factors, notably the plague of the 540s, which is likely to have had a more severe impact on urban communities than rural.

E. Summary

This survey of the economic impact of invasion on four regions of the empire has highlighted a number of more general points. First, there are dangers in generalizing about the economic impact of invasion on Roman territory at the empire-wide and regional levels. Secondly, these case studies have illustrated the difficulty of disentangling the economic impact of war from the economic impact of other significant factors, especially the sixth-century pandemic. Thirdly, the economic impact of war and invasion on imperial territory was not always as uniformly negative as ancient literary sources imply. Finally, it is apparent that regions did have the capacity to recover from the economically adverse effects of a period of invasion (cf. Mitchell 1993: 1.239–40 on the resilience of Anatolia during the mid third century); it was only when a region experienced repeated invasion over a significant period of time, as in Thrace, or when invasion coincided with other catastrophes, as in sixth-century Syria and Italy, that economic recovery proved difficult and that war can be considered to have had a lasting economic impact for the worse.

4.2.3. *The costs of lost territory*

As the negotiations revealed, Shapur required as our ransom five regions on the far side of the Tigris – Arzanene, Moxoene and Zabdicene together with Rehimene and Corduene – together with fifteen forts, as well as Nisibis,

> Singara and the Camp of the Mauri, a very valuable fortification. Although it would have been preferable to fight ten times over rather than surrender any of these, a group of flatterers pressed the apprehensive emperor [Jovian]... and without hesitation he handed over everything demanded. (Ammianus 25.7.9–11; cf. 25.9.7–11)

During the course of late antiquity the empire lost long-term control of territory at various points. Any loss of territory was a blow to imperial prestige, as the passage above implies, but some losses had much more serious economic consequences than others. During the mid third century imperial forces withdrew from two regions – the *Agri Decumates* (between the upper reaches of the Rhine and Danube) and the province of Dacia, north of the lower Danube. The most serious economic effect of these changes was probably losing the Dacian mines, which had been a valuable source of gold and other minerals for the previous century and a half; otherwise, however, the loss of this region did not have serious economic ramifications. During the fourth century, the only significant loss of territory was that alluded to above after the debacle of Julian's Persian expedition in 363 – effectively, some of the Transtigritane satrapies which the Romans had gained in 299 and the eastern half of the north Mesopotamian plain, between the Tigris and the Khabour (Lenski 2002a: 161–3). The main significance of this was more strategic than economic, since it included the handing over of the important fortress city of Nisibis, which had proved a consistent obstacle to Persian inroads during the first half of the fourth century (though of course one should not underestimate the economic benefits of this protection to northern Mesopotamia and Syria).

The fifth century saw the most significant losses of territory to date. The decision to withdraw from Britain early in the century was not a serious blow to the economic well-being of the empire – it was, after all, a region whose economic value had long been called into question (cf., e.g., Strabo *Geography* 4.200). The Vandal occupation of north Africa, on the other hand, proved to be a devastating blow. This was the wealthiest region of the western half of the empire and, it seems, continued to enjoy a reasonable level of prosperity under Vandal rule (Mattingly and Hitchner 1995: 211) – perhaps because no longer paying imperial taxes. However, its occupation by the Vandals deprived the western half of the empire of its valuable revenues, which explains why a number of concerted efforts were made by the empire during the mid fifth century to reconquer it, culminating in the debacle of 468. The longer north Africa remained outside imperial control, the greater the impact of that loss on imperial finances in the west. It became harder to sustain the armies of the west, increasing amounts of territory were lost to other Germanic peoples in Gaul and Spain, and the fiscal viability of the western half of the empire was steadily eroded – a downward spiral from which it proved impossible to escape.

The surviving eastern half of the empire suffered no significant losses of territory during the sixth century, and even managed to expand imperial territory, notably through the reconquest of north Africa, Italy, and a corner of Spain, as well as some additions in Transcaucasia as recompense for the assistance which the empire gave to Khusro II in his regaining control of the Persian throne in 591 (Michael Whitby 1988: 304). The early seventh century, on the other hand, saw dramatic setbacks as Persia conquered all of the eastern provinces, including Egypt, and threatened Constantinople itself in 626. These losses proved to be only temporary, as this grave crisis was seen off by Heraclius. However, he barely had time to recover before a new and unexpected enemy – Arab tribes energized by the new creed of Islam – conquered Syria, Palestine, and Egypt. These losses proved to be permanent, with that of Egypt – the wealthiest region of the empire – particularly devastating. Although the empire survived, it did so on a much reduced territorial scale (Anatolia and some of the Balkans) which necessitated fundamental changes to the empire's infrastructure during the seventh century, from which a very different entity eventually emerged (Haldon 1990a; Whittow 1996: 69–133).

4.2.4. *The costs of peace*

> At an earlier date the emperor [Justinian] had reduced Africa and the whole of Italy, becoming as a result of those epoch-making campaigns almost the first of the rulers of Constantinople to be emperor of the Romans in fact as well as in name. He had accomplished these and similar feats when he was still in the full vigour of his youth, but now in his declining years when old age was upon him he seemed to have wearied of vigorous policies and to prefer to play off his enemies against one another and, if necessary, to coax them away with gifts rather than rely on his own powers and expose himself to the hazards of a sustained struggle. (Agathias 5.14.1 [tr. Frendo, with revisions])

An alternative to the risks inherent in undertaking military campaigns and the losses that might arise from enemy raids and invasion was to purchase peace. The increasing willingness of emperors in late antiquity to give potential enemies "gifts" in return for security is one important difference in the empire's conduct of its relations with its neighbors compared with the Principate, and symptomatic of the more precarious position in which the empire found itself during this period of its history. As Agathias' comments above imply, however, this policy was one which met with criticism from some quarters. The attitude of many was well summed up by one senator, during the debate in 408 about Stilicho's proposal to persuade Alaric the Goth to remain in the Balkans, rather than invade Italy, by giving him 4,000 lb of gold: "this is not peace, but slavery" (Zosimus 5.29.9). Similarly, when organizing a truce with the Persians in 551, the Romans agreed to pay 2,000 lb of gold but were in two minds about the best arrangement for giving the money to the Persians: initially, Justinian favored handing it over in annual 400-lb installments so as to give Khusro an incentive to maintain the peace, but he was eventually persuaded to give it all in one lump sum (as the Persians wanted) "in order not to appear to be paying them tribute each year" (Procopius *Wars* 8.15.7). It was undoubtedly consciousness of this potential criticism which prompted Justin II's panegyrist to refer to Justinian's payments to the Avars as an act of generosity (Corippus *In Praise of Justin II* 3.349–50) – terminology which allowed him to maintain the façade of imperial superiority. To avoid the value-laden language of "gifts" and "bribes," modern scholars usually prefer the more neutral term "subsidies" (cf. C. D. Gordon 1949; Blockley 1985b).

Whatever term one uses, however, there is no doubt that these payments were a common feature of the empire's dealings with some states and peoples during the fifth and sixth centuries (Table 4.2). When one casts an eye over the figures involved, particularly when they entail annual amounts rather than one-off payments, one cannot but wonder about the economic wisdom of buying peace in this way. Yet further reflection may prompt a different conclusion. These figures need to be set alongside other figures already noted above – the estimated 100,000 *solidi* which Khusro extracted from Syrian cities in 540 and the more than 700,000 *solidi* lost as a result of the failed Vandal expedition in 468. When viewed against these figures, the majority of the amounts paid in subsidies do not seem excessive from an economic point of view (cf. Hendy 1985: 263–4). Of the specific figures at the high end of the scale, the 510,000 *solidi* paid to Alaric in 409 actually came out of the pockets of senators and from temple treasures, not the imperial treasury (Zosimus 5.41.4–7), and senators also made a significant contribution to the 432,000 *solidi* paid to Attila in 447; moreover, such amounts were well within the means of the senatorial aristocracy, on the basis of recorded figures for their incomes from earlier in the fifth century (Thompson 1948: 192–3). As for the largest figure of all – the 11,000 lb of gold paid to the Persians in 532, which equates to 792,000 *solidi* – there were specific circumstances which no doubt induced Justinian to agree in this instance. On the one hand, he must still have had at his disposal at least some of the huge surplus of 320,000 lb of gold which Anastasius had built up through careful financial stewardship and bequeathed to Justinian and his uncle in 518 (Procopius *Secret History* 19.7), while on the other, he must by this stage have been planning the Vandal expedition (for which the conclusion of peace with Persia was an essential prerequisite) and have calculated that, if successful, it was likely to bring in much greater wealth than he was having to lay out in order to secure peace with Persia.

Overall, then, while it is easy to exaggerate the costs of war, they do nonetheless often seem, on balance, to have outweighed any benefits in this period, and so there is good reason to think that, for the most part, purchasing peace through subsidies had less detrimental economic

Table 4.2 Subsidies paid by the empire to other states and peoples during late antiquity

Year	Recipient	Amount	Equivalent in *solidi*	Duration in years	Total in *solidi*	Reference
408	Goths (Alaric)	4,000 lb gold	288,000	1	288,000	Zosimus 5.29.9
409	Goths (Alaric)	5,000 lb gold 30,000 lb silver	360,000 150,000	1	510,000	Zosimus 5.41.4–7
c.422	Huns (Rua)	350 lb gold p.a.	25,200	15	378,000	Priscus fr. 2
c.437	Huns (Attila and Bleda)	700 lb gold p.a.	50,400	10	504,000	Priscus fr. 2
c.447	Huns (Attila)	6,000 lb gold (back payment)	432,000		432,000	Priscus fr. 9.3
473	Goths (Theodoric Strabo)	2,100 lb gold p.a.	151,200	3	453,600	Priscus fr. 9.3
	Goths (Theodoric Strabo)	2,000 lb gold p.a.	144,000	1	144,000	Malchus fr. 2
478	Goths (Theodoric the Amal)	1,000 lb gold 40,000 lb silver 10,000 *solidi* p.a.	72,000 200,000 10,000	1	282,000	Malchus fr. 18.3 (lines 25–6)
505	Persia	1,000 lb gold	72,000	1	72,000	Procopius *Wars* 1.9.4 (cf. Ps.-Zachariah *Church History* 7.5 [1,100 lb gold])
532	Persia	11,000 lb gold	792,000	1	792,000	Procopius *Wars* 1.22.3
545	Persia	2,000 lb gold	144,000	1	144,000	Procopius *Wars* 2.28.10
551	Persia	2,600 lb gold	187,200	1	187,200	Procopius *Wars* 8.15.3–7
561	Persia	30,000 *solidi* p.a.	30,000	10	300,000	Menander fr. 6.1 [lines 148–9]
574	Persia	45,000 *solidi*	45,000	1	45,000	Menander fr. 18.2
582	Avars	80,000 *solidi* p.a.	80,000	10	800,000	Theophylact 1.3.7
575	Persia	30,000 *solidi* p.a.	30,000	3	90,000	Menander fr. 18.3
583	Avars	100,000 *solidi* p.a.	100,000	15	1,500,000	Theophylact 1.4.5
598	Avars	120,000 *solidi* p.a.	120,000	5?	600,000	Theophylact 7.15.14

Notes: It is possible that some subsidies were never actually paid out, or lapsed earlier than indicated. It is also possible that the figures in the sources have been copied incorrectly in the manuscript transmission process.

consequences than war and was therefore a rational alternative, despite the odium it incurred in some quarters (with further possible implications for the debate about the capacity of imperial decision-makers to engage in strategic thinking). Indeed, some of the wealth paid out in subsidies may only have been lost temporarily, if it subsequently re-entered the empire as a result of trade.[10]

Further Reading

For good overviews of important aspects of **the late Roman economy** which give attention to war as one factor, see Corbier 2005, Whittaker and Garnsey 1998, and Ward-Perkins 2000a, 2000b. See also Wickham 2003, greatly expanded and developed in Wickham 2005. Hendy 1985 provides more detailed discussion of some aspects. Studies of the fate of **late Roman cities and towns** include Christie and Loseby 1996, Liebeschuetz 2001, and Lavan 2001. A number of valuable collections of essays on the **late Roman rural landscape** have appeared recently: Bowden et al. 2004 and Christie 2004; the former begins with a useful "bibliographic essay" by Chavarría and Lewit.

Helpful entrées to the issues affecting **specific regions** are provided by Michael Whitby 2000c; Poulter 2004 (Thrace and the lower Danube); Gatier 1994; Foss 1995, 1997; Wickham 2005: 443–54 (northern Mesopotamia and Syria); Wightman 1985; Van Ossel and Ouzalias 2000 (northern Gaul); and Christie 1996, Francovich 2002, and Arthur 2004 (Italy).

On **subsidies** in late Roman diplomacy, see C. D. Gordon 1949, Blockley 1985b, Hendy 1985: 260–4, and Delmaire 1989: 539–46.

5
THE EXPERIENCE OF WAR

Emperors were keen to promote a positive image of war and military success (cf. above, Chapter 1.2), but for those who experienced war at first hand (which did not, of course, include most emperors during the fifth and sixth centuries) it could be very different. One late Roman source referred to war as "a great evil, and the worst of evils" (*On Strategy* 4.9), while a number of others used the evocative phrase *lacrimabile bellum* – literally, "tearful war" or "war deserving (or accompanied by) tears."[1] Such language is a sobering reminder of the painful effects of war for many of the inhabitants of the empire and adjacent regions.

The previous two chapters have considered various aspects of the impact of war, including the consequences of the empire's military infrastructure and the economic benefits and costs of campaigns and invasions, and discussion of these aspects has necessarily been conducted at the largely impersonal level of broad trends. This chapter aims to investigate the impact of war at the human level of individual experience, or at least the experience of major categories of individual. There is of course a risk of such a discussion becoming merely anecdotal, but the question of the experience of war warrants attention nonetheless, given that the empathetic dimension of history has often been unduly neglected (cf. Runciman 1983: 15–21, 223–300).

Generalizing about the experience of war in late antiquity is fraught with difficulty (as is the case for any period of antiquity). War could take a variety of forms, from the high intensity of pitched battles, to the slower but remorseless pace of sieges, or the short, sharp shock of raiding, and the experience of individuals will have varied greatly according to their occupation and location, and the point in time when they were living. To take only the most obvious of contrasts, soldiers will have had a different perspective to non-combatants, and many civilians living away from the frontier regions of the empire will have had little if any direct experience of war. Nor will the experience of soldiers have been uniform, depending upon the type of unit in which they were enrolled (most obviously, the basic distinction between infantry and cavalry). All these variables make it impossible to avoid some degree of oversimplification.

Another problem in tackling this subject is the nature of the source material. Historians of more modern periods are able to draw on memoirs and diaries, whether of combatants or civilians caught up in conflict. Nothing remotely comparable survives from late antiquity. The papyri from Egypt which provide such valuable insights into other aspects of provincial social history are of little help for this subject, since Egypt during late antiquity experienced significant warfare (as opposed to the intermittent raiding of desert tribesmen) on only a limited number of occasions – the Palmyrene invasion of the early 270s, Diocletian's besieging of a rebellious Alexandria in the late 290s, and the Persian invasion of the early seventh century. The focal points for these events were Alexandria and the Delta region, whose damp climate is not conducive to the survival of papyrus documents.[2] Although narrative histories such as those of Ammianus Marcellinus and Procopius devote considerable attention to warfare, the potential value of this emphasis is offset, to some extent at least, by the influence of historiographical tradition on their presentation of events (see further below). In some respects, the most valuable sources for this subject, at least with respect to the experience of non-combatants, are the Syriac *Chronicle* attributed to Joshua the Stylite, which recounts, in unadorned style, the travails of north Mesopotamian communities during the war with Persia in the first decade of the sixth century (Trombley and Watt 2000: xi–li), and the letters of Pope Gregory the Great, which include much incidental detail about the consequences of warfare with the Lombards in late sixth- and early seventh-century Italy (Markus 1997: 97–107).

A further challenge in broaching this subject is that of deciding what, if anything, is distinctive about warfare in late antiquity. Clearly some aspects will have had much in common with warfare in other periods of antiquity, insofar as economic and technological change was limited. It is, however, possible to suggest some differences between the character of warfare during late antiquity and the centuries which immediately preceded it. One difference is that from the third century onward, some of the empire's neighbors proved to be stronger militarily and/or the empire proved less adept at repelling them, and therefore many inhabitants of the provinces near the frontiers (and, increasingly in the west, inhabitants of interior provinces also) experienced warfare at first hand more frequently than had been the case during the Principate. A second difference is that siege warfare became an increasingly important feature of warfare in late antiquity. During the Principate, no Germanic tribe had siege capability of any significance (Todd 1975: 178–9), and even the Parthians, while apparently possessing some technological capacity (Tacitus *Annals* 15.4–5, 10–13; cf. Leriche 1993: 86–8), did not use it very much against the Romans, perhaps because they lacked sufficient logistical infrastructure to sustain effective siege operations (cf. D. L. Kennedy 1996: 83–7). During late antiquity, by contrast, the Sasanian Persians demonstrated the organizational and technical skills to undertake effective sieges from an early stage.³ Some northern peoples may have possessed some siege capability in the mid third century,⁴ but if so, the fourth-century Goths, at least, shied away from attacking fortified centers (Ammianus 31.6.4). From the mid fifth century, northern peoples were once again attacking cities. The Huns successfully besieged Balkan cities like Naissus (Priscus fr.6.2), while sixth-century Avars launched assaults on cities like Thessalonica (*Miracles of St. Demetrius* 200) and Constantinople itself in 626 – even if their ability to undertake such operations was probably accomplished largely through exploiting, on the one hand, the knowledge of Roman prisoners and deserters (cf. John of Ephesus *Church History* 6.24), and on the other, the sheer numbers of subject peoples they controlled and were "content to sacrifice...in frontal assaults" (Michael Whitby 2000c: 709). Justinian's war in Italy and its aftermath meant that many cities in the peninsula also underwent siege at the hands of Roman, Gothic, or Lombard forces. Nor should the occurrence of sieges in the context of civil war be overlooked, such as Victorinus' investment of Autun in 269 (Drinkwater 1987: 36–9, 78–81), Diocletian's siege of Alexandria in the 290s (Eutropius 9.24; Malalas *Chronicle* pp. 308–9), that of Aquileia by Julian's generals in 361 (Ammianus 21.12), or that of Cyzicus by the usurper Procopius in 365 (Ammianus 26.8). This feature of late antique warfare was particularly significant for civilian populations. Whereas they were likely to have little, if any, involvement in pitched battles, they could not avoid being directly affected by fighting if their city or town found itself besieged.

In an effort to avoid the problem of generalization already noted, attention will be given to the experience of warfare from the perspective of a range of different social groups – soldiers, urban communities, rural communities, and women (a category which, while obviously overlapping with the previous two, deserves some specific consideration in an inevitably male-dominated subject such as this).

5.1. Soldiers

Missiles were hurled for a short time before the Germans rushed forward with more haste than thought, wielding their weapons in their right hands and throwing themselves upon our squadrons of horse with horrible grinding of their teeth and more than their usual savagery...Our men faced them resolutely, protecting their heads with shields, thrusting their swords or brandishing their javelins so as to intimidate them with the prospect of death. At the critical point in the battle, when our cavalry were bravely regrouping and the infantry were stoutly protecting their flanks with a wall of overlapping shields, thick clouds of dust arose...But while our left wing, advancing in close formation, had driven back by sheer force the columns of attacking Germans, and was advancing with shouts against the barbarians, our cavalry on the right unexpectedly gave way and fled. However, the first to flee impeded those behind them, and when they found themselves safe in the middle of the legions, they halted and renewed the fight. This had happened because, while their ranks were being reformed, the heavy cavalry saw their commander slightly wounded and one of their comrades slipping over the neck of his horse, which sank under the weight of his armor. They began scattering as best they could, and would have caused utter confusion by trampling on the infantry, had not the latter, who were drawn up in close order, stood their ground...

The Cornuti and Bracchiati, hardened by long experience of war, intimidated the enemy by their conduct and raised their mighty battle-cry... But the Alamanni, who enter wars enthusiastically, strove even harder, like inspired madmen, to destroy everything in front of them... They were stronger and taller, the Romans had the advantage in discipline from long practice. They were wild and uncontrollable, our men were deliberate and wary... They were ready to squander their lives for victory, and kept trying to find weak spots in the organization of our line... At last they gave way under the stress of disaster and put all their efforts into trying to escape... Our men hacked at the backs of the fleeing enemy... A great number lay mortally wounded, begging for the relief of a speedy death...; others slipped in the blood of their comrades on the muddy, treacherous ground, and were suffocated under the heaps of bodies which fell on them, and died without being wounded...(Ammianus 16.12.36–53)

Interest in the experience of battle from the perspective of front-line combatants in antiquity can be traced back to John Keegan's *The Face of Battle* (1976). Although Keegan did not give detailed attention to battle in the ancient world, the influence of his study has slowly filtered through into the study of warfare in the Roman world.[5] Most of this work has focused on the Roman army of the late Republic and Principate, but much of it is applicable to late antiquity because of continuities in the nature of warfare, and the limited nature of technological change already noted. On the other hand, certain shifts in emphasis – for example, smaller unit sizes, the higher profile of cavalry, and the greater prominence of siege warfare – will have made some difference, as will the particular enemy which an army faced.

Pitched battles were the exception rather than the rule in late antiquity: more often than not, warfare with Persia involved sieges, while northern peoples tended to favor dispersed raiding, which did not play to the strengths of the Romans. Pitched battles did, however, sometimes occur, and they were still the most intense and concentrated form of experience of warfare in this period. Insight into the nature of that experience relies heavily on the narrative histories of Ammianus, Procopius, and others. Their narrative character, complete with detailed descriptions of battles such as Ammianus' account of the battle of Strasbourg in 357 at the head of this section, can make it tempting to take those descriptions at face value. As already intimated in the introduction to this chapter, however, these historians were part of a long tradition of historical writing, and they were very conscious of that tradition, and of the expectations of their audiences with regard to content and style. As a result, although Ammianus, a former army officer, had first-hand experience of involvement in battle, and Procopius, as secretary to Justinian's leading general, Belisarius, had been an eyewitness of many military engagements, their accounts of battles cannot be treated as straight reportage.[6] Most notoriously, the speeches of commanders to their troops which almost invariably precede accounts of battles were an opportunity for the historian to display his rhetorical prowess for the edification and entertainment of his audience, and were not expected to bear any direct relationship to anything a commander may actually have said before battle. Similarly, there were certain stock images which recur in ancient battle accounts on which it would be unwise to place too much weight in any attempt to recover the experience of battle. In Ammianus' account of the battle of Strasbourg (above), this applies to such features as the enemy grinding their teeth, the ground being slippery with blood, and the heaps of corpses under which men are buried alive (Naudé 1958: 104–5), while the influence of rhetoric is evident in his formulaic contrasting of the relative advantages of the two sides.

The dictates of genre ought, however, to be thought of as providing a framework rather than as imposing a straitjacket. For it is apparent in the cases of Ammianus and Procopius that their personal experiences also had an important influence on their representation of battle. Alongside the stereotypical and rhetorical features already noted in Ammianus' account of Strasbourg, one finds significant elements whose very specificity must reflect the events of that particular battle: the attempted flight of some of the Roman cavalry, panicked by incidents which, although seemingly inconsequential, understandably caused concern and provide valuable insight into some of the combatants' edgy frame of mind; and the reference to specific units – the Cornuti and Bracchiati – and their effective use of their war-cry to steady morale. More generally, Ammianus' description of the attendant circumstances of fighting – the noise, the dust, the sense of confusion – rings true. Moreover, despite the influence of convention in the description of battles, it cannot at the same time have been uncommon for a certain spectrum of similar things to recur in such situations.[7]

Procopius' battle descriptions also contain their fair share of stock features, such as "the vast cloud" of arrows at the battle of Dara in 530 (*Wars* 1.14.35; cf. Naudé 1958: 104 for this commonplace). However, there are also examples of detail which are likely to reflect the realities of a particular engagement, perhaps most famously his description of the wounds suffered by certain soldiers during a skirmish with Gothic forces outside the Pincian Gate of Rome in 537:

> In this action Cutilas was struck in the middle of the middle of the head by a javelin, and he kept on pursuing with the javelin still embedded in his head. And after the rout [of the Goths] had taken place, he rode into the city about sunset together with the other survivors, the javelin in his head waving about,

a most extraordinary sight. During the same encounter Arzes, one of the guards of Belisarius, was hit by one of the Gothic archers between the nose and the right eye. And the point of the arrow penetrated as far as the neck behind, but it did not show through, and the rest of the shaft projected from his face and shook as the man rode. (Procopius *Wars* 6.2.15–17 [tr. Dewing]; cf. 6.2.25–7)

The sequel to this episode highlights another aspect of the realities of warfare – the potential and the limitations of Roman medical expertise in treating war wounds. The army of late antiquity inherited an infrastructure for military medical care that had developed during the Principate.[8] While the "medical corpsmen" (*depotatoi*) recommended by one late Roman military treatise (Ps-Maurice *Strategy* 2.9) cannot have been trained doctors, since they were selected from the ranks of each unit (7B.17), there are also references to doctors who may have been able to provide more skilled treatment of soldiers (e.g., Ammianus 16.6.2; Theophylact Simocatta 2.5.5–6; *P. Nessana* 36 (line 15) [sixth century]; *P. Munich* 9 (line 106) [Syene, 585]). In the case of Cutilas and Arzes from the episode in Procopius above, a doctor (who may in fact have been a civilian physician in the city rather than an army medic, as also in Ammianus 19.2.15) demonstrated great skill in removing the arrow from the latter without any serious consequences, but it is likely that Procopius included this case at least partly because its successful outcome for Arzes was unusual – in contrast with Cutilas' wound, which proved fatal (6.2.25–31).[9]

The ability of Ammianus and Procopius to instill their battle descriptions with a genuine sense of elements of the combatants' experience, despite the constraints of genre within which the writers operated, is also apparent when one compares battle narratives in other historians who are not known to have had first-hand familiarity with military campaigning. Procopius' continuator, Agathias, "was not at home in accounts of military actions" (Averil Cameron 1970: 48), while Theophylact Simocatta "lacked military expertise...; interesting stratagems or unusual incidents might attract his attention, but the inclusion of such items might merely obscure the rest of the military narrative" (Michael Whitby 1988: 322). Consider, for example, Theophylact's account of the battle of Solachon in 586 (2.4). He devotes most space to a ploy by one officer designed to regroup Roman soldiers in danger of being distracted by the opportunity for plunder, and to the question of whether an order to focus their attack on the Persian cavalry had emanated from another particular officer or from the heavens. Otherwise the account comprises minimal detail,[10] filled out with commonplaces such as the fact that "the battle line stood on the remains of the dead, since the face of the earth was covered because of the continuity of corpses upon its surface" (2.4.6 [trs. Whitby and Whitby]). The one detail of genuine interest is Theophylact's comment that the Roman cavalry dismounted at one point to engage in hand-to-hand combat (2.4.5).

Late Roman sources provide confirmation of continuities in the traditional strategies by which soldiers' morale in the face of the possibility of death was maintained and encouraged, such as the issuing of rewards for bravery,[11] care for the wounded (cf. above, p. 128), or proper burial of the dead: "After the battle the general should give prompt attention to the wounded and see to burying the dead. Not only is this a religious duty, but it greatly helps the morale of the living" (Ps.-Maurice *Strategy* 7B.6; cf. Agathias 2.10.7).[12] Statues honoring brave soldiers were set up on at least one occasion (Ammianus 19.6.12), although this appears to have been the exception rather than the rule. There was of course also the prospect of booty in the event of victory (e.g., Procopius *Wars* 4.1.11, 5.23.27; Agathias 2.10.7, 3.23.13; Theophylact Simocatta 2.6.11). However, late antiquity saw some new developments in this sphere, notably the use of Christian symbols to motivate troops, particularly icons in the later sixth and early seventh century, as when, before the battle of Solachon in 586, "the general paraded [the icon] through the ranks, thereby inspiring the army with greater and irresistible courage" (Theophylact Simocatta 2.2.6; cf. George of Pisidia *On the Persian Campaign* 1.139–54, 2.86). During the dark days of war against Persia in the early seventh century, the emperor Heraclius even appears to have promised eternal salvation to those who died in battle against the heathen enemy (cf. Howard-Johnston 1999: 39–40):

> "Be not disturbed, O brethren, by the multitude of the enemy. For when God wills it, one man will rout a thousand. So let us sacrifice ourselves to God for the salvation of our brothers. May we win the crown of martyrdom so that we may be praised in the future and receive our recompense from God." (Theophanes *Chronicle* pp. 310–11 [trs. Mango and Scott])

And what of the defeated? For soldiers on the losing side who failed to make good their escape and were not cut down in retreat, many were no doubt enslaved, as happened to civilians (see below), although as already noted (Chapter 4.1, p. 104), some might find themselves expected to fight on the Roman side on some distant frontier, while others might end up settled on vacant land, such as the Hunnic prisoners whom the historian Sozomen encountered cultivating the fields of Bithynia in the mid fifth century (*Church History* 9.5.7). There were also occasional instances of enemy prisoners being slaughtered in cold blood by the Romans immediately after a battle, such as the Persian prisoners after the battle of Dara in 530 and Gothic prisoners after the battle of Taginae in 552.[13] Similarly horrific was Julian's encouragement to his troops in Gaul to decapitate any barbarian enemy they killed and bring the severed heads back for reward.[14]

Siege warfare was at least as common an experience for soldiers in late antiquity as pitched battles.[15] For soldiers defending a city or town, being besieged will have involved many of the same elements experienced by the civilians within the fortifications, to be discussed below (cf. also Figs. 5.1 and 5.2). However, there were some features specific to the military personnel involved, whether attacking or defending, principally the greater exposure to danger from various quarters. So, for example, siege artillery could pose as serious a threat to those using it as to their targets, if insufficient care was taken, as in the following incident involving a torsion machine for throwing heavy projectiles, known as a "scorpion" or "wild ass" (cf. Matthews 1989: 291–3):

> In the course of these operations [the siege of Maozamalcha during Julian's Persian campaign in 363] one of our engineers, whose name I cannot recall, was by chance standing behind a "scorpion" when a stone which an artilleryman had placed insecurely in the sling was hurled backward. He was thrown on his back, his chest was crushed, and he was killed. His limbs were torn apart to such an extent that parts of his body were beyond recognition. (Ammianus 24.4.28)

Another example of technology backfiring with disastrous consequences occurred during the Roman siege of Petra in the Caucasus in the early 550s, when Persian defenders stationed on a wooden tower were trying to drop pots of burning sulfur and bitumen onto Roman battering rams below – a standard tactic (cf. Vegetius *Epitome of Military Science* 4.8; Ps.-Maurice *Strategy* 10.3; Ammianus 20.6.6). In this instance, however, a sudden gust of wind somehow set the wooden tower alight, with the result that fire "consumed the whole tower and the Persians who were in it. These were all burned to death, and their charred bodies fell, some inside the wall, others outside" (Procopius *Wars* 8.11.35–8, 61–2).

One of the most gruesome insights into the potential horrors of siege warfare for soldiers was provided by the archaeological investigations in the 1930s at the fort of Dura-Europos on the Euphrates, which uncovered the tunnels through which Persian attackers had sought to undermine a section of wall in 256, and the counter-mine through which the Roman defenders had tried to prevent them:

> The bodies of sixteen or eighteen [Roman] soldiers were found with the remains of their armour and clothing...In the easternmost part...the skeletons lay in contracted positions as if the men had tried to save themselves from a cave-in or had been crushed in positions of defence. One man appears to have been seated, his spinal column being markedly curved. Another lay, thrown backward, with his legs spread wide apart and folded under him as if he had made an attempt to rise. (du Mesnil du Buisson 1936: 194–5)

The original excavator concluded that when the Roman counter-mine broke into the Persian tunnel, the Persians got the better of the Romans, who then retreated, pursued by the enemy, and that

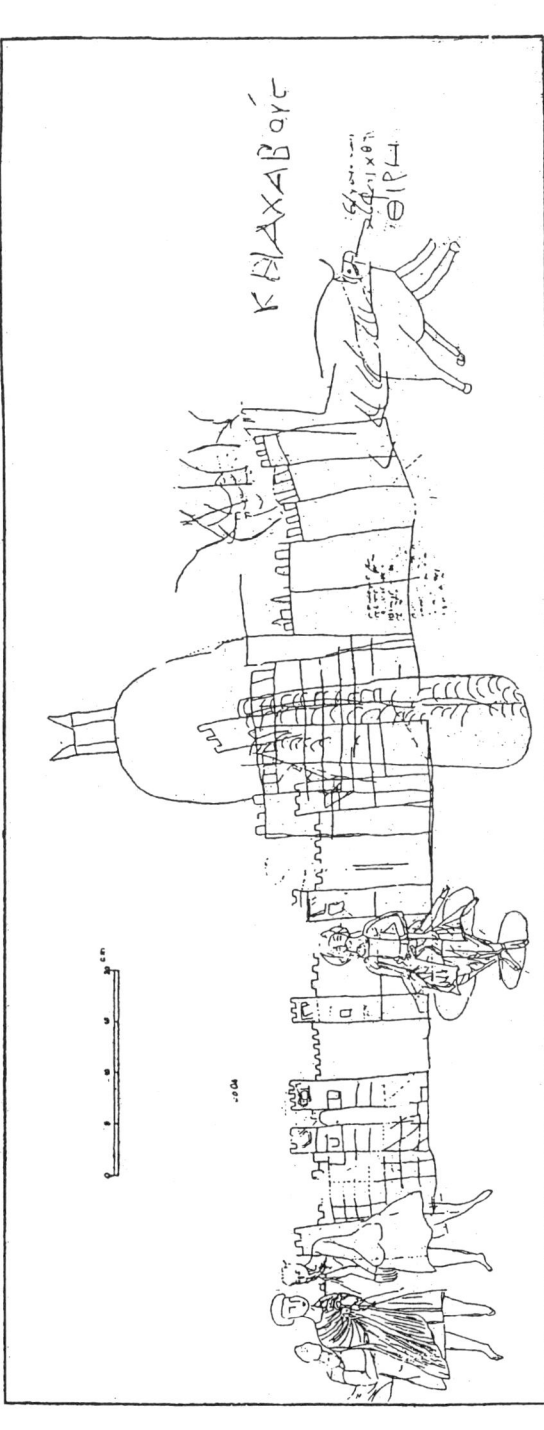

Figure 5.1 Graffito from Dura-Europos depicting a town under siege.
The substantial remains of the Roman fortress at Dura-Europos on the Euphrates have provided a wealth of material, visual and written evidence about life in a third-century frontier community. This evidence includes graffiti scratched by inhabitants on the walls of buildings, including this item (120 × 48 cm) found in the Temple of Bel, depicting a walled town under siege. The right-hand end of the town appears to be on fire, while toward the center there are portrayed various types of siege-works – a siege mound rising high above the walls, and tunnels which could be either mines dug by the attackers or counter-mines of the defenders. (Reproduced from du Mesnil du Buisson 1944: 35, by permission of the Société nationale des Antiquaires de France and the Département des Antiquités orientales du Musée du Louvre.)

Figure 5.2 Relief from the Arch of Constantine depicting the siege of Verona.

The Arch of Constantine was erected in the center of Rome between 312 and 315 to commemorate Constantine's victory over Maxentius outside Rome in 312. Among the numerous reliefs adorning the arch is a series of four representing various stages in Constantine's Italian campaign against Maxentius. The second of these reliefs depicts his siege of the north Italian city of Verona, one of Maxentius' strongholds and a major obstacle to Constantine's advance southward. It shows the city walls and towers, whose defenders are armed with spears and rocks to throw at the attackers. Constantine's forces advance from the left, while a wounded defender topples from the walls in front of them. (Image reproduced by permission of Wayne Boucher.)

the defenders of the city, seeing that the Roman auxiliaries were retreating in disorder and fearing that the Persians would emerge into the city, hastily blocked up the entrance into the counter-mine shutting up inside those who were wounded or were lagging behind. At the same time the Persians, who were undoubtedly too few in number to attempt to enter the city, and who had already attained their objective [viz., completing a mine under the wall], set fire to [the wooden supports in] the countermine and rapidly withdrew.

This fire resulted in the collapse of the counter-mine on top of the soldiers discovered there (du Mesnil du Buisson 1936: 198). A recent re-examination of the evidence has highlighted various inconsistencies in the earlier reconstruction of events, discounting the idea that other defenders sealed off the tunnel and entombed their comrades, and suggesting a more complex but equally harrowing scenario which included the Persians piling up the bodies of the Romans they had killed in their underground struggle, to form a barrier against further Roman interference before they collapsed the counter-mine and then their own tunnel (James 2005). From the perspective of the experience of war, however, the overall conclusion remains the same: "These gruesome deposits bring us as close as archaeology ever has to the immediacy, and the real horror, of ancient combat" (James 2005: 204).[16]

5.2. Urban Communities

Provision for food and water for the army and for the civilian population is both the beginning and the end of any plan of defence. (*On Strategy* 6 [tr. Dennis])

As already noted, war impinged most directly on the civilian populations of urban communities when cities or towns were besieged. Urban communities near the eastern frontier with Persia were particularly prone to this throughout late antiquity (with the exception of the fifth century, when relations between the two empires were largely quiescent), with Balkan cities affected increasingly from the mid fifth century onward, and Italian cities in the mid to late sixth century.

Civilians might sometimes be called upon to assist with the defense of their city or town, whether in the form of keeping watch or actively responding to enemy assaults.[17] However, for the majority of civilian inhabitants the most obvious immediate effect of a siege on their lives would be increasing food shortages.[18] The speed with which such shortages made themselves felt depended in part on whether there had been any forewarning of the siege which might allow the stockpiling of foodstuffs and in part on the effectiveness of the enemy blockade: it proved impossible for the Goths to effect the complete encirclement of Rome in 537 because of the sheer size of the city, which allowed Belisarius to send all the women and children away to Campania and thereby reduce the drain on food supplies (Procopius *Wars*

5.25.2; cf. the advice of Ps.-Maurice *Strategy* 10.3); during the third siege of Rome in 549, imperial forces also took advantage of Rome's size to grow grain within the city walls (Procopius *Wars* 7.36.2). Although Rome was an exceptional case, there are other examples of the expulsion of surplus population and the sowing of land within the town walls (notably Cremna in 278: Zosimus 1.69 with Mitchell 1995: 177–9). More often than not, however, the population of a city or town actually swelled on the eve of a siege as rural communities fled before the invaders and sought refuge in fortified centers (e.g., Zosimus 1.33.3 (Trabzon), Ammianus 19.6.1 (Ziata), Ps.-Joshua Stylites *Chronicle* 62 (Edessa)). Constantius II is said to have expanded the size of Amida on the upper Tigris specifically for this purpose (Ammianus 18.9.1), though his planning had clearly not anticipated the possibility that a Persian attack might coincide with the annual fair, as happened in 359 (Ammianus 18.8.13), with the result that an even larger number of people from neighboring areas were caught up in that fateful siege.[19]

Military manuals offered a range of sensible advice on maximizing available food resources during a siege (Vegetius *Epitome of Military Science* 4.7; Ps.-Maurice *Strategy* 10.2–3). However, as a siege dragged on and food began to run short, individuals typically found themselves increasingly having to resort to ersatz forms of sustenance, often of dubious nutritional value, on which the poor had traditionally relied in times of scarcity (cf. Garnsey 1999: 36–41 for "famine foods" in antiquity more generally; also Stathakopoulos 2004: 81–5). During Alaric's blockade of Rome in 409, people fell back on acorns, a long-standing grain substitute (Olympiodorus fr.10.1 [line 43]), presumably grinding them into a form of flour (cf. Procopius *Wars* 6.20.19; Garnsey 1999: 40–1); during the Gothic blockades of Clermont in the early 470s, inhabitants were forced to eat grass torn from cracks in the walls, and weeds, some of which proved to be noxious (Sidonius Apollinaris *Letters* 7.7.3; cf. Garnsey 1999: 39); various forms of plant life were likewise consumed during the sixth-century sieges of Rome and Milan including boiled nettles, as also the flesh of dead horses, mules, dogs, cats, mice, and other animals;[20] some of the besieged inhabitants of Amida in 504 are reported as somehow turning the leather of old shoes into a form of nourishment (sole soup?).[21] It is difficult to know what to make of claims that some individuals were so hungry that they were even prepared to eat human excrement (Ps.-Zachariah *Church History* 7.5; Procopius *Wars* 7.17.19).[22]

Mingled with some of these statements are allegations that desperate individuals resorted to cannibalism (Olympiodorus fr.7.1; Malchus fr.2; Ps.-Joshua Stylites *Chronicle* 77; Procopius *Wars* 7.16.3). Cannibalism is of course a highly emotive subject which has aroused fierce debate among anthropologists and others (see Hulme 1998 for an overview). While some have been highly skeptical about its incidence (most famously, Arens 1979), there are enough well-attested examples of survival cannibalism (as distinct from ritual cannibalism) in recent centuries for contemporary claims about its occurrence during late antique sieges not to be dismissed as the product of apocalyptically inclined imaginations.[23] Certainly there is no reason to doubt the report of individuals at their wits' end deciding that the only solution was to take their own life (Procopius *Wars* 7.17.19–22, including detail of one very specific and tragic instance). Needless to say, malnutrition left individuals more susceptible to disease, and in the often crowded conditions of a siege, disease could spread rapidly, with fatal consequences for many. Problems with the appropriate disposal of bodies in turn exacerbated insanitary conditions, as many of those at Amida in 359 and Rome in 409 found to their cost (Ammianus 19.4; Zosimus 5.39.2–3).

In such dire circumstances, maintenance of civilian morale was a challenge. An important theme in late antiquity was the way in which Christian inspiration came increasingly to play a role in this respect (Michael Whitby 1998), as in stories of divine deliverance for the inhabitants of Nisibis from successive Persian attacks in the first half of the fourth century (Lightfoot 1988), the bishop of Orleans inspiring the defenders of the city in the mid fifth century against the Huns of Attila until relief arrived from Aetius (Harries 1995: 228), or the divine protection of Thessalonica against Avars and Slavs with which St Demetrius was credited in the late sixth and early seventh centuries (Cormack 1985: 50–94; cf. also Averil Cameron 1979: 18–24 for the role of the cult of the Virgin in the defense of Constantinople in 626).

Sieges were not always successful, but if the besiegers achieved their objective and captured the city or town, then further horrors usually awaited the inhabitants – slaughter or enslavement. The fate of individuals often seems to have depended upon how long a siege had lasted. If a city fell or surrendered relatively quickly, then there was less likely to be a killing spree by the victors. In 359, however, the inhabitants of Amida had resisted the Persians for 73 days and inflicted heavy losses on their assailants (30,000 casualties, according to Ammianus [19.9.9]), thereby also disrupting the Persian king Shapur's larger plan for a speedy push toward Antioch, so it is hardly surprising to learn that when the Persians finally occupied the city, indiscriminate slaughter of the inhabitants ensued (Ammianus 19.8.4). Similarly, the capture of Amida by the Persians in 503 after a three-month siege and the reported loss of 50,000 of the besiegers (Ps.-Joshua Stylites *Chronicle* 53) was followed by "a great massacre of the Amidenes" (Procopius *Wars* 1.7.30). The siege of Milan by the Goths in 538–9 ended with the slaughter of all the male inhabitants (Procopius *Wars* 6.21.39), a reflection partly of the length of the siege – nine months (Stein 1949–59: II.355 n.1) – and partly of their being viewed as traitors to the Gothic regime in Italy (Procopius *Wars* 6.21.29; cf. the fate of the male inhabitants of Tibur in 544: Procopius *Wars* 7.10.22). Lest there be any doubt about the capacity of Roman forces to perpetrate comparable brutality, one need only consider their behavior following the capture of Naples in 535 after a siege of only 20 days' duration (Procopius *Wars* 5.10.29, 36).[24]

There were no doubt circumstances in which it was difficult to restrain soldiers from behaving in this way, whether out of anger, pent-up frustration, or sheer bloodlust, but in a world in which slavery remained an accepted institution it made economic sense to keep prisoners alive for use or sale as slaves, and this was the more common fate for civilians captured after the fall of a besieged city. Again, there was nothing new about this in late antiquity, but it was undoubtedly a more frequent experience for inhabitants of the empire in this period than it had been during the Principate. The Persians continued the practice of Near Eastern kings in earlier epochs of deporting large numbers of captives. In the great trilingual triumphal inscription which he had carved at Naqsh-i Rustam near Persepolis, Shapur I recorded details of the 37 Roman cities and towns he sacked in 256, and the further 36 which suffered the same fate in 260. Immediately following this second list, the text refers to his deporting of Romans and their being settled in various parts of the Persian empire (see Frye 1984: 371–3 and Dodgeon and Lieu 1991: 50, 57 for translations). Although these captives undoubtedly included soldiers from the defeated Roman army of Valerian, there must also have been civilian prisoners from the sacked cities (cf. Lieu 1986: 476–8). In the same way, Shapur II carried off large numbers of prisoners from Amida, Singara, and Bezabde in 359–60 (Ammianus 19.8.1–2, 20.6.7, 20.7.15), as did Kavad from Amida in 503 (Ps.-Joshua Stylites *Chronicle* 53), and Khusro I from Sura, Beroea, and Antioch in 540 and from Apamea and Dara in 573 (Procopius *Wars* 2.5.29, 2.7.11, 2.14.1; John of Ephesus *Church History* 6.6, 19); and when they conquered northern Mesopotamia and Syria in the early seventh century, Persian forces are said to have taken "an innumerable multitude of captives" from Dara and other locations (Theophanes *Chronicle* p. 293).

Something of the experience of such captives can be gleaned from the sources. They were, unsurprisingly, typically shackled,[25] and the journey itself to Persia could entail considerable hardship: "As they led away the multitude of prisoners [captured in 260] they did not give them more than the minimum amount of food needed to sustain life, nor did they allow them a sufficient supply of water, but once a day the guards drove them to water like cattle" (Zonaras 12.23 [tr. Dodgeon] (= Dodgeon and Lieu 1991: 64)). During the siege of Amida in 359, the defenders on the walls saw the Persians leading away prisoners from nearby forts which they had already captured; Ammianus (19.6.2) observed that "among them were many feeble old men and aged women. When their strength gave out for various reasons under the hardship of the long march and they lost any desire to live, their calves or hams were severed and they were left behind." Once they reached their destinations, it seems that the third-century deportees were set to work building irrigation dams and cities; one of Shapur I's new cities, Bishapur, was laid out on a Greco-Roman style, "Hippodamian," rectangular grid, suggesting the involvement of Roman surveyors, and his palace there was decorated with mosaic pictures whose execution and style point strongly to their being the work of Roman craftsmen.[26]

The Persian practice of deportation appears to have been part of a conscious policy to supplement the kingdom's workforce both numerically and in terms of skills (Lieu 1986; Morony 2004). Whether from motives of practicality or prestige, the Romans also sometimes deported the population of captured Persian cities and towns: both motives were evidently at work in Constantius II's transfer of the inhabitants of an unnamed Persian city to Thrace, since they were expected to help with the cultivation of the region, but had also been paraded through the streets of Antioch en route (Libanius *Orations* 59.83–6). Julian sent prisoners from Anatha on the Euphrates in 363 to be settled at Chalcis in Syria (Ammianus 24.1.9), perhaps making up for some of the manpower lost to Persia in 359–60, and Maurice resettled thousands of prisoners from forts in Arzanene on vacant land in Cyprus in 578 (Theophylact Simocatta 3.15.13–15; John of Ephesus *Church History* 6.15; Evagrius *Church History* 5.19). This is perhaps the appropriate point to mention the rather unusual case of the resettlement of the Roman inhabitants of the Mesopotamian cities of Nisibis and Singara, who, by the terms of the peace settlement imposed by the Persians in 363, were obliged to vacate their cities before those were handed over to the Persians. Although he exploits the dramatic possibilities of the scenario to full effect, Ammianus' description of the evacuation of Nisibis also provides a telling insight into the practical and emotional ramifications of this uprooting, which must also have been a part of the experience of those taken away as prisoners from captured cities in this period:

> The city was filled with lamentation and weeping, and throughout every part there was only the sound of everyone wailing. Women tore their hair at the thought of having to flee into exile from the homes in which they had been born and raised. Mothers who had lost their children or been widowed were driven away from the tombs of their loved ones, and the tearful crowd embraced the doorposts and thresholds of their homes as they wept. The different roads were filled as people scattered wherever they could. In their haste many people furtively took such of their goods as they thought they could carry, disregarding the rest of their property, however valuable and substantial, compelled to abandon it for lack of transport. (Ammianus 25.9.5–6)

Enslavement of urban civilians on a large scale was not confined to conflict with Persia. Despite their inexperience in waging siege warfare, a group referred to as the Borani crossed the Black Sea in the mid 250s and managed to capture the city of Trabzon on the northern coast of Anatolia – their success is attributed to the "laziness and drinking" of the city's soldiers – where they found "an immense amount of money and great numbers of slaves; for almost all the country-dwellers in the district had congregated in the city because of its fortifications" (Zosimus 1.33.3; cf. Gregory Thaumaturgus *Canonical Letter* 5, 7; Mitchell 1993: I.235–6). A few years after the Hunnic capture of Naissus in the 440s, a Roman embassy en route to Attila's camp "found the city empty of people" (Priscus fr.11.2 [line 51]), presumably because those of the population who had not perished – "the river bank was full of the bones of men killed in the fighting" – had been enslaved. Interestingly, when the embassy eventually reached the village where Attila was living at the time, they found the buildings there included a bath house built by a Roman prisoner from Sirmium (fr.11.2 [lines 364–72]), while the historian Priscus, a member of the embassy, had a famous exchange there with a former merchant from Viminacium who had been made a slave when the Huns captured the city (fr.11.2 [lines 407–510]). The biography of a holy man who lived on the upper Danube during the final years of the western half of the empire includes much circumstantial detail about the capture of towns by Germanic tribes and the enslavement of their inhabitants (Eugippius *Life of St. Severinus* 24, 27, with discussion in Ward-Perkins 2005: 17–20).

One almost inevitable consequence of such events was the break-up of families whose members were sold on to different buyers, as lamented by Gregory the Great following the capture of Croton by the Lombards in the 590s (*Letters* 7.23); after the Vandal sack of Rome in 455, the bishop of Carthage sold church plate in order to have the money to ransom prisoners and prevent the splitting of families (Victor of Vita *History of the Vandal Persecution* 1.25). Captives sometimes managed to return home, though whether as a result of escape or manumission is not usually known: there are instances from the fifth-century west (Leo *Letters* 159) and the sixth-century east, including a report that the Persian king Kavad released the Amidenes enslaved in 503 (Procopius *Wars* 1.7.34; cf. Ps.-Zachariah *Church History* 7.5; Trombley 1997: 203). The first of these cases, however, illustrates how what ought to have been the occasion for rejoicing could be the cause of yet further heartache. Men from Aquileia enslaved by the Huns in 452 eventually managed to return home about five years later (perhaps taking advantage of the turmoil into which his empire fell following Attila's death), only to find that some of their wives had given them up for dead and had remarried – prompting an appeal for papal adjudication.

5.3. Rural Communities

On the twenty-sixth of this month [November 502], [the Lakhmid Arab ruler] Nu'man also arrived from the south and entered the territory of the Harranites. He ravaged and plundered it, and took away captive men, cattle and goods from the whole territory of the Harranites. He even came as far as Edessa, ravaging, plundering, and taking captive all the villages. The number of people whom he led away into captivity was 18,500, not counting those who were killed, and the cattle, goods and spoil of all kinds. The reason so many people were in the villages is that it was the vintage season, when not only the villagers, but also many Harranites and Edessenes, had gone out for the vintage and were thus taken captive. (Ps.-Joshua Stylites *Chronicle* 52 [trs. Trombley and Watt])

Although the coincidence of Nu'man's raid with the grape harvest exacerbated the impact of his attack on the peasants of northern Mesopotamia, this description can be taken as fairly typical of the experience of war for inhabitants of rural communities. "They crossed the Danube and fell upon the country folk, who were busy with their harvest and had no thought of an enemy. Most of them were killed, and the rest they carried off home together with a large quantity of livestock" (Ammianus 29.6.6): a different region of the empire (Pannonia), a different enemy (the Quadi), a different century (the fourth – 374 to be precise), but the same basic, age-old story. For some of those who died during such attacks, death did not, it seems, come quickly. Archaeological excavation has provided gruesome insight into atrocities committed by Alamannic raiders in southern Germany in the mid third century. Thirteen inhabitants of one villa (at Regensburg-Harting) were brutally killed, their bodies dismembered and partially scalped before being dumped down wells, while at another villa (at Mundelsheim) there were found the remains of an older man and a teenage girl, both of whom had suffered burning and dog-bites.[27]

For those whose fields lay close to a fortified settlement, an obvious option was to try to flee there for safety. A poignant illustration of the confused circumstances which such flight entailed is provided by Ammianus' dramatic account of his experiences in northern Mesopotamia during the chaos arising from the Persian invasion in spring 359. A couple of miles from the fortress of Nisibis, Ammianus' party encountered a young boy standing in the middle of the road, in tears after becoming separated from his mother while hurrying toward the fort (Ammianus hastily carried the boy on his horse the rest of way to safety before proceeding to Amida: 18.6.10).

For those rural inhabitants who failed to reach fortified shelter, enslavement was probably the most common fate. The "many thousands of Italian prisoners" rescued from the homeward-bound Germanic Juthungi in about 260, as recorded in a recently discovered inscription from Augsburg (*AE* 1993.1231), are likely to have been peasants, given the general lack of aptitude of Germanic tribes for capturing cities and towns (cf. Zosimus 1.43.2), while the Romans whom Gregory the Great had seen being led away for sale in Gaul by the Lombards in 595, "bound with rope around their necks like dogs" (*Letters* 5.36), were presumably also peasants from Rome's hinterland rather than inhabitants of the city itself, since the Lombard siege had failed to effect the capture of the city. As for those who managed to avoid death or enslavement, they were likely to have to make do, for the time being at least, without any livestock, whose mobility made them an obvious and attractive target for raiders (Ammianus 29.6.6; Synesius *Letters* 130, 132; Malchus fr.18.4; Agathias 1.17.5; cf. Erdkamp 1998: 234–9).

In registering the misfortunes suffered by peasants living in Roman provinces, it is essential to appreciate that Roman forces behaved no differently when they mounted incursions into territory adjacent to the empire. So, for example, there was indiscriminate slaughter of Alamanni who had settled near the Rhine in 357 (Ammianus 16.11.9), and when they attacked Alamannic territory in 358, Julian's forces "burnt up the fields, carried off men and beasts, and cut to pieces without mercy any who offered resistance."[28] Roman troops raiding Persian territory in 504 pursued an even more systematic policy of destruction:

> The Romans ... were making forays into Persian territory, taking booty and captives and wreaking havoc ... They looted the property of all those who had fled, burned many villages, killed all the men in them of twelve years or above, and took captive the women and children ... [The commander] had detached some strong men from the soldiers, and also numerous villagers who joined them as they went down [into Persian territory], and after the roofs had been burnt and the fire had gone out, these people pulled down the walls [of houses]. They also cut down and destroyed the vineyards, olives and all other trees. (Ps.-Joshua Stylites *Chronicle* 79 [trs. Trombley and Watt]; cf. 75)

These references to devastation of crops highlight a further potential aspect of such warfare, although it is one which was by no means always present. Burning of wheat and comparable crops could only be accomplished when the grain was ripe (i.e., late May to early July, depending on the region), while destruction of olive trees and vines required considerable investment of time and manpower (V. D. Hanson 1998; Erdkamp 1998: 210–20). Instances of the firing of cornfields are not unknown in late antiquity,[29] but it is much rarer to find references to the cutting down of olive trees and vines. The empire's northern neighbors lived in regions mostly too cold for the cultivation of the olive and do not appear to have had any interest in viticulture, while the hallmarks of their incursions were speed and such devastation as was not labor-intensive.

Where there was serious plundering or destruction of sources of food in the countryside, food shortages could cause considerable hardship for those rural inhabitants who survived enemy depredations. Sometimes a wealthy patron was on hand to alleviate conditions, as happened in central Gaul and along the Rhone valley in the early 470s, where Patiens, bishop of Lyons and also a wealthy aristocrat, stepped in to avert serious problems in both countryside and cities, even allowing for Sidonius' evident desire to magnify Patiens' reputation:

After the Goths had finished their plundering and the cornfields had been consumed by fire, at your own personal expense you sent free grain to meet the general scarcity throughout the devastated parts of Gaul, although you would have been giving more than enough help to people wasting away from hunger if that produce had been for sale and not a gift. We have seen the roads congested with your grain; we have seen more than one granary along the banks of the Saone and the Rhone filled by you alone. (Sidonius Apollinaris *Letters* 6.12.5)

Similarly, rural refugees from a Persian invasion of eastern Anatolia in 575 found relief out of the grain reserves of a monastery near the city of Amaseia (*Life of St Eutychius* (*PG* 86.2344–5), discussed in Trombley 1985b: 53). However, these instances of providential deliverance are likely to have been the exception to the rule, with the deprivations described by Procopius in central Italy during the Gothic war, one suspects, more typical:

The inhabitants of that region [Emilia] left their homes and went to Picenum, thinking that, since that region was adjacent to the sea, it could not be suffering from a complete lack of food supplies. The inhabitants of Tuscany, no less than the others, were attacked by famine for the same reason, and the many who were living in the mountains ate loaves made from acorns off oak trees, which they ground up like grain. As was to be expected, many of these people fell victim to all manner of diseases, and there were only a few who threw them off and recovered. Indeed it is said that among the Roman farmers of Picenum no fewer than 50,000 perished from starvation, and a great many more north of the Adriatic Sea. (Procopius *Wars* 6.20.18–21 [tr. Dewing]; cf. 20.27–9 for reports of cannibalism)

In this instance, the crisis was precipitated less by direct enemy destruction of crops and more by shortage of manpower to plant and harvest (cf. Procopius *Wars* 6.20.15–17), no doubt partly as a result of Gothic farmers serving in the Gothic army, and partly as a result of the understandable flight of peasants from areas directly affected by the fighting. A further contributory factor may have been the flight of slaves, for whom the upheaval of war often provided the ideal opportunity for escape to a new life. A legal document from this period bequeathed land to the church, along with associated slaves, including "any of those who have run away during these disturbed times [who] can be found" (*P. Italy* 13 [553]).

5.4. Women

Look at this stele which bears witness to virtue, traveler. For there lies inside this tomb a young girl, Domitilla, who won the prize garland for chastity. For when the young girls were being carried off to be raped by the men whom the anger of the gods and fate brought from Pontus, she was the only one of those killed by barbarian hands at that time who was not afraid to die rather than

suffer wretched rape. She had enjoyed only seven months with her beloved husband when she relinquished the light of her girlhood at the age of fourteen.
(*SEG* 34 (1984) 1271 [Paphlagonia, mid third century])

Although two of the categories already discussed – urban inhabitants and peasants – obviously included females as well as males, the experience of women warrants additional separate consideration in relation to a number of more specific issues which particularly affected them as a result of their gender. Few sources written by women relevant to these issues have survived from late antiquity, and hence, as so often in the study of antiquity, the experience of women has, for the most part, to be studied through the imperfect and indirect medium of male reportage.

One group of women for whom the experience of war could be very personal was the wives of soldiers (for this difference between the army during the Principate and late antiquity, see further Chapter 6.1 below). In the more vulnerable parts of the empire, they faced the possibility of their husbands dying in the line of duty and, in the case of the wives of troops enrolled in field army units, lengthy periods of separation when the army was on campaign.[30] Although there are occasional references to wives accompanying husbands on campaign (e.g., Procopius *Wars* 7.23.1–2), various sources also give attention to issues arising from the extended absence of a soldier husband, the possibility that his absence was due to his death, and the wife's freedom to remarry. Writing in the latter half of the fourth century, Basil of Caesarea took the view that soldiers' wives who remarried in their absence without evidence of their husband's death were guilty of adultery, although he did also acknowledge that there was scope for a degree of leniency in such cases compared with those of "civilian" women who remarried when their husbands were away on a lengthy journey, since soldiers' wives had greater reason to suspect that their husband was dead (*Letters* 199.36).

The government also legislated on the subject. Unsurprisingly, it sought to protect the interests of the husband ahead of those of the wife, to her emotional cost. A law of the late 330s addressed the question of a soldier's wife who had received no news of her husband for a substantial period of time. It stipulated that a wife in such a position could only remarry after four years had elapsed and after notifying the relevant general in command of her husband's unit about her intention (so, by implication, ascertaining that he was dead) (*Justinianic Code* 5.17.7 [337]). Two centuries later Justinian decided that, in view of the hardships which soldier husbands underwent in the field of duty, four years was too short a period and extended it to an extraordinary ten years (Justinian *Novel* 22.14 [536]). He subsequently further tightened the process with the requirement that an officer from the man's unit swear an oath on the Gospels and complete a signed affidavit confirming the husband's death (*Novel* 117.11 [542]).

It is in this context that there survives one category of source material through which the voices of women can perhaps be heard – namely, epitaphs set up by wives for deceased soldier husbands, such as the following:

> To the spirits of the dead. Valerius Victorinus, holding the rank of *biarchus*, who served (*militavit*) in the sacred palace for seven years, lived for forty years, and fell in the battle of the Romans against their enemies at Chalcedon. For the sake of his reputation, he stipulated that he should be seen to be honored in perpetuity and that he should be consecrated by the proper burial of his remains. Matrona, his very dutiful wife (*coniux* [sic] *pientissima*), set up this epitaph for herself while still living and for her well deserving companion (*benemerenti conpari*). (*AE* 1976.631 [324, Scythia], with discussion in Speidel 1995 and Woods 1997)

> When I was young, I knew my sweet husband (*conpare[m dulcem]*) who earned all his successive distinctions, one by one: first, centurion, then officer, then tribune. Having reached the apex and trusting in his strength, he fell in worthless war, the fate allotted to him. (Drew-Bear et al. 2004 [mid fourth century, Maionia, western Anatolia])

The difficulty with trying to recapture the authentic expression of female sentiment through this sort of evidence, however, is that epitaphs had their own conventions and those set up by spouses tended to recycle certain stock epithets, of which *bene merens* was among the most common (cf. Treggiari 1991: 230–2, 243–9); the one element in the above examples which hints at something more genuine is their description of the husband as her *conpar* (lit. "equal to another").[31] At the same time, there was a limit to the scope for originality in such formulations, so that the recurrence of certain traditional phrases does not necessarily mean that a spouse was merely saying what was expected or that their relationship had lacked genuine affection.[32]

If it is often difficult to decipher the emotional content of an epitaph's language, however, there were undoubtedly circumstances in which news of a husband's death in action cannot have failed to induce considerable trauma. Such was the case after the battle of Adrianople in 378. The extent of Roman losses – two-thirds of the army involved, including the emperor Valens – meant that word must have spread quickly and that many were directly affected. In seeking to console a young widow whose officer husband had died as a result of illness, John Chrysostom drew attention to the relative advantages which she had had – being able to hear his last words, to embrace him as he died, and to bury him appropriately – compared with the hardship of the wives recently bereaved as a result of the carnage at Adrianople:

> These women have been deprived of all these things: they all sent out their husbands to war in the expectation of receiving them back again, instead of which they have received the bitter news of their death. Nor is it their mortal

remains which have been returned to them, but only words describing the manner of their death. There are even some who have been denied these details and who are not able to learn how they fell, since they disappeared in the great melée of the battle. (*To a Young Widow* 5)

The sources offer no hint of any provision by the state for the maintenance of soldiers' widows and their families (an absence perhaps corroborated by the legislation against too hasty remarriage noted above).[33] The church, of course, had a long tradition of charitable support for widows and orphans, but increasing pressures on its material resources meant that over the course of the late Roman period the criteria for helping widows became increasingly strict, including stipulations that women needed to be at least 60 years old, married only once, have no children able to support them, and be of exemplary character (Krause 1995: 11–26). Even if they satisfied the other criteria, the age rule alone must have disqualified most, if not all, widows of soldiers killed in the line of duty.

Women who experienced war without having any direct link with the army will usually have done so as refugees from enemy raids and as innocent bystanders caught up in sieges of cities in which they lived or in which they had taken shelter. There is little explicit evidence of women playing a direct part in the defense of cities, although it was clearly not unknown. Vegetius comments in general terms on how "from windows and rooftops people of all ages and both sexes overwhelm the invaders with stones and other kinds of missiles" (*Epitome of Military Science* 4.25), while Procopius reports one particular episode in the context of the Persian siege of Edessa in 544:

> The women and children, and the elderly also, were gathering stones for the fighters and assisting them in other ways. Some also filled numerous basins with olive oil, and after heating them over a fire a sufficient time everywhere along the wall, they showered the oil, while boiling fiercely, onto the enemy who were attacking the wall, using a sort of ladle, and in this way harassed them even more. (Procopius *Wars* 2.27.35–6 [tr. Dewing])

The inhabitants of Edessa managed to see off the Persians, but many other cities and towns during late antiquity were not so lucky in avoiding capture by the enemy. This is the context in which women are often mentioned, as being either slaughtered by the enemy or enslaved (cf. above, Chapter 5.2, pp. 136–8). To mention only one further notorious incident from the sixth century: following the capture of Milan by the Goths in 539 and the slaughter of all the male population, the female population was enslaved and handed over to the Burgundians as payment for their assistance with the siege (Procopius *Wars* 6.21.39).

Although explicit reference is rare in the ancient sources, one corollary of enslavement must regularly have been rape. It is a well-attested phenomenon in wartime throughout history (Brownmiller 1975: 31–113; Chang 1998:

89–96); with more specific reference to the second half of the twentieth century, it has been observed that "rape in war is pervasive. It may be officially permitted or forbidden. Its victims include civilians as well as troops, allies, and sometimes even nationals as well as enemies" (Morris 1996: 656 n.5). Even if the ideological factors which intensified its use in more recent contexts, such as the notorious behavior of the Red Army in Germany in 1945 (Beevor 2002: 28–32, 409–12), were absent in antiquity, it must nevertheless have been common practice on the part of both Roman and non-Roman soldiers. This is certainly the implication of the Gothic king Totila's apparently successful ban on his men mistreating any women when he recaptured Rome in 546, as a result of which he "won great renown for moderation" (Procopius *Wars* 7.20.29–31; cf. 7.6.4).

There is specific testimony to Roman women being raped by invaders in a variety of contexts during late antiquity. One third-century bishop issued specific instruction on the status of women who had been raped during Gothic raids into Pontus in the middle of that century: provided a woman's previous behavior had been above reproach, she was to suffer no discrimination because of events over which she had no control (Gregory Thaumaturgus *Canonical Letter* 1). The inscription from neighboring Paphlagonia at the head of this section, which commemorates a girl who died resisting the attempts of barbarians to abduct and rape her, may well relate to the same events (Lebek 1985; Mitchell 1993: I.236). Women captured by the Goths in Thrace in 377 took it for granted that they would be raped (Ammianus 31.8.8), while a bishop of Rome in the mid fifth century faced an issue analogous to that of Gregory Thaumaturgus after Vandal invaders of north Africa had raped nuns: he affirmed that while their bodies had been violated, they had not sinned in their hearts, although he was unable to resist observing that they ought now to be regarded as holding an intermediate status between "undefiled virgins" and widows (Leo *Letters* 12.8 and 11). Antiochene women are said to have killed themselves rather than risk rape at the hands of the Persians after their capture of the city in 540 (Procopius *Wars* 2.8.35). In the late 550s, a Hunnic attack into Thrace penetrated close to Constantinople itself, during the course of which they took many prisoners, including well-born women pursuing a monastic life who were "forcibly abducted from their cells and brutally raped" (Agathias 5.13.2–3).[34] While some of this material is undoubtedly animated by anti-barbarian prejudice and so might be suspected of containing elements of exaggeration, the responses of Gregory Thaumaturgus and Leo were clearly dealing with practical issues. There is, however, no indication of what happened to any children conceived through rape, though there must have been a strong likelihood of their experiencing some degree of social rejection.

As for the reverse situation, there are no explicit references to Roman soldiers in late antiquity raping the womenfolk of enemy peoples, but the argument from silence rarely constitutes a strong defense in any situation, and certainly not here. For one thing, the rape of captured women by soldiers had occurred in earlier periods of Roman history (Phang 2001: 254–6). Moreover, as will be seen in the next chapter (Chapter 6.3), there are references to Roman soldiers raping Roman women in late antiquity, and if some had no qualms about such behavior, then they are hardly likely to have exercised restraint when dealing with non-Romans. Nor is there good reason to think that such treatment will not have had emotional consequences for its victims, whether Roman or non-Roman, comparable to those experienced by mistreated women in more recent times: "Rape lives on in the anger, grief, depression, and adhesive shame that it leaves behind – a moral and psychological scorched earth" (Morrow 1996: 379).

Further Reading

For the **practicalities of battle** in late antiquity, see Crump 1975: 79–96 (fourth century); Elton 1996: 250–7 (fourth and early fifth century); Nicasie 1998: 199–219 (fourth century); Haldon 1999: 190–217 (sixth century and beyond); Rance 2005 (sixth century). For siege warfare, see Crump 1975: 97–113; Matthews 1989: 288–95; Elton 1996: 257–63; Southern and Dixon 1996: 148–67; Haldon 1999: 183–9.

For discussions of the **experience of combat** from the perspective of soldiers in late antiquity, see Matthews 1989: 279–303 (fourth century) and Lenski (forthcoming) (siege warfare in the fourth and sixth centuries).

The experience of war by **non-combatants** during late antiquity has not been the subject of any overall synthesis. Helpful treatments of particular aspects include Lieu 1986 and Morony 2004 (prisoners captured by the Persians in the third and fourth centuries, and the sixth and early seventh, respectively), Michael Whitby 1998 (the role of Christianity in siege-time morale), Trombley and Watt 2000 (commentary on one of the most valuable sources for the subject), and Ward-Perkins 2005: 13–31 (the fifth-century west). For comparanda from more modern periods, see the essays in Grimsley and Rodgers 2002.

6

SOLDIERS AND SOCIETY

Times of war brought the most intense forms of interaction between soldiers and civilians, but for a majority of the time Roman soldiers had dealings with civilians in circumstances undisturbed by warfare. The greater part of this chapter will investigate that interaction at both the elite and non-elite levels of society. First, however, attention will be given to an important aspect of the internal social dynamics of the army – the family life of soldiers.

6.1. Soldiers and their Families

> Even the ground is hard to their feet for lack of footwear; for they are obliged, of course, to spend their money on the wife and children – for every one of them has both. Nothing stops them getting married and they don't concern themselves with what the mothers and the children will have to live on. So when soldiers' rations are so sub-divided, where can a man get his fill? The harm resulting from this is a loss of military efficiency. This was not the case in those good old days which I commend. Then the officers hankered after glory, not cash, and no one would rob the soldiers of what was theirs. And the men themselves were sturdy and brave, specialists in warfare, and they remained unmarried: it was ensured that they would even have no need of marriage. (Libanius *Orations* 2.39–40 [tr. Norman])

Among the many ways in which the late Roman army differed from its early imperial precursor was in the important area of the marriage of soldiers. One of the first emperors – almost certainly Augustus – had prohibited soldiers from contracting legally recognized marriages (Phang 2001: 34–50 for earlier literature on the question of responsibility). The reasons for the introduction of the ban have been the subject of much debate. The most recent and detailed treatment of the question has reached the following conclusion:

> In promulgating the marriage ban, Augustus probably sought to dissociate himself from civil war and to associate himself with the restoration of order, including the discipline of the army. These immediate political motives faded,

but subsequent emperors maintained the ban out of tradition. Alleged practical motives, such as that women and children were a hindrance to troop transfers or that they were a drain on the soldiers' financial resources, may be informed by misogynistic cultural assumptions... Pragmatic reasons to keep the ban were financial (the army did not want to increase the soldiers' pay) and legalistic (the army was spared from administering soldiers' families legal claims and lawsuits). But the main reason for the ban was probably not pragmatic, but political: it maintained a distinction between soldier and civilian, separating the soldier from the civilians whom he subjected. (Phang 2001: 383)[1]

The ban did not prevent, nor did the authorities seek to discourage, soldiers from establishing liaisons with local women which sometimes developed into permanent cohabitation complete with offspring. From the perspective of Roman law, however, these family members had no recognized legal status and therefore no legal claim on the soldier in question with regard to property until such time as the soldier completed his military service.

The emperor Hadrian did make some concessions with regard to the inheritance rights of soldiers' children in 119: "Whereas offspring acknowledged during the period of military service are not legal heirs of their fathers, nevertheless I rule that they, too, can claim possession of property in accordance with that part of the edict by which this right is given also to blood relatives" (*BGU* 140 [trs. Lewis and Reinhold]). However, it was not until the reign of Septimius Severus that the marriage ban was removed – a step which incurred the criticism of at least one contemporary commentator:

> The soldiers too were given a very substantial sum of money and with this many other privileges that they had not had before, such as an increase in pay (which Severus was the first to give), permission to wear a gold ring and the right to live at home with their wives. All these things are usually considered to be inimical to military discipline and to a state of prompt readiness for action. Severus was certainly the first to undermine the tough austerity of their diet, their obedience in the face of hardship, and their disciplined respect for commanders, by teaching the men to be greedy for riches and seducing them into a life of luxury. (Herodian 3.8.5 [tr. Whittaker])

Herodian is incorrect in his claim that Septimius was the first to increase soldiers' pay (the emperor Domitian had set a precedent in the late first century), and his moralizing rhetoric also weakens the force of his claims. However, it is generally accepted that Septimius revoked the marriage ban and that this and the other measures were motivated above all by the need to secure the loyalty of the army in the aftermath of his rise to power in the context of civil war (Campbell 1984: 194–5, 302; Potter 2004: 130–1), although another, more practical consideration has also been suggested: "Severus' military reforms were not merely to indulge the army; he probably sought to increase recruitment after the Marcomannic war, the Antonine plague, and the civil wars of 193–197 had decimated the army. Military service was made more attractive by a pay raise and by the permission of legal marriage" (Phang 2001: 382).[2]

If this was one of his main objectives, it is not possible to say whether it was achieved, but as shown by the opening passage from Libanius, written in the late fourth century, critics continued to bemoan the disadvantages of soldiers being allowed to marry long after the change had become established. Libanius' gloomy assessment, however, needs to be treated with great care. First, there is the issue of context. The work in which this passage appears was written in 381 as a response to the author's critics whose "complaint is that I am constantly praising and longing for what is dead and gone, denouncing the present day, harping on the past prosperity and the present miseries of the cities, and that this is my tale, everywhere, every day" (26 [tr. Norman]). Libanius' response is effectively to reiterate what he sees as wrong with the contemporary situation, with the result that it is very difficult for him to avoid overdrawing the contrast between present and past. The sense that exaggeration is at play here is reinforced when one finds another of Libanius' speeches from no more than two years earlier endorsing the military effectiveness of Roman troops, despite the recent defeat at Adrianople – "let there be no talk of cowardice, weakness or lack of training ...The morale of the soldiers and their officers was like that of their forebears, and they were no whit inferior to them in skill and training" (Libanius *Oration* 24.5 [tr. Norman]). Secondly, the specific contrast between the pre-Severan and post-Severan period to which he refers apropos soldiers lay above all in the legal sphere. As already noted, many soldiers prior to the lifting of the marriage ban nevertheless effectively had de facto wives and children on whom they must have spent money, even if the incidence of (unofficial) marital relationships among soldiers during the Principate was not as high as among the civilian population of the empire (Saller and Shaw 1984: 133–4). In this respect, Libanius' contrast is a rather artificial one.[3]

A study of late Roman epitaphs from the west has produced further relevant conclusions. The samples analyzed are acknowledged to be "small, but are still sufficiently large to provide...a general profile of familial, and other, relationships in late imperial society in the west" (Shaw 1984: 469). Analysis of military epitaphs in the late Roman west "show[s] a distinct shift towards greater nuclear family emphasis compared with their pagan predecessors [of the Principate]" – consistent with the idea that the lifting of the ban encouraged more soldiers to marry. However, that movement toward a greater incidence of military marriages had definite limits. The epitaphs of late Roman soldiers show "the lowest emphasis on nuclear family as a whole" amongst all the groups in the late Roman material:

> Extended family relationships remain weak, whereas *amici* [friends] are very strongly represented (12%). So too, the *se vivo-sibi* category [i.e., epitaphs prepared by individuals for themselves while still living] is the highest attested

> for any Christian [i.e., late Roman] sample, and is also characteristic of soldiers in the Principate who, in lieu of family commemorators, demonstrated a far higher propensity than average to commemorate themselves before death. (Shaw 1984: 472)

Judging by the epigraphic evidence, then, significant numbers of soldiers remained unmarried in the late Roman west, and there is no reason to think the pattern in the east should have been significantly different, despite Libanius' (rhetorical) claim that every soldier in late fourth-century Syria was encumbered with a wife and children.

Notwithstanding this important qualification, however, it is also clear that many soldiers during late antiquity *were* married. In addition to the epigraphic evidence, late Roman legal sources take it for granted that there are soldiers with wives and children (e.g., *Theodosian Code* 3.5.5 [332], 7.1.3 [377]; *Justinianic Code* 5.4.21 [426]), and there is papyrological evidence of marriage contracts and divorce agreements involving soldiers (e.g., *P. Dura* 30, 32 [mid third century]), as well as birthday invitations for their children's parties (*P. Oxyrhynchus* 1214 [fifth century]). One might have expected surviving papyri to provide further enlightening evidence in the form of wills, but there appears to be only one definite example from late antiquity, that of a centurion in a cavalry unit, Valerius Aion, from the year 320 (*P. Columbia* 7.188). He seems to have been quite well off, since he has substantial amounts of money out on loan to various people, but the significant detail from the perspective of this chapter is that he names as heirs his wife and daughter, alongside his five siblings.[4]

It would be interesting to know something about the practicalities of living arrangements in military camps after the lifting of the ban on soldiers marrying. Initially, no doubt, families continued to inhabit the adjacent settlement (*canabae*), but with the growing insecurities of the mid third century and the corresponding emphasis on stronger fortifications, one would have expected some changes to have occurred. The emergence of the distinction between *comitatenses* and *limitanei* in the early fourth century will have introduced further complications in this respect. Identifying archaeological evidence for the presence of military families associated with the former category is bound to be difficult, given that the *comitatenses* were based in cities and towns, but even in the more explicitly military sites associated with the latter category of soldier, it remains problematic.[5]

When late Roman soldiers were on campaign, one would not normally have expected them to be accompanied by their families, which is certainly the assumption underlying legislation governing the remarriage rights of soldiers' wives (Chapter 5.4 above, p. 142; cf. John of Ephesus *Church History* 3.13). One could well imagine some soldiers taking advantage of this legal framework to have more than one wife in different parts of the empire, as indeed is reported in the story of "Euphemia and the Goth," set in the 390s but probably written in the mid fifth century (where the "Goth" of the title is not necessarily an ethnic Goth: the significant presence of Germans in the Roman army has resulted in "Goth" becoming a generic term for "soldier" in Syriac, the language in which this story was written (Jones 1964: 1263 n.53)). A soldier temporarily stationed in Edessa is said to have married the daughter of the family with whom he was billeted, only for his new wife to discover, on her returning westward with her husband to his usual base, that he already had a wife there, and that he proposed to make his new wife their slave – a predicament resolved only by the intervention of certain Edessene saints (Burkitt 1913: 129–53).

However, soldier husbands emerge in a better light in other incidents, which also provide examples of specific situations in which family ties in the army had the potential to create problems of different sorts. Most famously, because of its role in the background to Julian's usurpation, Constantius II's request that some of Julian's troops from the Rhine frontier be dispatched to the east, to strengthen the Roman response to a Persian invasion, prompted significant dissatisfaction among the chosen troops specifically because of fears about the safety of their wives and families: "We are to be driven off to the ends of the earth like condemned criminals while our nearest and dearest (*caritates nostrae*), whom we set free from their previous captivity after desperate fighting, again become slaves of the Alamanni" (Ammianus 20.4.10). According to another version of events, "those women especially who had borne children to the soldiers pointed to their children, not least to the babes at the breast, dandled then before them and begged their fathers not to desert them" (Libanius *Orations* 18.95 [tr. Norman]). Julian's response was to facilitate the soldiers' taking their families with them by granting them the jealously guarded privilege of using the wagons of the imperial transport system – a step for which there was a precedent of sorts in a law of the emperor Constans from a decade earlier, which countenanced (unspecified) situations where imperial approval might be given to assisting wives and children to join soldiers (*Theodosian Code* 7.1.3 [349]). Prolonged separation of soldiers from their families increased the risk of desertion, as happened during the Italian campaigns of the mid sixth century, when Roman units recruited from Illyricum suddenly abandoned their siege of a city and headed for home, partly because they were owed considerable arrears in pay, but also because they had learned that Huns had attacked their homeland and enslaved women and children (Procopius *Wars* 7.11.13–16). On the other hand, a soldier from Constantinople who had evidently taken his family with him during the same Italian campaigns found himself in no better a situation when his wife and two children were captured by the Goths after they retook Rome in 346 (Procopius *Wars* 7.23.1–2).

The presence and absence of family could both be problematic, then, but the relative infrequency with which such situations seem to have arisen suggests that these "problem cases" are the exception. All three instances occurred in the context of active campaigning, which will have occupied a relatively small proportion of their time in service for the great majority of soldiers. For most, a more settled existence is likely to have been the order of the day for much of their military life, allowing those soldiers who were married to enjoy a relatively stable family life without it necessarily impinging adversely on the effectiveness of the army. Even when circumstances in peacetime required a transfer of location, it was not necessarily a choice between leaving all the family behind or taking them all: when the Isaurian unit in which his father served was transferred from Cappadocia to Alexandria in the mid fifth century, his mother accompanied her husband to Egypt but their 5-year-old son Saba remained behind in the care of an uncle (Cyril of Scythopolis *Life of St. Saba* 1). Finally, it is worth noting that problems arising from the possible transfer of units to other parts of the empire were not specific to the centuries following Severus' abolition of the marriage ban: when Vespasian was proclaimed emperor in 69, he was able to ensure the support of the Syrian legions by putting it about that his opponent Vitellius was planning to relocate them to the Rhine frontier (Tacitus *Histories* 2.8).

With regard to the origin of wives, as one might have anticipated and as the Julian episode confirms, female members of the local populace where a unit was stationed were prime candidates to become wives of soldiers. One thinks also of the way in which significant numbers of soldiers in Belisarius' expeditionary force to north Africa in 533 quickly married Vandal women after the successful conclusion of the campaign (Procopius *Wars* 4.14.8), though how many of these relationships were formal marriages is unclear. There is, however, also evidence of another unsurprising pattern – soldiers marrying the daughters of other soldiers (MacMullen 1963: 102–3). The first pattern would have promoted integration of soldiers into their local communities, while the second would have contributed to making military units more insular, but in the absence of significant numbers of data, it is impossible to draw out more general trends (cf. Pollard 2000: 152–8).

The law of 349 referred to earlier, countenancing situations where the imperial transport system might be made available for the carriage of family members to join soldiers (*Theodosian Code* 7.1.3), included soldiers' slaves alongside wives and children – a reminder that another aspect of family life for soldiers was the fact that they often owned slaves. Unlike officially sanctioned marriages, this was not a phenomenon specific to the army in late antiquity – there is plenty of evidence for their presence in the army of the Principate (Speidel 1989) – but there is no doubt that it remained a feature of army life during the third to sixth centuries. Papyrus documents show soldiers engaging in the purchase and sale of slaves (e.g., *P. Euphrates* 9 [mid third century]; Mitteis and Wilcken 1912: 271 [359]), and the law codes take it for granted (e.g., *Theodosian Code* 7.1.3 [349], 7.13.16 [406]), as do narrative sources (e.g., Ammianus 16.11.14, 31.15.4; Zosimus 3.24.1,

4.11.2; Procopius *Wars* 5.25.2–3, 5.29.26) and military manuals (Vegetius *Epitome of Military Science* 3.6; Ps.-Maurice *Strategy* 5.1–2, 7.13). Just as the fact that some soldiers had wives and children does not appear to have affected their military effectiveness, despite Libanius' complaints, so also the presence of soldiers' slaves was more likely to have been an asset than a hindrance, judging by the record from the Principate (Speidel 1989) and episodes from late antiquity where soldiers' slaves made a positive contribution to the army's performance in crisis situations (Zosimus 4.11.2; Procopius *Wars* 5.25.2–3).

6.2. Interaction between Military and Non-Military Elites

> To Richomer: As I count one by one the blessings I have from the gods, my greatest blessing I find to be your friendship. I revere that day which brought it about, when first we saw each other, and had pleasure in each other's company and behaved as though we had known each other a long time and had long enjoyed such intimacy. And when I was forced to stay and you to go [when Richomer was recalled to hold the consulship in Constantinople in 384], this was done tearfully. Well, rumour used to bring you some items of news about me, that I deliver and compose my orations, that I sit surrounded by pupils who are either persuaded or forced to learn something of my art. But yours is a career of fame, renown, and greatness, of military commands, battles, victories, the suppression of tyranny, and the rescue of free men from slavery, as our emperor and yourself hasten to all deeds of high endeavour, and by wisdom or by main force win the day. Such conduct has received its meed of praise, and does and will do more; and the reward for your successes is this, just as Homer bestowed it on the deeds of those who went with Agamemnon. We pray the gods and yourself that you visit us, fulfil our desires and glorify Daphne [a fashionable suburb of Antioch] with the glory of the emperor [Theodosius I]. For even if we are not Rome, neither the mother city nor her daughter [Constantinople], still our city is not unworthy of such a benefaction, for she rejoices in our emperor's success and grieves that she has not yet beheld his divine person. (Libanius *Letters* 972 [tr. Norman])

One obvious avenue for the investigation of military–civilian relations is through the letters which passed between soldiers and civilians. Such letters have survived in two ways – first, where the actual letter has been preserved on papyrus, usually in Egypt, and secondly, where the author kept a copy of his letters, which were subsequently "published" either on the initiative of the author himself or on that of a relative or associate. The former category comprises exchanges at the non-elite level, whereas the latter relate predominantly to elite interactions: if letters were considered "publishable," this presupposes that their authors were well educated, but such authors are unlikely to have corresponded with the ordinary rank and file who would have had difficulty appreciating the literary qualities of such letters, assuming they were able to read them in the first place.[6] For these reasons, it is appropriate to give this latter body of material separate consideration, before turning in the next section to letters preserved on papyrus, as well as the other diverse material which bears on military–civilian relations at the non-elite level.

The letters which bear on interaction at the elite level can in turn be divided into two categories – those written by bishops and those written by non-ecclesiastical civilians – though this distinction is in some respects an artificial one, since the bishops in question were invariably the social and educational equals of their non-ecclesiastical counterparts. A brief survey of the main correspondents will help to establish the parameters of this material (cf. Table 6.1).[7] On the non-ecclesiastical side, there is the correspondence of Symmachus and Libanius (containing 44 and 29 letters to military officers respectively)[8] – the first a senatorial aristocrat active in Italy during the final decades of the fourth century, the second a respected teacher of rhetoric in Antioch, active from the 350s to the 390s, although nearly all his letters to individuals in the military come from the final decade of his life (the exceptions are his correspondence in the 350s with the *magister* Barbatio and with Sebastianus, the *dux* of Egypt at that time). On the ecclesiastical side, the most helpful corpora of letters are those of Basil of Caesarea (9 "military letters")[9] and Gregory of Nazianzus (7),[10] both bishops in Cappadocia in the second half of the fourth century; that of Theodoret of Cyrrhus, a Syrian bishop of the first half of the fifth century (18);[11] and that of Gregory the Great, bishop of Rome in the late sixth and early seventh century (28).[12] Also invaluable are the letters of Synesius of Cyrenaica (12),[13] which hold an unusual status in that some were produced when he was a philosophically inclined landowner and notable in his native Cyrenaica in the first decade of

Table 6.1 Correspondents with military officers of high rank: a summary

Letter writer	Status	Location	Time	No. of letters to military officers
Symmachus	Senator	Rome	c.340–402	43
Libanius	Rhetor	Antioch	314–c.393	29
Basil	Bishop	Caesarea (Cappadocia)	c.330–c.379	9
Gregory	Bishop	Nazianzus (Cappadocia)	329–89	7
Synesius	Philosopher, bishop	Ptolemais (Cyrenaica)	c.370–413	12
Augustine	Bishop	Hippo (Africa)	354–430	4
Theodoret	Bishop	Cyrrhus (Syria)	c.393–466	18
Severus	Bishop	Antioch	c.465–538	2
Pelagius I	Bishop	Rome	d.561	4
Gregory I	Bishop	Rome	c.540–604	28

Note: The letter writers are listed broadly in chronological order with reference to when they were most actively writing letters, with the two non-ecclesiastical writers first.

the fifth century, while some come from the period after he became a bishop in 411. These are the main corpora of material, though brief reference should also be made to a handful of other letter-writing bishops whose correspondence includes a few letters to military officers: Augustine of Hippo in north Africa, in the early decades of the fifth century, whose four letters to military officers include by far the longest of any considered here (his exhaustive explanation of the doctrinal differences between Donatism and Arianism in response to a request from the *comes* Bonifatius (*Letters* 185));[14] Severus of Antioch, in the early decades of the sixth century (two letters);[15] and Pelagius I, bishop of Rome in the mid sixth century (four letters).[16]

Viewing all this material as a whole, there are a number of broad qualifications to be noted regarding its utility as evidence for military–civilian relations in late antiquity. The first is that chronological coverage is uneven, with the greatest concentration of material falling in the second half of the fourth and first half of the fifth century, with only limited coverage thereafter until the end of the sixth century. A second qualification is that there is something of a geographical bias toward the eastern half of the empire. A third point is that the numbers of letters addressed to military men as a proportion of the various corpora is still quite small – in most cases, 5 percent or less (a little more in the cases of Synesius and Theodoret). The fourth and final restriction is perhaps the most important. As the foregoing comments imply, this correspondence is one-sided, in the sense that these collections preserve the letters of these individuals *to* military officers, but not the letters of the officers which sometimes elicited these letters, nor the officers' responses to them. In other words, the collections only allow these military figures to be viewed indirectly, not to speak for themselves.

Despite these limitations, this is a valuable body of material which warrants investigation. Because of the wide chronological gap and difference in historical circumstances between the main concentration of letters in the later fourth and earlier fifth century and those of Gregory the Great from the late sixth and early seventh century, Gregory's correspondence with military figures will be left until later for separate consideration and comparison. In order to gain some sense of the significance of the relationships which these letters represent, an important initial consideration is the circumstances in which the correspondence began. Very occasionally, it is clear that a particular letter marks the start of an acquaintance, as in Libanius' letter (1057) to the officer Moderatus, in which he begins by explaining that he is writing at the suggestion of a mutual friend who "has told me... that you would be very pleased with a letter from me"; but such initiatives are the exception (cf. also *Letters* 867). Uncertainties over the dating of letters sometimes create difficulties, notably in the case of Symmachus, but in a number of instances it can be concluded with varying degrees of probability that (unsurprisingly) the exchange of letters grew out of face-to-face encounters. The clearest such cases relate to two of Libanius' correspondents, Barbatio and Richomer. The former served under the Caesar Gallus in Antioch in the early 350s, and a later letter from Libanius to him alludes to their having met at that time (*Letters* 436); the latter was *magister militum per Orientem* in the early 380s and so based in Antioch, and in his *Autobiography*, Libanius is explicit about his meeting Richomer for the first time when the latter took up his post, even if one is skeptical of his claim that Richomer had "begged me to be his friend" (*Orations* 1.219). It is highly likely that the same circumstances applied to the cases of Sapores and Ellebichus, Richomer's predecessor and successor: the former visited Libanius when ill in 381 (*Orations* 2.9) while *Letters* 2 shows friendly relations with the latter in 383, the year Ellebichus succeeded Richomer, and all of Libanius' letters to both men postdate this year.

There is less certainty about Basil having met his military correspondents, but it is not implausible given that Iunius Soranus (*Letters* 155, 165) was a fellow-Cappadocian, Terentius (*Letters* 99, 214) and Traianus (*Letters* 148-9) both served in neighboring Armenia in the early 370s, and Arinthaeus (*Letters* 179) and Victor (*Letters* 152-3) were based in Antioch during much of the 360s and 370s as overall commanders of the eastern infantry and cavalry respectively (see *PLRE* I for details); on the other hand, since all five men were also Christians, Basil could have initiated correspondence with some or all of them on that basis and without prior acquaintance. The same consideration might equally apply to Gregory of Nazianzus, but his letters to Ellebichus (*Letters* 225), Modares (*Letters* 136-7), Saturninus (*Letters* 132, 181), and Victor (*Letters* 133-4) all postdate his short stint as bishop in Constantinople from 379 to 381, where Saturninus and Victor, at least, are known also to have been present in 380/1 (*PLRE* I.807).

Theodoret's correspondents, on the other hand, were not all orthodox Christians, notably two very powerful figures in the late 440s, the pagan Flavius Zeno (*Letters* 65, 71) and the Arian Aspar (*Letters* 140). Theodoret's most frequent military correspondent, Anatolius (*Letters* 45, 79, 92, 111, 119, 121, 139), spent more than a decade as *magister militiae Orientis*, presumably with substantial periods of residence in Antioch, not so far from Cyrrhus. Although the *magister* Areobindus (*Letters* XVIII, 23) served in the war against Persia in the early 420s, it is more likely that Theodoret made his acquaintance in the context of the land which Areobindus owned in the vicinity of Cyrrhus (*Letters* XVIII, 23). The *comes* Titus (*Letters* VI, XI) is known to have traveled to Antioch in person in 434 (*PLRE* II: 1123), while Theodoret dedicated one of his works (the *Compendium of Heretical Stories*) to the *comes* Sporacius, which implies close acquaintance. He may have met Zeno in Antioch when the latter was *magister* of the east, but it is less easy to suggest contexts in which he might have met Apollonius and Aspar.

Two of Synesius' military correspondents served as the *dux* of Libya – Anysius (*Letters* 6, 14, 37, 59, 77-8, 94) and Marcellinus (*Letters* 62) – while the third – Simplicius (*Letters* 24, 28, 130) – was a fellow-native of Synesius'

Cyrenaica who had achieved high rank further afield (the status of Uranius is uncertain: see *PLRE* II: 1186); it is likely that Synesius met the fourth, Paeonius (*PG* 66.1577), while on an embassy in Constantinople.

Finally, returning to the most problematic set of letters in this respect, Symmachus probably met the *magister* Theodosius (father of the future emperor) (*Letters* 10.1) while visiting his north African estates after the conclusion of his African governorship in 374, in the period when Theodosius was completing the suppression of the rebel Firmus, unless they had already encountered one another at the imperial court in Trier in 369/70 (Matthews 1971); Theodosius' execution in 375, however, put paid to any possibility of a substantial correspondence. The Frankish general Bauto (*Letters* 4.15–16) is known to have supported Symmachus' plea for the restoration of the Altar of Victory to the senate house in 384 and to have received a consular panegyric the following year from one of Symmachus' protégés (Croke 1976a: 536–7), which suggests that the two men may have become acquainted in the context of the imperial court in 384, a time when Symmachus held high office as prefect of Rome. On the other hand, the eastern generals Timasius (*Letters* 3.70–3) and Promotus (*Letters* 3.74–80) were both commanders of the forces which the emperor Theodosius brought west in 388 to defeat the usurper Maximus, and their visit to Rome that year provided an obvious opportunity for Symmachus to meet them; yet some of his letters to them appear to pre-date 388 (3.72–3, 76). Despite his western Frankish origins, the same seems to apply to Richomer ((*Letters* 3.54–69), who spent most of his career in the east, although once again he received some letters from Symmachus which pre-date his visit to Rome in 388 (3.59, 62–3, with Croke 1976a: 538). As for Stilicho (*Letters* 4.1–14), although best known for his position of dominance in the west after Theodosius' death in 395, his early career was also spent in the east and it is likely that Symmachus first made his acquaintance when Stilicho too came west in the context of the 388 campaign; in this case, however, there is no letter which can definitely be assigned to the period before this – but then, Stilicho did not yet hold high rank of the sort which Timasius, Promotus, and Richomer did in the 380s.

Despite Libanius' story of Richomer eagerly searching him out (*Orations* 1.219), many of these relationships seem to have begun as a result of the contingent circumstance of the military figure being posted to the vicinity of the civilian in question, rather than the military figure actively seeking to initiate contact. Moreover, Symmachus' letters indicate that the burden of maintaining the relationship lay with the civilian, if his polite remonstrances about the lack of communication from some of his military acquaintances are anything to go by (*Letters* 3.54, 70, 4.1, 10, 15; cf. Libanius *Letters* 556). Of course this might be attributed in part to cultural differences: the activity of letter writing, which presumably appealed to individuals like Symmachus and Libanius as an opportunity to demonstrate their literary prowess – it was not unknown for letters to be read out to an audience (e.g., Synesius

Letters 101) – was no doubt seen in a somewhat different light – as an unwelcome chore – by individuals like Richomer and Ellebichus, even with the help of secretaries.[17] However, since it is apparent that these military figures did sometimes send letters (the following are explicitly presented as responses to letters received: Symmachus *Letters* 3.55, 64, 71, 78, 4.16, 10.1; Libanius *Letters* 1059, 1060; Theodoret *Letters* 97), it may also be a question of what each party stood to gain from the relationship, a subject which leads on to investigation of the content of the letters.

In assessing their content, it is important to appreciate that the surviving text does not necessarily represent all that was communicated. This is particularly germane to Symmachus' correspondence, some of whose letters appear to contain little more than polite but empty formulae:

> It is clear... that the letters were not always intended to say everything that we might expect of them. In some cases, a surviving letter was merely the "covering note" attached to a *breviarium* or *indiculum* which would have contained detailed news and information. On other occasions, it was left to the bearer of a letter to convey by word of mouth information of a more personal or trivial nature than was appropriately set down in writing. (Matthews 1974: 63)

Having registered this point, however, analysis can obviously only proceed on the basis of what has actually been preserved, and the content of the letters as it stands is still often informative.

Letter writing in the late Roman world was conducted within a framework of accepted conventions and traditions with regard to appropriate subject matter and occasions for correspondence.[18] The letter from Libanius to Richomer which opened this section is representative of a number of common features, such as the way it extols the virtues of friendship (cf. Symmachus *Letters* 3.78–9; Libanius *Letters* 1057) and offers congratulations on success – in this case, Richomer's role in the victory over "the tyrant," Magnus Maximus (cf. Symmachus *Letters* 3.59, 61, 10.1; Libanius *Letters* 436, 491, 866, 1024; Synesius *Letters* 62, 78, 94). Other well-known types of letter which occur in the material under consideration here are letters of consolation (Theodoret *Letters* 65; cf. Libanius *Letters* 318), and letters of recommendation on behalf of an individual, couched in very generalized terms, such as the following:

> To Arinthaeus: That you are a lover both of freedom and of mankind the nobility of your nature and your accessibility to all sufficiently informs us. Therefore with confidence do we address you on behalf of a man who is indeed distinguished through long lineage and through his ancestors, but worthy through his own merit of greater honour, and respect because of the inherent gentleness of his character; so that at our exhortation you may assist him in his fight against a charge which, so far as the truth is concerned, deserves nothing but contempt, but for the rest is dangerous on account of the seriousness of the calumny. For it would be of great influence towards his safety if you would

deign to say a kind word on his behalf, since in the first place you would be assisting justice, and secondly to us your chosen friends you would be showing in this instance also your accustomed honour and favour. (Basil *Letters* 179 [tr. Deferrari])

Such letters (cf. Symmachus *Letters* 3.67, 72–3, 76–7, 4.3; Libanius *Letters* 925, 1055, 1057; Gregory of Nazianzus *Letters* 134, 137, 181; Synesius *Letters* 59; Theodoret *Letters* XI) reflect the continuing vitality of relations of patronage in the late Roman world, and the wider power and influence which attended high military rank. One interesting variation on this theme is provided by Symmachus' letters to Stilicho requesting and thanking him for practical help in connection with his son's staging of public games in Rome (4.7–8). Another interesting variation comprises Theodoret's two letters addressed to Areobindus (XVIII, 23), on behalf of groups rather than individuals, with specific, practical objectives in mind. In both instances Theodoret asks Areobindus to remit dues owed by local peasants, though insofar as the somewhat opaque language of the letters allows one to judge, it looks like he is appealing to the general in the latter's "private" capacity as the owner of the land on which the peasants work.

Synesius' letters are unusual in that, unlike the other individuals from this period of the later fourth and earlier fifth century, he faced military threats at first hand in the form of raiding by nomadic Saharan tribesmen (cf. Liebeschuetz 1991: 228–35). Given his experience of being at the "sharp end," it is not surprising to find some of his letters to officers dealing with the military needs of his community – notably his trenchant criticisms of the performance of the local commander Cerealis (*Letters* 130), and his plea on behalf of the unit of Hunnigardae that their status not be downgraded and that their numbers be supplemented (*Letters* 78).

One type of letter specific to episcopal correspondence is appeals for help in relation to ecclesiastical affairs. Three of Gregory's letters (132–3, 136) request support during a forthcoming church council, while a number of Theodoret's request help in relation to the fall-out from the notorious Council of Ephesus in 448 (119, 139–40), such as the following to Anatolius toward the end of that year (cf. also Theodoret *Letters* IV.25; Severus *Letters* 1.40):

> The very holy lord archbishop Domnus has arranged for the most pious bishops to repair to the imperial city, with a view to the complete refutation of the false accusation made against us all. At this time we stand in especial need of the aid of your Magnificence, since the Lord of all has endowed you with the gifts of pure faith, of warm zeal on its behalf, of intelligence and capacity, and power to carry out your prudent counsels. I beg you therefore to defend the cause of the wronged, to contend against lies, and champion the apostolic teaching now assailed. Without doubt the master and guide of the churches will bless your endeavour, will scatter the lowering cloud, and bless the nurslings of

the faith with clear sky. Even should he permit the tempest to prevail, your greatness will reap your perfect reward, and we shall bow our heads before the storm, ready to live with cheerfulness wheresoever it may drive us, and waiting the judgment of God and his true and righteous sentence. (*Letters* 92 [tr. Jackson)

On the face of it, this type of letter can be viewed as a variation on the traditional pattern noted above, and yet it is difficult not to see a certain novelty in the idea of trying to harness the influence of high-ranking military figures in the sphere of religious policy. Comparison with Libanius' correspondence is of interest here. Although his letter to Richomer at the head of this section makes reference to "the gods" and it is apparent that part of the basis of their friendship was a common reverence for traditional cults ("he was a man deeply attached to the religion of the gods" (Libanius *Orations* 1.219)), at no point is there any suggestion of Libanius seeking to engage Richomer in the active defense of paganism (cf. Symmachus' general avoidance of reference in his letters to the religious issues of the late fourth century (Matthews 1974: 85–91)). Nor is it easy to think of analogies or precedents from earlier centuries of Roman history, though this possibly reflects, at least in part, the relative dearth of letter collections from the late Republic and Principate compared with late antiquity (there survive only those of Cicero, Pliny, and Fronto). Of course, the essential background to these particular letters is the fact that nearly all of the recipients were committed Catholic Christians. The most intriguing exception to this is the Arian Aspar. His heterodox theological leanings did not, however, deter Theodoret from asking him to use his influence with the emperor Marcian and the empress Pulcheria to help bring about the calling of a new council to undo the results of the Council of Ephesus – perhaps tacit acknowledgement on Theodoret's part of Aspar's role in Marcian's elevation to the imperial throne (cf. Lee 2000b: 42–3). At any rate, his hopes were soon realized in the form of the Council of Chalcedon (451), as a result of which he was reinstated as bishop of Cyrrhus.

All this suggests that, in this period at least, the benefits from these relationships flowed only in one direction, from the military to civilians. However, such a conclusion risks overlooking evidence of counter-currents which advantaged the military recipients of these letters. Libanius is known to have written panegyrics in honor of Richomer and Ellebichus (Libanius *Orations* 1.220, 232), while his request that Promotus pass on to him as much information as possible about the campaign against Maximus in 388, as a "gift sent by a general to an orator" (*Letters* 867), has been interpreted as reflecting Libanius' "consolidat[ing] this newly formed friendship by requesting information on which to exercise his oratory" (Norman 1992: II.319; cf. Libanius *Letters* 436).[19] Symmachus was also a capable orator, though he is not known to have written panegyrics for anyone other than emperors; however, he did arrange for a gifted young rhetorician (Augustine) to produce an appropriate piece of oratory for Bauto at the time of his consulship in 385 (Croke 1976a: 536–7). The text of a short speech by Synesius extolling the exploits of the *dux* Anysius has survived (the so-called *Constitutio* [*PG* 66.1573–7]), while his letter to Marcellinus (62) is effectively a eulogy of his exploits for public consumption. Such texts may seem of trifling significance, but that would be to underestimate the importance of panegyric in the political culture of late antiquity (cf. Mary Whitby 1998a) and of its particular value to figures like the generals in question, in terms of enhancing their social standing at court and providing a gloss of cultural sophistication which their military backgrounds lacked – "officers did not normally come from the educated city aristocracies" (Liebeschuetz 1972: 114). It is presumably for this reason also that one finds Libanius including Homeric allusions in the letter to Richomer which opened this section, as a subtle strategy for appealing to and flattering the cultural aspirations of such men.[20]

Other practical benefits for the generals can also be discerned. Symmachus served as a useful conduit of information through which Stilicho was better able to gauge the mood of the senate in Rome, notably in Symmachus' report on the senatorial debate about Gildo's rebellion in Africa in 397 (*Letters* 4.5). Eugenius, a teacher of rhetoric and imperial official, was a mutual friend of Symmachus and Richomer (*Letters* 3.60–1), and given Eugenius' background, it is likely that the former introduced Eugenius to the latter; Richomer in turn introduced his nephew Arbogast, another general, to Eugenius (Zosimus 4.54.1), and when Arbogast launched his rebellion in 392, it was Eugenius whom he used as the figurehead for the regime (cf. Matthews 1975: 240; Tomlin 1976: 194).

When one turns to the episcopal correspondence, it is much less easy to discern any benefits which might accrue to the military correspondents of the various bishops, beyond the assurance of their prayers and of the blessing of God. Given the evident Christian commitment of many of the generals in question, they will perhaps have considered this more than enough, but it nonetheless stands in contrast to the situation in the late sixth century when it was possible for a bishop such as Gregory the Great in Rome to be the recipient of letters from military men seeking help on a variety of matters (see below, p. 163), and for another bishop, Gregory of Antioch, to offer very practical and timely help to the military hierarchy through his ability to resolve a serious mutiny in 588–9 (Evagrius *Church History* 6.10–13; Theophylact Simocatta 3.5.10; with discussion in Michael Whitby 1988: 287–8 and Lee 2007).

One interesting feature of a handful of the letters is the author's deliberate use of military metaphors. In one of his letters to Richomer (3.67), Symmachus "makes deft use of military clichés" (Tomlin 1976: 192) as he seeks the general's help on behalf of a retiring civil servant, although the significance of this is somewhat reduced by the fact that service in the late Roman bureaucracy was regarded as a type of *militia* (cf. Introduction, p. 2). More intriguing is Gregory of Nazianzus' effective use of military analogies in one of his letters (136) to the Gothic general Modares in 382:

> To us you are a kinsman, a member of the family, and all that one can say about such a person. For piety has united us, and also the well-known virtue which we have observed in you. You show clearly that the difference between being a Greek and a barbarian is a matter of the body, not the soul, of the distance between places, but not between character or purpose. Would that many of our race would imitate your upright conduct, and then everything would go well for us, I know, both in public affairs and individually. Just as you put an end to foreign conflict with your right hand and wisdom, taking a valiant stand in our defense, so I call on you also to resolve the war among ourselves; as far as you are able, strive to bring about a peaceful solution among the bishops now gathering. For you understand well that to gather frequently without finding an end to our troubles, but always to be adding disorder to disorder, only increases our shame.

What is surprising is that such language does not feature more frequently in letters to generals.[21] Indeed, in many cases, if the identity of the recipient were not known, one would have no idea that the recipient was military (cf., e.g., Basil's letter to Arinthaeus and Theodoret's to Anatolius, quoted above). This is partly because epistolary conventions kept many of the letters at a very generalized level of artificial pleasantries, partly because the letter writers were interested in these men not for their military expertise but for their political influence. But perhaps the absence of "military language" is also a small but telling indication of the extent to which these military men were integrated into wider society at elite level.

Turning to the correspondence of Gregory the Great from the last decade of the sixth century and the early years of the seventh century, one can observe certain similarities with the letters already considered. Military recipients of Gregory's letters comprised *duces* of various regions in or near Italy, such as Sardinia and Campania, *magistri militum* stationed in Italy, and most prominent of all, the exarchs of Italy and of Africa; although this last office combined responsibilities in both military affairs and civilian administration, the military side was very much to the fore in this period when the Lombards presented such problems in the Italian peninsula (for these different ranks, see T. S. Brown 1984: 48–56). Gregory can be found sending letters of congratulation (e.g., 1.72–3, 9.155) and of recommendation (e.g., 9.9, 71) to these individuals, on the pattern of earlier examples noted above. He also sought to engage these military men in helping to resolve church problems of one sort or another (e.g., 1.46, 72–3, 4.7, 13.34), not unlike the efforts of Gregory of Nazianzus and Theodoret (cf. also Pelagius *Letters* 60).

However, it is noticeable that Gregory the Great also took a much closer interest in military affairs, seeking information about developments and offering suggestions and help for containing the Lombard problem, and often adopting a more forceful tone than one encounters in the earlier correspondence, as in the following example to the *magister militum* Velox, who in 591 was based in Umbria, between Rome and Ravenna:

> We informed your Glory some time ago that soldiers had been made ready to come to your parts; but since your letter signified to us that the enemy had assembled and were marching in our direction, for this reason we have detained them here. But now it seems desirable that a certain number of soldiers should be sent to you. We therefore beg your Glory to admonish and exhort them to be prepared for hard work. And when you have an opportunity, confer with our glorious sons Mauricius and Vitalianus, and do whatever, with the help of God, you jointly decide is to the advantage of the state. Should you learn that the unspeakable Ariulph [Lombard ruler of Spoletum] is moving in this direction or to the area near Ravenna, get to work in his rear, as becomes brave men, so that your activity may further increase your renown in the state. (*Letters* 2.7 [tr. Dudden (1905: 2.9–10), with revisions]; cf. 2.27–8, with Markus 1997: 99–101)

In part this reflects the way in which military problems impinged much more directly on Gregory's affairs than was the case for the bishops of the later fourth and early fifth century. No doubt it also reflects the special authority associated with Gregory's particular see, and the greater degree of independence from imperial control which he enjoyed compared with bishops in the eastern Mediterranean, by virtue of Rome's distance from Constantinople. But it is also indicative of the fact that the position of bishops had grown in stature in the interim.

Another novel feature of Gregory's correspondence is the way it indicates that some of these military men were sometimes writing to Gregory requesting *his* help in relation to ecclesiastical problems germane to their locale, as when the *magister* Aldio asked Gregory to ordain priests and deacons for his (unnamed) city (9.103), the *magister* Bahan requested help with the organization of church affairs at Orsino (9.100), or the exarch Callinicus lobbied Gregory in support of a bishop of Salona (8.24, 9.156, 177, with discussion in Markus 1997: 157–9). This development, for which there is no precedent in the episcopal correspondence of the late fourth and early fifth century, is a further indication of a shift in the balance of power between the military and the church, albeit in fraught circumstances which required a greater degree of co-operation than was necessary further east.

6.3. Military–Civilian Interaction at Non-Elite Levels

> If you wish to be a tribune, or rather if you wish to remain alive, restrain the hands of your soldiers. No one is to steal another person's poultry or to touch his sheep. No one is to make off with grapes, pilfer the harvest, or exact oil, salt

or firewood: they are to be content with their own allowance (*annona*). They are to obtain their livelihood from the enemy's booty, not from the tears of the provincials... They ought to keep their pay in their pockets and not spend it in taverns... Let them behave respectably in their billets (*hospitia*), and let anyone who starts an altercation be flogged. (*Historia Augusta: Aurelian* 7.5–8 [tr. Magie])

This letter, attributed to the emperor Aurelian (270–5), appears as part of a series of imperial biographies which, while purporting to have been written during the Tetrarchy, is generally agreed to have been written toward the end of the fourth century. Despite the fictional character of much of their content – the anonymous author's motive remains a source of bafflement to scholars – this particular item nevertheless provides a valuable insight into the genuine apprehensions of civilians about the behavior of soldiers in late antiquity. However, before investigating those apprehensions and their validity further, the parameters and contexts within which civilians typically interacted with soldiers in this period need to be established.

The extent of contact between ordinary civilian inhabitants of the empire and soldiers varied widely from location to location, depending above all on the distribution of troops. It is therefore important to gain some sense of the pattern of that distribution. Although the combination of the increased size of the army in late antiquity and the smaller size of individual units must have meant that soldiers were dispersed more widely, it has proved difficult to plot that pattern in detail. Attempts to do so have drawn on a variety of evidence, including literary sources, papyri, and archaeological evidence. Each of these, however, has its limitations: archaeological remains (e.g., forts) can often be difficult to date with sufficient precision, relevant papyri derive almost exclusively from Egypt, and the incidental references in literary sources provide uneven coverage (cf. the material assembled in MacMullen 1988: 209–17).

The one source which offers the possibility of more systematic information is the *Notitia Dignitatum*, the administrative document whose listings of military officers and the units under their command are generally accepted as reflecting the situation in the late fourth and early fifth century. However, even this document presents difficulties: first, although it does provide a specific location for many units of the *limitanei*, a significant number of these locations cannot easily be identified, either because of gaps in modern knowledge of ancient place-names, or because the place-names have been corrupted in the transmission of the text from its no-longer-extant late Roman incarnation to the later medieval copies on which modern editions must rely (see Brennan 1998b for a valuable case study of the problems arising from the entries for one region, Armenia); and secondly, it provides no locations for units in the central field armies, because the mobility which was an essential part of their original *raison d'être* meant that they were by definition not tied to a specific location – for much of the fourth century, at any rate, they were usually based wherever the emperor happened to be. Over the course of the fourth century, there was a trend toward regionalization of field armies to the point where, toward the end of the century, the field armies in the eastern half of the empire comprised two armies based near Constantinople and designated *praesentales* because of their proximity to the imperial capital, with the other three assigned to Illyricum, Thrace, and the East; however, the *Notitia*, while reflecting this structure, still offers no clues as to the specific locations of the units which constituted these armies.

Out of this diverse and admittedly incomplete evidence, the following generally agreed picture has emerged. On the one hand, the *limitanei* were based in the frontier provinces of the empire, usually in forts located in and adjacent to cities, towns, or villages. Limitanean units of higher status (i.e., those on the *laterculum maius*, "the higher register") generally seem to have been stationed in larger urban centers, with those on the *laterculum minor* ("the lesser register") in smaller centers and villages. In some cases, archaeological research has corroborated and expanded the place-name data of the *Notitia*, notably in Syria, where late Roman forts are preserved at such sites such as Palmyra, Resafa, and Sura (see D. Kennedy and Riley 1990 and Pollard 2000: 285–300 for details), while in the case of Egypt, papyri sometimes provide additional valuable documentary material alongside the archaeological evidence, notably in the cases of Dionysias and Hermopolis (Bell et al. 1962; Bailey 1991; Keenan 1994; cf. also Kraemer 1958 for Nessana in the Negev, although it has not been identified in the *Notitia*). None of this should occasion surprise, since troops will necessarily have been situated at locations on major communication routes along which there were already bound to be civilian settlements. At the same time, it is worth noting that not all major urban centers in frontier provinces had troops stationed in them – to take the example of Syria again, Damascus and Heliopolis appear not to have had garrisons in late antiquity – while, conversely, the archaeological remains of significant late Roman military bases have been found in the east at locations which were not in or near towns (Isaac 1992: 281, citing the examples of Lejjun and Udruh in Transjordan).

The field armies, on the other hand, had a more peripatetic existence, moving to meet threats to the frontiers or to embark on expeditions. Sometimes this would entail camping in tents,[22] at other times taking up temporary residence in urban centers, as at Amida in 359 (Ammianus 18.9.3) and in the cities of northern Mesopotamia during the Persian war of 502–5 (Ps.-Joshua Stylites *Chronicle* 65, 86–7). However, since campaigning usually took place during the warmer months of the year, field army units must have had winter quarters when not on campaign. In the absence of any help from the *Notitia* about the location of these winter quarters, one must have recourse to the occasional circumstantial detail provided by narrative histories, notably that of Ammianus. He makes passing mention of units wintering in towns (*oppida*) near Adrianople in 354 (14.11.15), which is likely to refer to the Thracian field army (cf. Brennan 2001), while two years later Julian dispersed his troops among Gallic towns (*municipia*) for the winter, the specific reference to *scutarii* (literally "shield bearers") and *gentiles* (literally "foreigners") confirming their field army status (16.4.1). A few years later again, when Julian was advancing into the Balkans against Constantius in the spring of 361, one of the latter's generals, Lucillianus – a cavalry *magister* and therefore a field army commander - is said to have had his headquarters at Sirmium with his units in nearby abodes (*stationibus propinquis*) (21.9.5, 7).

This pattern is replicated in the sixth century, when field army forces engaged in the Persian war of 502–5 were "assigned... to the cities [of northern Mesopotamia] in which they were to pass the winter until the campaign season came" (Ps.-Joshua Stylites *Chronicle* 65 [trs. Trombley and Watt]), and, with the onset of winter in 553, the Roman commander in Italy, Narses, is reported to have "disbanded his army and ordered them to group themselves into companies and battalions and winter in the neighboring towns and fortresses" (Agathias 1.19.3 [tr. Frendo])[23] – a situation which became common in Italy in the later decades of the sixth century, when cities came increasingly to have permanent garrisons of troops because of the Lombard threat (T. S. Brown 1984: 43, 89). It is generally assumed that the two eastern praesental armies wintered in towns on either side of the Bosporus near Constantinople (Jones 1964: 609; Dagron 1974: 108), an assumption which perhaps finds some corroboration in literary references to the presence of military units at Selymbria (Malalas *Chronicle* pp. 337–8, 383; Candidus fr.1) and the late Roman epitaphs of soldiers at Panium (Asdracha 1998: 312–14 [nos. 137–8]; cf. 320 [no. 146], and also 292–3 [no. 120] from nearby Apros). Despite the understandable reluctance of modern scholars to accept many aspects of the tendentious summary of Constantine's military reforms given by the pagan historian Zosimus (2.34.2), it seems, then, that there was probably an element of truth at least in his claim that troops withdrawn from the frontiers were based in cities.[24]

One final important qualification to this general picture concerns the great metropoleis of the empire. If one lived in Rome, Constantinople, Antioch, or Alexandria, then encounters with the military were likely to have been comparatively rare, since military units were not usually stationed permanently in the great cities of late antiquity. Ammianus included regular reference to events in fourth-century Rome in the course of his narrative (e.g., Ammianus 15.7.2–5, 19.10.2–3), from which it is apparent that the prefects of the city did not have access to military forces when trying to deal with the periodic riots prompted by food shortages (Jones 1964: 693). Although the imperial palace in Constantinople was guarded by the units of the *scholae palatinae*, supplemented from the mid fifth century by the *excubitores*, no regular army units were based in the city (Jones 1964: 694; Dagron 1974: 108–13): an ecclesiastical crisis involving the bishop of Constantinople required the intervention of troops from beyond the city in 342 (Socrates *Church History* 2.13); the usurper Procopius was only able to launch his rebellion in 365 because of the presence of units passing through the city en route to Thrace who were lodging, significantly, in one of the bath complexes (implying that there were no barracks in the city) (Ammianus 26.6.12–14); and Justinian was eventually able to suppress the Nika riot of 532 only with the arrival of troops from Thrace (Procopius *Wars* 1.24.40–1).

Antioch had a garrison imposed on the city after the Riot of the Statues in 387, but "up to that rising it seems to have been deliberate policy not to use the army to control the population [and] this policy was resumed in later years," even though it "reduced the coercive powers of the authorities" (Liebeschuetz 1972: 117–18; cf. Pollard 2000: 300–3, *pace* Isaac 1992: 270–7); only on the eve of campaigns against Persia, it seems, was there a notable military presence of soldiers in the city, with eastern field army units normally living in villages in the hinterland (cf. Libanius *Orations* 47.4). As for Alexandria, soldiers did have to intervene on numerous occasions during late antiquity to re-establish public order (see below, Chapter 7.2, pp. 198–204), but it is likely that the troops were based in the military camp established by Augustus to the east of the city at Nicopolis, which continued to function as such in the fourth century (e.g., *P. Oxyrhynchus* 60 (323)); the Parembole ("military camp") to which there are occasional references in the fourth century (e.g., *P. London* 1914; *Notitia Dignitatum (East)* 28.19) is probably an alternative name for this military camp at Nicopolis rather than being a fixture within the city itself (Bell 1924: 64; Van Berchem 1952: 62; Worp 1991: 294).

For civilians the most important consequence of soldiers being billeted in cities and towns was the requirement that they make available part of their houses for occupation by troops – in effect, a form of military requisitioning, referred to in the legal sources by a variety of terms including the euphemistic *hospitium* and *hospitalitas* (Goffart 1980: 41–2). The military hierarchy included quartermasters (*mensores* or *metatores*), one of whose responsibilities was to "assign billets in cities" (*hospitia in civitatibus*)(Vegetius *Epitome of Military Science* 2.7; cf. Procopius *Wars* 3.21.10). They performed this task by "writing on the doorposts the names of those to be quartered" in individual properties, as is known from a law aimed at householders who quickly tried to remove this information after the quartermasters had been along their street (*Theodosian Code* 7.8.4 [393]). The need for this law, the willingness of some to resort to bribery in order to avoid having to offer accommodation (Isaac 1992: 297; cf. also Ps.-Joshua Stylites *Chronicle* 86), and the fact that certain categories of individual and property were explicitly exempted from having to take in soldiers (e.g., teachers, doctors, clergy, synagogues: Jones 1964: 631) are symptomatic of the unpopularity of the practice. Some cities and towns were even prepared to pay as a whole to avoid having soldiers billeted among them, a fact of which an enterprising commander took advantage in early fifth-century Cyrenaica, as Synesius complained: "he proceeded to extract money from their cities by conducting troops there and moving them, not where the greatest military advantage was, but where there was the most plunder. Burdened by this billeting of troops upon them, the cities paid in gold" (*Letters* 130 [tr. Fitzgerald]). When Libanius wanted to flatter a military officer, he did so by noting that "you command your troops so well and care so well for the cities that they are attached to the regiment billeted there and are afraid some other city may get it" (*Letters* 1057.2 [tr. Norman]) – clearly the exception to the rule.[25]

The unpopularity of billeting stemmed partly from the formal requirement to surrender such a substantial portion of the property – one third – for the duration of the soldiers' stay (*Theodosian Code* 7.8.5 [398]),[26] but above all from the behavior of soldiers once in occupation, as vividly evoked in a metaphor used to illustrate a point in a fourth-century sermon on the subject of virginity:

> A girl should avoid taking pleasure in sensual sights and sounds, for these are the first steps in the corruption of her virginity; one thing leads to another just as when a soldier comes into a city with his battalion, and prowls around looking for a place to lodge. Sometimes he is forcibly locked out by the master of the house, but once he is through the door he is well on the way to the inner chambers. He leaves his helmet or some piece of his armour inside and you think that he has left to join his companions. But the weapon that he has put down gives him reason to come in again, and in no time he is back bringing his companions into the house as well, treating the place as if it was their own. (Basil *On Virginity* 15 (*PG* 30.700d–701a) [tr. Mitchell (1993: II.75)])

One of the specific problems which arose from billeting was the usual determination of soldiers to extract from householders what was known in military jargon as *salgamum* – literally "pickles," but in fact a broader term encompassing any kind of additional goods, especially oil, wood, and bedding. As a succession of imperial laws indicates (*Theodosian Code* 7.9), despite there being no legal requirement for householders to provide anything beyond shelter, soldiers were in the habit of extorting such items, with violence if necessary, as illustrated in the following contemporary account of the abuses arising from the billeting of soldiers in Edessa and other cities and towns of northern Mesopotamia during and after the Persian war of 502–5:

> When those who came to our assistance ostensibly as saviours were going down and coming up, they looted us in a manner little short of enemies. They threw many poor people out of their beds and slept in them, leaving their owners to lie on the ground at a time of cold weather. They ejected others from their houses, going in and living in them. Others' cattle they led away by force as if plundering an enemy. They stripped some people's clothing off them and took

it away. They used rough treatment on others for the sake of obtaining anything whatever. In the streets they denounced and insulted others for the smallest reason. They brazenly plundered the meagre provisions which everyone had, and the stockpile belonging to a few individuals in the villages and cities. They attacked many on the roads... In full view of everyone they had their way over the women in the streets and houses. They took oil, wood, salt, and other things for their own needs from the old women, widowed or poor, and they stopped them doing their own work in order to serve them. In a nutshell, they oppressed everyone, nobles and commoners, and no one escaped receiving some of their wickedness. (Ps.-Joshua Stylites *Chronicle* 86 [trs. Trombley and Watt])[27]

As this passage also indicates, their use of violence extended to some soldiers' dealings with women. Although the sources are understandably more reticent about the incidence of Roman soldiers raping Roman women, this is not the only allusion to such mistreatment. In a speech delivered in honor of Constantius II and Constans in the 340s, Libanius conceded that "the dishonouring of women... had not been averted in earlier emperorships ... [and] the habit of violating women had become a custom... [on the part of] those who were keeping our enemies in check... They resembled excellent hounds with regard to the wolves, but they were savage towards the sheep" (*Orations* 59.157 [tr. Dodgeon);[28] a late fourth-century source took it for granted that soldiers would "commit adultery" with the wives of those on whom they were billeted (*Historia Augusta, Aurelian* 7.4); troops sent to Alexandria in the early 450s to quell a disturbance were "drunkenly abusive towards both the wives and daughters of the Alexandrians" (Evagrius *Church History* 2.5 [tr. Whitby]); and in 603 Gregory the Great wrote to the *dux* of Naples urging firm punishment of a soldier who had raped a nun, as an example to other troops (*Letters* 14.10; cf. also *Letters* 9.207, expressing concern about soldiers being billeted on nuns in Naples).[29]

As the penultimate example shows, the behavior of soldiers was not aided by a propensity to consume too much alcohol. Wine was a standard component of a soldier's rations in late antiquity (*Theodosian Code* 7.4.4, 6, 25; *P. Beatty Panopolis* 2.109–13 [300]; *PSI* 7.820 [309/14]; *CPL* 199 [399]), in part because it was a standard component of the ancient Mediterranean diet but perhaps also because it was recognized that it had the potential to play a positive role in military life. It has been pointed out, with reference to the conduct of soldiers in more recent centuries, that alcohol has "an entirely legitimate function in helping overwrought men to sleep"; "communal drinking also assists in the small-group bonding process"; and it serves as a way of "mitigating the stresses of battle" (Holmes 1985: 244–6). However, it is also the case that "soldiers in garrison in both peace and war tend to overindulge in alcohol as a means of making an unbearable existence more tolerable" (Holmes 1985: 245) – an observation borne out in the case of Roman soldiers in late antiquity. Soldiers sent to arrest a heterodox bishop in

Alexandria in 335 "came in a drunken state" (*P. London* 1914 [line 10]); Ammianus commented on the excessive consumption of alcohol by some of Julian's troops in Antioch in the winter of 362/3 (22.12.6); and some soldiers in early sixth-century Edessa became so drunk that they inadvertently killed themselves falling out of upper-story windows (Ps.-Joshua Stylites *Chronicle* 96).[30] When preaching against drunkenness, Basil used the behavior of the military as an illustration:

> What a pitiful spectacle for the eyes of Christians: a man in the prime of life, strong in body, renowned in the military ranks, is carried home on a litter because he is unable to hold himself upright or walk on his own two feet. A man who ought to be a terror to the enemy is the occasion for laughter among the children in the marketplace; without a sword in sight, he is laid low, in the absence of the enemy, he is slain. A soldier in the prime of life has become useless as a result of wine, ready to suffer whatever the enemy wishes. (Basil *Sermon against Drunkards* 7 (*PG* 31.457b))

Even more interesting is the scene of an officers' mess, brilliantly (if also tendentiously) evoked at length in one of Ambrose's sermons (only a summary of which can be presented in the space available here):

> The diners commence with cocktails, but these are merely the prelude to serious drinking and intended to stimulate thirst. When the dinner is served, the consumption of liquor begins in earnest. With every course the goblets are filled; often they are replenished between mouthfuls. It is the ambition of every soldier to show that he can drink the most; to refuse to engage in this revelry is considered disgraceful. The meal is followed by the drinking-bout proper. Huge mixing-bowls and silver beakers are brought in; a chairman is chosen; the proportions of mixing and the number of parts to be absorbed by each person are arranged. Then the company settles down to business. No one is allowed to leave off drinking. Should any reverse his goblet in token that he has had enough, he is pressed to start again; should he still refuse, he is held while wine is poured down his throat. There are regular toasts – "To the good health of the emperors," "the army," "our gallant comrades," "our children." It is the custom to swallow great quantities in a single draught; to take a breath is an offence, for which the drinker has to pay forfeit. Even the men with the strongest heads get drunk. Some fall asleep; some babble in a maudlin fashion about their martial exploits; some, pale and perspiring, are supported into the fresh air, and after an interval are led back again – to go on drinking. In the end such of the officers as are still capable of motion reel from the dining-room and are hoisted on to their horses, from which, after a moment of dizzy oscillation, they tumble into the arms of their grinning slaves. The rest are carried home, dead drunk, on their shields. (Ambrose *On Elijah and Fasting* 46–50, 62, 64, in the paraphrase of Dudden (1935: 2.468–9), with revisions)

Drunken, abusive behavior on the part of soldiers was not, of course, unique to late antiquity (cf. Campbell 1984: 246–54 for the Principate).

However, if, as seems to have been the case, there was a greater likelihood in this period of civilians having direct contact with soldiers, then the impact of poor behavior will have been greater. As already indicated, this impact is likely to have fallen most heavily on the communities of the frontier provinces and of the regions where the field armies were quartered during the winter. However, cities and towns in other, intermediate regions could still suffer at the hands of soldiers, albeit more briefly, as a result of the movements of armies to and from frontier areas. The famous petition from the Thracian village of Scaptopara to the emperor Gordian III in 238, preserved on stone, included, among various grievances, the fact that "soldiers who are despatched elsewhere leave their proper routes and appear among us and likewise press us hard to furnish them quartering and provisions without paying anything" – together with the veiled threat that if the villagers receive no alleviation, they will have to abandon the village, with all that that implied in terms of the loss of imperial revenue (*CIL* 3.12336 with *AE* 1994.1552 [tr. Hauken]). Similarly, in the mid 240s peasants on an imperial estate at Aragua on the Anatolian plateau appealed to the emperor Philip against the depredations of soldiers (among others): "On their travel through the territory of the Appians – leaving the main roads – soldiers, leading men from the town and your *Caesariani* [i.e., officials] are coming when leaving the main roads, and they drag us away from our work, requisition our ploughing oxen and extort what is not owed to them whatsoever" (*CIL* 3.14191 [tr. Hauken]). This is only one of a number of such complaints in the third century from this region, which was particularly exposed to the movement of troops back and forth to the eastern frontier (cf. Zosimus 1.36.1; Mitchell 1993: I.229–34).

The third century was a period of intensive military activity in the east as the empire sought to combat the emergence of an aggressive Sasanian regime in Persia, but movement of troops remained a problem here in subsequent centuries. Firmus, bishop of Cappadocian Caesarea in the first half of the fifth century, wrote to an individual of evident influence with the following request for help:

> Since it is natural for us to have recourse to your patronage, we have been led to hope also for the redress of our grievances. We ask that you judge us worthy of consideration, we and our homeland weakened by famine, so that the expenses occasioned by the soldiers which are now crushing us are lightened and it is stipulated that no army should pass through our territory. For if this befalls us, only a handful from among us will escape the utter ruin of the famine and survive. (*Letters* 12)

The *Life* of the late sixth-century holy man Theodore of Sykeon also refers to the holy man intervening to divert the passage of armies away from poorer villages in his homeland of central Anatolia (147).[31] The existence of the problem is corroborated by epigraphic evidence from the fifth and sixth century (Trombley 1997: 172); some communities even constructed and maintained special inns for passing soldiers as a strategy for avoiding having to billet them (Rémondon 1961: 61–5; Isaac 1992: 177–8; Gascou 1994; Trombley 2004: 85).

When recourse to more conventional means of prevention or redress, such as petition and patronage, was not possible or was ineffective, there were other, more unusual strategies. One fourth-century document refers to a householder stealing from billeted soldiers (*P. Oxyrhynchus* 3581), while the long-suffering inhabitants of early sixth-century Edessa eventually resorted to secretly posting public notices criticizing the soldiers' commander in a (successful) attempt to embarrass him into action (viz., withdrawal of the troops from the city) (Ps.-Joshua Stylites *Chronicle* 96). One ingenious individual in the fourth-century west evidently decided to strike back by lampooning the military through a clever parody of a soldier's will in the form of the so-called "Testament of the piglet" – "the only possible target is the semi-barbarous late Roman soldier, as viewed by an educated man" (Champlin 1987: 182). Although it loses much of its impact in translation, its opening gives some idea of the flavor of the piece, with its combination of legal knowledge and humor based on puns, comic exaggeration, and double entendre:

> M. Grunter Hyena the piglet has made this will. As I cannot write myself, I have dictated it. Butcher the cook said: "Come here, destroyer of the house, digger up of the soil, runaway, piglet, and today I take your life." Hyena the piglet said: "If I have done anything, if I have sinned in any way, if I have broken some little vessels with my feet, I petition you, master cook, I ask for my life, grant it to the petitioner." Butcher the cook said: "Come here, boy, hand me the knife from the kitchen in order that I may make a bloody end of this piglet." The piglet is seized by the assistants, led off on the fifteenth day before the first of the Herbal Month, when herbage is plentiful, in the consulship of Roastingtin and Peppersauce. And as he saw that he was going to die, he asked for an hour's reprieve and petitioned the cook in order to be able to make a will. (tr. Daube (1969: 78–9))

The fact that schoolboys are reported as reciting this text with great hilarity in the late fourth century (Jerome *Commentary on Isaiah* 12) suggests that it gained wide appreciation.[32]

Perhaps the most unusual riposte, however, was that apparently adopted by one Isidore of Pelusium, probably a clergyman in this important Egyptian port (see Évieux 1995 for a reconstruction of his career and context, and analysis of his letters). Among the edited extracts which have been preserved from his voluminous correspondence from the first half of the fifth century (which includes two letters to the emperor Theodosius II) are a number of communications to soldiers, the tone of which has been described as "vigorous and firm, even menacing" (Évieux 1995: 17). The following examples give some idea of his uncompromising attitude, even if the impact of his strictures remains unknown:

> To Turba, soldier: It is not appropriate to bear arms in peacetime, nor to wander around the middle of the marketplace in military dress, nor to go about the city with a sword. Creating fear and undertaking this sort of activity ought to be done in war against the enemy. So if you enjoy wearing your military gear and you think yourself worthy of having your name proclaimed and of being accorded honorific plaques, take yourself off to the army camp to fight with the barbarians, and do not purchase exemption and remain at home: this is the place for child's play, that is the place to pursue war. (*Letters* 1.40 (*PG* 78.208))

> To Esaia, soldier: If you consider pointed weapons and a helmet and breastplate to be a guarantee of safety so you can live well by plundering and laying waste the thoroughfares, consider the fact that many who protected themselves more securely than you still achieved a miserable death. There are recorded in our scriptures the cases of Horeb, Zeb, Salman, Abimelech, Goliath, Absalom, and others like them; and in other texts, Hector, Ajax, and those Spartans who are regarded as the greatest of all in strength, since they did not have a fair contest. So if you do not wish to be a rash soldier, quickly change your order of battle to spiritual warfare, and wage war, rather, against your own lack of discipline. (*Letters* 1.78 (*PG* 78.236))

While the anti-military sentiment which prevails in late Roman sources is undeniable, various qualifications ought nonetheless also to be noted. At the most general level, it has been pointed out with reference to late Roman military–civilian relations that "as so often, documentation follows trouble" (Bagnall 1993: 174). Well-behaved soldiers rarely merited comment, although interestingly, one of the sources offering the most vociferous and detailed criticism of military behavior conceded that "there were also others among them who lived in an orderly fashion, for in a large army like that there are certain to be some such people." In the context of an epidemic which struck Edessa a few years prior to the Persian war of 502–5, the same source comments in passing that "Roman soldiers established places [for those affected by the disease]; the ill slept in them and the soldiers took care of their expenses" (Ps.-Joshua Stylites *Chronicle* 96, 43 [trs. Trombley and Watt]). There are also occasional glimpses of billeted soldiers who apparently got on well with their "host," as clearly implied by the arrangements recorded in the following late fourth-century epitaph from northern Italy (cf. Tomlin 1972: 271): "To Flavius Fortunatus, officer (*augustalis*) from the unit of the Jovian soldiers: Vettius Serenianus, his host (*hospes*) and heir, in accordance with his will prepared a worthy sarcophagus from his own resources" (*ILS* 551).

Also of relevance is the evidence of the military defending the interests of peasants against landowners and government authorities. The most detailed information on this relates to the agricultural hinterland of Antioch in the late fourth century. In the pamphlet he wrote in the late 380s or early 390s protesting against "protection rackets" (*Orations* 47), Libanius complained about peasants enlisting the help of soldiers billeted in surrounding villages to resist the demands of landlords and of tax collectors, with the latter "collecting wounds instead of taxes" (47.8); in the event of complaints about the villagers' behavior being lodged with the governor, it seems that higher military officers intervened to protect the villagers' interests. Libanius was moved to write because he himself, as a landowner, was affected by this development, but the fact that imperial laws on the subject were issued in the 390s (*Theodosian Code* 11.24.3–5) shows that Libanius' experience was not unique, although it is apparent from the laws that such patronage (*patrocinium*) was also being exercised by influential civilians. Of course military involvement on behalf of the peasants was not altruistic – the soldiers received recompense in money or kind – but in circumstances where the demands on peasants from the imperial authorities were increasing, the presence of the military nevertheless offered peasants a welcome alternative source of patron as they sought to defend their interests against the encroachments of government and powerful individuals (Liebeschuetz 1972: 201–7; Krause 1987: 73–87; Garnsey and Woolf 1989). Moreover, an earlier law on the subject of patronage (*Theodosian Code* 11.24.1 [360]) implies that a similar phenomenon was also occurring in Egypt, again with military involvement (the law refers to *duces* as being among those offering protection to peasants).[33]

Another perspective is also provided by papyrus documentation relating to military units in late Roman Egypt, most famously the archive of material associated with Abinnaeus, the commander of the cavalry unit based at Dionysias in the Fayum in the mid fourth century (Bell et al. 1962; Barnes 1985b). Just as the letters discussed in the preceding section did not include any written by generals, so also the Abinnaeus archive comprises, almost exclusively, items sent to Abinnaeus, apart from a petition from him to the emperors of the day protesting against his removal from his post (*P. Abinnaeus* 1) and a memorandum reminding various debtors what they owe Abinnaeus' relatives (*P. Abinnaeus* 43). Despite this limitation, however, there is still much of value to be gained from the archive.

First, there is no doubt that Abinnaeus was seen as an influential figure in the local community, and he certainly received requests for help on various fronts. These petitions, however, generally concerned comparatively minor matters relating to the apprehension of perpetrators of petty theft or violence. The only hint of tension with civilian authorities in a manner analogous to the Syrian situation described by Libanius is in a letter of complaint from Chaeremon, the leader of a local council (probably that of Arsinoe) (*P. Abinnaeus* 18) – with, however, two important differences: on the one hand, Chaeremon threatens to take the matter up with

Abinnaeus' superior (whereas Libanius complained that senior officers were in cahoots with the troops), while on the other, the cause of Chaeremon's complaint seems to be Abinnaeus' conscription of villagers, which was presumably a legitimate activity on the part of his troops.

Secondly, while there are occasional complaints about the behavior of individual soldiers from Abinnaeus' unit in their relations with local civilians – one was prone to violent behavior and "goes out continually drunk into the fields and makes the village his prey" (*P. Abinnaeus* 28), while another was accused of the nocturnal fleecing of a villager's sheep (*P. Abinnaeus* 48) – there is no sense of the sort of widespread abuse of civilians familiar from Edessa in the early sixth century. Presumably this reflects the fact that Abinnaeus' unit was part of the *limitanei*: not only were they not billeted on locals, but they were also likely to have been recruited locally, which "should have made them fit fairly easily into the society they guarded" (Bagnall 1993: 177). This picture gains further credence from fifth-century papyri from Hermopolis, where another unit of *limitanei* was posted. Although it was a cavalry regiment of *Mauri* ("Moors"), which must originally have been recruited in north Africa, it is evident that by this time they too were recruited locally, and the archive of one of its soldiers, that of Taurinus, illustrates both how one fifth-century soldier rose through the ranks and also how he became the owner of land in the area, albeit on a modest scale (Keenan 1994).[34] Perhaps it came down to a simple matter of permanence versus transience – that soldiers based continuously in the same community were bound to be more conscious of the advantages of maintaining good relations with local inhabitants, whereas troops on campaign (above, pp. 171–2) did not have to live with the long-term consequences of any poor behavior on their part.

Further Reading

Soldiers' families in late antiquity are a subject which has received little previous attention: the best starting point is Phang 2001, whose primary focus is, however, on the Principate.

Correspondence between military and non-military elites has likewise received little previous attention, but Tomlin 1976 is an excellent starting point for the subject more generally.

Interaction between **soldiers and civilians at non-elite levels**, on the other hand, has been the subject of much previous work. Useful studies of different aspects are MacMullen 1963 and Pollard 2000.

7

ARMY, WARFARE, AND RELIGION

Late antiquity was a period of major religious upheaval and change in the Roman world. In the third century the religious life of the empire was characterized by a huge diversity of religious cults with little interference from the authorities. By the early fourth century, however, one religion – Christianity – began to enjoy a favored status, and by the end of that century, it had effectively become the official religion of the empire; other cults experienced growing discrimination, and Christianity increasingly impinged on all areas of life, including the military. This chapter investigates the effects of these religious changes on the late Roman army and on attitudes to war by examining a number of areas: first, the religious allegiances of those serving in the army; secondly, the role of the army as an instrument of religious policy; and thirdly, the impact of Christianity on both the empire's reasons for embarking on war and its military effectiveness.

7.1. The Changing Religious Complexion of the Army

7.1.1. Before Constantine

On the 3rd day before the Nones of January [3 January], because vows are discharged and pronounced both for the well-being of our Lord Marcus Aurelius Severus Alexander Augustus and for the perpetual continuance of the empire of the Roman people: to Jupiter the Best and Greatest an ox, to Queen Juno a cow, to Minerva a cow, to Jupiter the Victor an ox, ... to Mars the Father a bull, to Mars the Victor a bull, to Victory a cow...

On the 7th day before the Ides of January [7 January], because honorable discharge with enjoyment of privileges is given to those who have completed their service and pay is counted out to the soldiers: to Jupiter the Best and Greatest an ox, to Juno a cow, to Minerva a cow, to Well-being (*Salus*) a cow, to Mars the Father a bull... (*P. Dura* 54, col. 1, lines 2–9 [222/235])

Religious ritual permeated the life of the Roman army during the Republic, whether it was the totemic associations of legionary standards reflected in the dedication of a shrine for their reverence within military camps, or generals' practice of promising a sanctuary or some other form of dedication to a particular deity in return for that deity's aid in achieving success in a forthcoming campaign (Rüpke 1990). With the advent of monarchy from Augustus onward, there was added a regular cycle of religious observances within military camps for the purpose of consolidating and reinforcing the loyalty of soldiers toward the emperor, as reflected in the famous third-century calendar preserved on a papyrus from the Roman fortress on the Euphrates at Dura-Europos, a short excerpt from which appears above. It is generally accepted that this calendar was not specific to the particular unit stationed at Dura – the absence of any local deities is noteworthy – but rather was "a standard festival list for the army, simply one representative of a type issued to every camp and garrison" (Fink et al. 1940: 28; cf. Nock 1952; Campbell 1984: 99–101; Fishwick 1988). Study of the full text reveals a clear focus on the reigning emperor Severus Alexander and his forebears; also notable is the emphasis on sacrifice, and the prominence of deities associated with war and victory. Yet another important way in which religion impinged on military life was through the military oath, whose very name in Latin (*sacramentum*) implies its religious character. Although its precise wording before the fourth century is uncertain, it seems to have been repeated on a regular basis, near the start of each calendar year and on the anniversary of the accession of the emperor (Campbell 1984: 19–32; and more generally Helgeland 1978; Clauss 1986: 1073–94; Beard et al. 1998: I.324–7).

The religious observances associated with the Dura calendar and the military oath were obviously official initiatives, but it is apparent that the authorities also allowed scope for individual religious preferences on the part of soldiers, as reflected in the evidence for a host of non-official cults in the vicinity of military camps during the Principate. The most widespread of these was the cult of Mithras, whose male exclusivity and strongly hierarchical character clearly exercised a particular appeal for soldiers (Clauss 2000: 33–7; R. L. Gordon 1972), although other cults, notably that of Jupiter Dolichenus, also enjoyed prominence in military contexts (Speidel 1978; Brennan 1987).

Mithraism and most of the other non-official cults practiced by soldiers did not make exclusive claims on the allegiance of adherents – unlike the monotheistic cults of Judaism and Christianity. One might have expected their monotheistic character to preclude the possibility of finding adherents of either creed in the army, particularly given the requirements of "official" religious ritual, and indeed as far as Jews are concerned, there is little if any evidence of their serving in the Roman army during the Principate.[1]

Christians, on the other hand, were undoubtedly present in the army by the third century, although it is very difficult to gauge their numbers, and whether they were predominantly individuals who became Christians before or after enlisting. General considerations argue against there having been large numbers of Christians entering the third-century army: soldiers tended to be drawn predominantly from rural regions, where Christianity historically was slower to make an impact than in urban communities, while the army's most important recruiting area in the third century – the Balkans – was also one of the least Christianized parts of the empire (cf. Jones 1963: 24; MacMullen 1984: 44–5). Of course, once in the army, soldiers may have found themselves posted to a part of the empire where they were more likely to come into contact with Christians, as presumably might have happened at Dura-Europos, where there was some sort of Christian community by the early third century, reflected in the archaeological evidence of a house church located in the "non-military" sector of the site (Kraeling 1967, who notes (90, 92, 96) Christian graffiti from the structure which include names otherwise known only from the military population of Dura).

When it comes to questions of quantification in Roman history, the first port of call is usually epigraphic evidence, because of the sheer numbers of inscriptions which have survived. On the specific issue of Christians in the pre-Constantinian army, however, they are of limited help, since there are not many more than a dozen examples of soldiers' epitaphs extant from the first three centuries AD which also contain an indication of Christian allegiance (Tomlin 1998: 24, 43 n.22). While this tends to corroborate initial minimizing assumptions based on recruitment patterns, it does not exhaust the available relevant evidence. One must also take into account discussions of the appropriate Christian attitude to service in the army by a range of theologians from the late second century onward. Had they, for example, been more or less uniform in their condemnation of Christians serving in the army, this would have provided further corroboration for the minimizing view. A survey of their views, however, reveals a range of stances whose variety implies that this was a live issue confronting more than just a handful of individuals at any one point in time.

These varied stances no doubt in part reflect the fact that the New Testament itself did not provide unequivocal guidance on this issue. On the one hand, it included injunctions to love one's enemies (Matthew 5.38–48; Luke 6.27–38) and against killing and physical violence, such as Jesus' encouragement to turn the other cheek and his strictures about those who live by the sword dying by the sword (Matthew 5.39, 26.52), which might seem to preclude military service; on the other hand, the New Testament emphasized respect for secular authority (Romans 13.1–5), and included anecdotes involving soldiers, such as those instructed by John the Baptist to refrain from intimidation and extortion, but not, by implication, from service in the army altogether (Luke 3.14); the centurion whose daughter Jesus healed and whose expression of faith through the phrase "Just give the command" drew Jesus' approval (Matthew 8.5–13); and the God-fearing centurion Cornelius to whom at no point did the apostle Peter suggest he should resign his commission (Acts 10).

As a result, there were some early Christian theologians, such as Clement of Alexandria, writing in the late second and early third century, who took it for granted that there were Christians serving in the army and who offered no explicit criticism of those who did: "If you are a farmer, we say, till the earth, but acknowledge the God of farmers; if you love seafaring, sail on, but remember to call upon the celestial Helmsman. Have you been seized by the knowledge of God while engaged in military service? Then obey the Commander who gives just commands" (Clement of Alexandria *Exhortation to the Greeks* 10.100.2). Others like Origen (mid third century), argued that the most effective way for Christians to contribute to the defense of the empire was through prayer for the emperor and his armies:

> he more pious a man is, the more effective he is in helping the emperors – more so than the soldiers who go into the lines and kill all the enemy troops they can... We who by our prayers destroy all daemons which stir up wars, violate oaths, and disturb the peace, are more help to the emperors than those who seem to be doing the fighting... And though we do not become fellow-soldiers with him, even if he presses us, yet we are fighting for him and composing a special army of piety through our intercessions to God. (Origen *Against Celsus* 8.73 [tr. Chadwick])

Writing at about the same time, Hippolytus adopted an uncompromising position:

> A soldier who is in authority must be told not to execute men; if he should be ordered to do it, he shall not do it. He must be told not to take the military oath. If he will not agree, let him be rejected... If a catechumen or a baptized Christian wishes to become a soldier, let him be cast out, for he has despised God. (*Apostolic Tradition* 16.17, 19 [tr. Dix])

That different stances on this issue could be justified is most strikingly illustrated by the case of Tertullian, a contemporary of Clement, who did not at first see the presence of Christians in the army as problematic: "We live in the world sharing with you the forum, the market, the baths, the shops, the factories, the inns, the market days, and all other commercial activities. We, no less than you, sail the sea, serve in the army, farm the land, buy and sell" (Tertullian *Apology* 42.2–3). Later, however, after embracing the rigorist teachings of Montanism, he became strongly opposed to Christian involvement in the military:

> But the question now is whether a member of the faithful can become a soldier, and whether a soldier can be admitted to the Faith even if he is a member of the rank and file who are not required to offer sacrifice or decide capital cases. There can be no compatibility between an oath made to God and one made to man, between the standard of Christ and that of the devil, between the camp of light and the camp of darkness. The soul cannot be beholden to two masters, God and Caesar... Even if soldiers came to John and got advice on how they

ought to act, even if the centurion became a believer, the Lord, by taking away Peter's sword [in the garden of Gethsemane], disarmed every soldier thereafter. We are not allowed to wear any uniform that symbolizes a sinful act. (Tertullian *On Idolatry* 19.1–3 [tr. Swift (1983: 41–2)])

As these examples show, those who opposed Christian involvement did not do so on uniform grounds: some emphasized the necessity to refrain from killing, others the need to avoid participation in the "official" religious rituals which were so integral to army life.[2]

The upshot of all this was that church teaching did not present a united front of opposition to discourage Christians from enlisting, and indeed a number of these theological discussions presuppose that there were Christians in the army. Accounts of martyrdoms from the third century shed further light on these issues. The church historian Eusebius reports the case of a soldier named Marinus, probably from the early 260s, who was due to be promoted to the rank of centurion until a jealous rival denounced him as a Christian; when Marinus, encouraged by the local bishop, refused to renounce his Christianity, he was duly executed (Eusebius *Church History* 7.15). What is intriguing about this case is its implication that Marinus had served long enough to warrant promotion and must therefore have existed quite happily in the army for some time prior to this without apparently facing any crisis of conscience (did he go through the motions of participating in army rituals, or did his fellow soldiers turn a blind eye when he refrained from doing so?). From the late 290s, there is a second instance of an individual, Marcellus, who had already attained the rank of centurion, until qualms about involvement in military religious festivities prompted him effectively to renounce his involvement in the army (*Acts of Marcellus* [= Musurillo 1972: 252–9]) – but again, in view of his rank, he must have been serving for some time prior to this without, it seems, seriously questioning the compatibility of military service with his commitment.[3]

From a few years earlier, there is an account of the trial of a young man, Maximilian, who was presented for enlistment in the ranks, but who objected on the grounds of his Christian allegiance. The particular point of interest in this case lies in the fact that, as part of his efforts to persuade Maximilian to change his mind, the governor stated that "in the sacred retinue (*comitatus*) of our lords Diocletian and Maximian, Constantius and Maximus [= Galerius], there are soldiers who are Christians and they undertake military service." Such a claim might be viewed skeptically as the desperate attempt of an official keen to resolve a problematic situation as expeditiously as possible, but it finds independent corroboration from a number of other sources. One is an epitaph for the wife of a soldier, in which her husband, Aurelius Gaius, takes the opportunity to provide a detailed account of his military career under Diocletian, including service in the *comitatus*, before bidding farewell to his wife "until the resurrection."[4] The other is a report by the Christian scholar Lactantius about events leading up to the initiation of the "Great Persecution" in 303. A few years earlier, when priests were inspecting the entrails of a sacrifice in the presence of the emperor Diocletian, they complained that the presence of "profane persons" was inhibiting the successful performance of the ritual, which was taken to be a reference to Christians in the emperor's entourage. This in turn led Diocletian to initiate a more general purge of Christians from the army (Lactantius *On the Deaths of the Persecutors* 10; cf. Eusebius *Church History* 8.1, 4) – probably the context in which Aurelius Gaius found himself having to terminate his military career (cf. Drew-Bear 1979: 140–1). This purge was a clear indication that by the end of the third century, Christians were a noticeable element in the army (though presumably not so substantial that their dismissal would compromise the army's effectiveness).

It is also worth noting Maximilian's telling response to the governor's statement about the presence of Christians in the imperial *comitatus* – "What they do is their own business." It confirms what one would have expected – that those in the army who considered themselves Christians took differing views as to what constituted compromise. Tertullian articulated this even more clearly when describing the reaction of some Christian soldiers to the resolute stance taken by one of their brethren in 211, when he objected very publicly to an aspect of army ceremonial which had religious connotations, namely the wearing of a wreath when receiving an imperial donative:

> It was then that the gossips started: maybe they were not all Christians, for they certainly talked very much like pagans! "Why does he have to make so much trouble for the rest of us Christians over the trifling matter of dress? Why must he be so inconsiderate and rash and act as if he were anxious to die? Is he the only brave man, the only Christian among his fellow soldiers?"... In a word, they grumble because our soldier was endangering the long and comfortable peace they had been enjoying. (Tertullian *On the Wreath* 1.4–5 [tr. Quain])

7.1.2. The fourth century

> The Day of Salvation then, which also bears the names of Light Day and Sun Day, he taught all the military to revere devoutly. To those who shared the divinely given faith he allowed free time to attend unhindered the church of God, on the assumption that with all impediment removed they would join in the prayers. To those who did not yet share in the divine Word he gave order in a second decree that every Lord's Day they should march out to an open space just outside the city, and that there at a signal they should all together offer up to God a form of prayer learnt by heart; they ought not to rest their hopes on spears or armour or physical strength, but acknowledge God over all, the giver of all good and indeed of victory itself... Furthermore he caused the sign of the saving trophy to be marked on their shields, and had the army led on parade, not by any of the golden images, as had been their past practice, but by the saving trophy alone. (Eusebius *Life of Constantine* 4.18.3–21 [trs. Cameron and Hall])

The preceding section has suggested that it is possible to over-minimize the Christian presence in the third-century army, particularly toward the end of that century. Nevertheless, this is a matter of relative degrees at the lower end of the scale, and it remains the case that the army of the early fourth century was for the most part pagan in its religious allegiances. This must particularly have been the case with the army which Constantine led against Maxentius in 312, recruited as it was primarily from Gaul and Germany, where Christianity's impact will at that stage have been limited. The fact that Constantine's dramatic victory over Maxentius persuaded him to support the Christian god did not automatically mean that the rank and file of the army did so en masse as well, even if, as he later claimed, his troops had also witnessed the celestial sign which prompted him to turn to Christ for assistance (Eusebius *Life of Constantine* 1.28.2). Military success under the aegis of the Christians' deity no doubt encouraged soldiers to view Christianity in a more favorable light than previously, but success of this sort could also be accommodated within a pagan mindset; indeed, if it took Constantine himself some years to appreciate the full ramifications of adherence to Christianity, with the aid of clerical advisers (Averil Cameron 1983), then it was going to be an even slower process for the ordinary untutored soldier, assuming he was interested in the first place.

Until he gained control of the whole empire in 324, at the very earliest, Constantine could certainly not afford to alienate the army by introducing wholesale changes with regard to religious practices – a situation reflected in the report that on one occasion Constantine reluctantly participated in pagan rites in Rome "out of fear of the soldiers" (Zosimus 2.29.5, with discussion in Paschoud 1971: it is unclear whether this episode should be assigned to 312, 315, or 326). If, as seems likely, he did not prohibit the observance of traditional religious ritual in the army camps,[5] this did not apparently hold him back from introducing various measures designed to inculcate Christianity into the army, as described in the passage which opens this section.

In the midst of Eusebius' enthusiastic reportage, it is possible to lose sight of the obstacles which Constantine's measures had to overcome, particularly the sheer conservatism and loyalty to traditions which are an integral part of any military culture, as well as the practical problem of ensuring that officers in charge of units posted in parts of the empire removed from Constantine's direct presence maintained the observance of these practices on a regular basis, when the great majority of those officers are unlikely to have been Christians themselves (cf. Julian's later reliance on officers to win Christian soldiers back to paganism: Gregory of Nazianzus *Orations* 4.64). On the other hand, it is worth recalling the importance of ritual and symbolism in the traditional religious life of the army, so that regular recitation of what was essentially a Christian prayer by the troops who did not yet consider themselves Christian, and familiarity with Christian symbols, especially in the context of military standards and the reverence which they had traditionally

ARMY, WARFARE, AND RELIGION

attracted (if one assumes that the "saving trophy" in the final line of the opening passage above is the famous *labarum* bearing the *chi-rho* monogram), had the potential to have some sort of effect on the soldiers. Constantine is also credited with providing each unit with its own mobile tent to serve as a chapel, complete with associated priests and deacons (Sozomen *Church History* 1.8). If this is true, the presence of such personnel would have held out the greatest hope of effecting the "re-education" of the rank and file, but in the absence of any corroborative evidence for "military chaplains" before the fifth century (particularly Eusebius' silence on the subject), alongside the fact that the source for Constantine's creation of them was himself writing in the mid fifth century, scholars have generally been skeptical about their existence in the fourth century (see further below, pp. 191–2). Even if, therefore, some older soldiers in the 360s claimed to recall receiving instruction in the Christian faith from Constantine himself (Theodoret *Church History* 4.1.6), it was also the case that a group of them had no hesitation about greeting the emperor in 326 with the pagan acclamation "May the gods preserve you," in a context where it was not in their interests to antagonize him (they were seeking confirmation of their privileges) (*Theodosian Code* 7.20.2), and the likelihood is that Christianity made only slow progress among the ranks during the half century after Constantine's own conversion in 312.[6]

The accession of Julian in 361 provides the clearest confirmation of this conclusion. Had a majority of the army embraced Christianity by this stage, one might have expected there to have been a negative reaction to the advent of an emperor who quickly made known his true, pagan religious sympathies and who lost little time in promoting traditional rituals and undoing Constantine's measures to support the church. In fact, however, he seems to have been able to gain the support of the troops without too much difficulty, although there was some difference in attitude between those from the less Christianized west and those from the more Christianized east, and he had to resort to wily tactics to win over some of the latter. Even while the outcome of his challenge to the reigning emperor Constantius II remained in the balance, Julian was able to report from Naissus in the Balkans that "I worship the gods openly, and the whole mass of the troops who are returning with me [from Gaul] worship the gods – I sacrifice oxen in public" (*Letter* 26 [Bidez]). Another source, however, draws a contrast between, on the one hand, the soldiers "that he had with him originally" – that is, those who had served under him in Gaul – "[who] entered the fight with the names of the gods on their lips," and on the other, "his recent acquisitions" – that is, those who had been part of Constantius II's eastern army:

> Feeling that their morale was lowered not just by bad leadership but also because they went into battle without the gods supporting them, he stayed where he was [in Antioch] for nine months [before embarking on his Persian

campaign in 363] procuring for them the turning of the scales, for he considered superiority in numbers, force of steel, strength of shield, and every single thing to be quite pointless if the gods were not on his side. His actions were designed to secure their active support: he induced the hand that grasped the spear to grasp offerings of incense and libation, so that they would be able to pray, when the weapons were flying, to those who had it in their power to forestall them. If persuasion proved insufficient, gold and silver co-operated to ensure adherence, and through this petty profit the soldiery secured the greater gain: by accepting a piece of gold, they won the friendship of the gods, the lords of war. (Libanius *Orations* 18.166–8 [tr. Norman])

Contemporary Christian commentators subsequently emphasized the resistance of some Christian soldiers to Julian's blandishments, but it is generally agreed that much of this is special pleading and that the overwhelming majority of soldiers were willing to embrace, or at the very least acquiesce in, Julian's changes in religious policy (see, e.g., Tomlin 1998: 32–5; Lenski 2002b: 275–6). The fact that the troops raised no objection to the resumption of Christian emperors after Julian's death strongly suggests that it is in fact more appropriate in this period to speak of the "relative indifference to religious changes" on the part of the army (Nock 1952: 226; cf. Jones 1963: 24–5; Gabba 1974: 104; Tomlin 1998: 33–6).

One important area of military life where Christianity did have a clear impact during the fourth century was the military oath (*sacramentum*). According to a military manual probably compiled during the reign of Theodosius I (379–95) (Milner 1996: xxxvii–xli), the wording of the oath by this period had acquired a clear Christian element:

> They swear by God, Christ and the Holy Spirit, and by the Majesty of the Emperor which second to God is to be loved and worshipped by the human race. For since the Emperor has received the name of Augustus, faithful devotion should be given, unceasing homage paid him as if to a present and corporeal deity. For it is God whom a private citizen or a soldier serves, when he faithfully loves him who reigns by God's authority. The soldiers swear that they will strenuously do all that the Emperor may command, will never desert the service, nor refuse to die for the Roman state. (Vegetius *Epitome of Military Science* 2.5 [tr. Milner])

It is not known which emperor introduced this change, though in the light of his other religious policies, Theodosius must be a strong candidate (cf. Lippold 1973: 942).[7] Vegetius says nothing to suggest that this oath was only to be sworn by those from a Christian background, and one should not underestimate the slow but cumulative impact of new recruits being inducted into military service through this explicitly Christian formula within a culture and tradition where the oath had far-reaching connotations (cf. above, Chapter 2.1.1, p. 52).

Theodosius' religious policies most famously included a final ban on pagan sacrifice in 391. Presumably this ban was implemented within the military context as much as elsewhere (which is not to say that its implementation generally was not uneven and very much dependent on the attitude and sympathies of local officials (cf. Bradbury 1994: 132–9) – and, in the case of the army, officers). One possible, albeit small, indication of implementation in the military context might be the series of Mithraic shrines in Britain destroyed in fourth-century contexts, which some have interpreted as a reflection of policy, rather than just being random.[8]

At the same time, there is also evidence from the late fourth century for the construction of churches within military forts at sites along the northern frontier – at Zurzach, Kaiseraugst, Boppard, and Koblenz on the Rhine (Petrikovits 1971: 203), and at Richborough in Britain (P. D. C. Brown 1971), with further possibilities at South Shields (Bidwell and Speak 1994: 45, 103–4), Housesteads (Crow 1995: 96–7), and, from the mid fourth century, at Saldum and nearby Zanes (Donje Butork) on the middle Danube, where, interestingly, what look like chapel-shaped structures have been integrated into the design of forts of apparently Valentinianic date (Petrović 1980). As has been observed, however, "overall [this evidence] does seem rather slight, compared with the hundreds of pagan temples that clustered around the forts of the Principate" (Tomlin 1998: 28).[9]

On the other hand, it is also worth noting that a significant portion of the fourth-century army – the *comitatenses* – did not reside in forts, but were instead resident in cities and towns when not on campaign (cf. Chapter 6.3 above, pp. 165–6), and one would not therefore normally expect to be able to identify such churches as individuals from these units may have frequented. A possible exception is perhaps provided by the church at Anemurium, on the south-east coast of Asia Minor, which contains mosaic inscriptions dedicated by three army officers (and perhaps a fourth), able to be dated with considerable precision on the basis of associated coin finds to around the year 400. One records a certain Bibianos (Vivianus?), who held the rank of *ducenarius* (a "commander of 200 men"), having dedicated a water channel in fulfillment of a vow, while another, intriguingly, was made by a "newly baptized" Flavius Telpullius in return for "the salvation of the unit (*numerus*)," perhaps more likely a reference to physical protection of his men rather than group conversion. If, as suggested by the inscriptions' editor, the unit was part of the *legio I Armeniaca*, then these are troops from the *comitatenses* under the command of the *magister militum per Orientem* (*Notitia Dignitatum (East)* 7.49) (Russell 1999, with further detail on the inscriptions in Russell 1987: 85–8 and Gibson 1998: 44–6).[10]

One further area for brief consideration is the religious complexion of the army's high command in the fourth century. A clear overall picture is elusive because, while the religious allegiance of some individuals is clear, that of others is unknown, and there are also cases where potentially relevant circumstantial detail is ambiguous. This has left plenty of scope for differing emphases. The most detailed study presents quite an optimistic view of the infiltration of Christianity among the senior ranks (von Haehling 1978: 527–606), although the study as a whole (which also deals with those holding high-ranking civilian posts) has lost some of its credibility as a result of the identification of methodological flaws (Barnes 1995).[11] Another recent study is more cautious in its assessment (Salzman 2002: 128–32), although the significance of its conclusions are limited by the fact that it deals only with the western half of the empire. What is not in doubt is that, irrespective of the precise number, there were generals from Constantius II's reign onward who were Christians, which must have at least some implications for the wider Christianization of the army. At the same time, it is evident that pragmatism sometimes prevailed over ideology when it came to military appointments: even Julian retained Christians as generals, just as subsequent Christian emperors retained the services of some commanders who were pagans.

Had the advent of Christian emperors resulted in a more uniformly positive view of military service in church teaching during the fourth century, then one might have expected a stronger influx of Christians into the ranks of the army. However, the range of stances which characterized the pre-Constantinian period persisted. The transitional figure of Lactantius was emphatic that "a just man may not be a soldier" (*Divine Institutes* 6.16), even if a possible hint of subsequent relaxation of attitude has been detected (Nicholson 1993), while in the late fourth century, Paulinus, bishop of Nola, can be found urging a soldier to leave the army in highly emotive language and in terms which rejected any rapprochement between church and state:

> If we love this world more, and prefer to be a soldier for Caesar rather than for Christ, we shall later be transported not to Christ but to hell, where the cause of the princes of this world rests . . . Therefore do not any longer love this world or its military service, for Scripture's authority attests that "whoever is a friend of this world is an enemy of God." He who is a soldier with the sword is a servant of death, and when he sheds his own blood or that of another, this is the reward for his service. He will be regarded as guilty of death either because of his own death or because of his sin, because a soldier in war, fighting not so much for himself as for another, is either conquered and killed, or conquers and wins a pretext for death – for he cannot be a victor until he first sheds blood. So the Lord says: "You cannot serve two masters," the one God and mammon, that is, Christ and Caesar, even though Caesar himself is now keen to be Christ's servant so that he may deserve kingship over a few peoples. (Paulinus of Nola *Letters* 25.1, 3 [tr. Walsh])

Basil of Caesarea, on the other hand, was more positive, while also expressing reservations about some aspects of the soldier's activities. Although quite prepared to urge one acquaintance to give up the military for the ascetic life (*Letters* 116), he nevertheless included "those who are enrolled in military service" alongside "our brethren who are sojourning abroad" and "those who speak out boldly for the sake of the name of the Lord" in a list of categories of people for whom the church had a responsibility to offer prayers (*Letters* 155), while elsewhere he stated that "our fathers did not consider killing in war as murder because, in my view, they forgave those who defended wisdom and piety. Nevertheless, it is perhaps good to advise them to abstain from communion for three years, since their hands are unclean" (*Letters* 188.).[12] Augustine took a favorable view of military service in his comments to an acquaintance of his, the military officer Bonifatius, while also making clear that war needed to be waged for the right reasons:

> You must not think that no-one who serves as a soldier, using arms for warfare, can be acceptable to God. The holy David was one such, and the Lord offered a great witness to him. Very many other just men of the same period were also soldiers... [However,] peace ought to be what you want, war only what necessity demands. Then God may free you from necessity and preserve you in peace. For you don't seek peace in order to stir up war; no – war is waged in order to obtain peace. Be a peacemaker, therefore, even in war, so that by conquering them you bring the benefit of peace even to those you defeat... And just as you use force against the rebel or opponent, so you ought now to use mercy toward the defeated or the captive, and particularly so when there is no fear that peace will be disturbed. (*Letters* 189.4, 6 [tr. Atkins, in Atkins and Dodaro 2001: 216–17])[13]

Church councils during this period offer another perspective on ecclesiastical attitudes to military service. The earliest pronouncement is also the most problematic. The third canon of the Council of Arles (314) laid down the exclusion from communion of soldiers who in peacetime *arma proiciunt*. While the meaning of the reference to peacetime has occasioned some debate – is it simply peacetime as opposed to war, or is it perhaps a reference to the fact that, with the emergence of a Christian emperor in the person of Constantine, the church now enjoyed peace from persecution? – it is the interpretation of *proiciunt* which has proved most contentious. Traditionally this has been taken to mean soldiers who throw away their weapons, thereby implying the church's condemnation of deserters and endorsement of military service. However, *proiciunt* can also mean "thrust out," in which case this becomes a condemnation of soldiers using their weapons to disturb the peace – a more coherent and plausible interpretation.[14] Subsequent councils accepted the presence of Christians in the army, but also imposed restrictions of one sort or another on them, particularly in the event of their wishing subsequently to pursue a career in the church. So the Council of Rome (386) ruled that military service after baptism was forbidden to anyone who wished to become a member of the clergy (Canon 3), and the Council of Toledo (400) decided that anyone who had undertaken military service could assume an office no higher than deacon (Canon 8) (Noethlichs 2001: 21 n.90).[15] In a similar vein, the absence of a triumphalist spirit has been noted in fourth-century liturgies (Taft 1995: 29–31). Reservations about the compatibility of Christianity and military service clearly persisted.

7.1.3. The fifth and sixth centuries

> Whether the unit is in service with the rest of the army or is camping someplace by itself, the *Trisagion* ["the threefold holy" (a hymn)] must be sung, and the other customary practices observed, early in the morning before any other duty and again in the evening after supper and the dismissal... Prayers should be said in camp on the actual day of battle before anyone goes out the gate. All, led by the priests, the general, and the other officers, should recite the *Kyrie eleison* ["Lord have mercy"] for some time in unison. Then, in hopes of success, each unit should shout the *Deus nobiscum* ["God with us"] three times as it marches out of camp. (Ps.-Maurice *Strategy* 7B.17, 2.18 [tr. Dennis])

Theodosius' ban on pagan sacrifice in 391 did not, of course, result in the prompt elimination of pagan ritual from the Roman world or the rapid emergence of a thoroughly Christianized empire. The long history of traditional cults, deeply embedded into local cultures, ensured that they maintained an ongoing, if less obvious, existence for a long time to come, as did the problems presented by the sheer size of the empire and the practical difficulties of enforcing imperial law. But while acknowledging the longevity of traditional cults, even into the sixth century and beyond, it is also apparent that the religious orientation of the empire did undergo a slow but steady transformation during the fifth and sixth centuries, and one would expect this to have been reflected in the religious complexion of the army.[16] Indeed it ought, in principle, to have been somewhat easier to monitor and enforce the ban on sacrifice within the framework of the army than it was in society more generally. One reflection of change is provided by the military manual attributed to the emperor Maurice from which the passage which opens this section comes: notwithstanding its status as a handbook of recommendations and advice for generals, it presupposes that by the late sixth century military life was conducted within a framework of Christian ritual.

Mapping this change in the military, however, is rather less easy. The fifth century in particular presents difficulties on this front, owing to the relative paucity of surviving evidence compared with the fourth and sixth centuries, although one of the bishop Theodoret's letters (145) is relevant: Theodoret wrote in response to a request from a group of soldiers seeking elucidation of a rather rarefied theological question concerning the nature of God; not only is it significant that these soldiers wrote on a matter of theology, but Theodoret wrote back at length and with a degree of detail which presupposes considerable theological knowledge on their part. By the sixth century there are further indications that the rank and file were Christianized in more than just a superficial manner. It is not just a question of the performance of certain Christian rituals by those in leadership in the presence of an army, such as the patriarch of Constantinople praying for a blessing on the expedition against the Vandals in 533 before it left Constantinople for north Africa (Procopius *Wars* 3.12.2), the general Belisarius invoking God's assistance on the eve of important battles in north Africa (Procopius *Wars* 3.19.11, 4.1.21), or another general, Philippicus, parading an icon before the troops to inspire them in the battle of Solachon in 586 (Theophylact Simocatta 2.3.4–6). These are situations where it is not possible to deduce the attitude of the troops themselves to what is going on, even if the apparently enthusiastic response of the troops to the display of the icon at Solachon is potentially significant.

More telling with regard to the religious complexion of the army in this period are circumstantial details which imply something about the religious stance of the rank and file. In his description of the events leading up to the battle with a Persian force at Callinicum on the Euphrates in the early spring of 531, Procopius refers to the Roman soldiers having been weakened by their observation of the fast on the eve of Easter (*Wars* 1.18.15–16, 37) – an action on their part which, because of the self-denial involved, is a significant indicator of religious allegiance.[17] Similarly, in his account of the background to the conflict between Roman forces and the north African Laguatan on the "Plains of Cato" in 548, Corippus describes the Roman soldiers as being occupied with their "customary rites" (*solitis sacris*) on the Sunday before the battle (*Iohannis* 8.213–23, 254–6, 321–9; cf. Theophylact Simocatta 2.2.7, where Persian forces deliberately attack Roman troops on a Sunday in 586 on the assumption that, "out of respect for its sanctity," they will be resting and therefore unprepared). That such examples are not more common is more likely to reflect the reluctance of authors writing within "classicizing" traditions of history and panegyric to compromise their genres by including too much detail about "unclassical" Christianity (cf. Michael Whitby 1998: 194).

This gradual change in the army's religious complexion can be accounted for in a number of ways. If the empire at large was gradually Christianized, including rural areas, then this will have been reflected increasingly in the army's recruits, even if it is apparent that pockets of rural paganism survived in the mid sixth century (Trombley 1985a). There is also the question of the role of legislation. One historian refers to a law from the early fifth century which prohibited pagans from serving in the army (Zosimus 5.49), but it is difficult to find an unambiguous law to this effect in the *Theodosian Code* from this period (cf. Paschoud's discussion of this passage in the Budé edition of Zosimus). There are laws banning pagans from imperial *militia* which have been taken by some as referring to the army (e.g., Clauss 1986: 1108; Noethlichs 1986: 1165), but this term could of course equally refer to service in the bureaucracy, as indeed seems to be the case with the most likely candidate, a law from 416:

189

> Those persons who are polluted by the profane false doctrine or crime of pagan rites, that is, the pagans, shall not be admitted to the imperial service (*militia*), and they shall not be honoured with the rank of administrator or magistrate. (*Theodosian Code* 16.10.21 [tr. Pharr])

This stands in contrast with another law from around the same time which very explicitly banned Jews from military service:

> We decree that those persons who are bound to the perversity of this race and who are proved to have sought armed imperial service (*militia armata*) shall unquestionably be released from the belt of office (*cingulum*), and they shall not be protected by the patronage of their earlier merits. (*Theodosian Code* 16.8.24 [tr. Pharr])

If there was a ban on pagans serving in the army in the early decades of the fifth century, then it does not appear to have been observed with regard to the highest ranks of the army, since a number of avowed pagans are found in senior positions until the middle of the fifth century, viz. Apollonius (*magister militum praesentalis*, 443–51: Theodoret *Letters* 73), Flavius Zeno (*magister militum Orientis*, 447–51: Theodoret *Letters* 71), Litorius (military officer in Gaul in the late 430s: *PLRE* II.685), and Marcellinus (commander in Dalmatia in the mid fifth century: McGeorge 2002: 42–6 for the evidence of his pagan associations).

It is in relation to the early sixth century that there is less ambiguous evidence for Christianizing legislation applied to the army. Two later Syriac sources refer to a law, apparently issued in the early years of the reign of Justin I, which required soldiers to adhere not just to Christianity, but to the doctrinal stance associated with the Council of Chalcedon (451) (see Gray 2005 for an overview of the theological issues), with the penalty for non-adherence being loss of rations (*annona*) and other privileges arising from their military service (Jacob of Edessa *Chronicle* p. 240; Michael the Syrian *Chronicle* 9.16). Vasiliev (1950: 242–3) has argued that an associated part of this legislation is preserved in the *Justinianic Code*:

> Nobody can be enrolled into the army unless three witnesses on the Holy Gospels testify that he is an orthodox Christian; the transaction is to take place in the presence of the commander under whom he is to serve; and a fee of two *nomismata* is to be paid for this [transaction]. But if this [edict] is violated, the commander shall pay fifty pounds of gold, his staff twenty, and the person enrolled ten; he shall be dismissed, and the false witnesses shall undergo corporal punishment. And penalties are to be paid to the imperial treasury at the peril of the count (*comes*). (*Justinianic Code* 1.4.20 [tr. Vasiliev])

This law raises a number of issues. First, the fact it stipulates adherence not just to Christianity *per se* but to orthodox Chalcedonian Christianity raises the question of the presence in the late Roman army of individuals and groups who adhered to heterodox versions of Christianity, a subject which will be considered later in this section. Secondly, there is the broader question of the extent to which it was possible to enforce legislation such as this, even if one of the late Syriac sources says that the majority adhered to the requirement (Michael the Syrian *Chronicle* 9.16). Certainly the specificity of the requirements – the three witnesses, an oath on the gospels, the presence of the commander, and the calibrated penalties – implies serious intent on the part of the government.[18] On the other hand, in an age when there was never an abundance of military manpower, it is difficult to imagine most officers in, say, staunchly Monophysite Egypt turning away a suitable recruit on the grounds of his religious allegiances.

While one might have legitimate doubts about the efficacy of a legislative strategy, however, there may have been more scope for the role of education in bringing about religious change. One of the most interesting developments apropos the religious life of soldiers in the fifth century is the evidence for the existence of what have been referred to as "military chaplains." As noted earlier (Chapter 7.1.2, p. 183), the church historian Sozomen claimed that Constantine created them, but in the absence of any corroborative evidence, it is generally assumed that they emerged as an institution in the first half of the fifth century (when, indeed, Sozomen was writing). The most detailed evidence about them derives from a letter from Theodoret, bishop of Cyrrhus, to Eusebius, bishop of Ancyra, probably written during the 440s:

> The promise of our God and Saviour is true, for he promised that the teaching of God's word should be diffused over all the world, and the facts cry out, bearing witness to this saying. For the foster sons of piety and those deemed worthy of the priesthood direct not only provinces, cities, villages, estates and farms; but the regiments of soldiers stationed in cities and villages themselves too have consecrated shepherds. Among these is the very devout deacon Agapetus, who claims as his city the metropolis of our province [Hierapolis], and has been appointed to guide a military regiment in things divine. That is why he has started for Thrace; for his unit happens to be stationed there. (Theodoret *Letters* II [tr. Jones (1953)])

Theodoret's letter is of great interest because it implies that these "military chaplains" were widespread among military units, if not universal, while it also suggests a conscious and potentially practical strategy for advancing the Christianization of the army. There is corroborative evidence for the existence of the office in Cyril of Scythpolis' *Life of St. Saba* (9), who reports that when Saba visited Alexandria in the late 450s or early 460s, he happened to encounter his father, who was now commander of unit there and who tried to persuade him to undertake military service by becoming the priest (*presbuteros*) of his unit (see Jones 1953 for this reading of the text, against the editor's unnecessary emendation). Presumably, too, the priest referred to by Corippus as conducting the eucharist on the eve of the battle of the "Plains of Cato" in 548 (*Iohannis* 8.221, 326, 363) was a military chaplain, as also the priests leading troops in the *Kyrie eleison* in the *Strategikon* attributed to Maurice (2.18).[19]

To all this can be added various items of documentary evidence. First, there is epigraphic testimony, in the form of an epitaph from Panium in Thrace, erected in commemoration of his wife by a certain Ioannes, deacon of the *numerus Defensorum* (Asdracha 1998: 320 [no. 146]). This is a unit attested in the *Notitia Dignitatum* (*East* 5.57) as one of the elite units of *auxilia palatina* under the command of one of the two *magistri militum praesentales*, whose forces were based in the hinterland of Constantinople (cf. Chapter 6.3, p. 165) – entirely consistent with this epitaph's location in Panium. The inscription can only be dated very broadly to the fifth or sixth centuries, but it remains important as the only epigraphic evidence for the office thus far. Secondly, there are some items of papyrological evidence. The most important of these is a (partially preserved) document from the late fifth or early sixth century listing individuals under the commander responsible for the southern half of Egypt, including a "first priest" (*protopresbuteros*) and at least four priests (*presbuteroi*) alongside individuals holding more obvious military ranks such as those of *domesticus* and *protector* (*CPR* 24.15 with discussion in Palme 2002: 90–7). There is also a sixth-century papyrus from the village of Nessana in the Negev (*P. Nessana* 35). This document is a list of the members of the military unit based there to whom camels or dromedaries have been assigned, and it includes a dromedary for "the holy church of the camp" (*hagia ekklesia tou kastrou*), and, on the next line, a camel for "Faysan the priest" (*presbuteros*). The church is taken by the editor of the text to be that of Saints Sergius and Bacchus (appropriate military saints) built against the north wall of the fort. The fact that military chaplains never feature in the narratives of Procopius and other sixth-century histories ought not to occasion surprise, since the classicizing canons according to which they wrote would have precluded mention of such an unclassical institution.[20]

Discussion to this point has focused on Christianization of the army vis-à-vis adherence to traditional pagan cults. However, as Justin's law about Chalcedonian orthodoxy highlights, there is the further issue of the presence in the empire's armed forces of individuals who subscribed to heterodox versions of Christianity, which warrants brief comment. Although Theodosius I took steps early in his reign to resolve the Arian controversy which had been one of the main theological disputes of the fourth century, its significance in relation to the army actually increased from around this time, essentially because of the influx of Gothic units into the army and the fact that the majority of Goths had converted to Arian Christianity (see Lenski 1995 for a survey of the debate about the timing of this development). Gothic units continued to play a major role in the eastern army throughout the fifth century. Partly because the empire needed their manpower and partly because of the military power they controlled, there was an understandable reluctance on the part of the authorities to discriminate too strictly against Arianism. The importance of the Arian component in the army of the fifth century is reflected in the number of barbarian generals in this period who were also Arians, most famously Aspar (who was, however, an Alan rather than a Goth). As a result, Arian clerics and churches continued to exist in the hinterland of Constantinople (Greatrex 2001).

Although Justin I was known for his upholding of orthodoxy, he made an exception in relation to Arian Goths serving in the armed forces (*Justinianic Code* 1.5.12.17). However, just over a decade later, the Arian churches in the east were finally seized by the government (Malalas *Chronicle* p. 479), partly as a result of successful campaigning by Justinian's forces against Arian regimes in north Africa and Italy (which included the seizure of Arian churches in those parts); partly because of the fact that most Arian units were probably by this stage in north Africa, where they had proceeded to revolt; and partly because of the government's ever-present need for funds (Greatrex 2001). Even then, it is apparent that there continued to be an Arian presence in the army, perhaps as a result of subsequent recruitment, for in the late 570s, the wives of Gothic soldiers dispatched to the eastern frontier requested that the emperor Tiberius assign them a church in Constantinople where they could worship according to Arian principles (John of Ephesus *Church History* 3.13).[21]

7.2. The Army and Religious Policy

The religious changes of late antiquity did not just affect the army in terms of military ritual and the religious allegiances of soldiers. These changes also had far-reaching implications for the roles that the army was expected to play in late Roman society. In particular, soldiers are found implementing policies which discriminated, at different times, against Christians and pagans, and enforcing imperial decisions about church politics. These areas of involvement prompt a number of questions: to what extent were these novel functions for the army? What was the attitude of soldiers to such involvement? And how effective was the use of military force in these contexts?

7.2.1. *The army and persecution*

When this day dawned during the consulship of both the old men [Diocletian and Maximian, 303]..., suddenly while it was still twilight, the prefect came to the church [in Nicomedia] with military leaders (*duces*), tribunes and accountants; they forced open the doors and searched for the image of God; they found the scriptures and burnt them; all were granted booty; the scene was one of plunder, panic and confusion...Then the praetorians came in formation, bringing axes and other iron tools, and after being ordered in from every direction they levelled the lofty edifice to the ground within a few hours. (Lactantius *On the Deaths of the Persecutors* 12.2–5 [tr. Creed])

During the third and early fourth centuries, there were three major persecutions of Christians by the imperial authorities – those of Decius (249–51), Valerian (257–60), and Diocletian (303–11). These persecutions differed from earlier instances in two important and related ways: they were instigated centrally and they were empire-wide, rather than being localized responses to pressure from specific communities.[22] As such, they can legitimately be viewed as examples of religious policies in a way which earlier persecutions were not. Soldiers undoubtedly featured in the more localized persecutions of the pre-Decian period, whether as apprehenders, guards, or executioners of Christians (Lopuszanski 1951), and continued to perform such tasks in the Decian, Valerianic, and Diocletianic persecutions (e.g., Eusebius *Church History* 6.40.4–6, 7.11.22; *Martyrdom of Felix* 31 [= Musurillo 1972: 270]), but they also assumed more prominent roles: "the beginning of systematic and comprehensive suppression [of Christianity] in the mid third century... brought more active participation by the military forces" (Nippel 1995: 107). This was particularly the case during the so-called "Great Persecution" of the early fourth century, by virtue of the wider range of measures which Diocletian tried to implement. One novel aspect of Diocletian's measures was the destruction of church buildings, which, in the case of Nicomedia, certainly involved a significant body of troops, as the passage above shows. Another incident involving substantial numbers of soldiers is reported by the church historian Eusebius (cf. Mitchell 1993: II.57):

> A little Christian town in Phrygia was encircled by legionaries, who set it on fire and completely destroyed it, along with the entire population – men, women, and children – as they called on Almighty God. And why? Because all the inhabitants of the town without exception – the chief magistrate himself and the other magistrates, with all the officials and the whole populace – declared themselves Christians and absolutely refused to obey the command to commit idolatry. (Eusebius *Church History* 8.11.1 [tr. Williamson])

Eusebius also refers to the use of military tribunes and centurions in the drawing up of detailed lists of inhabitants in the east, in preparation for the implementation of the fourth edict in 305 which required everyone to offer sacrifice (Eusebius *Martyrs of Palestine* 4.8 [long recension]). While such episodes can be seen as a simple extension of past practice with regard to the use of the army in relation to religious policy, there is also a sense in which they represent a qualitative shift.

Although the advent of Christian emperors did not immediately result in reciprocal policies of persecution of pagans across the board, the destruction of cult statues and shrines was something which did occur periodically during the fourth century, often again with the involvement of soldiers, even if not always with direct imperial approval. So, for example, although Constantine did not order the destruction of all temples in the empire (cf. Libanius *Orations* 30.6), he did act against a small number which he regarded as particularly reprehensible for one reason or another:

> The emperor... perceived from afar a dire trap for souls lurking in the province of Phoenicia. This was a grove and precinct... founded for the hateful demon Aphrodite in the mountainous part of Lebanon at Aphaca... On the emperor's command the devices of licentious error were at once destroyed and a detachment of soldiers saw to the clearing of the site. (Eusebius *Life of Constantine* 3.55 [trs. Cameron and Hall])

To this instance can be added Constantine's destruction of the temple of Asclepius in Cilicia, "pulled down by a military force" (Eusebius *Life of Constantine* 3.56; cf. also 3.57, with its more general reference to how "forbidden innermost sanctuaries of temples were trodden by soldiers' feet"). There are further cases from later in the fourth century, even if the role of imperial initiative in these episodes is sometimes less clear: the looting of the Serapeum in Alexandria in 360, with the aid of troops under the authority of the military commander (*dux*) of Egypt (Sozomen *Church History* 4.30); the attacks of the praetorian prefect Cynegius Maternus on Syrian temples during the mid 380s, with the aid of military units (Fowden 1978: 62–4); the attacks of the governor of Egypt on the Serapeum in 391 (Fowden 1978: 69–70: Haas 1997: 159–69); and the demolition of temples in Gaza in 402, in which military units played a leading role (Mark the Deacon *Life of Porphyry* 63, 65).[23]

It is difficult to find parallels for this sort of military activity against religious sites – whether pagan or Christian – prior to the late Roman period. Potential precedents for consideration include Titus' destruction of the temple in Jerusalem in 70, and perhaps also, from a decade earlier, Suetonius Paulinus' cutting down of the sacred groves of the Druids on the island of Anglesey in Wales (Tacitus *Annals* 14.30). One might also add the demolition of temples of Isis and Serapis in the city of Rome on various occasions during the late Republic and first century AD (Beard et al. 1998: I.161), and going back further, the destruction of Bacchic shrines in Italy on the order of the senate in 186 BC (Livy 39.18). Yet there do seem to be differences between these instances from the Republic and Principate, on the one hand, and the late Roman examples on the other. In the cases of the temple of Jerusalem and the Druids' groves, where the army had a clear role in the destruction, it is apparent that Roman actions were motivated primarily by political rather than religious concerns – they were part of a concerted effort to suppress opposition to Roman rule, not to eliminate the particular religion or cult on religious grounds. With regard to the shrines of Isis, Serapis, and Bacchus, the sources are silent about military involvement, though admittedly, the episodes involving Isis and Serapis are only known from generally brief notices anyway; the Bacchic episode, on the other hand, receives very full treatment from Livy, who nonetheless says nothing about how the shrines were destroyed beyond the fact that the task was entrusted to the consuls, while elsewhere in his account, responsibility for preventing Bacchic assemblies was given to civilian officials (specifically aediles and *triumviri capitales*: 39.18.14). Perhaps more importantly, however, recent analyses of Roman action against these cults have also placed the emphasis on the political anxieties which they occasioned (Beard et al. 1998: I.272). By contrast, during the later third and fourth century religious allegiances became increasingly polarized – a development in which Decius' edict has been seen as marking a critical stage: "it was only when a 'religion of the Empire' had been defined and its boundaries set that there could be a systematic persecution of people who transgressed those boundaries" (Rives 1999: 153). In this climate, religious motivations appear to be predominant in the destruction of religious buildings, whether Christian or pagan, and the use of the army to enforce these religious policies can be seen, correspondingly, as a new departure.

How did soldiers react to their involvement in the implementation of these religious policies? As far as persecution of Christians is concerned, there are occasional indications that Christian soldiers sometimes found it too much to stand by silently while fellow-believers were tortured or executed, preferring to make an open declaration of their faith and suffer the consequences (e.g., Eusebius *Church History* 6.41.16, 22). With regard to the more specific policy of destruction of churches during the Diocletianic persecution, there will have been rather less difficulty, for the simple reason that a purge of Christians from the army had been conducted a few years prior to 303 (Eusebius *Church History* 8.4; cf. p. 181 above).

Destruction of cult statues and shrines in the fourth century, on the other hand, ought to have presented more problems, given the relatively slow Christianization of the army during that period (cf. Chapter 7.1.2 above). Yet the various surviving episodes of temple destruction contain no hint of opposition or reluctance on the part of the soldiers involved. A number of considerations may help to explain this apparent paradox. The first is the chronological spread of known incidents. Although it is not possible to compile a comprehensive catalogue of all such incidents, owing to the likelihood of gaps in the source record, it does look like such incidents became more frequent in the final decades of the fourth century – a pattern which is certainly consistent with the more general tenor of imperial policy toward pagan cults in this period, which undoubtedly saw a hardening of attitudes in the 380s and 390s. By this stage, there will have been more time for Christianity to have had an impact on those serving in the army and on the regions from which they were recruited. A second consideration is the geographical distribution of known incidents involving military units – namely, they all come from the eastern provinces of the empire.[24] As already noted (pp. 182–3), the eastern half of the empire was Christianized more rapidly than the west, and although troops serving in the east had not necessarily been recruited from that half of the empire, there is nevertheless a potentially interesting correlation here. With regard to the west, by contrast, it has been noted that in the accounts of the activities of western bishops such as Martin of Tours and Maximus of Turin, "there is no good evidence that either was ever supported by the civil authorities or the army" (Fowden 1978: 71).

Of course if the fourth century army was largely religiously indifferent (cf. Chapter 7.1.2 above, pp. 183–4), then perhaps the explanation for their willingness to participate in the destruction of temples and cult objects is less problematic. On the other hand, indifference is one thing in situations where all that is required is acquiescence, whereas destruction of sacred sites and their paraphernalia involves more active agreement. One might invoke the argument that military habits of obedience overcame any residual objections, in which case the outlook of the individual in command becomes more important. It is of interest, therefore (though perhaps unsurprising), that where the identity of the individual in command is known, he was often an avowed Christian – so, the *dux* Artemius in Alexandria in 360, the praetorian prefect Cynegius Maternus in the mid 380s, and another Cynegius who oversaw the destruction in Gaza in 402.[25]

Accounts of some of these episodes, however, suggest another, more persuasive explanation for the willingness of soldiers who might otherwise have hesitated about engaging in the destruction of cult statues and shrines – the prospect of booty. Temples were usually the repositories of quantities of votive offerings, a proportion of which was likely to be made of precious metals – the quantities and proportion would obviously correlate with the reputation and fame of a particular shrine, though even relatively insignificant temples might accrue substantial amounts with the passage of time, judging by the inventory from a minor Egyptian temple (*P. Oxyrhynchus* 1449). Although Constantine stripped temples of much of their treasure in order to finance the development of Constantinople (Libanius *Orations* 30.6), it is apparent that temples either retained some of their treasure or acquired fresh offerings during the decades after Constantine. In describing the attack on the Serapeum in 360, one source refers to the soldiers' involvement in "robbing the images and votive offerings and decoration in the temples" (Sozomen *Church History* 4.30), while the account of the destruction in Gaza includes the following detail:

> The admirable Cynegius arrived [in Gaza] after ten days, along with the provincial governor, the military commander (*dux*), and a great military and civilian host... On the following day, Cynegius, having called together the

inhabitants, in the presence of the commander and the governor, promulgated the imperial rescript which ordered that the places of idol worship be torn down and given over to the flames. As soon as the idol worshippers heard this, they raised a loud lament, so that the leaders became angry and, with threats, sent soldiers against them to beat them with clubs and cudgels... After the soldiers had been given the order, in company with the Christians of the city and of the coastal region that belonged to it, they moved against the places of idol worship... Some they tore down, others they gave over to the flames, plundering all the precious furnishings in them. But St Porphyry had pronounced in church a condemnation on any Christian citizen who took anything at all from the places of idol worship for his own gain. Therefore none of the faithful citizens took anything, except the soldiers and the foreign residents who were present there. (Mark the Deacon *Life of Porphyry* 63, 65 [tr. Rapp])[26]

The potential conflict of interests on the part of soldiers ordered to assist in the destruction of sacred objects and sites presumably became increasingly less problematic during the fifth century,[27] although specific examples of troops being involved in the destruction of temples after 402 are few.[28] Even the most famous instance is something of a conundrum: troops are said to have been ordered by Justinian to dismantle the temple of Isis at Philae in southern Egypt in 529 (Procopius *Wars* 1.19.37), but the building in fact remained standing following its conversion into a church during the sixth century (Nautin 1967).[29]

7.2.2. *The army and church controversies*

While we were keeping vigil in the Lord's house and engaged in our prayers..., suddenly about midnight, the most illustrious *dux* Syrianus attacked us and the church with many units of soldiers, armed with naked swords, javelins and other warlike instruments, and wearing helmets on their heads. While we were actually praying and while the lessons were being read, they broke down the doors. When the doors burst open under the violence of the multitude, he gave the command and some of them were shooting, other shouting, their arms rattling, and their swords flashing in the light of the lamps; and immediately, virgins were being slain, men trampled down and falling over one another as the soldiers came upon them, and several were pierced with arrows and perished. Some of the soldiers were helping themselves to plunder and were stripping the virgins, who were more afraid of even being touched by them than they were of death. (Athanasius *History of the Arians* 8.81.6 [tr. Robertson])

An increasingly common phenomenon during the fourth century and beyond was the use of the army to intervene in internal disagreements within the church, as in this episode from Alexandria in 356. Athanasius' presentation of the incident is, of course, highly tendentious (cf. more generally Barnes 1993), but it remains the case that military force was deployed to enforce the will of the emperor Constantius II in the removal of Athanasius from his see and his replacement with Constantius' preferred candidate, the Arian sympathizer George of Cappadocia. Assisting in the removal of a bishop and his replacement with the imperially approved alternative was probably the most common way in which the army played a role in church politics during late antiquity, but there were also other roles, such as the related duty of accompanying a displaced bishop into exile, and acting to disperse supporters of an out-of-favor doctrinal position (see Table 7.1 for a summary of the evidence).

It is difficult to find any precedent before the fourth century for military intervention in the context of ecclesiastical disputes. The one possibility is perhaps the controversy surrounding Paul of Samosata in the late 260s and early 270s (Eusebius *Church History* 7.30, with Millar 1971). Paul was bishop of Antioch, but there was growing concern about his doctrinal stance (it seems that he did not recognize Christ as the son of God) and about his general behavior (it seems that he conducted himself like an imperial official, and not with the humility expected of a bishop). These concerns culminated in his excommunication by a church council in about 270. There remained a problem, however. Paul was an early pioneer of the "sit in" – he continued to occupy the church building in Antioch and he refused to vacate it. This in turn prompted church leaders to appeal to the emperor Aurelian, who gave judgment against Paul. As a result, Paul was "driven out" of the church (Eusebius *Church History* 7.30.19). Unfortunately, Eusebius does not elaborate on how he was driven out. The use of imperial troops must be a possibility, particularly given that one of the accusations against Paul was that he paraded around Antioch with a bodyguard (Eusebius *Church History* 7.30.8). However, in the absence of any explicit statement in the ancient sources, the use of the army in this situation can remain no more than surmise, and in fact there was an important difference between this episode and the doctrinal disputes of the fourth century and later. The point at issue as far as Aurelian was concerned was not religious – after all, he could not have been expected to appreciate the doctrinal niceties at stake; from his perspective, it was, rather, a question concerning ownership of property (cf. Watson 1999: 199).

Apart from this episode, in which any part played by the army must remain uncertain, it is difficult to suggest any other plausible precedent in Roman history for military intervention in the context of ecclesiastical disputes. Since traditional Roman cults emphasized ritual over belief, and since written texts did not play the pre-eminent role which they did in Christianity, there was much less scope for analogous situations to arise in pagan contexts. The closest potential parallel might be philosophical debates, but philosophical disagreements are not known to have provoked military intervention on any occasion in the Roman world. Nor are these interventions close analogies to military action to re-establish public order in situations of unrest created, for example, by the activities of the circus factions,[30] since in the case of

Table 7.1 Military intervention in church affairs in late antiquity

Date	Place	Details	Reference
317	Carthage	*Dux* Ursatius and soldiers attack Donatist churches allegedly in connivance with Caecilianus, with many killed, including two bishops	*Sermon on the Suffering of Donatus* (PL 8.752ff.)
339	Alexandria	Constantius replaces Athanasius as bishop with Gregory who is accompanied by troops; Athanasius flees before there is any bloodshed	Sozomen *Church History* 3.6
342	Constantinople	Constantius' attempt to remove the Nicaean bishop Paul with military force backfires, with the general Hermogenes being lynched by a mob	Socrates *Church History* 2.13; Sozomen *Church History* 3.7
344	Constantinople	Praetorian prefect Philippus expels Paul with military force who kill significant number of crowd	Socrates *Church History* 2.16; Sozomen *Church History* 3.9
347	Numidia	Donatists attack imperial officials distributing funds to Catholic churches; troops are called in and bloodshed ensues	Optatus 3.4; cf. *Acts of Maximian and Isaac* (PL 8.767–74; *Acts of Marculus* (PL 8.760–6) (but authenticity?)
356	Alexandria	Constantius replaces Athanasius as bishop with George, who is accompanied by the *dux* Syrianus, with 5,000 troops; Athanasius flees before there is any bloodshed	Athanasius *History of the Arians* 8.81.6; Socrates *Church History* 2.11
356	Alexandria	*Dux* Sebastianus expels Athanasius' supporters from churches	Athanasius *Acephalous History* 2.2
357	Alexandria	*Dux* Sebastianus and 3,000 soldiers disperse gathering of Athanasius' supporters from cemetery to west of city	Athanasius *In Defence of his Flight* 6–7
358	Alexandria	*Dux* Sebastianus and troops recover control of churches which Athanasius' supporters had occupied	Athanasius *Acephalous History* 2.4
358/9	Paphlagonia	With imperial approval, Macedonius, bishop of Constantinople, sends troops on abortive expedition to Paphlagonia to force Novatians to become Arians	Socrates *Church History* 2.38; Sozomen *Church History* 4.21
370	Constantinople	Troops sent from Nicomedia to oversee the exile of Evagrius	Socrates *Church History* 4.15; Sozomen *Church History* 6.13
370	Antioch	Valens uses troops to disperse Nicene congregation from meeting outside the city	Theodoret *Church History* 4.24.4
373	Alexandria	With imperial approval, the count of the sacred largesses Magnus takes a military force from Syria and imposes the Arian Lucius in place of the Nicene Peter; Lucius subsequently uses troops against Nicene monks	Socrates *Church History* 4.21; Theodoret *Church History* 4.19, 21

Date	Place	Event	Source
375	Edessa	On imperial instruction, praetorian prefect Modestus collects troops (normally used for collecting taxes) to disperse the Nicene congregation, though in the end he arrests leaders and sends them into exile	Theodoret *Church History* 4.17–18
380	Constantinople	Theodosius I deploys troops to ensure that Nicaean Christians regain control of the cathedral without opposition	Gregory of Nazianzus *Poem* 11 (*On his own life*) 1325–41
386	Milan	Troops try unsuccessfully to gain control of a church which Ambrose and supporters have occupied to prevent its use by Arians	Ambrose *Letters* 76 (20); Augustine *Confessions* 9.7
404	Constantinople	Soldiers are used to disperse supporters of John Chrysostom during services	Sozomen *Church History* 8.21, 23
404	Anatolia	Soldiers conduct John Chrysostom into exile at Pityus	Sozomen *Church History* 7.28
440s	Egypt	The exiled Nestorius is conducted by soldiers from Panopolis to Elephantine	Evagrius *Church History* 1.7
449	Ephesus	Bishops are forced to sign their agreement with the conclusions of the council, surrounded by soldiers with drawn swords	Evagrius *Church History* 2.18; Theophanes p. 101
451–2	Alexandria	After the removal of Dioscorus and his replacement by the pro-Chalcedonian Proterius as bishop, troops try to disperse angry mobs, without success; Marcian sends fresh troops from Constantinople to restore order	Evagrius *Church History* 2.5
453	Jerusalem	On imperial instruction, *dux* Dorotheus and troops depose Theodosius as bishop and replace him with Juvenalis	Ps.-Zachariah *Church History* 3.5
515/518	Syria	On imperial instruction, *dux* Asiaticus advances with troops to depose Severian of Arethusae and Cosmas of Epiphania, but when he sees the strength of public support for them, he warns the emperor of the likelihood of bloodshed, and the emperor relents	Evagrius *Church History* 3.34
535	Alexandria	Aristomachus, commander of troops, brings Theodosius book from exile and ejects Gainas; fighting between soldiers and populace ensues	John of Nikiu 92.4–5; Liberatus *Breviary* 20
539	Alexandria	Justinian sends Paul of Tinnis as new bishop, accompanied by troops	*History of the Patriarchs* 1.13 (*PO* 1, pp. 466–7)
552	Alexandria	Apollinarius requires military support to deal with popular opposition to his appointment as bishop	Liberatus *Breviary* 23

ecclesiastical controversies, it was more often than not military intervention itself which was responsible for generating rioting.

What of the attitude of soldiers to military interventions in doctrinal disputes and ecclesiastical politics (cf. MacCoull 1995)? In some ways, this is less problematic in the fourth century than soldiers assisting in the destruction of temples, since if one accepts that a majority of soldiers remained un-Christianized for much of the fourth century, then intervention for or against this or that particular party within the church will presumably have presented few moral dilemmas for them. This seems to have been the case, for example, when troops intervened against the supporters of John Chrysostom in Constantinople in 404:

> Under protest, on the grounds of what was likely to result, the *magister* granted them [i.e., the bishops opposed to John] the services of a certain Lucius, reputed to be a pagan, who was the leader of a unit of armed men... Lucius set off immediately, in the second watch of the night, accompanied by the clergy in the party of Acacius... He had with him four hundred newly enlisted Thracian swordsmen, completely reckless. With them and with the clergy as guides, he eagerly attacked the crowd. With his flashing sword, he cut his way through to the sacred waters [of baptism]. He prevented the celebration of the Saviour's resurrection and, seizing the deacons, he poured out the sacramental elements. Priests, already advanced in age, he beat about the head with clubs, and the font was stained with blood... Women, stripped for baptism, ran away to the sides of their husbands, forgetting their shame in fear of murder or dishonour. Here a man fled, crying and with a wounded hand, there another dragged off a virgin, tearing her clothes as he goes. They were all appropriating the treasures which they had seized as booty. (Palladius *Dialogue on the Life of John Chrysostom* pp. 57–8 [tr. Gregory (1979: 60), with revisions])

In this instance, the commander, Lucius, was certainly thought to be a pagan, and one modern commentator has stated that "the soldiers used in the attack were undoubtedly also pagans" (Gregory 1979: 61), though the sources are not explicit about this; indeed, if, as has been suggested (Liebeschuetz 1983: 21 n.136), "Thracians" is actually Palladius' way of referring to Goths, then they are more likely to have been Arian Christians.

A noteworthy feature of episodes from the fourth and early fifth century is the frequency with which there is, again, reference to the soldiers seizing booty: it occurs in the passage at the head of this section, and that relating to John Chrysostom above. It is of course interesting that the same theme is present in some accounts of temple destruction. This might incline one to suspect the deployment of a standard *topos* about military behavior, but some accounts are sufficiently detailed to make this unlikely.[31]

Even as those in the army became increasingly Christianized during the fifth and sixth centuries, is it realistic to expect them to have been *au fait* with the doctrinal disagreements which divided clergy? It seems that even members of the general public who were relatively uneducated nevertheless took a lively interest in doctrinal issues, if Gregory of Nyssa's famous complaint about the preoccupations of the populace of Constantinople in the early 380s is anything to go by:

> Everywhere throughout the city [Constantinople] is full of such things – the alleys, the squares, the thoroughfares, the residential quarters; among cloak salesmen, those in charge of the money-changing tables, those who sell us our food. For if you ask about change, they philosophize to you about the Begotten and the Unbegotten. And if you ask about the price of bread, the reply is, "The Father is greater, and the Son is subject to him." If you say, "Is the bath ready?," they declare the Son has his being from the non-existent. (Gregory of Nyssa *On the Divinity of the Son and the Holy Spirit* (*PG* 46.557))

The idea that the uneducated had some knowledge of doctrinal issues acquires plausibility from what is known of the efforts of theologians to disseminate their ideas through popular media. In the early fourth century Arius wrote popular ballads which reflected his theology, ballads which took the form of travel songs for journeys by land and sea, and work songs for the mill (Philostorgius *Church History* 2.2; cf. de Ste. Croix 1981: 450), while Augustine wrote an anti-Donatist ballad explicitly for popular consumption in the late fourth century (*Psalm against the Donatist faction* (*CSEL* 51.1–15); cf. Jones 1959: 327 n. 65). So one ought not to dismiss too quickly the possibility that soldiers were also exposed to and increasingly influenced by the theological currents of the late Roman period. Justin's law requiring soldiers to indicate their approval of the Council of Chalcedon presupposes awareness in the early sixth century, and the increasing presence of Arian Germans in the army will have been another way in which knowledge of doctrinal differences was disseminated within the military context.

There are a number of incidents which suggest that some soldiers at least had views about theological controversies in this period. Eusebius hints at the military taking sides in an ecclesiastical dispute in Antioch as early as the 320s (*Life of Constantine* 3.59.2); soldiers in Alexandria sympathetic to another heterodox group, the Meletians, hid Meletian clergy on one occasion in the mid 330s when supporters of Athanasius, aided by other soldiers, came looking for them (*P. London* 1914); and Julian seems to have suspected that it was the loyalty of Alexandrian soldiers to Athanasius which prevented his arrest (*Letters* 112).

Indirect corroboration of at least some soldiers having views on the doctrinal controversies of the day can perhaps also be found in various episodes, where the authorities seem to have gone to the trouble of using troops from outside of the locality. This is likely to have been the point of using troops stationed outside Alexandria to arrest Athanasius on one occasion (Athanasius *Acephalous History* 1.10; Sozomen *Church History* 4.9), as also the use of the Thracians to deal with the supporters of John Chrysostom in the passage quoted above – there must have been a concern that troops from nearby might have been influenced by John's persuasive rhetorical gifts (cf. Gregory 1979: 61). Likewise in the middle of the fifth century, the emperor Marcian sought to ensure that individuals sympathetic to the conclusions of the Council of Chalcedon occupied the key episcopal seats in the eastern Mediterranean. Chalcedon was particularly unpopular in Alexandria, and the new bishop there, Proterius, required military support in the face of popular opposition. When this support proved inadequate, Marcian sent fresh troops from Constantinople (Evagrius *Church History* 2.5). Presumably at least part of the rationale for sending them from the vicinity of the imperial capital rather than from somewhere geographically closer, such as Palestine, was that they could be relied upon to be sympathetic to Chalcedon. Even so, opposition from the populace of Alexandria to Proterius was such that he urged the emperor to send further military support (Gregory 1979: 187). Similarly, Justinian sent his appointee Paul of Tinnis to Alexandria accompanied by troops from Constantinople in 539 (Severus *History of the Patriarchs* 1.13 (*PO* 1.466–7)). An analogous rationale may have been in operation during the final years of the emperor Anastasius' reign in the early sixth century when it came to trying to remove two bishops from towns in the province of Syria II, Severian of Arethusae and Cosmas of Epiphania (Evagrius *Church History* 3.34): the task was entrusted to Asiaticus, commander of troops in Phoenicia Libanensis, perhaps because of concerns about the sympathies (whether theological or personal) of more locally based troops.

A final issue which bears on both this section and the preceding one is that of how effective the army was as an instrument of religious policy. It is difficult to avoid a mainly negative conclusion. Persecution of Christians ultimately failed, and the churches that the army had helped to destroy were rebuilt under the patronage of Constantine. Likewise the use of the army in the context of doctrinal disputes tended only to aggravate already highly tense situations, and certainly did not serve to bring those hostile to whichever doctrinal stance currently enjoyed imperial favor back into the fold. This was the case with the Donatists in north Africa, who remained a presence there even after the end of Vandal rule and Justinian's reconquest in the sixth century (Frend 1952: 300–314), as also with the Monophysites in Egypt and elsewhere (Frend 1972a: 255–95, 316–53); as for Arianism, although Theodosius I deployed troops to ensure that Nicaean Christians regained control of the cathedral in Constantinople without opposition (Gregory of Nazianzus *Poem* 11 (*On his own life*) 1325–41), he does not seem to have had to rely on the army to install orthodox bishops elsewhere in the eastern Mediterranean during the 380s.

The one area where the army's intervention could be argued to have achieved some success was in the destruction of pagan temples and shrines. Very gradually, the empire *was* Christianized, and the elimination of the physical focus of pagan allegiances played a part in that change, even if destruction of the physical context of pagan cult did not necessarily mean the immediate end of such loyalties. The use of the army to help effect religious change in this period was, then, a rather blunt instrument deployed with only mixed results, though of course there were many other factors influencing people's religious allegiances.

7.3. A Christian Empire at War

This chapter has concentrated on the impact of religion, especially Christianity, on the late Roman army as an institution and as an instrument of religious policy within the empire. This final section shifts the focus from "internal" matters to the external dimension, by considering two issues of fundamental importance: the impact of Christianity on reasons for going to war, and on the military effectiveness of the empire.

7.3.1. Religiously motivated warfare in late antiquity

> The all-powerful God has now designed to demonstrate through our agency something for his praise and name beyond all the many marvelous works which have happened in this age: Africa has received from us freedom in such a short time, after 105 years of captivity by the Vandals! These had been the enemies of souls at the same time as of bodies, for they transferred to their false belief the souls of those who did not resist various tortures and punishments, rebaptizing them, and they subjected their bodies to the barbarian yoke. Moreover, they polluted the sacrosanct churches of God with their false belief and converted some of them into stables. We have seen holy men whose tongues have been cut out at the root and who testify eloquently to the sort of atrocity which they have experienced; and others who, after various tortures, have passed their lives in exile, scattered in different provinces. By what words and by what deeds are we able to render suitable thanks to God, who has judged it good to avenge the wrongs done against his Church and to release the people of such great provinces from the yoke of slavery through my action who is his most humble servant? (*Justinianic Code* 1.27.1 [April 534])

As this passage implies, Christianity sometimes provided a very powerful motivation for embarking on war during late antiquity. Here Justinian explains his decision to invade the Vandal kingdom of north Africa in 533 in terms of his desire to avenge the discriminatory measures which the Arian Vandals had implemented against Nicene Christians. The potential for Christianity to provide this motivation became apparent as early as the reign of Constantine, who at the time of his death in 337 was apparently planning to invade Persia. Eusebius describes

> how on his campaign against Persia he took with him bishops and a tent to form a church... Once the decision was made he set military officers to work,

and also discussed the campaign with the bishops at his court, planning that some of those needed for divine worship should be there with him. They said they would only too gladly accompany him as he wished, and not shrink back, but would soldier with him and fight at his side with supplications to God. (Eusebius *Life of Constantine* 4.56 [chapter heading], 56.2–3 [trs. Cameron and Hall])

This has been seen against the background of Constantine writing to the Persian king Shapur in the late 320s in terms which constituted a veiled warning to Shapur that he should take care not to persecute the substantial numbers of Christians who lived in Persian territory, and has prompted one commentator to argue that when Shapur subsequently initiated discriminatory measures against Persian Christians, "Constantine proposed to conduct his Persian expedition as a religious crusade" (Barnes 1985a: 132; cf. Fowden 1993: 94–7; McLynn 2004: 240–1). Similarly, the Roman invasion of Persia in the early 420s, which came at least in part as a response to Persian persecution of Christians living in Persia, has been seen as a religiously motivated crusade (Holum 1977).

It is difficult to find parallels for this sort of religiously motivated warfare in earlier periods of Roman history. Virgil famously presented Octavian's clash with Antony and Cleopatra at the battle of Actium in 31 BC in terms of a conflict between Mars, Neptune, and Apollo on the one hand, and "barking Anubis" and other repugnant Egyptian deities (*Aeneid* 8.671–713) on the other, but this has more to do with the influence of Octavian's propaganda during the late 30s BC than with that particular war having a genuine religious dimension. One might also give thought to the traditional Republican procedure for ensuring that Rome embarked on a "just war," through the institution of the fetial priests and their associated rituals (Rich 1976; Rüpke 1990: 97–122), particularly given that the examples from late antiquity noted above might be interpreted more cynically as emperors using religion as a justification for war (Justinian's statement about the rationale for the Vandal war, e.g., was issued after the event).

There are, however, a number of reasons for thinking that religion provided a genuine motivation in late antiquity in a way that had not been the case in earlier periods of Roman history. First, the three emperors involved in the relevant episodes – Constantine, Theodosius II, and Justinian – were all noted for their particular interest in theological matters. Secondly, what has been described as the "universalist" character of Christian monotheism provided a dynamic which was largely absent from the polytheism of traditional Roman cults (Fowden 1993). Thirdly, in all three late Roman cases the presence of co-religionists resident within the enemy state was a critical factor in the equation, a factor for which there was no precedent. Finally, Persia's official support for Zoroastrianism and the Vandal regime's zealous policies on behalf of Arianism must have served to sharpen the sense

7.3.2. Christianity and Roman military effectiveness

> As the happiness of a *future* life is the great object of religion, we may hear without surprise or scandal, that the introduction, or at least the abuse, of Christianity, had some influence on the decline and fall of the Roman empire. The clergy successfully preached the doctrines of patience and pusillanimity; the active virtues of society were discouraged; and the last remains of military spirit were buried in the cloyster: a large portion of public and private wealth was consecrated to the specious demands of charity and devotion, and the soldiers pay was lavished on the useless multitudes of both sexes, who could only plead the merits of abstinence and chastity. Faith, zeal, curiosity, and the more earthly passions of malice and ambition, kindled the flame of theological discord; the church, and even the state, were distracted by religious factions, whose conflicts were sometimes bloody, and always implacable; the attention of emperors was diverted from camps to synods; the Roman world was oppressed by a new species of tyranny; and the persecuted sects became the secret enemies of their country. (Gibbon 1994 [1776–88]: II.510–11)

Edward Gibbon famously placed a major part of the responsibility for the fall of the empire on Christianity's negative impact on Roman military effectiveness in late antiquity.[32] Since Gibbon remains a figure of enormous significance in the study of late antiquity (cf. Bowersock et al. 1977; McKitterick and Quinault 1997), and since his views on this particular issue have received some measure of endorsement by more recent scholars,[33] it is appropriate to conclude this chapter and this study with some consideration of his claims.

As ever, Gibbon's prose is brilliantly persuasive, but its seductive momentum can mask weaknesses of argument. At the most general level, his critique falls foul of the same problem which besets so many universalizing explanations of the empire's problems during late antiquity – namely, that they did not affect both halves of the empire equally. With specific reference to the impact of Christianity, one would have expected any negative effects arising from its advent to be felt even more acutely in the east than the west, given that the east had Christianized more rapidly, yet the east did not collapse in the fifth century.

Gibbon's particular criticisms linking Christianity with the empire's military effectiveness can be summarized under three headings:

1 the church preached pacifism and so the empire's "military spirit" disappeared;

2   material resources were diverted from soldiers' pay into the church, especially into unproductive monasteries;
3   theological controversies distracted emperors from their military duties.

Taking each of these points in turn, "military spirit" is a very vague concept which is impossible to measure with any accuracy, and as has been noted above at various points, the church did not preach pacifism uniformly. In lamenting a decline in military spirit, it is likely that Gibbon had in mind an implicit comparison with the Republican period, when vigorous military expansion was the order of the day.[34] However, the fact that the empire was not expanding during late antiquity, and was increasingly losing control of territory in the west, need not have had anything to do with a dilution of "military spirit," whatever that might mean, and could reasonably be accounted for by a range of other, more obvious considerations, such as the empire now having to confront more powerful and aggressive neighbors.

The emergence of the church as a major institution within the empire which received imperial support in various ways must have had some impact on imperial resources, both human and material (cf. Momigliano 1963a; de Ste. Croix 1981: 495–7). Constantine did provide churches with substantial endowments of land, and he did also institute subsidies to help with the church's charitable work with the poor. However, while the scale of the subsidies is unknown, they were reduced to a third of their original size when Jovian reinstituted them following Julian's death, and the church relied heavily on other sources of income – congregational giving and private bequests (Jones 1964: 898–9; cf. also Liebeschuetz 1991: 222); nor should one overlook the way in which the church became a net provider of financial support to the empire during the dire emergency of Heraclius' Persian campaigns, through the melting down of gold and silver vessels to provide pay for the troops (Kaegi 2003: 110–11). The image of monasteries as net consumers of resources also minimizes the way that many monasteries strove to be self-sufficient,[35] while monks were involved in Basil of Caesarea's schemes to provide practical social support within their communities (Gain 1985: 282–3). It has also been argued that holy men played a role in the survival of the eastern half of the empire during the fifth century (Frend 1972b).

There is no doubt that theological controversies did occupy emperors' time in a way which was without precedent in Roman history, yet a detailed consideration of the incidence of church councils does not support Gibbon's implication that they had a deleterious effect on the involvement of emperors in military affairs. Before the advent of non-campaigning emperors in the late fourth century, Constantine and his successors remained militarily active despite involvement in church affairs. Constantius II, for example, called numerous councils during his reign, yet can hardly be accused of neglecting the military needs of the empire (cf. Blockley 1989). Much of this was made possible through emperors' delegation of practicalities to episcopal representatives. One emperor, Valentinian I, is even credited with eschewing any involvement in doctrinal affairs on the grounds of his lacking the appropriate expertise (Sozomen *Church History* 6.21.7).

After 395, the retreat from active campaigning should in principle have given emperors greater time to devote to church affairs, although in the first half of the fifth century, the main factor responsible for non-campaigning – youth and inexperience – will also have militated against emperors seizing the initiative in the ecclesiastical sphere. No plausible argument can be mounted to suggest that Valentinian III's successors in the west struggled militarily because of preoccupation with church affairs – circumstances did not allow them time for such matters, and doctrinal controversies were much less of a problem in the west by this time anyway. In the east, Marcian managed to organize the holding of the Council of Chalcedon in 451 while also coping well with the Hunnic threat, while Zeno's formulation of the *Henotikon* ("Formula of Union") was an important element in his survival. Justinian took a close interest in ecclesiastical affairs, yet this did not prevent him from overseeing a wide range of military initiatives; the fact that some of these were less successful than others had more to do with overambition and the impact of the pandemic than with his forays into theological controversies. As for Gibbon's parting shot about "persecuted sects becoming the secret enemies of their country," this can only be a reference to Monophysite Christians in Egypt, Palestine, and Syria, and the suggestion that they welcomed Arab invaders in the seventh century because of disillusionment with the Chalcedonianism of Constantinople. This is an argument which has, however, been persuasively rebutted (Jones 1959).

It is, furthermore, possible to identify ways in which Christianity made a positive contribution to the military effectiveness of the empire in late antiquity, particularly in relation to the maintenance of morale. This can be seen with reference to the performance of soldiers in battle in the sixth and early seventh centuries, for instance, through the use of icons as a motivational device (Theophylact Simocatta 2.3.4–7; George of Pisidia *On the Persian Campaign* 1.139–54. 2.86) and the emperor Heraclius' promise of eternal salvation for those who died in battle against the Persians (cf. Howard-Johnston 1999: 39–40):

> "Be not disturbed, O brethren, by the multitude of the enemy. For when God wills it, one man will rout a thousand. So let us sacrifice ourselves to God for the salvation of our brothers. May we win the crown of martyrdom so that we may be praised in the future and receive our recompense from God." (Theophanes *Chronicle* pp. 310–11 [trs. Mango and Scott])

Christian inspiration also proved to be very important in the maintenance of civilian morale in the context of the sieges which became such a common feature of warfare in late antiquity (Michael Whitby 1998), whether it be stories of divine deliverance for the inhabitants of Nisibis from successive Persian attacks in the first half of the fourth century (Lightfoot 1988), the bishop of Orleans inspiring the defenders of the city in the mid fifth century against the Huns of Attila until relief arrived from Aetius (Harries 1995: 228), or the divine protection of Thessalonica against Avars and Slavs with which St Demetrius was credited in the late sixth and early seventh centuries (Cormack 1985: 50–94).

Analysis of Gibbon's claims, then, indicates that Christianity's impact on the empire's capacity to wage war effectively in late antiquity was by no means as negative as Gibbon wished to believe. Explanations for the empire's military difficulties in late antiquity are better sought in the military sphere itself, although not necessarily in the most immediately obvious direction within that sphere. It is tempting to assume that the greater incidence of military setbacks and catastrophes in late antiquity than in the Principate must reflect a deterioration in the effectiveness of imperial armies, but as with Gibbon's views about the impact of Christianity, this proposition proves less easy to maintain when analyzed in detail; apart from anything else, the empire's military record in late antiquity was not one of unmitigated disaster (cf. Elton 1996: 265–8; Lee 1998: 232–7; Nicasie 1998: 257–64; Michael Whitby 2000a: 308–14). A more persuasive explanation is to be found in the empire's changed geopolitical circumstances from the third century onward – the emergence of Sasanian Persia, the succession of increasingly powerful tribal groupings along the empire's northern frontiers, and finally the unexpected impact of Arab tribes, energized by the new creed of Islam and able to take advantage of the war-weary condition of the Roman and Persian states after their recent prolonged conflict in the early decades of the seventh century (a conflict which had, incidentally, demonstrated their ability to conduct sustained military operations in very testing circumstances). If religion has any place in the analysis, it is in this final phase – a phase which ultimately transformed the world of late antiquity beyond recognition.

Further Reading

The best discussion of **Christianity and the Roman army** during the third to fifth centuries is Tomlin 1998. The closely related subject of Christian attitudes to war – a contentious subject – is discussed from various perspectives by Harnack 1981, Helgeland 1979, Swift 1983, and Noethlichs 2001. Note also Haensch 2004 (which only became available after the completion of this chapter).

There is no study of the **army's role in implementing religious policies**, but Fowden 1978 and Gregory 1979 provide useful starting points, and Kaegi 1981: 73–88 also has some helpful discussion.

For discussion of different aspects of **Christianity's impact on the empire's military effectiveness**, see de Ste. Croix 1981: 495–7, Liebeschuetz 1991: 237–52, and Michael Whitby 2004: 176–9. For the Islamic invasions of the 630s, see Whittow 1996: 69–95 and (in more detail) Kaegi 1992.

NOTES

Introduction

1. These are the most commonly accepted chronological parameters for late antiquity, although some scholars have argued for a broader chronological definition: for the debate, see Bowersock et al. 1999: vii–xiii; Averil Cameron 2002. "Late antiquity" is sometimes also referred to as "early Byzantium," a reflection of the period's transitional status between the ancient world and medieval Byzantium, at least with respect to the eastern Mediterranean.
2. For this theme in Roman history, see Heckel and Yardley 2004: 299–302 for relevant ancient sources, with Spencer 2002: 189–200 for discussion. For debate about whether Julian was seeking to emulate Alexander, see Lane Fox 1997: 248–52; Lendon 2005: 290–305.
3. For an alternative view which minimizes the military threat from the Rhine Germans in the fourth century, see Drinkwater 1996, 1997, 1999.
4. For studies of the Berbers, see Brett and Fentress 1996, and Modéran 2003; for the Lombards, Christie 1995; for the Avars, Pohl 1988; and for the Slavs, Curta 2001, including (at 116–17) a tabulation of recorded attacks along the lower Danube between the late fifth and early seventh centuries, with an average of one at least every three years.
5. For differing interpretations of the Bacaudae (to whom there are also references in the late third century), see Thompson 1952b; Van Dam 1985a: 25–56; Drinkwater 1984, 1989, 1992; Wickham 2005: 529–33.
6. See Lenski 1999 for a convenient overview.
7. Cf. pagan support for the revolts of Eugenius in 392 (Matthews 1975: 238–47) and Illus in 484 (Lee 2000a: 134–5), and the doctrinal differences which played a part in Vitalian's rebellion against Anastasius in 513–15 (Lee 2000b: 56–7).
8. For discussion of the emergence of the so-called system of *themes*, and the intense scholarly debate which it has occasioned, see Haldon 1990a: ch. 6.
9. The Roman navy is not discussed here, since it was generally of limited importance during late antiquity. The most detailed treatment can be found in Reddé 1986: 572–652, with a more concise overview of the contexts in which naval warfare was of some significance during late antiquity in Lee 2002a: 93–104. Pryor and Jeffreys 2006 includes detailed consideration of the imperial navy in the sixth and seventh centuries.
10. For the terms *limes* and *limitanei*, see Isaac 1988. See also Brennan 2001 for some provocative thoughts on the traditional dichotomy between

comitatenses and *limitanei*, and suggestions for a more nuanced understanding of the spectrum of troop statuses.
11 See, however, Adams 2003: 599–608 for the problems raised by the notion of Latin as the "official" language of the army.
12 This is not to overlook the importance of other languages in certain parts of the empire, such as Syriac and Coptic; for a good overview of the linguistic diversity of the Roman empire in late antiquity, see Mango 1980: 13–24.
13 Elsewhere, the author comments on the desirability of having some soldiers proficient in both Greek and Latin (as well as Persian, if possible) (12B.7).
14 These (and comparable works by other historians) are usually described as "literary sources," because historical writing in classical antiquity was regarded as a literary genre and authors of histories usually had aspirations to literary sophistication in the presentation of their narratives.

Chapter 1   Emperors and Warfare

1 The exception was Macrinus, whose reign (217–18) was brief and who, as an equestrian of high standing, was not so far removed socially from the senatorial aristocracy – despite the jibes of Cassius Dio (78.11.1, 14.1), himself a senator.
2 See Millar 1977: 15–40 and Halfmann 1986 for details of imperial movements, with corrections of the latter and detailed comments in Barnes 1989a.
3 Diocletian did make use of adoption and marriage ties to strengthen bonds between imperial colleagues in what has been described as "a bureaucratic type of dynasticism that privileged the office rather than its holder" (Fowden 1993: 51).
4 Generally poor relations between the two men are clear from Zos. 4.53, with Arbogast opposing his involvement in military affairs, hinted at by Ambrose *On the Death of Valentinian II* 22–7 and John of Antioch fr.187; cf. Seeck 1920–3: V.240.
5 The Greek word *rastone*, translated above as "indolent dispositions," can be translated less pejoratively as "ease" – but the term appears four other times in this work (Pref. 2.14, 2.15, 3.51, 3.56), and in all four cases it carries the more negative sense of indolence.
6 The general Constantius, who was married to Honorius' sister and proclaimed co-emperor in January 421, certainly had the military expertise to have led the army in person, having fought successfully on a number of fronts during the preceding decade, but he is not known to have embarked on any campaign during his short-lived seven-month reign (Matthews 1975: 377–8).
7 For his known movements outside Constantinople, see Dagron 1974: 85–6 with Roueché 1986. Interestingly, he is reported to have planned to travel to Rome in 425 to proclaim in person the accession of his cousin Valentinian III as emperor in the west, but was prevented by illness from proceeding further than Thessalonica (Socrates *Church History* 7.24).
8 Marcian may have led a brief military expedition to counter a Hunnic raid into the Balkans in 451 (Seeck 1920–3: V.273, 301). The evidence for this – his request that the ecumenical council of 451 be relocated from Nicaea to Chalcedon (and so closer to Constantinople) – is, however, not sufficiently

precise to be certain: it may in fact be that Marcian was "involved in a morale-boosting demonstration of imperial authority after the devastation caused by Attila...rather than an active campaign" (Michael Whitby 2005: 368).

9   It has also been noted that imperial non-involvement in campaigning had benefits when it came to diplomatic negotiations, which could be conducted more effectively in the "controlled" environment of the palace complex in Constantinople, in contrast to the less predictable circumstances of the frontier (Michael Whitby 2005: 371–2); but how far this was a conscious factor in the thinking of emperors and their advisers in the fifth century, as opposed to an unintended, contingent development, is less certain.

10 One sixth-century source, which survives only in a Syriac translation, reports that "when [Anastasius] was a *palha*, he was acquainted with the empress Ariadne who wished to make him emperor and did so" (Ps.-Zachariah *Church History* 7.1). The word *palha* is translated "soldier" in the 1899 English translation of F. J. Hamilton and E. W. Brooks, as also in Brooks's 1924 Latin translation (*miles*), which might suggest that Anastasius had had some military background. There are, however, a number of countervailing considerations: the word *palha* can also carry the more general sense of "worker," and it seems unlikely that a mere soldier would have acquaintance with the empress and on that basis be promised the throne. Moreover, Brooks qualifies his 1924 translation of *miles* with the note *sensu civili*, no doubt reflecting the fact that service in the late Roman bureaucracy was regarded as a form of *militia*; this would be consistent with Anastasius' position at court as a silentiary, which is explicitly referred to in one source as a *strateia*, the Greek equivalent of *militia* (Constantine Porphyrogenitus *Book of Ceremonies* 1.86 (one of a number of chapters in this tenth-century work written in the sixth century)). Indeed Jones (1964: 572) suggests that Anastasius must have been one of the four silentiaries attached to the empress, and that it was in this capacity that he became sufficiently well acquainted with her for Ariadne to consider him a suitable candidate for the throne.

11 Matthews (2000: 189) interprets this somewhat cryptic comment as referring to "sarcastic remarks about (non-existent) Sarmatian victories." Alternatively, the phrase can be translated as "victories *of* Goths and Sarmatians," in which case "the martyr is...credited with Lactantius' own tendency to class the persecuting emperors as barbarians" (Creed 1984: 94).

12 For elucidation of Ammianus' comments about "letters wreathed in laurel" and the reports being the occasion for extraction of money from the provinces, see McCormick 1986: 44, 190–1.

13 Note that Rösch 1978 covers the period from Constantine onward; Kneissel 1969 focuses on the Principate and so is incomplete for the late Roman period (Barnes 1999: 570 n.26), but includes data on the victory titles of third-century emperors and tetrarchs.

14 Identification of the plate with Valentinian II is the more appealing option since its emphasis on military success would be more significant in relation to an emperor without any military experience.

15 This arch has been interpreted as a celebration of Diocletian's *decennalia* and the formation of the Tetrarchy in 293 (Kleiner 1992: 409), rather than commemorating any particular military victory, but the surviving reliefs include significant emphasis on victory and defeated enemies.

16 Columns associated with Constantine, Theodosius II, Marcian, Leo, Justin II, and Phocas are also known, either from material or epigraphic evidence (Mango 1993), but it is less certain whether they were intended to celebrate military success.

17 For further discussion of this item (including the fifteenth-century drawing of the statue preserved in a manuscript), see Mango 1993; the reference to Achilles is elucidated in Downey 1940.

18 One might also add here one of the reliefs at the base of the obelisk of Theodosius I in Constantinople, which depicts foreign peoples offering public submission and gifts to the emperor, albeit in a civic rather than military context (see Leppin 2003: 188–95 for further details and references).

19 Kent (1994: 47) also expresses doubts about this possible correlation because of the speed with which the new type was implemented after Theodosius' death.

Chapter 2 Military Loyalties and Civil War

1 It does receive passing mention in a number of fifth-century laws (*Theodosian Code* 7.8.15 (430/3), Theodosius II *Novel* 4.1.2 (438), Valentinian III *Novel* 15.1 (444/5)).

2 As noted by Creed (1984: 99), "this passage is of great interest as the first contemporary account of a transfer of imperial power since Herodian's account of the imperial vicissitudes of AD 238. The formal approval of the senate is no longer of significance, and the official conferment of power takes place in the presence of the army, now seen as the legitimizing body." Surviving sources for Diocletian's proclamation of Maximian as co-emperor in 286, and their joint proclamation of Constantius and Galerius as junior emperors in 293, are very short on detail, making it impossible to confirm the reasonable assumption that the army also played a role on these occasions (cf. Kolb 2001: 26).

3 Valentinian II was also proclaimed emperor in 375 in the military camp where his recently deceased father Valentinian I had been preparing for a military campaign against the Quadi (Ammianus 30.10), although the specific circumstances might be regarded as more akin to a coup by senior military officers.

4 In the case of Gratian's accession, Valentinian was en route to Trier, probably to start a campaign, but he was not actually on campaign at the time.

5 Grand speeches were a standard feature of classicizing historiography which gave authors an opportunity to display their rhetorical skills for the benefit of their audience, so one should never treat them as if they were an accurate record of what was said; on the other hand, their broad content presumably reflects something of the sentiments expressed at the time.

6 Theodosius was formally proclaimed emperor in 402 when still a baby, but his reign is not normally regarded as having begun until the death of his father Arcadius in 408.

7 This passage is preserved in a tenth-century work compiled on the orders of the emperor Constantine VII Porphyrogenitus (913–59) under the title *The Book of Ceremonies*, most of whose content postdates late antiquity. However, the final 12 chapters of Book 1 comprise material from a sixth-century work on court ceremonial, almost certainly written by Justinian's long-serving *magister*

officiorum, Peter the Patrician, and his account of Leo's accession is in turn probably based on a contemporary account from 457 (Bury 1923: I.216 n.2).

8   Martialis had been *magister officiorum* in 449, but others had since held the post; although it is possible that the term *magister* in this text "is used loosely of him as a former holder of the post" (*PLRE* II.729), it seems more likely that he held it for a second time in 457, since it is clear that this official became closely involved in the supervision of ceremonial occasions during the fifth and sixth centuries and it is otherwise difficult to see why he should receive special mention in this way.

9   The *labarum* (pl. *labara*) was a special military standard, introduced by Constantine, bearing the monogram of Christ.

10 The proclamations of Maurice in 582 and Phocas in 602 did take place at the Hebdomon, but both occasions were rather different to those of the fourth and fifth centuries: Maurice was declared successor to Tiberius II inside the imperial palace at the Hebdomon where the ailing emperor happened to be at the time, while Phocas was crowned emperor by the patriarch inside a church at the Hebdomon.

11 John of Ephesus *Church History* 3.11, where the usual five *solidi* and pound of silver have been commuted into nine *solidi*. Late sixth-century coin hoard evidence from the lower Danube has provided possible archaeological corroboration of the distribution of accession (and quinquennial anniversary) donatives in this period and as late as 641: Curta 2001: 177–8.

12 Fourth century: *Martyrdom of Julius the Veteran* 2.5 (= Musurillo 1972: 262), Ammianus 15.6.3 with Jones 1964: 1259 n.32, Libanius *Orations* 22.4; fifth century: Michael the Syrian *Chronicle* 9.9; sixth century: Marcellinus *Chronicle s.a.* 500, Ps-Zachariah *Church History* 7.8, Procopius *Secret History* 24.27–8.

13 Honorius' use of the term in a letter to troops in Spain (*ZPE* 61 (1985) 274) could be regarded as a case of the imperial chancellery taking a little time to adjust to new circumstances, while Leo's use of it at his accession (above, p. 55) was warranted by the fact that he had until very recently been a serving soldier.

14 This is not to deny that the text and images on coins have their own limitations as historical evidence and that their use can be problematic (notably on the vexed issue of responsibility for selection of motifs and slogans, on which see Howgego 1995: 67–75).

15 Trajan and Marcus Aurelius, both of whom were militarily active, did also use it on one or two issues of theirs; Trajan's, however, appeared early in his reign (*RIC* II.276), when he was perhaps still establishing his position, while Marcus only became militarily active in his final years under force of circumstances.

16 Constantine's showdown with Maxentius in 312 might be thought to fall into this category as well, but Maxentius was a self-proclaimed emperor without any recognized status from any of the tetrarchs.

17 In both scenarios, on the other hand, it was not usually the initial usurpation or mutiny which resulted in civil war, but rather the determination of an existing emperor to suppress the usurpation or mutiny.

18 The obvious exception is Julian, about whose background and possible motives a great deal can be said, not least because of the substantial body of writings from his own hand (which is not to say that these are unproblematic).

19 Cf. similar reactions among auxiliary units in the Roman army posted far from home during the Principate (Campbell 2002: 30), and the analogous case of Scots recruited into the British army post-1745: "For the most part, they enlisted... on the understanding – often erroneously given by their own lairds – that they would not have to serve overseas. They also considered themselves Scotsmen and clansmen... and thus presumed they would be organized and outfitted in a manner which sustained this salient self-image. The mutinies which took place generally occurred when the English violated either of these two basic ethnic preconditions. In particular, Highland Scottish soldiers objected when it was rumoured that they were about to be shipped to the West Indies, where tropical heat and disease were known to take as great a toll on soldiers as the fiercest enemy" (Enloe 1980: 35).
20 This particular episode is further complicated by Valentinian's death – Arbogast was suspected of complicity, although suicide is the more likely explanation (Croke 1976b) – and by Arbogast using Eugenius as a figurehead for his regime once the inevitability of conflict with Theodosius became clear (cf. Chapter 6.2, p. 161).
21 Analogous reasoning can perhaps be detected in Julian's sending Lupicinus on an expedition to Britain in 360 (Ammianus 20.1.2, 20.9.9), even if this was more to do with preventing interference in Julian's own plans for usurpation.
22 In addition to their entries in *PLRE*, see also, for Stilicho, Matthews 1975: 253–83; for Aetius, O'Flynn 1983: 74–103, Stickler 2002; and for Aspar, Scott 1976, Croke 2005.
23 Note, however, the reservations about this expressed by Drinkwater 1994.
24 For shortages of pay for imperial troops in Italy in the late sixth century, see Gregory the Great *Letters* 2.45, 5.30. For the link between pay shortages and mutiny in a more recent historical context (seventeenth-century England), see Gentles 1975.

Chapter 3   The Infrastructure of War

1 For discussions of this issue, see Jones 1964: 679–86; Luttwak 1976: 188–90; MacMullen 1980; Treadgold 1995: 43–64; Nicasie 1998: 74–6, 202–7; Carrié 1999: 636–9; Potter 2004: 455–9; Michael Whitby 2004: 159–60.
2 E.g, his claim that the Vandal expedition in 468 comprised 400,000 troops (*On the Magistracies* 3.43).
3 Nicasie 1998: 203–7, including a valuable table collating data on the sizes of late Roman field armies until the mid sixth century (omitting, however, the important figure of 52,000 for the army sent against Kavad's invasion of 502 (Ps.-Joshua Stylites *Chronicle* 54)), with Michael Whitby 1995: 100–2 for figures from the later sixth century; cf. also Rance 2005: 447–9.
4 The most important question for which it is less satisfactory is determining whether the fourth-century army was significantly larger than that of the Principate, though this is also complicated by the fact that there is an equally wide range of estimates for the size of the army in the late second/early third century – from 350,000 (MacMullen 1980: 454), to 400,000 (Potter 2004: 126), to 430,000 (A., R. Birley 1983: 43), to 500,000 (Hassall 2000: 321).

5 Carrié also investigates other scenarios involving a larger total population and a larger army, with the necessary caveats and acknowledgment of the range of variables involved. It ought perhaps to be added that the basis for his most optimistic demographic scenario is Burn 1953, which, as he himself notes, has since been much criticized for lack of methodological rigor.
6 It is of course possible that Belisarius exaggerated these soldiers' small numbers and inexperience in order to increase the likelihood of Justinian sending reinforcements.
7 For differing evidence about the precise minimum age for recruitment, see Nicasie 1998: 88–9. With regard to social background, military families had long been regarded as having an obligation to serve in the army, though this was probably no longer obligatory by this stage (see further below) – reference to it here perhaps implies a privileged status (Jones 1964: 669); as for those of "curial or praesidial rank," the army had traditionally been a refuge for those from the families of local elites seeking to escape the burdens associated with that status (where "praesidial" is taken to be a reference to *cohortales*: Jones 1964: 669).
8 The best discussions of recruitment in late antiquity are Jones 1964: 614–23, 668–79, Michael Whitby 1995 (the latter is much broader in coverage than its title indicates), and Brennan 1998a (despite its title), with Haldon 1979: 20–39, Elton 1996: 128–54, and Nicasie 1998: 83–96 providing valuable treatment of more specific aspects.
9 For documentary examples from fourth-century Egypt, see *P. London* 5.1655, *P. Oxyrhynchus* 4373, with Rea 1997a.
10 A more specific argument for a decisive move away from the use of conscription during the 370s (Zuckerman 1998) has been rejected independently by Carrié 2004 and Michael Whitby 2004: 170–2.
11 This is not to deny that the sons of soldiers had become a source of recruits during the Principate (Campbell 2002: 26).
12 See de Ste. Croix 1981: Appendix 3 for a catalogue.
13 For discussions of *laeti*, see Jones 1964: 620; Whittaker 1982; Nixon and Rodgers 1994: 142–3; Elton 1996: 129–33; Brennan 1998a: 200–2.
14 At another point, Ammianus refers to *laeti* making an attack on Lyons (16.11.4). Both the Loeb and Penguin translations interpret the *laeti* here as foreign raiders and add the word "tribe," even though there is nothing in the Latin to warrant this (cf. Elton 1996: 132 n.12). It is more consistent with Ammianus' other references to see these raiders as unruly conscripted barbarians trying to seize an opportunity for self-aggrandizement (cf. Brennan 2001: 262).
15 A law issued by Theodosius II concerning Scirian prisoners has sometimes been taken as showing the presence of *laeti* in the eastern half of the empire (*Theodosian Code* 5.6.3 [409], with Elton 1996: 129–30), but the 20-year moratorium on the requirement to provide recruits is as likely to be a reference to general conscription from among the peasantry, particularly since the captured Sciri were to be distributed randomly as a supplement to the workforce of landowners rather than being settled *en bloc*. For reservations about the idea that Valens might have viewed the Goths as potential *laeti* in 376, see Lenski 2002a: 343.
16 In addition to the case noted above from Gregory of Nazianzus *Letters* 225, cf. also *P. Hermopolis* 7 (with Zuckerman 1995, who dates the letter to c.381), from which it appears that one potential recruit had enlisted the services of an

anchorite to help him bribe his way out of the draft. On the other hand, contrast Firmus of Caesarea *Letters* 6 (early fifth century), in which the bishop appears to decline a request to intercede on behalf of a family member for exemption from military service (a reference I owe to Pierre-Louis Gatier).

17 Jones 1964: 617–19; Lee 1998: 220–1; Nicasie 1998: 90–1; with Zuckerman 1995: 184–7 for the specific evolution of tattooing and of imperial policy with regard to digit amputees.
18 Jones 1964: 618–19; Bagnall 1993: 176; Elton 1996: 153–4; Brennan 1998b: 196; Nicasie 1998: 92–4.
19 I owe my original acquaintance with this study to Keith Hopwood.
20 For discussions of Isauria in late antiquity, see Matthews 1989: 355–67; Shaw 1990; Hopwood 1990, 1999b; Lenski 1999. For Roman use of Isaurians in the army, see the references in Lenski 1999: 426–7, 437–8. Roman use of the inhabitants of the Balkan highlands and of Armenia in the late Roman army also has many analogies with the "Ghurka syndrome."
21 For good discussions of the subject, see Elton 1996: 136–52 and Nicasie 1998: 97–116 (focusing on the fourth century) and Michael Whitby 1995: 103–110 (focusing on the sixth century). Note also Cosentino 2004 for the use of Iranians, a salutary supplement to the usual focus on Germans.
22 For a good discussion of the issues raised by "Roman" identity in late antiquity, see Greatrex 2000.
23 For the period 476–641, the identity of 207 *magistri* is known, of whom 165 were definitely (63) or probably (102) Roman, and 42 were definitely (21) or probably (21) non-Roman. "Definites" are those for whom a source provides an explicit indication of place or people of origin, "probables" are based on names. As with previous analyses, this conclusion must necessarily be hedged about with various caveats concerning reliance on onomastic evidence in those cases where nothing else is known about the background of individuals. *PLRE* entries which indicate an element of uncertainty about whether an individual held the post were excluded, as were "Anonymi" unless they had a definite indication of place of origin. For a more general discussion of the presence of foreign soldiers in the sixth-century army, which argues against those who have claimed a significant increase in the second half of the century, see Michael Whitby 1995: 103–10.
24 Such were the burdens of the office that there were in fact multiple praetorian prefects, with responsibility for different regions of the empire. During Heraclius' Persian campaigns in the early seventh century, the additional pressures of that momentous conflict prompted the emperor to separate responsibility for military expenditure from the prefect's duties and entrust it to an official termed a *logothetes* (literally "accountant" or "auditor") (Howard-Johnston 1999: 35).
25 Cf. also Augustine *City of God* 18.18.10 about a man who dreamt he was a horse which, together with other pack animals, was carrying grain to troops in Raetia (modern-day Switzerland), though the origin of the grain is not indicated. With regard to meat, note the claim in one (admittedly hostile) source that, prior to his entry to the church, the fourth-century Arian bishop George of Cappadocia had been involved in the supply of pork meat to the army (Gregory of Nazianzus *Orations* 21.16).
26 Poulter 1999: 166–74, 177–8; cf. also pp. 109–11 below (Chapter 4.2.2A) on the sixth-century *quaestura exercitus*. For storehouses at the fortress of Dara

on the eastern frontier, see Michael Whitby 1986b: 750, and for archaeological evidence of late Roman military granaries in the west, see Rickman 1971: 264–70. For archaeological evidence of river transport on the Rhine and Danube, see Höckmann 1997.

27 There is papyrological evidence from the early seventh century indicating that Heraclius may have reinstituted this tax, presumably because of financial pressures arising from his Persian campaigns (MacCoull 1994).

28 In a subsequent, but much briefer, discussion (1989: 18), Hendy suggested that "something of the order of 50–75% of [tax income] was ... redistributed to the army in the form of annual pay" – seemingly a significant advance on his previous estimate; however, no reasons are offered for this higher range.

29 Wickham 2005: 73–4, taking Hendy's conclusion as the lower limit in relation to the later date. For another attempt to tackle this subject, which does not, however, try to come up with an estimate of military expenditure as a proportion of revenue, see Elton 1996: 118–27. As for the burden of taxation itself, opinions range from the pessimistic to the more optimistic; for a convenient discussion of the spectrum of views, see Wickham 2005: 62–72.

30 The one location for which such a specification is lacking is Suessones (Soissons) in northern Gaul (*Notitia, West* 9.35), probably due to a lacuna in the text (James 1988: 258).

31 The greater number of *fabricae* specializing in cavalry armor in the east fits with the presence of more units of heavy cavalry in that half of the empire; on the other hand, the absence of any *fabricae* producing bows and arrows in the east is problematic.

32 James (1988: 260) argues that the Egyptian arsenals mentioned in a late third-century papyrus (*P. Beatty Panopolis* 1.213–16, 314–46) must refer to temporary establishments set up during Diocletian's suppression of the revolt of Alexandria. On the other hand, it has also been suggested that the absence of *fabricae* from north Africa, Spain, and Britain in the *Notitia* catalogue implies that smaller-scale production within the context of military forts must have continued to meet the needs of troops stationed in those regions (Bishop and Coulston 1993: 188).

33 With reference to this specific issue, in addition to the data assembled in James 1988, note also the reference in a sixth-century papyrus to camels transporting iron within Egypt in a military context, even if the point of origin of the camel train is not known to have possessed iron deposits (Gascou 1989: 307). Although the *Notitia* does not detail any *fabricae* in Egypt in the late fourth century, it seems that they existed in Alexandria by the sixth century (James 1988: 282).

34 For the debate as to whether or not the *fabricae* had originally been under the authority of the praetorian prefect during the fourth century, see James 1988: 290–4 and Delmaire 1995: 88 (both of whom favor the view that the master had this responsibility from the creation of the office by Constantine, against the older opinion that oversight was only transferred in the 390s).

35 Evidence for the *fabricae* after the time of the *Notitia* is much more limited: see James 1988: 281–7, though note Delmaire's (1995: 90) reservations about James's interpretation of Justinian *Novel* 85; note also that the passage from the *Book of Ceremonies* which refers to *fabricae* workers in Constantinople can be

36 A series of receipts for delivery of quantities of pork and chaff to the Egyptian port of Pelusium in the summer of 361 (*P. Oxyrhynchus* 4598–4603) has also been linked with Constantius' preparations for this campaign (Coles 2001: 191).

dated much more precisely than James allows, to August 11, 559 (cf. Haldon 1990b: 264–5). The instruction in Ps.-Maurice *Strategy* (12B.7) that each unit should assign soldiers to specific duties, including those of armorers, weapon makers, bow makers, and arrow makers, may indicate that there had been a reversion to a more decentralized system of production by the end of the sixth century.

37 Jones 1964: 628 implies that this development was linked with emperors no longer campaigning in person (and presumably therefore requiring the presence of the praetorian prefect himself at the imperial court).

38 Presented as it is in the form of a panegyric, this work has prompted much scholarly debate as to its reliability and value: see Averil Cameron 1985: 84–112, Michael Whitby 1986a, 1986b, and the special issue of the journal *Antiquité tardive* 8 (2000), containing a series of important papers on this text, including that by Denis Feissel correlating the epigraphic evidence for Justinian's building work.

39 For discussions of the design and function of late Roman fortifications (which are not a concern of this section or indeed volume), see Pringle 1981; Johnson 1983; Elton 1996: 155–74; Southern and Dixon 1996: 127–47. Only the first two discuss issues of funding.

40 Cf. Treadgold 1995: 193: "Most of Justinian's fortifications would have been built cheaply from local materials by soldiers on regular pay" (although no sources are cited in support).

41 For other (rare) figures relating to the costs of construction of fortifications, see Trombley and Watt 2000: 110 n.511 (60 *solidi* for a tower in the late fifth century) and Pringle 1981: 91 (1,000 *solidi* for the construction of a fort in the early sixth century, though this seems expensive compared with the figure for Edessa above, which appears as one of a number of quite specific figures; by contrast, the very round 1,000 *solidi* appears in a saint's life whose author might have had reason to exaggerate the emperor's generosity).

42 Jones 1964: 462. During the Principate, "one of the more severe legal punishments was *damnatio ad opus publicum*, being condemned to labour on public works" (Duncan-Jones 1990: 174).

Chapter 4 The Economic Impact of War

1 Calculation of the figure for gold is straightforward, with 72 *solidi* per pound of gold a standard equivalence from Constantine onward (Jones 1964: 439, 444–5). Calculation of the figure for silver is less easy, since silver was not used for coinage after the fourth century; the figure of 5 *solidi* for a pound of silver which prevailed at the end of the fourth century (Jones 1964: 439) has been used. For a useful tabulation of sundry data about amounts of gold recorded in late Roman sources, see Banaji 2001: 227–9.

2 The contents of the Persian treasury at Ctesiphon were captured by Heraclius in 628, including substantial quantities of spices of all kinds, silver, silk garments,

carpets, and hangings, but their sheer weight prompted Heraclius to have most of these goods burnt (Theophanes *Chronicle* pp. 321–2), presumably because it was not considered logistically feasible to transport them back to Constantinople

3 I am indebted to John Drinkwater for a number of the points in this paragraph.
4 By way of comparison, it is interesting to note that Ghurkas first entered the British army in the early nineteenth century when Britain was in the process of conquering Nepal and "Ghurka prisoners were given the option of entering British military service" (Enloe 1980: 40).
5 See Hordern 2005 for an overview of the issues and previous literature on this subject, with Stathakopoulos 2004: 113–24 for specific discussion of chronology.
6 Indeed, only a decade or so after the author of the *Description* was writing his positive assessment, the region applied to Julian for a remission of taxes (on what grounds is unknown), which the emperor granted in part (*Letters* 73 [362]).
7 See Frye 1984: 371–2 or Dodgeon and Lieu 1991: 50 for translations of Shapur's famous trilingual inscription at Naqsh-i Rustam near Persepolis.
8 This destruction was not due to the behavior of Magnentius' supporters, but to Magnentius' withdrawal of forces from the Rhine frontier for his campaign against the emperor Constantius which left northern Gaul exposed to external attack.
9 Once again, I am indebted to John Drinkwater for helpful suggestions on this subject.
10 John Drinkwater has suggested to me that the forced collection of bullion to pay subsidies might also have been a way by which economically sterile hoards were effectively "de-thesaurized."

Chapter 5 The Experience of War

1 Jerome *Chronicle* 378, Orosius 7.33.13, and Jordanes *History of the Goths* 138, all with reference to the Goths and Adrianople in 378 (with Jerome no doubt drawing on Virgil *Aeneid* 7.604, and Orosius and Jordanes perhaps drawing their phraseology from Jerome); John of Biclaro *Chronicle* 578.3, with reference to the Lombards in sixth-century Italy.
2 One might contrast the Jewish revolt in Egypt under the emperor Trajan (115–17), which extended south of the Delta and where the survival of some of the correspondence between a local official and his wife from Middle Egypt provides an invaluable civilian perspective on the experience of war (Tcherikover and Fuks 1960: 225–60).
3 Notably during the siege of Dura-Europos in 256: Leriche 1993; James 2004: 30–9, James 2005; cf. Procopius *Wars* 8.11.27 on Persian siege engineers as a long-standing institution.
4 The sketchy sources for this period leave it unclear in most cases whether their success in capturing some towns and cities was due to the neglected state of fortifications, surprise, abandonment, or some technological knowledge on the part of the attackers. There are reports of machinery being brought against the walls of Philippopolis and Thessalonica in the late 260s (Dexippus fr.27; Zosimus 1.43.1), but the latter source also mentions many centers which the attackers failed to capture. They may have relied on the expertise of captured Roman soldiers to assist them in the construction of siege towers and the like.

5 See Matthews 1989: 279–303; Goldsworthy 1996: 171–282; Lee 1996; Sabin 2000; Trombley 2002; Lenski (forthcoming). Some reservations have been expressed about this trend: see, e.g., Wheeler 1998; Rance 2005: 425 n.1.
6 It has recently been suggested that Procopius may have been a military engineer, rather than a lawyer (Howard-Johnston 2000), but see the reservations of Greatrex 2003: 58–61.
7 It is important to note that Ammianus himself was not present at the battle of Strasbourg and was dependent for his knowledge of the course of this particular battle on the oral reports and written accounts of contemporaries. Nevertheless, this should not detract from the importance of his own experiences of battle on other occasions in imbuing his account with a strong sense of the realities of battle. For further discussion of Ammianus' account of Strasbourg, see Crump 1975: 85–9; Blockley 1977; Matthews 1989: 297–8; Nicasie 1998: 219–33.
8 See Guillermand 1982: 113–50; Jackson 1988: 112–37; R. Davies 1989; Salazar 2000: 25–32; with Baker 2004 for cautionary comments about the dangers of overgeneralizing and assuming uniformity of practice and provision throughout the army of the Principate.
9 On the other hand, it is the case that at least one late Roman medical writer included detailed discussion of the treatment of war wounds (Paul of Aegina 6.88). For observations on the psychological impact of wounds on the wounded and their comrades in more recent periods of warfare, see Holmes 1985: 181–8.
10 Cf. the admission by one scholar that in presenting a reconstruction of the battle, the lack of detail in Theophylact's account has forced him to use his imagination on the basis of what is plausible from other sixth-century battle narratives (Haldon 2000: 149).
11 Ammianus 19.6.11–12, 24.4.24; Procopius *Wars* 7.1.8, 8.31.9; Theophylact Simocatta 2.6.10–11; cf. the archaeological evidence for inscribed clasps, rings, torques, and belt buckles (MacMullen 1962: 161) which may be examples of such rewards.
12 It was not always possible to organize burial, however, as references to sites full of bleached bones testify: Ammianus 31.7.16; Priscus fr.11, 2 [lines 54–5]).
13 Procopius *Wars* 1.14.52, 8.32.20. In the former instance, Procopius' phraseology is rather coy, suggesting embarrassment at what happened, perhaps because Belisarius was in command. For cases from more recent times, see Holmes 1985: 381–92.
14 The practice is referred to with approval by Libanius (*Orations* 18.45) in the context of illustrating Julian's ability to raise the morale and effectiveness of his men. It does not seem to have been practiced more generally, although reliefs on Trajan's column provide a precedent from the early second century. Cf. Zos. 4.11, 22.
15 Discussions of siege warfare in late antiquity (or portions thereof) from different perspectives: Crump 1975: 97–113; Matthews 1989: 288–95; Chevedden 1995; Elton 1996: 257–63; Southern and Dixon 1996: 148–67; Haldon 1999: 183–9; Syvänne 2004: 295–312 (with a useful catalogue of sieges in the sixth and early seventh centuries at 490–506). Despite its title, Kern 1999 concludes his study with the Roman siege of Jerusalem in 66–70.
16 For quite a detailed description of another tunneling operation during the Roman attempts to recapture Amida from the Persians in 504, see Ps.-Joshua Stylites *Chronicle* 71 (possibly based on an oral report from one of the soldiers

involved: Trombley and Watt 2000: xxxviii), and for an example of a more successful Roman counter-mine at Dara in 540, see Procopius *Wars* 2.13.20–7. The site of Cremna in central Anatolia offers an intriguing case study where archaeological evidence of siege warfare can to some extent be correlated with written sources relating to events in the 270s, albeit concerning an internal rebellion (Mitchell 1995: 177–218); the material remains are not, however, as impressive or informative as those from Dura.

17 E.g., Millar 1969 (Dexippus and Athens, 260s); Ps.-Zachariah *Church History* 7.4 (monks on guard at Amida, 503); Procopius *Wars* 5.20.5, 25.2, 12 (Rome, 537), 2.27.35–6 (Edessa, 544), 7.10.19 (Tibur, 544); Vegetius *Epitome of Military Science* 4.25 (general observation on the role of citizens in defense of besieged cities). The possibility has been raised that some of those who died in the counter-mine at Dura-Europos may have been civilian miners (James 2005: 204).

18 The recent catalogue of famines and epidemics during late antiquity assembled in Stathakopoulos 2004 includes many instances of famine arising from siege (summarized at 46–7).

19 Ammianus (19.2.14) gives a total figure of 20,000 soldiers and civilians; since the former is said to have comprised seven "legions," and a "legion" in this period was probably about 1,000 men, the number of civilians may well have been about 12,000.

20 Procopius *Wars* 6.3.10–12, 7.17.12, 19, 7.17.13, 7.21.26; cf. also Malchus fr.2 (Gothic siege of Arcadiopolis in 473: horses and pack-animals); cats were also consumed during the two-year Avar siege of Sirmium in the 580s (John of Ephesus *Church History* 6.32); cf. Garnsey 1999: 83–5 for more general comments on consumption of "non-standard" forms of meat in antiquity.

21 Ps.-Joshua Stylites *Chronicle* 77; Ps.-Zachariah *Church History* 7.5; cf. Theophanes *Chronicle* p. 118 (siege of Rome, 472); cf. also Appian *Mithridatic Wars* 38: the defenders of Athens in 87/86 BC had "devoured all their cattle, boiled the hides and skins and licked what they could get therefrom." Stathokopoulos 2004: 85 cites a modern example of the consumption of leather *in extremis* in the context of the nineteenth-century American frontier.

22 Stathakopoulos 2004: 85 refers to evidence of this phenomenon during the German occupation of Athens in 1941–2.

23 See Petrinovich 2000: chs. 1–4 for a useful collection of data, with Askenasy 1994: 59–82 and Figes 1996: 777–8 for examples in the specific context of famine, the latter with much heart-rending detail from Soviet Russia in the early 1920s (cf. also Garnsey 1999: 37, 83–4, 140; Stathakopoulos 2004: 85–7). Southern and Dixon (1996: 151) dismiss the case mentioned by Procopius on the grounds that "according to the chronology of events outlined by Procopius, the besieged started eating each other before they tried nettles!"; however, they have overlooked the fact that Procopius attributes the cannibalism to the inhabitants of Placentia (7.16.2), while the nettle eating (7.17.13) took place in Rome (to which his narrative switches at 7.16.4).

24 Procopius tried to mitigate the damage to Roman honor by attributing the worst behavior to troops recruited from among the barbarian Massagetae and by having Belisarius intervene to curb their excesses. Note also the episode on the eastern frontier in 584 when a shortage of water led Roman forces to kill adult

prisoners, both male and female (Theophylact Simocatta 1.13.8–12). More generally, see Holmes 1985: 389–93 for brief discussion of the psychology behind atrocities against civilians in twentieth-century warfare, such as the notorious My Lai massacre during the Vietnam War.

25 E.g., Ammianus 19.9.2; *Life of the Younger St Symeon the Stylite* 62–3. Cf. also the shackles found with the Neupotz booty, implying the presence of captured Roman provincials with the Germanic raiders (Künzl 1993: I.365–78).

26 See Ghirshman 1962: 137–47, including color images of the mosaics; see also Greatrex 1998: 93 for the probable destinations and work of Kavad's captives in 503.

27 Fuchs 1998: 345–6 (with pictures of some of the skulls); Schröter 2000: 180–1 (with pictures at 176); Carroll 2001: 138. (I owe these references to John Drinkwater.)

28 Ammianus 17.10.6–7; cf. 17.13.14, 27.10.7, 29.4.5, 30.3.1. Agathias (4.19) reports (in highly critical terms) an episode of extreme brutality by Roman troops against a village of the Mismian people in the Caucasus in the 550s, during which they slaughtered all the inhabitants, including babies, and burnt the village to the ground, as reprisal for the Mismians having killed envoys sent by the Roman commander (4.15.7).

29 In addition to the examples already noted, see also Ammianus 24.1.14, 27.10.7; Synesius *Letters* 130; Sidonius Apollinaris *Letters* 6.12.5. Note also Ammianus 18.7.3–4, where Roman fields in northern Mesopotamia are deliberately set on fire by the Roman authorities in 359 in order to deny fodder to invading Persian forces.

30 Cf. Tritle 2000: 79–100 for reflections on the theme of "waiting wives and mothers" in the context of ancient Greek and modern warfare.

31 Cf. Treggiari 1991: 249–53 on expressions of partnership and agreement where, significantly, this term does not feature as a commonplace.

32 Compare the contemporary situation with wedding ceremonies: the fact that the many hundreds celebrated in churches every weekend use the same form of words does not mean that couples making their wedding vows do not love one another (an observation which I owe to Al Bertrand).

33 P. *Edfu* 9 (sixth century) includes reference to a widow receiving some sort of payment from the army, but it is likely that this refers to back-pay owed to her husband prior to his death rather than any ongoing support for her following the loss of her spouse (Rémondon 1961: 54–5). Similarly, the reference in the same document to payments to orphans is best seen in the context of recruitment practices, rather than any broader concern on the part of the army for the welfare of the offspring of deceased soldiers (Rémondon 1961: 59–61). Cf. Miller 2003: 30: "Despite the importance of its legions, the [pre-Constantinian] Roman state never developed any welfare program for the orphans of its fallen soldiers," and although the influence of Christianity did result in the establishment of orphanages during late antiquity (Miller 2003: 49–77), the surviving evidence provides no indication of any specific provision for military offspring. Miller (2003: 17) notes that before the impact of Christianity made itself felt, Romans considered an orphan to be a child without a living father.

34 One further, somewhat unusual instance relates to the siege of Cremna in central Anatolia in 278. The leader of the rebellion expelled those of the population

unable to contribute to the city's defense, but retained women "to satisfy their common desires" (Zosimus 1.69). Interestingly, an informer who assisted Roman forces besieging the city was female.

Chapter 6 Soldiers and Society

1 Note also the persuasive suggestion of Colin Wells that the Augustan ban should be linked to his more general legislation on marriage, which was clearly intended to increase the birthrate in Italy: "It would not help the Italian birthrate, if husband [on military service] and wife were apart during the wife's best reproductive years" (Wells 1998: 187).
2 As previously noted (p. 81 in Chapter 3.1), late Roman emperors went a step further by tying any male offspring of soldiers' marriages into military service when they reached their late teens.
3 There has been debate on the specific question of whether the wives and children of late Roman soldiers were entitled to military supplies in their own right: on the basis of the *Theodosian Code* and of papyri, some have argued that this was so (Jones 1964: 630–1, Zuckerman 1998), but it has been pointed out that the term *familia* can have a range of meanings in the military context of which "family" is only one, the legal evidence is ambiguous, and the references to *familia* in the papyri associate the term, not with the soldiers as individuals, but with units, which suggests that the term more probably refers to slaves who helped with the unit's baggage (Mitthof 2001: 236–8, Carrié 2002: 429).
4 Another possible example of a late Roman military will is *CPR* 6.76, although its date can only be determined very approximately and may be as early as the end of the second century or the early third century (cf. Migliardi Zingale 1997: 79–81). A check of a very recent catalogue of Roman wills (Salomons 2006: 236) reveals no other examples of military wills. This is less surprising when it is appreciated that "wills of the period from 300 to 700 are notably scarce" (Bagnall 1986: 1; cf. Grönewald et al. 2003: 186–8).
5 See MacMullen 1963: 128 and Daniels 1980 for some possibilities from British sites. For critiques of Daniels's interpretation of the archaeological data, see Bidwell 1992 and Coello 1996: 52–6.
6 Note, however, the following letters apparently to ordinary soldiers: Basil *Letter* 106 (but see below, p. 230 n.12); Theodoret *Letters* 145, which contains lengthy discussion of complex theological issues; and more than forty letters from Isidore of Pelusium to soldiers (cf. Évieux 1995), including one (*Letters* 2.203 (*PG* 78.645–8)) which contains a quotation from Plato *Phaedo* 107cd, and another (1.78 (*PG* 78.236)) with allusions to Homeric heroes and the 300 Spartans at Thermopylae.
7 Letters addressed to the holders of the posts of *comes* and *tribunus* can present difficulties of identification, in so far as these titles can refer to either a military or a civilian responsibility, though other evidence sometimes helps to resolve the uncertainty in specific cases. Where uncertainty remains, these letters have been excluded from consideration here.
8 Symmachus' recipients: Bauto (4.15–16), Promotus (3.74–80), Richomer (3.54–69), Stilicho (4.1–14), Theodosius senior (10.1), Timasius (3.70–3);

Libanius' recipients: Addaeus (1062), Bacurius (1060), Barbatio (436, 491, 556–7), Demonicus (1054–5), Ellebichus (2, 868, 884, 898, 925), Moderatus (1057, 1059), Promotus (867), Richomer (866, 972, 1007, 1024), Sapores (957), Saturninus (857, 897), Sebastianus (318, 350, 520, 596), Varanes (1104), an unnamed *comes* of Isauria (426). (The numeration followed here is that of Foerster).

9 Arinthaeus (179), Terentius (99, 214), Traianus (148–9), Soranus (155, 165), Victor (152–3).
10 Ellebichus (225), Modares (136–7), Saturninus (132, 181), Victor (133–4).
11 Anatolius (45, 79, 92, 111, 119, 121, 139), Apollonius (73, 103, accepting *PLRE*'s identification of the recipient of these two letters as being the same individual), Areobindus (XVIII, 23), Aspar (140), Flavius Zeno (65, 71), Sporacius (97), Titus (VI, XI), and an unnamed *magister militum* (IV.25) (probably Dionysius, *magister* of the east in the late 420s and early 430s: Azéma 1998: 37–9). The numeration of Theodoret's letters is more complicated than that of others: the first volume of the (standard) *Source chrétiennes* edition uses Roman numerals for the individual letters (which are preserved in one manuscript); the second and third volumes use Arabic numerals (these letters are preserved in a separate manuscript tradition); while the fourth volume, published much later than the others and comprising letters which survive in the records of church councils of the mid fifth century, uses the Roman numeral IV to indicate the volume number, and then Arabic numerals for the individual letters.
12 Callinicus (9.155), Eupaterius (9.71), Gennadius (1.59,72–3, 4.7, 6.62, 7.3, 9.9), Gudescalus (10.5), Guduin (14.1), Gulfaris (9.16), Maurentius (9.17, 53, 65, 124, 159, 162), Mauricius and Vitalianus (2.27–8), Romanus (1.32, 3.31, 5.19), Smaragdus (13.34), Theodorus (1.46), Velox (2.4), Zabardas (4.25), Zittas (10.1).
13 Anysius (6, 14, 34, 59, 77–8, 94), Marcellinus (62), Paeonius (*PG* 66.1577), Simplicius (24, 28, 130). Uranius, the recipient of *Letters* 37, may have been a general, but might equally have been a landowner whom Synesius was flattering with military allusions (cf. *PLRE* II.1186).
14 Bonifatius (185, 189, 220), Cresconius (113). The status of Florentinus, recipient of *Letters* 114, is unclear.
15 Hypatius (1.40), Timostratus (1.8).
16 Narses (60, 90), Sindula (31, 73). As for one other possible candidate for inclusion, Sidonius Apollinaris, Gallic aristocrat and bishop, did write a letter to Ecdicius praising his bravery during the siege of Clermont in 471 (3.3), but Ecdicius was acting in a private capacity before his appointment to military office in 474 (and, in addition, he was Sidonius' brother-in-law, so that the latter had good personal reasons to write to him); Sidonius also wrote to the *comes* Arbogast in 477 (4.17), but Arbogast was based in Trier, which was by this time under Frankish control, making it unlikely he was a Roman appointee.
17 Julian apparently observed to Libanius that "letters from generals are short because of their life of action" (Libanius *Letters* 369.5 [358]).
18 For a valuable introduction to letter writing in the Greco-Roman world, see Trapp 2003: 1–46, esp. 38–42; also useful is Stowers 1986.
19 Libanius also claimed to have played a part in the *magister* Lupicinus' gaining the consulship in 367 (*Orations* 1.166), although Lupicinus' effective support for

the emperor Valens during the revolt of Procopius (Ammianus 26.8.4, 9.1) is likely to have been sufficient recommendation.

20 Other examples of panegyrics in honor of generals include Corippus' *Iohannis* for John Troglyta and the fragmentary panegyric, preserved on papyrus, in praise of a certain Germanus and his victories over the Blemmyean tribesmen of southern Egypt, perhaps in the early fifth century (Page 1942: 590–5).

21 See Libanius *Letters* 925 and Theodoret *Letters* IV.25 ll.19ff. for two further instances.

22 Soldiers' tents: Ammianus 17.13.33, 18.2.10, 20.11.6, 24.1.11, 24.3.9, 24.4.2, 25.1.18, 29.5.55, 31.7.15; Malalas 330–1, 336; Ps.-Zachariah *Church History* 7.5; Procopius *Wars* 2.19.32, 2.30.12, 3.17.10, 6.23.9–10, 7.28.12; *Theodosian Code* 7.1.13 [391]; Vegetius *Epitome of Military Science* 2.7, 3.8; Urbicius 13; Ps.-Maurice *Strategy* 12B.20, 22. Commander's tent: Ammianus 24.6.15, 25.3.10 (cf. Malalas p. 332); Procopius *Wars* 2.21.3; Theophylact Simocatta 2.8.6, 3.1.9, 3.2.1, 7.10.1. Note also the sixth-century epitaph of a tent-maker (*papulionarius*) from Adrianople whose products were "perhaps destined for the army" (Feissel 1995: 383).

23 Cf. also Ammianus 16.11.15, 17.10.10, 21.12.22; Theodoret *Church History* 5.6.4; Socrates *Church History* 6.6.20. for other references to winter quarters and the temporary dispersal of troops likely to have been *comitatenses*.

24 This should not be taken to imply acceptance of Zosimus' accompanying claim about the corrupting effect which city life supposedly had on soldiers – a long-standing *topos* comprehensively refuted by Wheeler 1996.

25 Cf. also Procopius *Wars* 3.21.10 for the exemplary conduct of Belisarius' troops billeted in Carthage in 533. See Hopkins 1934: 38–40 for an example of a house at Dura-Europos where surviving graffiti implies its use for billeting in the early third century.

26 A law of Justinian's further stipulated that soldiers were not to occupy the main rooms of houses in which they were billeted, but to leave those for the use of the householders (*Novel* 130.9 [545]).

27 For interesting comparative material for the seventeenth-century French army and its relations with the communities on which it was billeted, see Parrott 2001: 516–26.

28 Cf. the comment of P.-L. Malosse in the Budé edition of this speech (212–13) that this must be a reference to women living within the empire, not to barbarian females; John Chrysostom also likened soldiers to wolves more generally in one of his sermons (*Homilies on Matthew* 61.2 (*PG* 58.590).

29 "The French army had, by long tradition, an enlightened and practical policy on brothels ... Brothels catered for the needs of French soldiers in two World Wars, and far-flung garrisons were sustained by BMCs (*Bordels Militaires de Campagne*), with the specific aim of cutting down on rape, desertion and disease" (Holmes 1985: 97). For discussion of the (very limited) evidence for prostitution in the Roman army during the Principate, see Phang 2001: 244–51; the only case of a possible military brothel is at third-century Dura-Europos (cf. Pollard 2000: 53–4). For the (similarly limited) evidence of soldiers' raping female inhabitants of the empire during the Principate, see Phang 2001: 251–60.

30 For other references to drunkenness on the part of soldiers, which did not, however, impinge on civilians, see Libanius *Orations* 18.199; Ammianus 24.1.16; Procopius *Wars* 3.12.8–10, 4.4.15–19, 29.

31 Although not a case involving military movements, this is perhaps an appropriate point to mention a sixth-century instance involving soldiers of the *dux* of Palestine harassing peasants and ejecting them from churches, in response to which the local bishop and civic notables proposed to write direct to the emperor (not without some concern about possible reprisals from the *dux*): Barsanuphius and John of Gaza *Letters* 831.
32 For a recent alternative interpretation of this text, see Aubert 2005.
33 There is also evidence of parallel developments in Gaul in the early fifth century without, however, specific evidence of military involvement (Garnsey and Woolf 1989: 164, citing Salvian *On the Government of God* 5.38–45; cf. also Krause 1987: 233–83; Whittaker 1993: 284–5; Wickham 2005: 527–9).
34 This land seems to have been leased out to others to farm, so provides no support for the idea of the *limitanei* as "soldier farmers." For the modest size of military land-owning in fourth-century Egypt, see Bagnall 1992.

Chapter 7   Army, Warfare, and Religion

1 Josephus *Jewish Antiquities* 14.10.12 highlights the practical difficulties that practicing Jews would have faced in the army, viz. being required to travel and work on the Sabbath, and obtaining ritually pure food. *Theodosian Code* 16.8.24 (418) banned Jews from military service, which implies that there were Jews present in the army in the early fifth century, and presumably this was not a novel phenomenon; cf. the late fourth-century inscription from Concordia in northern Italy which refers to a military unit of "the royal Emesene Jews" (*CIL* 5.8764, with discussion in Noy 1993–5: I.8–11).
2 For succinct overviews of the individuals referred to here, see Helgeland 1979: 733–55; Clauss 1986: 1094–8; Haldon 1986: 155–9. There are many more detailed discussions of this subject, including Harnack 1981 [1905]; Helgeland et al. 1985; Pucciarelli 1987; I have not been able to see Ubiña 2000. For helpful surveys of the historiography of this issue, specifically the ways in which the confessional backgrounds of scholars have influenced their interpretation of the ancient sources, see Helgeland 1979: 725–33; Gracie 1981.
3 The veracity of early Christian martyr acts has occasioned considerable discussion. Some are clearly later confections, manufactured for improving purposes, but others are undoubtedly genuine, based on short-hand records of actual trials: cf. de Ste. Croix 1984: 18–20 for specific comment on the accuracy of the records relating to Marcellus, and also Maximilian (see below). For detailed discussion of the latter case, see Brock 1994.
4 *AE* 1981.777, with Drew-Bear 1979, who notes (138–9) that the iconography of the stele is consistent with the identification of Aurelius as a Christian.
5 The evidence for Constantine's policy regarding sacrifice in the empire more generally is notoriously problematic: for an overview, with further references, see Averil Cameron and Hall 1999: 243–4, 247–8.
6 Intriguingly, the compilers of the *Theodosian Code* in the 430s apparently found nothing odd about the reference to "the gods" in *Theodosian Code* 7.20.2, since it was not emended to "May God preserve you!" until the early 530s (*Justinianic Code* 12.46.1) (cf. Jones 1963: 24).

7 Interestingly, soldiers are reported as swearing by Jupiter "the usual soldier's oath" when they acclaimed the usurper Procopius in 365 (Ammianus 26.7.17), even if this oath was of a different sort from the oath of enlistment to which Vegetius refers.

8 See Thomas 1981: 133–6 for the evidence and discussion of different interpretations; some commentators have assigned their destruction to the first half of the fourth century, in which case they could not be linked specifically to Theodosian policies. There is further discussion of destruction of Mithraic shrines in northwest Europe (though not specifically in military contexts) in Sauer 1996, with a critique in R. L. Gordon 1999 and response in Sauer 2003: 165–73.

9 These examples all derive from the less Christianized west. In the eastern provinces a church was constructed against the (exterior of the) wall of the fort at Nessana in the Negev in the middle of the fifth century (Colt 1950: 16–18), while the church inside the fort at Lejjun in Transjordan has been dated to the late fifth century – though the pagan shrine for the unit's standards may also have continued in use beyond this time (Schick 1987).

10 There are also a number of instances of military officers constructing churches in the fourth century, though it is not known whether they were for the use of soldiers: Flavius Jovinus, *magister equitum* in the 360s, built a church at Reims (*CIL* 13.3256); Flavius Bonus, *comes* and *dux* in Arabia in the early 390s, built a church in the province (*PLRE* I: 164); and an unnamed general of Honorius' built a church in northern Italy around the end of the fourth century (Maximus of Turin *Sermon*s 87.2). Another possibility from fourth-century Isauria is discussed in Hill 1985, but note the reservations about dating in Feissel 1989: 496.

11 Note that among those individuals included in von Haehling's data, the common identification of the *magister* Sebastianus as a Manichaean has been refuted by Tardieu 1988 (a reference I owe to Tony Birley).

12 Also relevant may be *Letter* 106, "To a soldier" (*stratiotes*), in which Basil commented that, as a result of their acquaintance, "we have come to know a man who proves that even in military life (*stratiotikos bios*) one may preserve the perfection of love for God, and that a Christian should be marked, not by the fashion of his clothing, but by the disposition of his soul." If the recipient of the letter was an ordinary soldier, however, it is odd that Basil should address him as "your Honor" (*timiotes*). It is possible that he was a military officer, in which case it remains relevant here. However, it is also possible that he was a civilian bureaucrat, service as which was often referred to as *militia* (or *strateia* in Greek) and which could entail wearing military-style dress. It is also possible that the details of the recipient were an educated guess supplied by a later editor confronted with a letter lacking an addressee, or that Stratiotes was the individual's name, not his occupation (cf. *Lexicon of Greek Personal Names*, IIIB, for one instance of the name, possibly from the imperial period) – suggestions which I owe respectively to Alan Sommerstein and Andrew Bayliss.

13 For the development of Augustine's ideas about "just war," see Markus 1983, and more succinctly Markus 1988: 115–16, where he notes that "far from throwing the weight of his authority into the scales against the Christian 'pacifism' of the first three centuries, Augustine brought back something of that reserve into the wholly changed world of the Christian Empire of Theodosius and his successors."

14 For discussion, see Harnack 1981 [1905]: 99–100; Bainton 1946: 200; Noethlichs 2001: 11–12.
15 The various references to soldiers taking communion raises the interesting question of how common it was for Christian soldiers in the fourth century to have been baptized, since baptism was the prerequisite for eligibility to receive communion. Clearly, some soldiers had been baptized, but in view of the reluctance of emperors and high officials to receive baptism until close to their deaths, because of concerns about forgiveness for their having imposed capital punishment as part of their duties, one might have thought that soldiers, too, would refrain because of their potential involvement in killing. On the other hand, the possibility of they themselves being killed in battle might have outweighed such concerns (cf. the (unlikely) story that Constantius II required his troops to undergo baptism before the battle of Mursa because of such concerns (Theodoret *Church History* 3.3.7)). A few individual cases of soldiers who were baptized while in military service are known from the fourth century, the most famous being Martin of Tours in the 350s (Sulpicius Severus *Life of Martin* 3.5–6); epigraphic examples: *ILS* 9841 (Salona) and Russell 1987: 85 (Anemurium, Cilicia, with Russell 1999 for date). On the eve of the Vandal expedition in 533, the patriarch of Constantinople placed a newly baptized soldier on board the fleet (Procopius *Wars* 3.12.2), though it is difficult to know how to interpret this: is it indicative of the fact that soldiers in the sixth century were not usually baptized, or was the fact of this soldier's recent baptism somehow seen as a lucky omen?
16 Cf. Jones 1963: 25: "Under a succession of Christian emperors the general tone of the army must have become more and more Christian."
17 Even if one suspects Procopius of engaging in a certain amount of special pleading on behalf of his patron Belisarius – the soldiers' weakened state becomes part of the explanation for Belisarius' defeat in the ensuing battle – there is no reason to doubt that they had been fasting, particularly since other sources confirm that the battle occurred on Easter Saturday (Malalas *Chronicle* p. 463).
18 Cf. Justinian *Novel* 109 (541), whose preamble reiterated the ban on heretics serving in the army or the bureaucracy.
19 The subject is made even more interesting by the existence of documentary evidence from eastern provinces in the third and early fourth century attesting the presence of pagan priests as part of the establishment in military units (see Brennan 1987: 119 and Palme 2002: 95–7 for details). The latest item derives from Egypt in 323 (i.e., just prior to Constantine's acquisition of the east from Licinius), raising the intriguing, if unlikely, scenario of a seamless transition from pagan to Christian army chaplains (cf. Palme 2002: 97).
20 It has been suggested that there is evidence for the existence of chaplains at the beginning of the fifth century, at least for the units of imperial guards stationed in Constantinople (the so-called *scholae palatinae*): Woods 1991: 42, Tomlin 1998: 45 n.54, and Palme 2002: 94–5, relying on Palladius *Dialogue on the Life of John Chrysostom* 71–2 and John Chrysostom *Letters* 213, 218 (*PG* 52.729, 731–2). The argument hinges on the interpretation of the word *schola* in these texts (which refer to priests who were supporters of John Chrysostom being driven out of "the *schola*" after John's fall and exile); since the word can also mean a "school" for catechumens (i.e., individuals preparing for baptism

(cf. Lampe *A Patristic Greek Lexicon*), there remains room for uncertainty, particularly since Palladius is careful in the same passage to describe a soldier in the *scholae palatinae* as a "soldier of the *scholae* attached to the emperor."

21 As for the outcome, although Tiberius was initially sympathetic to the request, John's account implies that it was not ultimately granted.

22 This is not to deny that the Decian persecution may well have been an originally unintended consequence of a decision by that emperor to unite the empire in a mass expression of religious devotion to the gods (Rives 1999), or that there has been much debate as to whether the initiative in the Diocletianic persecution actually lay with Galerius (see P. S. Davies 1989 for discussion of the issues).

23 There is debate about the authenticity of this last source: see Van Dam 1985b; Barnes 1989b; Trombley 1993: 246–82.

24 Note, however, that according to Augustine (*City of God* 18.54), the *comites* Jovius and Gaudentius destroyed temples and cult statues in Carthage in March 399, while another source refers to them undertaking similar action more widely in north Africa (Quodvultdeus *Book of Promises* 3.38.41); these claims are essentially corroborated by a law sent by the emperor Honorius to the governor of Africa in the summer of the same year (*Theodosian Code* 16.10.18) to the effect that temples were not to be destroyed, although cult statues could be removed. None of these sources refers explicitly to the involvement of troops, and the reference to the office of *comes* is ambiguous as to whether these men were civilian or military; however, Gaudentius is known from other sources to have followed a career in the army, which makes the use of troops likely.

25 The religious stance of the *comes Aegypti* Romanus in 391 is unknown.

26 Note, however, that the emperor Theodosius apparently specified that the proceeds from the destruction of the Serapeum in Alexandria in 391 were to be used to help the poor of the city, while the cult statues were melted down and fashioned into vessels for use in the city's churches (Socrates *Church History* 5.16).

27 Note the lead apparently taken by a Christian soldier in 391 when the Christian laity momentarily hesitated to destroy the cult statue in the Serapeum (Rufinus *Church History* 11.24).

28 Cf. Noethlichs 1986 for a convenient survey of anti-pagan measures during late antiquity.

29 Justinian's order may have been quietly ignored, or perhaps the original announcement was primarily rhetorical in intent, designed to promote the emperor's image as a Christian ruler to the inhabitants of Constantinople who, on account of Philae's remote location, would be unable to verify easily whether the measure had in fact been implemented; indeed, the dispatch of the temple's cult statues to the capital, on which Procopius also comments, would have provided plausible corroboration.

30 On which see Michael Whitby 1999, with references to previous literature.

31 E.g., Sozomen *Church History* 8.23: "The soldiers, as is usual on such occasions, went beyond their orders, and forcibly stripped the women of their ornaments, and carried off as booty their chains, their golden girdles, necklaces, and their collars of rings; they pulled off the lobes of the ear with the earrings."

32 Coming as the quoted passage does in the "General Observations on the Fall of the Roman Empire in the West," which he interposed after Chapter 38

(his discussion of the establishment of the Frankish and Saxon kingdoms in Gaul and Britain respectively), his strictures obviously relate particularly to the end of the empire in the west during the fifth century.

33 Cf. Momigliano 1963a and Ward-Perkins 2005: 40–41, who cites Gibbon's claims with evident approval alongside Jones's argument about the role of "idle mouths" in the decline of the empire (1964: 1045–8), which Ward-Perkins describes as "Gibbon's 'specious demands of charity and devotion' expressed in measured twentieth-century prose." It is worth noting that Jones's argument is more nuanced than Gibbon's – in particular, he concedes that the burden was greater in the east than the west, yet the east survived (1064) – and he ends up placing the main emphasis on external factors in his analysis of the decline of the empire.

34 Cf. the following statement on the first page of the work: "The principal conquests of the Romans were atchieved under the republic... by the policy of the senate, the active emulation of the consuls, and the martial enthusiasm of the people" (Gibbon 1994 [1776–88]: I.31), where "martial enthusiasm" bears a close resemblance to "military spirit."

35 Rousseau 1985: 149–73 for Pachomian monasteries in Egypt, and Rousseau 2000: 755 for Syria. Gibbon was not unaware of this aspect of monasticism (1994 [1776–88]: II.422–3), but he underplayed it in favor of the wealth which some monasteries accrued through bequests.

BIBLIOGRAPHY OF ANCIENT SOURCES

This bibliography provides details of editions of the original text of ancient sources used, and English translations where available. (Note, however, that some of these translations, particularly those produced in the nineteenth and early twentieth century, were published before the production of a modern edition of the original text, and so are not always totally reliable.) Where the most recent edition of a work remains that published in *PG*, *PL*, or *PO*, it is usually not included below since the reference to the relevant volume is given when a passage is quoted or cited. In general, the series in which an edition or translation appears has been indicated, in preference to place of publication. For editions of papyri, see the standard checklist available on-line at http://odyssey.lib.duke.edu/papyrus/texts/clist.html.

Agathias, *History*, ed. R. Keydell (Berlin, 1967); tr. D. Frendo (Berlin, 1975)
Ambrose, *Letters*, ed. M. Zelzer, *CSEL* 82 (1982); tr. W. Liebeschuetz (TTH, 2005)
Ambrose, *On the Death of Valentinian II*, ed. O. Faller, *CSEL* 73 (1955); tr. W. Liebeschuetz (TTH, 2005)
Ammianus Marcellinus, ed. W. Seyfarth (Teubner, 1978); trs. J. C. Rolfe (Loeb, 1935–9), W. Hamilton (Penguin, 1986)
Anonymous Valesianus, tr. J. C. Rolfe in vol. 3 of Loeb Ammianus
Appian, *Mithridatic Wars*, tr. H. White (Loeb, 1912–13)
Athanasius, *Acephalous History*, ed. and French tr. A. Martin, *SC* 317 (1985)
Athanasius, *History of the Arians*, ed. H.-G. Opitz (Berlin, 1935–41); tr. A. Robertson (NPNCF, 1891)
Athanasius, *In Defence of his Flight*, ed. H.-G. Opitz (Berlin, 1935–41); tr. A. Robertson (NPNCF, 1891)
Augustine, *The City of God*, eds. B. Dombart and A. Kalb, *CCSL* 47–8 (1955); tr. H. Bettenson (Penguin, 1972)
Augustine, *Confessions*, ed. L. Verheijen, *CCSL* 27 (1981); tr. H. Chadwick (Oxford, 1991)
Augustine, *Letters*, ed. A. Goldbacher, *CSEL* 34, 44, 57–8 (1895–1923)
Aurelius Victor, *On the Caesars* (*De Caesaribus*), ed. and French tr. P. Dufraigne (Budé, 1975); tr. H. W. Bird (TTH, 1994)

BIBLIOGRAPHY OF ANCIENT SOURCES

Barsanuphius and John of Gaza, *Letters*, eds. and French trs. F. Neyt, P. de Angelis-Noah, and L. Regnault, *SC* 426–7, 450–1, 468 (1998–2002)

Basil of Caesarea, *Letters*, ed. and French tr. Y. Courtonne (Budé, 1957–66); trs. R. J. Deferrari and M. R. P. McGuire (Loeb, 1926–39)

Calendar of Polemius Silvius, ed. A. Degrassi, *Inscriptiones Italiae*, vol. 13.2 (Rome, 1963), 263–76

Candidus, *History*, ed. and tr. R. C. Blockley, *The Fragmentary Classicising Historians of the Later Roman Empire: Eunapius, Olympiodorus, Priscus and Malchus*, vol. 2 (Liverpool, 1983)

Cassiodorus, *Miscellanies (Variae)*, ed. T. Mommsen *MGH.AA* 12 (1894); tr. (selection) S. J. B. Barnish (TTH, 1992)

Claudian, *Poems*, ed. T. Birt, *MGH.AA* 10 (1892); tr. M. Platenauer (Loeb, 1922); tr. of *Panegyric on the Fourth Consulate of Honorius*, W. Barr (Liverpool, 1981)

Clement of Alexandria, *Exhortation (Protrepticus)*, eds. and French trs. A. Plassart and C. Mondésert, *SC* 2bis (1949); tr. G. W. Butterworth (Loeb, 1919)

Constantine Porphyrogenitus, *Book of Ceremonies*, ed. J. J. Reiske (Berlin, 1829)

Corippus, *In Praise of Justin II*, ed. and tr. A. Cameron (London, 1976)

Corippus, *Iohannis*, ed. J. Diggle (Cambridge, 1970); tr. G. W. Shea (Lewiston, 1998)

Cyril of Scythopolis, *Life of St. Saba*, ed. E. Schwartz (Berlin, 1939); tr. R. M. Price in *Lives of the Monks of Palestine* (Kalamazoo, 1991)

Description of the Whole World (Expositio Totius Mundi), ed. and French tr. J. Rougé (Budé, 1966)

Dexippus, ed. F. Jacoby, in *Die Fragmente der griechischen Historiker*, no. 100

Easter Chronicle (Chronicon Paschale), ed. L. Dindorf (Bonn, 1832); trs. M. Whitby and M. Whitby (TTH, 1989)

Eugippius, *Life of St. Severinus*, ed. R. Noll (Berlin, 1963); tr. L. Bieler, *FoC* 55 (1965)

Eunapius, *History*, ed. and tr. R. C. Blockley, *The Fragmentary Classicising Historians of the Later Roman Empire: Eunapius, Olympiodorus, Priscus and Malchus*, vol. 2 (Liverpool, 1983)

Eusebius, *Church History*, ed. and French tr. G. Bardy, *SC* 31, 41, 55 (1952–60); tr. G. A. Williamson (Penguin, 1965)

Eusebius, *Life of Constantine*, ed. F. Winkelmann (Berlin, 1975); trs. A. Cameron and S. G. Hall (Oxford, 1999)

Eusebius, *Martyrs of Palestine*, ed. and French tr. G. Bardy, in Eusebius *Church History* vol. 3, *SC* 55 (1960), 121–74

Eutropius, ed. H. Droysen, *MGH.AA* 2 (1879); tr. H. W. Bird (TTH, 1993)

Evagrius, *Church History*, eds. J. Bidez and L. Parmentier (London, 1898); tr. M. Whitby (TTH, 2000)

Firmus of Caesarea, *Letters*, eds. and French trs. M.-A. Calvet-Sebasti and P.-L. Gatier, *SC* 350 (1989)

George of Pisidia, *Poems and Panegyrics*, ed. A. Pertusi (Ettal, 1960)

Greek Anthology, ed. H. Beckby, 2nd edn. (Munich, 1965–8); tr. W. R. Paton (Loeb, 1916–18)

Gregory the Great, *Letters (Registrum Epistolarum)*, eds. P. Ewald and L. Hartmann, *MGH Epistolae* 1–2 (1887–99)

Gregory of Nazianzus, *Letters*, ed. and French tr. P. Gallay (Budé, 1964–7)

BIBLIOGRAPHY OF ANCIENT SOURCES

Gregory of Nazianzus, *Orations*, eds. and French trs. J. Bernardi, G. Lafontaine, J. Mossay, et al., *SC* 247, 250, 270 et al. (1978–95) (incomplete)

Gregory of Nazianus, *Poem* 11 (*On his own life*), ed. and German tr. C. Jungck (Heidelberg, 1974); tr. D. M. Meehan, *FoC* 75 (1987)

Gregory of Nyssa, *Letters*, ed. and French tr. P. Maraval, *SC* 363 (1990)

Gregory of Tours, *History of the Franks*, eds. W. Arndt and B. Krusch, *MGH Scriptores Rerum Merovingicarum* (1884); tr. L. Thorpe (Penguin, 1974)

Gregory Thaumaturgus, *Canonical Letter*, trs. P. Heather and J. Matthews, *The Goths in the Fourth Century* (TTH, 1991)

Herodian, ed. and tr. C. R. Whittaker (Loeb, 1969–70)

Hippolytus, *The Apostolic Tradition*, eds. and trs. G. Dix and H. Chadwick (London, 1968)

Historia Augusta, ed. E. Hohl (Teubner, 1927); tr. D. Magie (Loeb, 1922–32)

History of the Monks (*Historia Monarchorum in Aegypto*), ed. A.-J. Festugière (Brussels, 1961); tr. N. Russell, *The Lives of the Desert Fathers* (Kalamazoo, 1980)

Isidore of Pelusium, *Letters*, *PG* 78; ed. and French tr. (incomplete) P. Évieux, *SC* 422, 454 (1997–2000)

Jacob of Edessa, *Chronicle*, in *Chronica Minora*, ed. and Latin tr. E. W. Brooks, I. Guidi, and I.-B. Chabot (Corpus Scriptorum Christianorum Orientalium, Scriptores Syri 6, 1907)

Jerome, *Chronicle*, eds. R. Helm and U. Treu (Berlin, 1984)

Jerome, *Commentary on Isaiah*, ed. M. Adriaen, *CCSL* 73 (1963)

John Chrysostom, *To a Young Widow*, ed. and French tr. B. Grillet, *SC* 138 (1968)

John of Antioch, ed. C. Müller, *Fragmenta Historicorum Graecorum*, vol. 5 (Paris, 1883)

John of Biclaro, *Chronicle*, ed. T. Mommsen, *MGH.AA* 11 (1894); tr. K. B. Wolf (TTH, 1991)

John of Ephesus, *Church History*, tr. R. Payne-Smith (Oxford, 1860)

John of Nikiu, *Chronicle*, tr. R. H. Charles (London, 1916)

John the Lydian, *On the Magistracies of the Roman State*, ed. and tr. A. C. Bandy (Philadelphia, 1983); tr. T. F. Carney in *Bureaucracy in Traditional Society* (Lawrence, KS, 1971)

John the Lydian, *On the Months*, ed. R. Wünsch (Leipzig, 1898)

Jordanes, *History of the Goths* (*Getica*), ed. T. Mommsen, *MGH.AA* 5 (1882)

Josephus, *Jewish Antiquities*, trs. H. Thackeray, R. Marcus, and L. Feldman (Loeb, 1930–65)

Julian, *Works*, eds. and French trs. J. Bidez and C. Lacombrade (Budé, 1932–64); tr. W. C. Wright (Loeb, 1913–23) (with different numbering of the *Letters*)

Justinian, *Edicts* – see Justinian, *Novels*

Justinian, *Novels*, eds. R. Schoell and G. Kroll, 7th edn (Berlin, 1963)

Justinianic Code, ed. P. Krueger, 14th edn (Berlin, 1967)

Lactantius, *Divine Institutes*, eds. S. Brandt and G. Laubmann, *CSEL* 19, 27 (1890–7); trs. A. Bowen and P. Garnsey (TTH, 2003)

Lactantius, *On the Deaths of the Persecutors*, ed. and tr. J. L. Creed (Oxford, 1984)

Latin Panegyrics, ed. R. A. B. Mynors (Oxford, 1964); trs. C. E. V. Nixon and B. S. Rodgers (Berkeley, 1994)

Leo, *Letters*, *PL* 54; tr. E. Hunt, *FoC* 34 (1957)

Libanius, *Letters*, ed. R. Foerster (= *Works* vols. 10–11) (1921–2); ed. and tr. (selection, with different numbering) A. F. Norman (Loeb, 1992)

BIBLIOGRAPHY OF ANCIENT SOURCES

Libanius, *Orations*, ed. and tr. (selection) A. F. Norman (Loeb, 1969–77); *Oration* 59, tr. M. Dodgeon in Lieu and Montserrat 1996: 147–209

Liberatus, *Breviary* (*Short Account of the Affair of the Nestorians and Eutychians*), PL 68. 963–1052

Life of St Pachomius (Bohairic), tr. A. Veilleux (Cistercian Publications, 1980)

Life of St Theodore of Sykeon, ed. and French tr. A. J. Festugière (Brussels, 1970); trs. N. Baynes and E. Dawes in *Three Byzantine Saints* (London, 1948)

Life of the Younger St Symeon the Stylite, ed. P. van den Ven (Brussels, 1962–70)

Livy (Books 36–40), ed. P. G. Walsh (Oxford, 1999); tr. H. Bettenson (Penguin, 1976)

Majorian, *Novels* – see Theodosian Code

Malalas, *Chronicle*, ed. I. Thurn (Berlin, 2000); trs. E. Jeffreys, M. Jeffreys, and R. Scott (AABS, 1986)

Malchus, *History*, ed. and tr. R. C. Blockley, *The Fragmentary Classicising Historians of the Later Roman Empire: Eunapius, Olympiodorus, Priscus and Malchus*, vol. 2 (Liverpool, 1983)

Marcellinus, *Chronicle*, ed. T. Mommsen, *MGH.AA* 13 (1898); tr. B. Croke (AABS, 1995)

Mark the Deacon, *Life of Porphyry of Gaza*, eds. and French trs. H. Grégoire and M.-A. Kugener (Paris, 1930); tr. C. Rapp in T. Head (ed.), *Medieval Hagiography* (New York, 2001)

Maximus of Turin, *Sermons*, ed. A. Mutzenbecher, *CCSL* 23 (1962)

Menander, *History*, ed. and tr. R. C. Blockley (Liverpool, 1985)

Michael the Syrian, *Chronicle*, ed. and French tr. J. B. Chabot (Paris, 1901)

Miracles of St. Demetrius, ed. P. Lemerle (Paris, 1979)

Notitia Dignitatum, ed. O. Seeck (Berlin, 1876)

Olympiodorus, *History*, ed. and tr. R. C. Blockley, *The Fragmentary Classicising Historians of the Later Roman Empire: Eunapius, Olympiodorus, Priscus and Malchus*, vol. 2 (Liverpool, 1983)

On Military Affairs (*De Rebus Bellicis*), ed. R. Ireland (Teubner, 1984); tr. R. Ireland in Hassall 1979

On Strategy (*Peri strategias*), ed. and tr. G. T. Dennis in *Three Byzantine Military Treatises* (Vienna, 1985)

Optatus, *Against the Donatists*, ed. C. Ziwsa, *CSEL* 26 (1893); tr. M. Edwards (TTH, 1997)

Orientius, *The Admonition* (*Commonitorium*), ed. R. Ellis, *CSEL* 16 (1888); tr. M. D. Tobin (Washington, DC, 1945)

Origen, *Against Celsus*, ed. and French tr. P. M. Borret, *SC* 132, 136, 147, 150, 227 (1967–76); tr. H. Chadwick (Cambridge, 1953)

Orosius, *History*, ed. C. Zangemeister, *CSEL* 5 (1882); tr. R. J. Deferrari, *FoC* 50 (1964)

Palladius, *Dialogue on the Life of John Chrysostom*, eds. and French trs. P. J. Leclercq and A.-M. Malingrey, *SC* 341–2 (1988); tr. R. T. Meyer, *ACW* 45 (1985)

Paul of Aegina, in *Corpus Medicorum Graecorum*, vol. 9 (1921)

Paulinus of Nola, *Letters*, ed. W. Hartel, *CSEL* 29 (1894); tr. P. Walsh, *ACW* 35–6 (1967)

Pelagius I, *Letters*, eds. P. M. Gasso and C. M. Batlle (Montserrat, 1956)

Philostorgius, *Church History*, ed. J. Bidez (Berlin, 1913); tr. E. Walford (London, 1855)

Polemius Silvius, *Calendar*, ed. A. Degrassi, *Inscriptiones Italiae*, vol. 13.2 (Rome, 1963), 263–76
Priscian, *Panegyric*, ed. and French tr. A. Chauvot (Bonn, 1986); tr. P. Coyne (Lewiston, 1991)
Priscus, *History*, ed. and tr. R. C. Blockley, *The Fragmentary Classicising Historians of the Later Roman Empire: Eunapius, Olympiodorus, Priscus and Malchus*, vol. 2 (Liverpool, 1983)
Procopius, *Buildings*, eds. J. Haury and G. Wirth (Teubner, 1964); trs. H. B. Dewing and G. Downey (Loeb, 1940)
Procopius, *Secret History*, eds. J. Haury and G. Wirth (Teubner, 1963); tr. G. A. Williamson (Penguin, 1966)
Procopius, *Wars*, eds. J. Haury and G. Wirth (Teubner, 1962–3); tr. H. B. Dewing (Loeb, 1914–28)
Procopius of Gaza, *Panegyric*, ed. and French tr. A. Chauvot (Bonn, 1986)
Pseudo-Joshua the Stylite, *Chronicle*, trs. F. R. Trombley and J. W. Watt (TTH, 2000)
Pseudo-Maurice, *Strategy* (*Strategikon*), ed. G. T. Dennis (Vienna, 1981); tr. G. T. Dennis (Philadelphia, 1984)
Pseudo-Zachariah, *Church History*, trs. F. J. Hamilton and E. W. Brooks (London, 1899)
Quodvultdeus, *The Book of the Promises and Prophecies of God*, ed. R. Braun, *CCSL* 60 (1976)
Rufinus, *Church History*, *PL* 21; tr. P. R. Amidon (Oxford, 1997) (Books 10–11)
Sebeos, *Armenian History*, tr. R. W. Thomson (TTH, 1999)
Severus, *Novels* – see Theodosian Code
Sidonius Apollinaris, *Letters and Poems*, ed. C. Luetjohann, *MGH.AA* 8 (1887); tr. W. B. Anderson (Loeb, 1936)
Socrates Scholasticus, *Church History*, ed. G. C. Hansen (Berlin, 1995); tr. A. C. Zenos (NPNCF, 1891)
Sozomen, *Church History*, eds. J. Bidez and G. C. Hansen (Berlin, 1960); tr. C. D. Hartranft (NPNCF, 1891)
Strabo, *Geography*, tr. H. L. Jones (Loeb, 1917–32)
Suidas, ed. A. Adler (Leipzig, 1928–38)
Sulpicius Severus, *Life of Saint Martin*, ed. and French tr. J. Fontaine, *SC* 133–5 (1967–9)
Symmachus, *Works*, ed. O. Seeck, *MGH.AA* 6 (Berlin, 1883); tr. of *Memoranda*, R. H. Barrow (Oxford, 1973); French tr. of *Letters*, J. Callu (Budé, 1972–2002)
Synesius, *Letters*, ed. A. Garzya (Rome, 1979); tr. A. Fitzgerald (London, 1926)
Synesius, *On Kingship* (*Peri basileias/De regno*), ed. and French tr. C. Lacombrade (Budé, 1951); tr. A. Fitzgerald (London, 1930)
Tacitus, *Annals*, ed. C. D. Fisher (Oxford, 1906); tr. A. J. Woodman (Indianapolis, 2004)
Tacitus, *Histories*, ed. C. D. Fisher (Oxford, 1910); tr. K. Wellesley (Penguin, 1964)
Tertullian, *Works*, eds. E. Dekkers, J. G. P. Borleffs, R. Willems, et al., *CCSL* 1–2 (1954); *Apology*, tr. T. R. Glover (Loeb, 1931); *On Idolatry*, tr. J. C. M. van Winden (Leiden, 1987); *On the Wreath*, tr. E. A. Quain, *FoC* 40 (1959)
Theodoret, *Church History*, ed. L. Parmentier (Berlin, 1954)
Theodoret, *Letters*, ed. and French tr. Y. Azéma, *SC* 40, 98, 111, 429 (1955–98); tr. B. Jackson (NPNCF, 1892)

BIBLIOGRAPHY OF ANCIENT SOURCES

Theodosian Code, ed. T. Mommsen, 2nd edn. (Berlin, 1954); tr. C. Pharr (Princeton, 1952)

Theodosius II, *Novels – see Theodosian Code*

Theophanes, *Chronicle*, ed. C. de Boor (Leipzig, 1883–85); trs. C. Mango and R. Scott (Oxford, 1997)

Theophylact Simocatta, *History*, eds. C. de Boor and P. Wirth (Teubner, 1972); trs. M. Whitby and M. Whitby (Oxford, 1986)

Urbicius, *Invention* (*Epitedeuma*), eds. and trs. G. Greatrex, H. Elton, and R. Burgess (= *Byzantinische Zeitschrift* 98 (2005) 35–74)

Valentinian III, *Novels – see Theodosian Code*

Vegetius, *Epitome of Military Science*, ed. C. Lang (Teubner, 1885); tr. N. P. Milner (TTH, 1996)

Victor of Vita, *History of the Vandal Persecution*, ed. C. Halm, *MGH.AA* 3 (1879); tr. J. Moorhead (TTH, 1992)

Zosimus, ed. and French tr. F. Paschoud (Budé, 1971–89); tr. R. T. Ridley (AABS, 1982)

BIBLIOGRAPHY OF MODERN WORKS

Adams, J. N. (2003) *Bilingualism and the Latin Language* (Cambridge)
Alston, R. (2002) "Managing the frontiers: supplying the frontier troops in the sixth and seventh centuries" in P. Erdkamp (ed.), *The Roman Army and the Economy* (Amsterdam), 398–419
Ando, C. (2000) *Imperial Ideology and Provincial Loyalty in the Roman Empire* (Berkeley)
Arens, W. (1979) *The Man-Eating Myth: Anthropology and Anthropophagy* (New York)
Arthur, P. (2002) *Naples: From Roman Town to City-State* (London)
Arthur, P. (2004) "From *vicus* to village: Italian landscapes, AD 400–1000" in Christie 2004: 103–33
Asdracha, C. (1998) "Inscriptions chrétiennes et protobyzantines de la Thrace orientale et de l'ile d'Imbros (IIIe–VIIe siècles): presentation et commentaire historique," *Arkhaiologikon Deltion 49–50 (1994–1995) Meros A' – Meletes* (Athens), 279–356
Askenasy, H. (1994) *Cannibalism: From Sacrifice to Survival* (New York)
Atkins, E. M., and Dodaro, R. J. (2001) *Augustine: Political Writings* (Cambridge)
Aubert, J.-J. (2005) "*Du lard ou du cochon?* The *Testamentum porcelli* as a Jewish anti-Christian pamphlet" in J.-J. Aubert and Z. Várhelyi (eds.), *A Tall Order: Writing the Social History of the Ancient World. Essays in Honor of William V. Harris* (Leipzig), 107–41
Azéma, Y. (1998) *Théodoret de Cyr: Correspondance* IV (Paris)
Bachrach, B. S. (2001) *Early Carolingian Warfare: Prelude to Empire* (Philadelphia)
Bagnall, R. S. (1986) "Two Byzantine legal papyri in a private collection" in R. S. Bagnall and W. V. Harris (eds.), *Studies in Roman Law in Memory of A. Arthur Schiller* (Leiden), 1–9
Bagnall, R. S. (1992) "Military officers as landowners in fourth-century Egypt," *Chiron* 22: 47–54
Bagnall, R. S. (1993) *Egypt in Late Antiquity* (Princeton)
Bagnall, R. S. (1995) *Reading Papyri, Writing Ancient History* (London)
Bagnall, R. S., and Palme, B. (1996) "Franks in sixth-century Egypt," *Tyche* 11: 1–10
Bailey, D. M. (1991) *British Museum Expedition to Middle Egypt: Excavations at El-Ashmunein, IV. Hermopolis Magna: Buildings of the Roman Period* (London)

BIBLIOGRAPHY OF MODERN WORKS

Bainton, R. (1946) "The early Church and war," *HTR* 39: 188–212
Baker, P. A. (2004) *Medical Care for the Roman Army on the Rhine, Danube and British Frontiers in the First, Second and Early Third Centuries* AD (Oxford)
Banaji, J. (2001) *Agrarian Change in Late Antiquity: Gold, Labour, and Aristocratic Dominance* (Oxford)
Barnes, T. D. (1976) "Imperial campaigns, AD 285–311," *Phoenix* 30: 174–93
Barnes, T. D. (1982) *The New Empire of Diocletian and Constantine* (Cambridge, MA)
Barnes, T. D. (1985a) "Constantine and the Christians of Persia," *JRS* 75: 126–36
Barnes, T. D. (1985b) "The career of Abinnaeus," *Phoenix* 39: 368–74
Barnes, T. D. (1989a) "Emperors on the move," *JRA* 2: 147–61
Barnes, T. D. (1989b) "The baptism of Theodosius II," *Studia Patristica* 19: 8–12
Barnes, T. D. (1993) *Athanasius and Constantius: Theology and Politics in the Constantinian Empire* (Cambridge, MA)
Barnes, T. D. (1995) "Statistics and the conversion of the Roman aristocracy," *JRS* 85: 135–47
Barnes, T. D. (1998) *Ammianus Marcellinus and the Representation of Historical Reality* (Ithaca, NY)
Barnes, T. D. (1999) "Latin epigraphy and the history of the western Roman empire after Constantine," *XI Congresso Internazionale di Epigrafia Greca e Latina: Roma, 18–24 settembre 1997* (Rome), II.565–76
Barnish, S. J. B. (1987) "Pigs, plebeians and *potentes*: Rome's economic hinterland, c. 350–600 AD," *PBSR* 55: 157–85
Barnish, S. J. B., Lee, A. D., and Whitby, M. (2000) "Government and administration" in Cameron et al. 2000: 164–206
Bassett, S. (2004) *The Urban Image of Late Antique Constantinople* (Cambridge)
Bastien, P. (1988) *Monnaie et "donativa" au Bas-Empire* (Wetteren)
Bayard, D., and Piton, D. (1979) "Un bâtiment public du Bas-Empire à Amiens: 1973–1978 – six ans de recherches au square Jules Bocquet et au logis du Roy," *Cahiers archeologiques de Picardie* 6: 153–68
Bean, G. E., and Mitford, T. B. (1970) *Journeys in Rough Cilicia, 1964–1968* (Vienna)
Beard, M., North, J., and Price, S. (1998) *Religions of Rome* (Cambridge), 2 vols.
Beevor, A. (2002) *Berlin: The Downfall, 1945* (London)
Bell, H. I. (1924) *Jews and Christians in Egypt* (Oxford)
Bell, H. I., Martin V., Turner, E. G., and van Berchem, D. (1962) *The Abinnaeus Archive: Papers of a Roman Officer in the Reign of Constantius II* (Oxford)
Bellinger, A. R. (1966) *Catalogue of Byzantine Coins in the Dumbarton Oaks Collection and in the Whittemore Collection*, vol. 1: *Anastasius I to Maurice, 491–602* (Washington DC)
Bidwell, P. T. (1992) "Later Roman barracks in Britain" in V. A. Maxfield and M. J. Dobson (eds.), *Roman Frontier Studies 1989* (Exeter), 9–15
Bidwell, P. T., and Speak, S. (1994) *Excavations at South Shields Roman Fort*, vol. 1 (Newcastle)
Birley, A. R. (1983) "The economic effects of Roman frontier policy" in A. King and M. Henig (eds.), *The Roman West in the Third Century* (Oxford), 39–53
Birley, E. (1969) "Septimius Severus and the Roman army," *Epigraphische Studien* 8: 63–82
Bishop, M. C., and Coulston, J. C. (1993) *Roman Military Equipment from the Punic Wars to the Fall of Rome* (London)

Blockley, R. C. (1977) "Ammianus Marcellinus on the battle of Strasburg: art and analysis in the *History*," *Phoenix* 31: 218–31

Blockley, R. C. (1981) *The Fragmentary Classicising Historians of the Later Roman Empire*, vol. 1 (Liverpool)

Blockley, R. C. (1985a) *The History of Menander the Guardsman* (Liverpool)

Blockley, R. C. (1985b) "Subsidies and diplomacy: Rome and Persia in late antiquity," *Phoenix* 39: 62–74

Blockley, R. C. (1989) "Constantius II and Persia" in C. Deroux (ed.), *Studies in Latin Literature and Roman History*, vol. 5 (Brussels), 465–90

Bodel, J. P. (ed.) (2001) *Epigraphic Evidence: Writing Ancient History from Inscriptions* (London)

Bowden, W., Lavan, L., and Machado, C. (eds.) (2004) *Recent Research on the Late Antique Countryside* (Leiden)

Bowersock, G., Clive, J., and Graubard, S. (eds.) (1977) *Edward Gibbon and the Decline and Fall of the Roman Empire* (Cambridge, MA)

Bowersock, G., Brown, P., and Grabar, O. (eds.) (1999) *Late Antiquity: A Guide to the Postclassical World* (Cambridge, MA)

Bowman, A. K., Garnsey, P., and Rathbone, D. (eds.) (2000) *The Cambridge Ancient History* XI: *The High Empire, AD 70–192* (Cambridge)

Bowman, A. K., Garnsey, P., and Cameron, A. (eds.) (2005) *The Cambridge Ancient History* XII: *The Crisis of Empire, AD 193–337* (Cambridge)

Bradbury, S. (1994) "Constantine and the problem of anti-pagan legislation in the fourth century," *Classical Philology* 89: 120–39

Brennan, P. (1980) "Combined legionary detachments as artillery units in late-Roman Danubian bridgehead dispositions," *Chiron* 10: 553–67

Brennan, P. (1987) "Jupiter Dolichenus and religious life in the Roman army" in G. H. R. Horsley (ed.), *New Documents Illustrating Early Christianity: A Review of the Greek Inscriptions and Papyri published in 1979* (Sydney), 118–26

Brennan, P. (1996) "The *Notitia Dignitatum*" in C. Nicolet (ed.), *Les litteratures techniques dans l'antiquité romaine* (Geneva), 153–69

Brennan, P. (1998a) "The last of the Romans: Roman identity and the Roman army in the late Roman Near East" in G. Clarke (ed.), *Identities in the Eastern Mediterranean in Antiquity* (= *Mediterranean Archaeology* 11), 191–203

Brennan, P. (1998b) "A user's guide to the *Notitia Dignitatum*: the case of the *Dux Armeniae* (*ND Or.* XXXVIII)," *Antichthon* 32: 34–49

Brennan, P. (1998c) "Divide and fall: the separation of legionary cavalry and the fragmentation of the Roman empire" in T. W. Hillard, R. A. Kearsley, C. E. V. Nixon, and A. E. Nobbs (eds.), *Ancient History in a Modern University* (Grand Rapids, MI), II.238–44

Brennan, P. (2001) Review of Nicasie (1998), *Tijdschrift voor Geschiedenis* 114: 261–6

Brennan, P. (forthcoming) "Zosimos 2.34.1 and the 'Constantinian reform'" in A. Lewin (ed.), *L'Esercito tardo antico nel vicino oriente* (Potenza)

Brett, M., and Fentress, E. (1996) *The Berbers* (Oxford)

Brock, P. (1994) "Why did Maximilian refuse to serve in the Roman army?" *Journal of Ecclesiastical History* 45: 195–209

Brown, P. D. C. (1971) "The church at Richborough," *Britannia* 2: 225–31

Brown, P. R. L. (1971) *The World of Late Antiquity* (London)

Brown, T. S. (1984) *Gentlemen and Officers: Imperial Administration and Aristocratic Power in Byzantine Italy, A.D. 554–800* (Rome)
Browning, R. (1975) *The Emperor Julian* (London)
Brownmiller, S. (1975) *Against Our Will: Men, Women and Rape* (London)
Bruun, P. (1966) *The Roman Imperial Coinage*, vol. 7: *Constantine and Licinius*, AD 313–337 (London)
Burkitt, F. C. (1913) *Euphemia and the Goth* (London)
Burn, A. R. (1953) "*Hic breve vivitur*: a study of the expectation of life in the Roman empire," *P&P* 4: 2–31
Burnett, A. (1989) Review of Bastien (1988), *Numismatic Chronicle* 149: 254–5
Bury, J. B. (1923) *History of the Later Roman Empire from the Death of Theodosius I to the Death of Justinian* (London), 2 vols.
Butler, H. C. (1929) *Early Churches in Syria: Fourth to Seventh Centuries* (Princeton)
Callu, J. P. (1995) "Le butin de Neupotz," *JRA* 8: 514–20
Cameron, Alan, and Schauer, D. (1982) "The last consul: Basilius and his diptych," *JRS* 72: 126–45
Cameron, Alan, and Long, J. (1993) *Barbarians and Politics at the Court of Arcadius* (Berkeley)
Cameron, Averil (1970) *Agathias* (Oxford)
Cameron, Averil (1979) "Images of authority: elites and icons in late sixth-century Byzantium," *P&P* 84: 3–35
Cameron, Averil (1983) "Constantinus Christianus," *JRS* 73: 184–90
Cameron, Averil (1985) *Procopius and the Sixth Century* (London)
Cameron, Averil (1993a) *The Later Roman Empire, AD 284–430* (London)
Cameron, Averil (1993b) *The Mediterranean World in Late Antiquity, AD 395–600* (London)
Cameron, Averil (ed.) (1995) *The Byzantine and Early Islamic Near East* III: *States, Resources and Armies* (Princeton)
Cameron, Averil (2002) "The 'long' late antiquity: a late twentieth-century model" in T. P. Wiseman (ed.), *Classics in Progress: Essays on Ancient Greece and Rome* (Oxford), 165–91
Cameron, Averil, and Garnsey, P. (eds.) (1998) *The Cambridge Ancient History* XIII: *The Late Empire, AD 337–425* (Cambridge)
Cameron, Averil, and Hall, S. G. (1999) *Eusebius: Life of Constantine* (Oxford)
Cameron, Averil, Ward-Perkins, B., and Whitby, M. (eds.) (2000) *The Cambridge Ancient History* XIV: *Late Antiquity: Empire and Successors, AD 425–600* (Cambridge)
Campbell, J. B. (1984) *The Emperor and the Roman Army 31 BC–AD 235* (Oxford)
Campbell, J. B. (1987) "How to be a general," *JRS* 77: 13–29
Campbell, J. B. (2002) *War and Society in Imperial Rome, 31 BC–AD 284* (London)
Campbell, J. B. (2005) "The army" in Bowman et al. 2005: 110–30
Carrié, J.-M. (1977) "Le rôle économique de l'armée dans l'Egypte romaine" in *Armées et fiscalité dans le monde antique* (Paris), 373–93
Carrié, J.-M. (1986) "L'esercito: trasformazioni funzionali ed economie locali" in A. Giardina (ed.), *Società romana e impero tardoantico: istituzioni, ceti, economie* (Rome), 449–88
Carrié, J.-M. (1999) "L'Empire-monde et les bases restaurées de la puissance" in Carrié and Rousselle 1999: 563–650

Carrié, J.-M. (2002) "L'armée romaine tardive dans quelques travaux récents. 3e partie: fournitures militaires, recrutement et archéologie des fortifications," *AnTard* 10: 427–42

Carrié, J.-M. (2004) "Le système de recrutement des armies romaines de Dioclétien aux Valentiniens" in Le Bohec and Wolff 2004: 371–88

Carrié, J.-M., and Janniard, S. (2000) "L'armée romaine tardive dans quelques travaux récents. 1re partie: l'institution militaire et les modes de combat," *AnTard* 8: 321–41

Carrié, J.-M., and Rousselle, A. (1999) *L'Empire romain en mutation: des Sévères à Constantin, 192–337* (Paris)

Carroll, M. (2001) *Romans, Celts and Germans: The German Provinces of Rome* (Stroud)

Champlin, E. (1987) "The testament of the piglet," *Phoenix* 41: 174–83

Chang, I. (1998) *The Rape of Nanking: The Forgotten Holocaust of World War II* (London)

Chavarría, A., and Lewit, T. (2004) "Archaeological research on the late antique countryside: a bibliographic essay" in Bowden et al. 2004: 3–51

Chevedden, P. E. (1995) "Artillery in late antiquity: prelude to the Middle Ages" in I. Corfis and M. Wolfe (eds.), *The Medieval City under Siege* (Woodbridge), 131–73

Christie, N. (1995) *The Lombards: The Ancient Langobards* (Oxford)

Christie, N. (1996) "Barren fields? Landscapes and settlements in late Roman and post-Roman Italy" in G. Shipley and J. Salmon (eds.), *Human Landscapes in Classical Antiquity: Environment and Culture* (London), 254–83

Christie, N. (ed.) (2004) *Landscapes of Change: Rural Evolutions in Late Antiquity and the Early Middle Ages* (Aldershot)

Christie, N., and Loseby, S. T. (eds.) (1996) *Towns in Transition: Urban Evolution in Late Antiquity and the Early Middle Ages* (Aldershot)

Christol, M. (1999) "L'ascension de l'ordre equestre: un theme historiographique et sa réalité" in S. Demougin, H. Devijver, and M.-Th. Raepsaet-Charlier (eds.), *L'Ordre équestre: histoire d'une aristocratie (IIe siècle av. J.-C.–IIIe siècle ap. J.-C.)* (Rome), 613–28

Clark, E. A., and Hatch, D. F. (1981) *The Golden Bough, the Oaken Cross: The Virgilian Cento of Faltonia Betitia Proba* (Chico, CA)

Clauss, M. (1986) "Heerwesen (Heeresreligion)," *RAC* 13: 1073–113

Clauss, M. (2000) *The Roman Cult of Mithras: The God and his Mysteries*, tr. R. Gordon (Edinburgh)

Coello, T. (1996) *Unit Sizes in the Late Roman Army* (Oxford)

Coles, R. A. (ed.) (2001) *The Oxyrhynchus Papyri*, vol. 67 (London)

Colt, H. D. (1950) *Excavations at Nessana*, vol. 1 (Princeton)

Corbier, M. (2005) "Coinage, society and economy" in Bowman et al. 2005: 393–439

Corcoran, S. (1996) *The Empire of the Tetrarchs: Imperial Pronouncements and Government, AD 284–324* (Oxford)

Cormack, R. (1985) *Writing in Gold: Byzantine Society and its Icons* (London)

Cornell, T., and Matthews, J. (1981) *Atlas of the Roman World* (London)

Cosentino, S. (2000) "The Syrianos's *Strategikon*: a 9th-century source?" *Bizantinistica* 2: 248–61

Cosentino, S. (2004) "Iranian contingents in the Byzantine army" in *La Persia e Bisanzio* (= *Atti dei Convegni Lincei* 201) (Rome), 245–61

Coulston, J. N. C. (2002) "Arms and armour of the late Roman army" in D. Nicolle (ed.), *A Companion to Medieval Arms and Armour* (Woodbridge), 3–24

Courcelle, P. (1964) *Histoire litteraire des grandes invasions germaniques* (3rd edn.: Paris)

Creed, J. L. (1984) *Lactantius: De Mortibus Persecutorum* (Oxford)

Croke, B. (1976a) "The editing of Symmachus' letters to Eugenius and Arbogast," *Latomus* 35: 535–49

Croke, B. (1976b) "Arbogast and the death of Valentinian II," *Historia* 25: 235–44

Croke, B. (2005) "Dynasty and ethnicity: emperor Leo and the eclipse of Aspar," *Chiron* 35: 147–203

Crow, J. (1995) *The English Heritage Book of Housesteads* (London)

Crump, G. A. (1975) *Ammianus Marcellinus as a Military Historian* (Wiesbaden)

Curta, F. (2001) *The Making of the Slavs: History and Archaeology of the Lower Danube Region, c. 500–700* (Cambridge)

Cutler, A. (1991) "Barberiniana" in *Tesserae: Festschrift für Josef Engemann* (Munster), 329–39

Dąbrowa, E. (ed.) (1994) *The Roman and Byzantine Army in the East* (Cracow)

Dagron, G. (1969) "Aux origines de la civilisation byzantine: langue de culture et langue d'état," *RH* 241: 23–56

Dagron, G. (1974) *Naissance d'une capitale: Constantinople et ses institutions de 330 à 451* (Paris)

Daniels, C. (1980) "Excavations at Wallsend and the fourth-century barracks on Hadrian's Wall" in W. S. Hanson and Keppie 1980: 173–93

Daube, D. (1969) *Roman Law: Linguistic, Social and Philosophical Aspects* (Edinburgh)

Davies, R. (1989) "The Roman military medical service" in his *Service in the Roman Army* (eds. D. Breeze and V. Maxfield) (Edinburgh), 209–36

Davies, P. S. (1989) "The origin and purpose of the persecution of AD 303," *JTS* 40: 66–94

Davis, R. (2000) *The Book of the Pontiffs ("Liber Pontificalis"): The Ancient Biographies of the First Ninety Roman Bishops to AD 715* (2nd edn.: Liverpool)

de Blois, L. (1976) *The Policy of the Emperor Gallienus* (Leiden)

de Ste. Croix, G. E. M. (1981) *The Class Struggle in the Ancient Greek World: From the Archaic Age to the Arab Conquests* (London)

de Ste. Croix, G. E. M. (1984) "A worm's-eye view of the Greeks and Romans and how they spoke: martyr-acts, fables, parables and other texts," *Teaching Latin* 37/4: 16–30

Delmaire, R. (1989) *Largesses sacrées et* res privata: *l'*aerarium *imperial et son administration du IVe au VIe siècle* (Rome)

Delmaire, R. (1995) *Les institutions du bas-empire romain, de Constantin à Justinien* (Paris)

Demandt, A. (1989) *Die Spätanike: Römische Geschichte von Diocletian bis Justinian, 284–565 n. Chr.* (Munich)

Dennis, G. T. (1985) *Three Byzantine Military Treatises* (Washington, DC)

Dodgeon, M., and Lieu, S. N. C. (1991) *The Roman Eastern Frontier and the Persian Wars, AD 226–363* (London)

Downey, G. (1940) "Justinian as Achilles," *Transactions of the American Philological Association* 71: 68–78

Downey, G. (1961) *A History of Antioch in Syria* (Princeton)

Drew-Bear, T. (1979) "Les voyages d'Aurélius Gaius, soldat de Dioclétien" in T. Fahd (ed.), *La Géographie administrative et politique d'Alexandre à Mahomet* (Strasbourg), 93–141

Drew-Bear, T., Malay, H., and Zuckerman, C. (2004) "L'épitaphe de Valeria, veuve du tribun Dassianus" in Le Bohec and Wolff 2004: 409–17

Drinkwater, J. F. (1984) "Peasants and Bagaudae in Roman Gaul," *Echos du monde classique/Classical Views* 3: 349–71

Drinkwater, J. F. (1987) *The Gallic Empire* (Wiesbaden)

Drinkwater, J. F. (1989) "Patronage in Roman Gaul and the problem of the Bagaudae" in A. Wallace-Hadrill (ed.), *Patronage in Ancient Society* (London), 189–203

Drinkwater, J. F. (1992) "The Bacaudae in fifth-century Gaul" in Drinkwater and Elton 1992: 208–17

Drinkwater, J. F. (1994) "Silvanus, Ursicinus and Ammianus: fact or fiction?" in C. Deroux (ed.), *Studies in Latin Literature and Roman History*, vol. 7 (Brussels), 568–76

Drinkwater, J. F. (1996) "The 'Germanic threat on the Rhine frontier': a Romano-Gallic artefact?" in R. W. Mathisen and H. Sivan (eds.), *Shifting Frontiers in Late Antiquity* (Aldershot), 20–30

Drinkwater, J. F. (1997) "Julian and the Franks and Valentinian I and the Alamanni: Ammianus on Romano-German relations," *Francia* 24: 1–15

Drinkwater, J. F. (1998) Review of Paschoud and Szidat (1997), *Francia* 25: 304–6

Drinkwater, J. F. (1999) "Ammianus, Valentinian and the Rhine Germans" in J. W. Drijvers and D. Hunt (eds.), *The Late Roman World and its Historian: Interpreting Ammianus Marcellinus* (London), 127–37

Drinkwater, J. F. (2000) "The revolt and ethnicity of the usurper Magnentius (350–353) and the rebellion of Vetranio (350)," *Chiron* 30: 131–59

Drinkwater, J. F. (2005) "Maximinus to Diocletian and the 'crisis'" in Bowman et al. 2005: 28–66

Drinkwater, J. F., and Elton, H. (eds.) (1992) *Fifth-Century Gaul: A Crisis of Identity?* (Cambridge)

du Mesnil du Buisson, R. (1936) "The Persian mines" in M. Rostovtzeff, A. R. Bellinger, C. Hopkins, and C. B. Welles (eds.) (1986) *The Excavations at Dura-Europos: Preliminary Report of Sixth Season of Work, October 1932–March 1933* (New Haven, CT), 188–205

du Mesnil du Buisson, R. (1944) "Les ouvrages du siège à Doura-Europos," *MSNAF* 9th series, 1: 5–60

Dudden, F. H. (1905) *Gregory the Great: His Place in History and Thought* (New York), 2 vols.

Dudden, F. H. (1935) *The Life and Times of St. Ambrose* (Oxford), 2 vols.

Duncan-Jones, R. (1978) "Pay and numbers in Diocletian's army," *Chiron* 8: 541–60 (= Duncan-Jones 1990: 105–19)

Duncan-Jones, R. (1990) *Scale and Structure in the Roman Economy* (Cambridge)

Duncan-Jones, R. (2004) "Economic change and the transition to late antiquity" in Swain and Edwards 2004: 20–52

BIBLIOGRAPHY OF MODERN WORKS

Elton, H. (1996) *Warfare in Roman Europe, AD 350–425* (Oxford)
Elton, H. (2005) "Military supply and the south coast of Anatolia in the third century AD" in S. Mitchell and C. Katsari (eds.), *Patterns in the Economy of Roman Asia Minor* (Swansea), 289–304
Enloe, C. H. (1980) *Ethnic Soldiers: State Security in Divided Societies* (Athens, GA)
Erdkamp, P. (1998) *Hunger and the Sword: Warfare and Food Supply in Roman Republican Wars (264–30 BC)* (Amsterdam)
Évieux, P. (1995) *Isidore de Péluse* (Paris)
Feissel, D. (1989) "Bulletin épigraphique: inscriptions chrétiennes et byzantines," *Revue des études grecques* 102: 481–509
Feissel, D. (1995) "Une épitaphe d'Adrinople sous Justin II," *Bulletin de correspondance hellénique* 119: 379–86
Feissel, D. (2000) "Les édifices de Justinien au témoinage de Procope et de l'épigraphie," *AnTard* 8: 81–104
Ferris, I. M. (2000) *Enemies of Rome: Barbarians through Roman Eyes* (Stroud)
Fiches, J. L. (ed.) (1996) *Le IIIe siècle en Gaule Narbonnaise: données régionales sur la crise de l'Empire* (Antibes)
Figes, O. (1996) *A People's Tragedy: The Russian Revolution 1891–1924* (London)
Fink, R. O., Hoey, A. S., and Snyder, W. F. (1940) "The *Feriale Duranum*," *Yale Classical Studies* 7: 1–222
Fishwick, D. (1988) "Dated inscriptions and the *Feriale Duranum*," *Syria* 65: 349–61
Fitz, J. (1983) *Honorific Titles of Roman Military Units in the 3rd Century* (Budapest)
Foss, C. (1995) "The Near Eastern countryside in late antiquity: a review article" in J. H. Humphrey (ed.), *The Roman and Byzantine Near East: Some Recent Archaeological Research* (Ann Arbor, MI), 213–34
Foss, C. (1997) "Syria in transition, AD 550–750," *DOP* 51: 189–270
Fouracre, P. (ed.) (2005) *The New Cambridge Medieval History* I: *c. 500–c. 700* (Cambridge)
Fowden, G. (1978) "Bishops and temples in the eastern Roman empire, AD 320–435," *JTS* 29: 53–78
Fowden, G. (1993) *Empire to Commonwealth: Consequences of Monotheism in Late Antiquity* (Princeton)
Fowden, G. (1995) "Late Roman Achaea: identity and defence," *JRA* 8: 549–67
Francovich, R. (2002) "Changing structures of settlements" in C. La Rocca (ed.), *Italy in the Early Middle Ages* (Oxford), 144–67
Freeman, P., and Kennedy, D. (eds.) (1986) *The Defence of the Roman and Byzantine East* (Oxford)
Frend, W. H. C. (1952) *The Donatist Church* (Oxford)
Frend, W. H. C. (1972a) *The Rise of the Monophysite Movement* (Cambridge)
Frend, W. H. C. (1972b) "Monks and the survival of the east Roman empire in the fifth century," *P&P* 54: 3–24
Frier, B. W. (2000) "Demography" in Bowman et al. 2000: 787–816
Frye, R. N. (1984) *The History of Ancient Iran* (Munich)
Fuchs, K. (ed.) (1998), *Die Alamannen* (Mainz)
Gabba, E. (1974) *Per la storia dell'esercito romano in età imperiale* (Bologna)
Gagé, J. (1933) "La théologie de la victoire impériale," *RH* 171: 1–43
Gain, B. (1985) *L'Église de Cappadoce au IVe siècle d'après la correspondance de Basile de Césarée (330–379)* (Rome)

Garnsey, P. (1999) *Food and Society in Classical Antiquity* (Cambridge)
Garnsey, P., and Woolf, G. (1989) "Patronage of the rural poor in the Roman world" in A. Wallace-Hadrill (ed.), *Patronage in Ancient Society* (London), 153–70
Gascou, J. (1989) "La table budgétaire d'Antaeopolis (*P. Freer* 08.45 c–d)" in J. Lefort and C. Morrisson (eds.), *Hommes et richesses dans l'empire byzantin* I, *IVe–VIIe siècle* (Paris), 279–313
Gascou, J. (1994) "Deux inscriptions byzantines de Haute-Egypte," *Travaux and mémoires* 12: 323–45
Gatier, P.-L. (1994) "Villages du Proche-Orient protobyzantin (4ème–7ème s.): étude régionale" in G. R. D. King and A. Cameron (eds.), *The Byzantine and Early Islamic Near East* II: *Land Use and Settlement Patterns* (Princeton), 17–48
Geary, P. J. (1999) "Barbarians and ethnicity" in Bowersock et al. 1999: 107–29
Gentles, I. (1975) "Arrears of pay and ideology in the army revolt of 1647" in B. Bond and I. Roy (eds.) *War and Society: A Yearbook of Military History* (London), 44–66
Ghirshman, R. (1962) *Iran: Parthians and Sassanians* (trs. S. Gilbert and J. Emmons) (London)
Gibbon, E. (1994) [1776–88] *The History of the Decline and Fall of the Roman Empire* (ed. D. Womersley) (London), 3 vols.
Gibson, S. (1998) *The Mosaics of Anemurium* (Toronto)
Goffart, W. (1980) *Barbarians and Romans, AD 418–584: The Techniques of Accommodation* (Princeton)
Goldsworthy, A. (1996) *The Roman Army at War, 100 BC–AD 200* (Oxford)
Goodburn, R., and Bartholomew, P. (eds.) (1976) *Aspects of the* Notitia Dignitatum (Oxford)
Gordon, C. D. (1949) "Subsidies in Roman imperial defence," *Phoenix* 3: 60–9
Gordon, R. L. (1972) "Mithraism and Roman society," *Religion* 2/2: 92–121 (= Gordon 1996: Study 3)
Gordon, R. L. (1996) *Image and Value in the Graeco-Roman World* (Aldershot)
Gordon, R. L. (1999) "The end of Mithraism in the northwest provinces," *JRA* 12: 682–8
Grabar, A. (1936) *L'Empereur dans l'art byzantin: recherches sur l'art officiel de l'empire d'Orient* (Paris)
Gracie, D. M. (1981) "Translator's introduction" in Harnack 1981: 9–24
Gray, P. T. R. (2005) "The legacy of Chalcedon: Christological problems and their significance" in Maas 2005: 215–38
Greatrex, G. (1996) "Flavius Hypatius, *quem vidit validum Parthus sensitque timendum*: an investigation of his career," *Byzantion* 66: 120–42
Greatrex, G. (1998) *Rome and Persia at War, 502–532* (Leeds)
Greatrex, G. (2000) "Roman identity in the sixth century" in G. Greatrex and S. Mitchell (eds.), *Ethnicity and Identity in Late Antiquity* (London), 267–92
Greatrex, G. (2001) "Justin I and the Arians," *Studia Patristica* 34: 72–81
Greatrex, G. (2003) "Recent work on Procopius and the composition of *Wars* VIII," *BMGS* 27: 45–67
Greatrex, G. (forthcoming) "Roman frontiers and foreign policy in the East" in M. Choat and P. Edwell (eds.), *Aspects of the Roman East*
Greatrex, G., and Lieu, S. N. C. (2002) *The Roman Eastern Frontier and the Persian Wars, Part II: AD 363–630* (London)

Greatrex, G., Elton, H., and Burgess, R. (2005) "Urbicius' *Epitedeuma*: an edition, translation and commentary," *Byzantinische Zeitschrift* 98: 35–74

Gregory, T. E. (1979) Vox Populi: *Popular Opinion and Violence in Religious Controversies of the Fifth Century AD* (Columbus, OH)

Gregory, T. E. (1983) "Urban violence in late antiquity" in R. T. Marchese (ed.), *Aspects of Graeco-Roman Urbanism* (Oxford), 138–61

Grimsley, M., and Rodgers, C. J. (eds.) (2002) *Civilians in the Path of War* (Lincoln, NE)

Grönewald, M., et al. (2003) *Kölner Papyri (P. Köln)*, vol. 10 (= *Papyrologica Coloniensia vol.* VII/10) (Paderborn)

Guillermand, J. (1982) *Histoire de la medicine aux armies*, vol. 1: *De l'Antiquité à la Révolution* (Paris)

Haas, C. (1997) *Alexandria in Late Antiquity* (Baltimore)

Haensch, R. (2004) "La christianisation de l'armée romaine" in Le Bohec and Wolff 2004: 525–31

Haldon, J. F. (1979) *Recruitment and Conscription in the Byzantine Army c. 550–950* (Vienna)

Haldon, J. F. (1984) *Byzantine Praetorians: An Administrative, Institutional and Social Survey of the Opsikion and Tagmata, c. 580–900* (Bonn)

Haldon, J. F. (1986) "Ideology and social change in the seventh century: military discontent as a barometer," *Klio* 68: 139–90

Haldon, J. F. (1990a) *Byzantium in the Seventh Century* (Cambridge)

Haldon, J. F. (1990b) *Constantine Porphyrogenitus: Three Treatises on Imperial Military Expeditions* (Vienna)

Haldon, J. F. (1999) *Warfare, State and Society in the Byzantine World, 565–1204* (London)

Haldon, J. F. (2000) *The Byzantine Wars* (Stroud)

Haldon, J. F. (2005) "Feeding the army: food and transport in Byzantium, ca 600–1100" in W. Mayer and S. Trzcionka (eds.), *Feast, Fast or Famine: Food and Drink in Byzantium* (Brisbane), 85–100

Halfmann, H. (1986) Itinera principum: *Geschichte und Typologie der Kaiserreisen im römischen Reich* (Stuttgart)

Halsall, G. (2003) *Warfare and Society in the Barbarian West, 450–900* (London)

Halsall, G. (2005) "The barbarian invasions" in Fouracre 2005: 35–55

Hanson, V. D. (1998) *Warfare and Agriculture in Classical Greece* (2nd edn: Berkeley)

Hanson, W. S., and Keppie, L. J. F. (eds.) (1980) *Roman Frontier Studies 1979* (Oxford)

Harnack, A. von (1981) [1905] *Militia Christi: The Christian Religion and the Military in the First Three Centuries*, tr. D. M. Gracie (Philadelphia)

Harries, J. D. (1995) *Sidonius Apollinaris and the Fall of Rome, AD 407–485* (Oxford)

Hassall, M. W. C. (ed.) (1979) *De Rebus Bellicis* (Oxford)

Hassall, M. W. C. (2000) "The army" in Bowman et al. 2000: 320–43

Hauken, T. (1998) *Petition and Response: An Epigraphic Study of Petitions to Roman Emperors, 181–249* (Bergen)

Heather, P. (1991) *Goths and Romans, 332–489* (Oxford)

Heather, P. (1995) "The Huns and the end of the Roman empire in western Europe," *English Historical Review* 110: 4–41

Heather, P. (2005) *The Fall of the Roman Empire* (London)
Heckel, W., and Yardley, J. C. (2004) *Alexander the Great: Historical Sources in Translation* (Oxford)
Helgeland, J. (1978) "Roman army religion," *ANRW* II.16.2: 1470–1505
Helgeland, J. (1979) "Christians and the Roman army from Marcus Aurelius to Constantine," *ANRW* II.23.1: 724–834
Helgeland, J., Daly, R. J., and Burns, J. P. (1985) *Christians and the Military: The Early Experience* (Philadelphia)
Hendy, M. F. (1985) *Studies in the Byzantine Monetary Economy, c. 300–1450* (Cambridge)
Hendy, M. F. (1989) "Economy and state in late Rome and early Byzantium: an introduction" in M. F. Hendy, *The Economy, Fiscal Administration and Coinage of Byzantium* (Northampton), Study I
Hill, S. (1985) "Matronianus, *comes Isauriae*: an inscription from an early Byzantine basilica at Yanikhan, Rough Cilicia," *Anatolian Studies* 35: 93–7
Höckmann, O. (1997) "Roman river patrols and military logistics on the Rhine and Danube" in A. N. Jørgensen and B. L. Clausen (eds.), *Military Aspects of Scandinavian Society in a European Perspective, AD 1–1300* (Copenhagen), 239–47
Hoffmann, D. (1961/2) "Der *numerus equitum Persoiustinianorum* auf einer Mosaikinschrift von Sant'Eufemia in Grado," *Aquileia Nostra* 32–3: 81–98
Hoffmann, D. (1969–70) *Das spätrömische Bewegunsheer und die* Notitia Dignitatum (Dusseldorf), 2 vols.
Holmes, R. (1985) *Acts of War: The Behaviour of Men in Battle* (New York)
Holum, K. G. (1977) "Pulcheria's crusade AD 421–22 and the ideology of imperial victory," *GRBS* 18: 153–72
Honoré, T. (1978) *Tribonian* (London)
Hopkins, C. (1934) "Private houses" in M. I. Rostovtzeff (ed.), *The Excavations at Dura-Europos: Preliminary Report of the Fifth Season of Work* (New Haven, CT), 31–72
Hopwood, K. (1990) "The indigenous populations of Roman Rough Cilicia under Roman rule" in *X. Türk Tarih Kongresi'nden ayribasim* (Ankara), 337–45
Hopwood, K. (ed.) (1999a) *Organised Crime in Antiquity* (London)
Hopwood, K. (1999b) "Bandits between grandees and the state" in Hopwood 1999a: 179–84
Hordern, P. (2005) "Mediterranean plague in the age of Justinian" in Maas 2005: 134–60
Howard-Johnston, J. (1994) "The official history of Heraclius' Persian campaigns" in Dąbrowa 1994: 57–87
Howard-Johnston, J. (1995) "The two great powers in late antiquity: a comparison" in Averil Cameron 1995: 157–222
Howard-Johnston, J. (1999) "Heraclius' Persian campaigns and the revival of the East Roman Empire, 622–630," *War in History* 6: 1–44
Howard-Johnston, J. (2000) "The education and expertise of Procopius," *AnTard* 8: 19–30
Howgego, C. J. (1995) *Ancient History from Coins* (London)
Hulme, P. (1998) "Introduction: the cannibal scene" in F. Barker, P. Hulme, and M. Iversen (eds.), *Cannibalism and the Colonial World* (Cambridge), 1–38

Hunt, D. (1999) "The outsider inside: Ammianus on the rebellion of Silvanus" in D. Hunt and J. W. Drijvers (eds.), *The Late Roman World and its Historian: Interpreting Ammianus Marcellinus* (London), 51–63

Hyland, A. (1990) *Equus: The Horse in the Roman World* (London)

Isaac, B. (1988) "The meaning of the terms *limes* and *limitanei*," *JRS* 78: 125–47

Isaac, B. (1992) *The Limits of Empire: The Roman Army in the East* (revised edn: Oxford)

Jackson, R. (1988) *Doctors and Diseases in the Roman Empire* (London)

James, S. (1988) "The *fabricae*: state arms factories of the later Roman empire" in J. C. Coulston (ed.), *Military Equipment and the Identity of Roman Soldiers* (Oxford), 257–331

James, S. (2004) *The Excavations at Dura-Europos, Final Report VII: The Arms and Armour and Other Military Equipment* (London)

James, S. (2005) "The deposition of military equipment during the final siege at Dura-Europos, with particular regard to the Tower 19 countermine," *Carnuntum Jahrbuch 2005*: 189–206

Janin, R. (1964) *Constantinople byzantine: développement urbain et répertoire topographique* (2nd edn: Paris)

Janniard, S. (2001) "L'armée romaine tardive dans quelques travaux récents. 2e partie: stratégies et techniques militaires," *AnTard* 9: 351–61

Johnson, S. (1983) *Late Roman Fortifications* (London)

Jones, A. H. M. (1953) "Military chaplains in the Roman army," *HTR* 46: 239–40

Jones, A. H. M. (1959) "Were ancient heresies national or social movements in disguise?" *JTS* 11: 280–98

Jones, A. H. M. (1963) "The social background to the struggle between paganism and Christianity" in Momigliano 1963b: 17–37

Jones, A. H. M. (1964) *The Later Roman Empire, 284–602: A Social, Economic and Administrative Survey* (Oxford)

Kaegi, W. E. (1981) *Byzantine Military Unrest, 471–843: An Interpretation* (Amsterdam)

Kaegi, W. E. (1982) "Two studies in the continuity of late Roman and Byzantine military institutions," *Byzantinische Forschungen* 8: 87–113

Kaegi, W. E. (1992) *Byzantium and the Early Islamic Conquests* (Cambridge)

Kaegi, W. E. (2003) *Heraclius, Emperor of Byzantium* (Cambridge)

Karagiorgou, O. (2001) "LR2: a container for the military *annona* on the Danubian border?" in S. Kingsley and M. Decker (eds.), *Economy and Exchange in the Eastern Mediterranean during Late Antiquity* (Oxford), 129–66

Keegan, J. (1976) *The Face of Battle: A Study of Agincourt, Waterloo and the Somme* (Harmondsworth)

Keenan, J. G. (1994) "Soldier and civilian in Byzantine Hermopolis," *Proceedings of the 20th International Congress of Papyrologists, Copenhagen 23–29 August 1992* (Copenhagen), 444–51

Kelly, C. (1998) "Emperors, government and bureaucracy" in Averil Cameron and Garnsey 1998: 138–83

Kelly, C. (2004) *Ruling the Later Roman Empire* (Cambridge, MA)

Kennedy, D., and Riley, D. (1990) *Rome's Desert Frontier from the Air* (London)

Kennedy, D. L. (1996) "Parthia and Rome: eastern perspectives" in D. L. Kennedy (ed.), *The Roman Army in the East* (Ann Arbor, MI), 67–90

Kent, J. P. C. (1994) *The Roman Imperial Coinage*, vol. 10: *The Divided Empire and the Fall of the Western Parts, AD 395–491* (London)
Kern, P. B. (1999) *Ancient Siege Warfare* (Bloomington)
Kiilerich, B. (1993) *Late Fourth Century Classicism in the Plastic Arts: Studies in the so-called Theodosian Renaissance* (Odense)
King, C. E. (1990) Review of Bastien (1988), *JRS* 80: 253–4
Kleiner, D. E. E. (1992) *Roman Sculpture* (New Haven, CT)
Kneissel, P. (1969) *Die Siegestitulatur der römischen Kaiser: Untersuchungen zu den Siegerbeinamen des ersten und zweiten Jahrhunderts* (Göttingen)
Kolb, F. (2001) *Herrscherideologie in der Spätantike* (Berlin)
Kraeling, C. J. (1967) *The Excavations at Dura-Europos, Final Report VIII, Part II: The Christian Building* (New Haven, CT)
Kraemer, C. J. (1958) *Excavations at Nessana*, vol. 3: *The Non-literary Papyri* (Princeton)
Krause, J.-U. (1987) *Spätanike Patronatsformen im Westen des römischen Reiches* (Munich)
Krause, J.-U. (1995) *Witwen und Waisen im römischen Reich*, vol. 4: *Witwen und Waisen im frühen Christentum* (Heidelberg)
Krautheimer, R. (1980) *Rome: Profile of a City, 312–1308* (Princeton)
Künzl, E. (ed.) (1993) *Die Alamannenbeute aus dem Rhein bei Neupotz: Plünderungsgut aus dem römischen Gallien* (Mainz), 4 vols.
Lane Fox, R. (1997) "The itinerary of Alexander: Constantius to Julian," *Classical Quarterly* 47: 239–52
Lavan, L. (ed.) (2001) *Recent Research in Late-antique Urbanism* (Portsmouth, RI)
Leader-Newby, R. (2004) *Silver and Society in Late Antiquity* (Aldershot)
Le Bohec, Y., and Wolff, C. (eds.) (2004) *L'Armée romaine de Dioclétien à Valentinien Ier* (Lyons)
Lebek, W. D. (1985) "Das Grabepigramm auf Domitilla," *ZPE* 59: 7–8
Lee, A. D. (1993) *Information and Frontiers: Late Roman Foreign Relations* (Cambridge)
Lee, A. D. (1996) "Morale and the Roman experience of battle" in A. B. Lloyd (ed.), *Battle in Antiquity* (London), 199–217
Lee, A. D. (1998) "The army" in Averil Cameron and Garnsey 1998: 211–37
Lee, A. D. (2000a) *Pagans and Christians in Late Antiquity: A Sourcebook* (London)
Lee, A. D. (2000b) "The eastern empire: Theodosius to Anastasius" in Averil Cameron et al. 2000: 33–62
Lee, A. D. (2002a) "Naval intelligence in late antiquity" in J. Andreau and C. Virlouvet (eds.), *L'Information et la mer dans le monde antique* (Rome), 93–112
Lee, A. D. (2002b) "Decoding late Roman law," *JRS* 92: 185–94
Lee, A. D. (2007) "Episcopal power and perils in the late sixth century: the case of Gregory of Antioch" in J. F. Drinkwater and R. B. S. Salway (eds.), *Festschrift for Wolf Liebeschuetz* (London), 99–106
Lendon, J. E. (2005) *Soldiers and Ghosts: A History of Battle in Classical Antiquity* (New Haven, CT)
Lenski, N. (1995) "The Gothic civil war and the date of the Gothic conversion," *GRBS* 36: 51–87
Lenski, N. (1999) "Romanization and revolt in the territory of Isauria," *Journal of the Economic and Social History of the Orient* 42: 413–65

Lenski, N. (2000) "The election of Jovian and the role of the late imperial guards," *Klio* 82: 492–515

Lenski, N. (2002a) *Failure of Empire: Valens and the Roman State in the Fourth Century AD* (Berkeley)

Lenski, N. (2002b) "Were Valentinian, Valens and Jovian confessors before Julian the Apostate?" *Zeitschrift für Antikes Christentum* 6: 94–117

Lenski, N. (2004) "Valens and the monks: cudgelling and conscription as a means of social control," *DOP* 58: 93–117

Lenski, N. (forthcoming) "The face of battle in the late Roman Near East: the sieges of Amida 359 and 502" in A. Lewin (ed.), *L'Esercito tardo antico nel vicino oriente* (Potenza)

Leppin, H. (2003) *Theodosius der Große* (Darmstadt)

Leriche, P. (1993) "Techniques de guerre sassanides et romaines à Doura-Europos" in Vallet and Kazanski 1993: 83–100

Liebeschuetz, J. H. W. G. (1972) *Antioch: City and Imperial Administration in the Later Roman Empire* (Oxford)

Liebeschuetz, J. H. W. G. (1983) "The fall of John Chrysostom," *Nottingham Medieval Studies* 29: 1–31

Liebeschuetz, J. H. W. G. (1991) *Barbarians and Bishops: Army, Church and State in the Age of Arcadius and Chrysostom* (Oxford)

Liebeschuetz, J. H. W. G. (2001) *The Decline and Fall of the Roman City* (Oxford)

Lieu, S. N. C. (1986) "Captives, refugees and exiles: a study of cross-frontier civilian movements and contacts between Rome and Persia from Valerian to Jovian" in Freeman and Kennedy 1986: 475–505

Lieu, S. N. C., and Montserrat, D. (eds.) (1996) *From Constantine to Julian: Pagan and Byzantine Views: A Source History* (London)

Lightfoot, C. S. (1988) "Facts and fiction: the third siege of Nisibis (AD 350)," *Historia* 37: 105–25

Lippold, A. (1973) "Theodosius I," *RE Suppl.* 13: 837–961

Lopuszanski, G. (1951) "La police romaine et les chrétiens," *Antiquité classique* 20: 5–46

Louis, E. (2004) "A de-Romanised landscape in northern Gaul: the Scarpe valley from the 4th to the 9th century" in Bowden et al. 2004: 479–505

Luttwak, E. N. (1976) *The Grand Strategy of the Roman Empire, from the First Century AD to the Third* (Baltimore)

MacCail, R. C. (1978) "*P. Gr. Vindob.* 29788C: hexameter encomium on an unnamed emperor," *Journal of Hellenic Studies* 98: 38–63

MacCormack, S. (1981) *Art and Ceremony in Late Antiquity* (Berkeley)

McCormick, M. (1986) *Eternal Victory: Triumphal Rulership in Late Antiquity, Byzantium and the Early Medieval West* (Cambridge)

MacCoull, L. S. B. (1994) "BM 1079, CPR IX 44 and the *Chrysargyron*," *ZPE* 100: 139–43

MacCoull, L. S. B. (1995) " 'When Justinian was upsetting the world': a note on soldiers and religious coercion in sixth-century Egypt" in Miller and Nesbitt 1995: 106–13

McGeorge, P. (2002) *Late Roman Warlords* (Oxford)

McKitterick, R., and Quinault, R. (eds.) (1997) *Edward Gibbon and Empire* (Cambridge)

McLynn, N. (2004) "The transformation of imperial churchgoing in the fourth century" in Swain and Edwards 2004: 235–70
MacMullen, R. (1959) "Roman imperial building in the provinces," *HSCP* 64: 207–35
MacMullen, R. (1962) "The emperor's largesses," *Latomus* 21: 159–66
MacMullen, R. (1963) *Soldier and Civilian in the Later Roman Empire* (Cambridge, MA)
MacMullen, R. (1976) *Roman Government's Response to Crisis, AD 235–337* (New Haven, CT)
MacMullen, R. (1980) "How big was the Roman imperial army?" *Klio* 62: 451–60
MacMullen, R. (1984) *Christianizing the Roman Empire, AD 100–400* (New Haven, CT)
MacMullen, R. (1988) *Corruption and the Decline of Rome* (New Haven, CT)
Maas, M. (ed.) (2005) *The Cambridge Companion to the Age of Justinian* (Cambridge)
Mango, C. (1980) *Byzantium: Empire of the New Rome* (London)
Mango, C. (1993) "The columns of Justinian and his successors" in *Studies on Constantinople* (Aldershot), Study X
Mann, J. C. (1979) "Power, force and the frontiers of the empire," *JRS* 69: 175–83
Marfoe, L., Algaze, G., Ataman, K., et al. (1986) "The Chicago Euphrates archaeological project 1980–1984: an interim report," *Anatolica* 13: 37–148
Markus, R. A. (1983) "Saint Augustine's views on the 'just war,'" *Studies in Church History* 20: 1–13
Markus, R. A. (1988) "The Latin fathers" in J.H. Burns (ed.), *The Cambridge History of Medieval Political Thought, c. 350–c. 1450* (Cambridge), 92–122
Markus, R. A. (1997) *Gregory the Great and his World* (Cambridge)
Matthers, J. (ed.) (1981) *The River Qoueiq, Northern Syria, and its Catchment: Studies arising from the Tell Rifa'at Survey 1977–79* (Oxford)
Matthews, J. F. (1971) "Symmachus and the *magister militum* Theodosius," *Historia* 20: 122–8
Matthews, J. F. (1974) "The letters of Symmachus" in J. W. Binns (ed.), *Latin Literature in the Fourth Century* (London), 58–99
Matthews, J. F. (1975) *Western Aristocracies and Imperial Court, AD 364–425* (Oxford)
Matthews, J. F. (1989) *The Roman Empire of Ammianus* (London)
Matthews, J. F. (2000) *Laying Down the Law: A Study of the Theodosian Code* (New Haven, CT)
Mattingly, D. J., and Hitchner, R. B. (1995) "Roman Africa: an archaeological review," *JRS* 85: 165–213
Michaelides, D. (1970) *"Sacramentum" chez Tertullien* (Paris)
Migliardi Zingale, L. (1997) *I testamenti romani nei papyri e nelle tavolette d'Egitto: Silloge di documenti dal I al IV secolo d.C.*, (3rd edn: Turin)
Millar, F. (1969) "P. Herennius Dexippus: the Greek world and the third-century invasions," *JRS* 59: 12–29
Millar, F. (1977) *The Emperor in the Roman World, 31 BC–AD 337* (London)
Millar, F. (1982) "Emperors, frontiers and foreign relations, 31 BC to AD 378," *Britannia* 13: 1–23
Miller, T. S. (2003) *The Orphans of Byzantium: Child Welfare in the Christian Empire* (Washington, DC)

Miller, T. S., and Nesbitt, J. (eds.) (1995) *Peace and War in Byzantium: Essays in Honor of George T. Dennis* (Washington, DC)
Milner, N. P. (1996) *Vegetius: Epitome of Military Science* (2nd edn: Liverpool)
Mitchell, S. (1987) "Imperial building in the eastern Roman provinces," *HSCP* 91: 333–65
Mitchell, S. (1993) *Anatolia: Land, Men, and Gods in Asia Minor* (Oxford), 2 vols.
Mitchell, S. (1995) *Cremna in Pisidia: An Ancient City in Peace and in War* (London)
Mitchell, S. (2006) *A History of the Later Roman Empire,* AD *284–641* (Oxford)
Mitteis, L., and Wilcken, U. (1912) *Grundzüge und Chrestomathie der Papyruskunde*, II Bd. *Juristischer Teil*, II Hälfte *Chrestomathie* (Berlin and Leipzig)
Mitthof, F. (2001) *Annona militaris: Die Heeresversorgung im spätantike Ägypten. Ein Beitrag zur Verwaltungs- und Heeresgeschichte des Römischen Reiches im 3. bis 6. Jh n. Chr.* (Florence), 2 vols.
Modéran, Y. (2003) *Les Maures et l'Afrique romaine (IVe–VIIe siècle)* (Rome)
Momigliano, A. (1963a) "Introduction: Christianity and the decline of the Roman empire" in Momigliano 1963b: 1–17
Momigliano, A. (ed.) (1963b) *The Conflict between Paganism and Christianity in the Fourth Century* (Oxford)
Morony, M. G. (2004) "Population transfers between Sasanian Iran and the Byzantine empire" in *La Persia e Bisanzio* (= *Atti dei Convegni Lincei* 201) (Rome), 161–80
Morris, M. (1996) "By force of arms: rape, war and military culture," *Duke Law Journal* 45: 651–781
Morrow, L. (1996) "Rape" in R. Cowley and G. Parker (eds.), *The Osprey Companion to Military History* (London), 378–9
Mulvin, L. (2004) "Late Roman villa plans: the Danube-Balkan region" in Bowden et al. 2004: 377–410
Musurillo, H. (1972) *The Acts of the Christian Martyrs* (Oxford)
Naudé, C. P. T. (1958) "Battles and sieges in Ammianus Marcellinus," *Acta Classica* 1: 92–105
Nautin, P. (1967) "Le conversion du temple de Philae en église chrétienne," *Cahiers archéologiques* 17: 1–43
Nicasie, M. J. (1998) *Twilight of Empire: The Roman Army from the Reign of Diocletian until the Battle of Adrianople* (Amsterdam)
Nicholson, O. (1993) "Lactantius on military service," *Studia Patristica* 24: 175–83
Nippel, W. (1995) *Public Order in Ancient Rome* (Cambridge)
Nixon, C. E. V., and Rodgers, B. S. (1994) *In Praise of Later Roman Emperors: The "Panegyrici Latini"* (Berkeley)
Nock, A. D. (1952) "The Roman army and the Roman religious year," *HTR* 45: 186–252 (= Nock 1972: II.736–90)
Nock, A. D. (1972) *Essays on Religion and the Ancient World* (Oxford), 2 vols.
Noethlichs, K. L. (1986) "Heidenverfolgung," *RAC* 13: 1149–90
Noethlichs, K. L. (2001) "Die 'Christianisierung' des Krieges vom Spätantike bis zum frühmittelalterlichen und mittelbyzantinischen Reich," *Jahrbuch für Antike und Christentum* 44: 5–22
Norman, A. F. (1992) *Libanius: Autobiography and Selected Letters* (Cambridge, MA, and London), 2 vols.

BIBLIOGRAPHY OF MODERN WORKS

Noy, D. (1993–5) *Jewish Inscriptions of Western Europe* (Cambridge), 2 vols.

Noyé, G. (1994) "Villes, économie et société dans la province de Bruttium-Lucanie du IVe au VIIe siècle" in R. Francovich and G. Noyé (eds.), *La Storia dell' Alto Medioevo italiano (VI–X secolo) all luce dell'archeologia* (Florence), 693–733

O'Flynn, J. M. (1983) *Generalissimos of the Western Roman Empire* (Edmonton)

Page, D. L. (1942) *Greek Literary Papyri* I (London and Cambridge, MA)

Palme, B. (ed.) (2002) *Corpus Papyrorum Raineri*, vol. 24 (*Griechische Texte* XVII) (Vienna)

Parrott, D. (2001) *Richelieu's Army: War, Government and Society in France, 1624–1642* (Cambridge)

Paschoud, F. (1971) "Zosime 2.29 et la conversion de Constantin," *Historia* 20: 334–53 (= Paschoud 1975: 24–62)

Paschoud, F. (1975) *Cinq études sur Zosime* (Paris)

Paschoud, F., and Szidat, J. (eds.) (1997) *Usurpationen in der Spätantike* (Stuttgart)

Percival, J. (1992) "The fifth-century villa: new life or death postponed?" in Drinkwater and Elton 1992: 156–64

Petrikovits, H. von (1971) "Fortifications in the north-western Roman empire from the third to the fifth centuries AD," *JRS* 61: 178–218

Petrinovich, L. (2000) *The Cannibal Within* (New York)

Petrović, P. (1980) "Les forteresses du Bas-empire sur le *limes* danubien en Serbie" in Hanson and Keppie 1980: 757–73

Phang, S. E. (2001) *The Marriage of Roman Soldiers (13 BC–AD 235): Law and Family in the Imperial Roman Army* (Leiden)

Pohl, W. (1988) *Die Awaren: Ein Steppenvolk in Mitteleuropa, 567–822 n. Chr.* (Munich)

Pollard, N. (2000) *Soldiers, Cities and Civilians in Roman Syria* (Ann Arbor, MI)

Potter, D. S. (2004) *The Roman Empire at Bay, AD 180–395* (London)

Poulter, A. G. (1995) *The Roman, Late Roman and Early Byzantine City of Nicopolis ad Istrum: The British Excavations 1985–1992* (London)

Poulter, A. G. (1999) "The transition to late antiquity on the lower Danube: an interim report (1996–8)," *Antiquity* 79: 145–83

Poulter, A. G. (2002) "Economic collapse in the countryside and the consequent transformation of city into fortress in late antiquity" in L. de Blois and J. Rich (eds.), *The Transformation of Economic Life under the Roman Empire* (Amsterdam), 244–66

Poulter, A. G. (2004) "Cataclysm on the lower Danube: the destruction of a complex Roman landscape" in Christie 2004: 223–53

Pringle, D. (1981) *The Defence of Byzantine Africa from Justinian to the Arab Conquest* (Oxford), 2 vols.

Pryor, J. H., and Jeffreys, E. M. (2006) *The Age of the* Dromōn: *The Byzantine Navy*, ca *500–1204* (Leiden)

Pucciarelli, E. (1987) *I Cristiani e servizio militare: testimonianze dei primi tre secoli* (Florence)

Rance, P. (2005) "Narses and the battle of Taginae (Busta Gallorum) 552: Procopius and sixth-century warfare," *Historia* 54: 424–72

Rathbone, D. (1996) "Monetisation, not price-inflation, in third-century AD Egypt?" in C. E. King and D. G. Wigg (eds.), *Coin Finds and Coin Use in the Roman World* (Berlin), 321–39

Rea, J. R. (1997a) "Order to deliver: *P. Lond.* V 1655 revised," *ZPE* 115: 187–8
Rea, J. R. (1997b) "Letter of a recruit: *P. Lond.* III 982 revised," *ZPE* 115: 189–93
Reddé, M. (1986) Mare nostrum: *les infrastructures, le dispositif et l'histoire de la marine militaire sous l'empire romain* (Rome)
Rémondon, R. (1961) "Soldats de Byzance d'après un papyrus trouvé à Edfou," *Recherches de papyrologie* 1: 41–93
Rich, J. W. (1976) *Declaring War in the Roman Republic in the Period of Transmarine Expansion* (Brussels)
Rickman, G. (1971) *Roman Granaries and Store Buildings* (Cambridge)
Rives, J. B. (1999) "The decree of Decius and the religion of the empire," *JRS* 89: 135–54
Roberts, M. (2002) "Creation in Ovid's *Metamorphoses* and the Latin poets of late antiquity," *Arethusa* 35: 403–15
Rösch, G. (1978) *ONOMA BAΣIΛEIAΣ: Studien zum offiziellen Gebrauch der Kaisertitel in spätantiker und frühbyzantinischer Zeit* (Vienna)
Roth, J. (1999) *The Logistics of the Roman Army at War (264 BC–AD 235)* (Leiden)
Roueché, C. (1986) "Theodosius II, the cities and the date of the *Church History* of Sozomen," *JTS* 37: 130–2
Roueché, C. (2002) "The image of victory: new evidence from Ephesus," *Travaux et mémoires* 14: 527–46
Rousseau, P. (1985) *Pachomius: The Making of a Community in Fourth-Century Egypt* (Berkeley)
Rousseau, P. (2000) "Monasticism" in Averil Cameron et al. 2000: 745–80
Runciman, W. G. (1983) *A Treatise on Social Theory*, vol. 1: *The Methodology of Social Theory* (Cambridge)
Rüpke, J. (1990) *Domi militiae: Die religiöse Konstruktion des Krieges in Rom* (Stuttgart)
Russell, J. (1987) *The Mosaic Inscriptions of Anemurium* (Vienna)
Russell, J. (1999) "The military garrison of Anemurium in the reign of Arcadius," *XI Congresso Internazionale di Epigrafia Greca e Latina: Roma, 18–24 settembre 1997* (Rome), II.721–8
Sabin, P. (2000) "The face of Roman battle," *JRS* 90: 1–17
Sabin, P., van Wees, H., and Whitby, M. (eds.) (forthcoming) *The Cambridge History of Greek and Roman Warfare* (Cambridge)
Salazar, C. F. (2000) *The Treatment of War Wounds in Graeco-Roman Antiquity* (Leiden)
Saller, R. P., and Shaw, B. D. (1984) "Tombstones and Roman family relations in the Principate: civilians, soldiers and slaves," *JRS* 74: 124–56
Salomons, R. P. (2006) "Testamentaria," *ZPE* 156: 217–41
Salzman, M. R. (2002) *The Making of a Christian Aristocracy: Social and Religious Change in the Western Roman Empire* (Harvard, MA)
Sande, S. (1987) "The equestrian statue of Justinian and the *schema Achilleion*," *Acta ad archaeologiam et atrium historiam pertinentia* 6: 91–111
Sauer, E. (1996) *The End of Paganism in the North Western Provinces of the Roman Empire: The Example of the Mithras Cult* (Oxford)
Sauer, E. (2003) *The Archaeology of Religious Hatred in the Roman and Early Medieval World* (Stroud)
Scharf, R. (1991) "*Praefecti praetorio vacantes*: Generalquartiermeister des spätrömischen Heeres," *Byzantinische Forschungen* 17: 223–33

Scharf, R. (2001) Foederati: *Von der völkerrechtlichen Kategorie zur byzantinischen Truppengattung* (Vienna)
Schick, R. (1987) "The church at el-Lejjūn" in S. T. Parker (ed.), *The Roman Frontier in Central Jordan: Interim Report on the "Limes Arabicus" Project, 1980–1985* (Oxford), 353–83
Schmitt, O. (1994) "Die *buccellarii*: Eine Studie zum militärischen Gefolgschaftswesen in der Spätantike," *Tyche* 9: 147–74
Schröter, P. (2000) "Mensch und Umwelt: Anthropolgie der Römerzeit" in L. Wamser (ed.), *Die Römer zwischen Alpen und Nordmeer* (Mainz), 176–81
Scott, L. R. (1976) "Aspar and the burden of barbarian heritage," *Byzantine Studies/ Études byzantines* 3: 59–69
Seeck, O. (1919) *Regesten der Kaiser und Päpste für die Jahre 311 bis 476 n. Chr.* (Stuttgart)
Seeck, O. (1920–3) *Geschichte des Untergang der antiken Welt* (Stuttgart), 6 vols.
Shaw, B. D. (1984) "Latin funerary epigraphy and family life in the later Roman empire," *Historia* 33: 457–97
Shaw, B. D. (1990) "Bandit highlands and lowland peace: the mountains of Isauria-Cilicia," *Journal of the Social and Economic History of the Orient* 33: 199–233, 237–70
Shaw, B. D. (1999) "War and violence" in Bowersock et al. 1999: 130–69
Sheridan, J. A. (1998) *Columbia Papyrus IX: The* Vestis Militaris *Codex* (Atlanta, GA)
Sidebottom, H. (2004) *Ancient Warfare: A Very Short Introduction* (Oxford)
Small, A. M., and Buck, R. J. (1994) *The Excavations of San Giovanni di Ruoti*, vol. 1: *The Villas and their Environment* (Toronto)
Sodini, J.-P. (1994) "Images sculptées et propaganda impériale du IVe au VIe siècle: recherches récentes sur les colonnes honorifiques et les reliefs politiques à Byzance" in A. Guillou and J. Durand (eds.), *Byzance et les images* (Paris), 41–94
Southern, P., and Dixon, K. (1996) *The Late Roman Army* (London)
Speidel, M. P. (1978) *The Religion of Iuppiter Dolichenus in the Roman Army* (Leiden)
Speidel, M. P. (1989) "The soldiers' servants," *Ancient Society* 20: 239–48
Speidel, M. P. (1995) "A horse guardsman in the war between Licinius and Constantine," *Chiron* 25: 83–7
Spencer, D. (2002) *The Roman Alexander: Reading a Cultural Myth* (Exeter)
Stäcker, J. (2003) Princeps *und* miles: *Studien zum Bindungs- und Nahverhältnis von Kaiser und Soldat im 1. und 2. Jahrhundert n. Chr.* (Hildesheim)
Stathakopoulos, D. C. (2004) *Famine and Pestilence in the Late Roman and Early Byzantine Empire: A Systematic Survey of Subsistence Crises and Epidemics* (Aldershot)
Stein, E. (1949–59) *Histoire du Bas-Empire*, tr. J.-R. Palanque (Paris), 2 vols.
Stickler, T. (2002) *Aëtius: Gestaltungsspielräume eines Heermeisters im ausgehenden Weströmischen Reich* (Munich)
Stowers, S. K. (1986) *Letter Writing in Greco-Roman Antiquity* (Philadelphia)
Straub, J. A. (1939) *Vom Herrscherideal in der Spätantike* (Stuttgart)
Stroheker, K. F. (1970) "*Princeps clausus*: Zu einigen Berührungen der Literatur des fünften Jahrhunderts mit der *Historia Augusta*" in A. Alföldi (ed.), *Bonner Historia-Augusta-Colloquium 1968/1969* (Bonn), 273–83
Swain, S., and Edwards, M. (eds.) (2004) *Approaching Late Antiquity: The Transformation from Early to Late Empire* (Oxford)
Swift, L. J. (1983) *The Early Fathers on War and Military Service* (Wilmington)

Syme, R. (1971) *Emperors and Biography: Studies in the "Historia Augusta"* (Oxford)
Syvänne, I. (2004) *The Age of the Hippotoxotai: Art of War in Roman Military Revival and Disaster (491–636)* (Tampere)
Taft, R. F. (1995) "War and peace in the divine liturgy" in Miller and Nesbitt 1995: 17–32
Tardieu, M. (1988) "Sebastianus étiqueté comme manichéen," *Klio* 70: 494–500
Tate, G. (1992) *Les campagnes de la Syrie du Nord du iie au viie siècle* I (Beirut)
Tate, G. (1996) "A titre de comparaison, les manifestations économiques de la crise dans le nord de la Syrie" in Fiches 1996: 71–81
Tcherikover, V. A., and Fuks, A. (eds.) (1960) *Corpus Papyrorum Judaicarum*, vol. 2 (Cambridge, MA)
Thomas, C. (1981) *Christianity in Roman Britain to AD 500* (London)
Thompson, E. A. (1948) *A History of Attila and the Huns* (Oxford)
Thompson, E. A. (1952a) *A Roman Reformer and Inventor* (Oxford)
Thompson, E. A. (1952b) "Peasant revolts in late Roman Gaul and Spain," *P&P* 2: 11–23
Todd, M. (1975) *The Northern Barbarians, 100 BC–AD 300* (London)
Todd, M. (1996) Review of Künzl (1993), *Britannia* 27: 481–2
Tomlin, R. S. O. (1972) "*Seniores–iuniores* in the late Roman field army," *American Journal of Philology* 93: 253–78
Tomlin, R. S. O. (1976) "*Notitia dignitatum omnium, tam civilium quam militarium*" in Goodburn and Bartholomew 1976: 189–209
Tomlin, R. S. O. (1987) "The army of the late empire" in J. Wacher (ed.), *The Roman World* (London), 107–20
Tomlin, R. S. O. (1998) "Christianity and the Roman army" in S. N. C. Lieu and D. Montserrat (eds.), *Constantine: History, Hagiography and Legend* (London), 21–51
Tomlin, R. S. O. (2000) "The legions in the late empire" in R. J. Brewer (ed.), *Roman Fortresses and their Legions* (Cardiff), 159–81
Torbatov, S. (1997) "*Quaestura exercitus*: Moesia Secunda and Scythia under Justinian," *Archaeologia Bulgarica* 1: 78–87
Trapp, M. (2003) *Greek and Roman Letters: An Anthology with Translation* (Cambridge)
Treadgold, W. (1995) *Byzantium and its Army, 284–1081* (Stanford, CA)
Treggiari, S. (1991) *Roman Marriage: iusti coniuges from the time of Cicero to the time of Ulpian* (Oxford)
Tritle, L. A. (2000) *From Melos to My Lai: War and Survival* (London)
Trombley, F. R. (1985a) "Paganism in the Greek world: pagan survivals in the sixth century," *HTR* 78: 327–52
Trombley, F. R. (1985b) "Monastic foundations in sixth-century Anatolia and their role in the social and economic life of the countryside," *Greek Orthodox Theological Review* 30: 45–59
Trombley, F. R. (1993) *Hellenic Religion and Christianization, c. 370–529*, vol. 1 (Leiden)
Trombley, F. R. (1997) "War and society in rural Syria, c. 502–613 AD," *BMGS* 21: 154–209
Trombley, F. R. (2002) "Military cadres and battle during the reign of Heraclius" in G. J. Reinink and B. H. Stolte (eds.), *The Reign of Heraclius (610–641): Crisis and Confrontaion* (Leuven), 241–59

Trombley, F. R. (2004) "Epigraphic data on village culture and social institutions: an interregional comparison (Syria, Phoenice Libanensis and Arabia)" in Bowden et al. 2004: 73–101

Trombley, F. R., and Watt, J. W. (2000) *The Chronicle of Pseudo-Joshua the Stylite* (Liverpool)

Ubiña, J. F. (2000) *Cristianos y Militares: la iglesia antigua ante el ejército y la guerra* (Granada)

Vallet, F., and Kazanski, M. (eds.) (1993) *L'Armée romaine et les barbares du IIIe au VIIe siècle* (Rouen)

Van Berchem, D. (1937) "L'annone militaire dans l'empire romain au IIIe siècle," *MSNAF* 8th series, 10: 117–202

Van Berchem, D. (1952) *L'Armée de Dioclétien et la réforme constantinienne* (Paris)

Van Dam, R. (1985a) *Leadership and Community in Late Antique Gaul* (Berkeley)

Van Dam, R. (1985b) "From paganism to Christianity in late antique Gaza," *Viator* 16: 1–20

Van Ossel, P., and Ouzoulias, P. (2000) "Rural settlement economy in northern Gaul in the Late Empire: an overview and assessment," *JRA* 13: 133–60

Vasiliev, A. A. (1950) *Justin the First* (Cambridge, MA)

Viljamaa, T. (1968) *Studies in Greek Encomiastic Poetry of the Early Byzantine Period* (Helsinki)

von Haehling, R. (1978) *Die Religionszugehörigkeit der hohen Amtsträger des römischen Reiches seit Constantins I. Alleinherrschaft bis zum Ende der Theodosianischen Dynastie* (Bonn)

Wardman, A. E. (1984) "Usurpers and internal conflicts in the 4th century AD," *Historia* 33: 220–37

Ward-Perkins, B. (2000a) "Land, labour and settlement" in Averil Cameron et al. 2000: 315–45

Ward-Perkins, B. (2000b) "Specialized production and exchange" in Averil Cameron et al. 2000: 346–91

Ward-Perkins, B. (2005) *The Fall of Rome and the End of Civilization* (Oxford)

Watson, A. (1999) *Aurelian and the Third Century* (London)

Wells, C. (1998) "Celibate soldiers: Augustus and the army," *American Journal of Ancient History* 14: 180–90

Wheeler, E. L. (1993) "Methodological limits and the mirage of Roman strategy," *Journal of Military History* 57: 7–41, 215–40

Wheeler, E. L. (1996) "The laxity of Syrian legions" in J. H. Humphrey (ed.), *The Roman Near East* (Portsmouth, RI), 229–76

Wheeler, E. L. (1998) "Battles and frontiers," *JRA* 11: 644–51

Whitby, Mary (1994) "A new image for a new age: George of Pisidia on the emperor Heraclius" in Dąbrowa 1994: 197–225

Whitby, Mary (1998a) *The Propaganda of Power: The Role of Panegyric in Late Antiquity* (Leiden)

Whitby, Mary (1998b) "Defender of the Cross: George of Pisidia on the emperor Heraclius and his deputies" in Mary Whitby 1998a: 247–73

Whitby, Michael (1986a) "Procopius and the development of Roman defences in Upper Mesopotamia" in Freeman and Kennedy 1986: 717–35

Whitby, Michael (1986b) "Procopius' description of Dara (*Buildings* 2.1–3)" in Freeman and Kennedy 1986: 737–83

Whitby, Michael (1988) *The Emperor Maurice and his Historian: Theophylact Simocatta on Persian and Balkan Warfare* (Oxford)
Whitby, Michael (1992a) "Greek historical writing after Procopius: variety and vitality" in A. Cameron and L. I. Conrad (eds.). *The Byzantine and Islamic Near East*, vol. 1: *Problems in the Literary Source Material* (Princeton), 25–80
Whitby, Michael (1992b) "From frontier to palace: the personal role of the emperor in diplomacy" in J. Shepard and S. Franklin (eds.), *Byzantine Diplomacy* (Aldershot), 295–303
Whitby, Michael (1994) "The Persian king at war" in Dąbrowa 1994: 227–63
Whitby, Michael (1995) "Recruitment in Roman armies from Justinian to Heraclius (ca. 565–615)" in Averil Cameron 1995: 61–124
Whitby, Michael (1998) "*Deus nobiscum*: Christianity, warfare and morale in late antiquity" in M. M. Austin, J. D. Harries, and C. J. Smith (eds.), Modus operandi: *Essays in Honour of Geoffrey Rickman* (London), 191–208
Whitby, Michael (1999) "The violence of the circus factions" in Hopwood 1999a: 229–53
Whitby, Michael (2000a) "The army, c. 420–602" in Averil Cameron et al. 2000: 288–314
Whitby, Michael (2000b) "Armies and society in the later Roman world" in Averil Cameron et al. 2000: 469–96
Whitby, Michael (2000c) "The Balkans and Greece, 420–602" in Averil Cameron et al. 2000: 701–30
Whitby, Michael (2000d) "Pride and prejudice in Procopius' *Buildings*: imperial images in Constantinople," *AnTard* 8: 59–66
Whitby, Michael (2004) "Emperors and armies, AD 235–395" in Swain and Edwards 2004: 156–86
Whitby, Michael (2005) "War and state in late antiquity: some economic and political connections" in B. Meißner, O. Schmitt, and M. Sommer (eds.), *Krieg – Gesellschaft – Institutionen: Beiträge zu einer vergleichenden Kriegsgeschichte* (Berlin), 355–85
Whittaker, C. R. (1982) "Labour supply in the later Roman empire," *Opus* 1: 171–9
Whittaker, C. R. (1993) "Landlords and warlords in the later Roman empire" in J. Rich and G. Shipley (eds.), *War and Society in the Roman World* (London), 277–302
Whittaker, C. R. (1994) *The Frontiers of the Roman Empire: A Social and Economic Study* (Baltimore)
Whittaker, C. R., and Garnsey, P. (1998) "Rural life in the later Roman empire" in Averil Cameron and Garnsey 1998: 277–311
Whittow, M. (1996) *The Making of Orthodox Byzantium, 600–1025* (London)
Wickham, C. (2003) "Studying long-term change in the west, AD 400–800" in L. Lavan and W. Bowden (eds.), *Theory and Practice in Late Antique Archaeology* (Leiden), 386–423
Wickham, C. (2005) *Framing the Early Middle Ages: Europe and the Mediterranean 400–800* (Oxford)
Wightman, E. M. (1985) *Gallia Belgica* (London)
Wild, J. P. (1976) "The gynaecea" in Goodburn and Bartholomew 1976: 51–9
Wipszycka, E. (1969) "Un papyrus d'Egypte et la guerre de Théodose le Grand contre la réaction paienne en occident," *Eos* 56: 350–60

Witschel, C. (2004) "Re-evaluating the Roman west in the 3rd c. AD," *JRA* 17: 251–81
Woods, D. (1991) "The Christianization of the Roman army in the fourth century," unpublished PhD thesis, Queen's University, Belfast
Woods, D. (1997) "Valerius Victorinus again," *Chiron* 27: 85–93
Worp, K. A. (1991) "Observations on some military camps and place names in Lower Egypt," *ZPE* 87: 291–5
Zuckerman, C. (1988) "*Legio V Macedonica* in Egypt," *Tyche* 3: 279–87
Zuckerman, C. (1995) "The hapless recruit Psois and the mighty anchorite, Apa John," *Bulletin of the American Society of Papyrologists* 32: 183–94
Zuckerman, C. (1998) "Two reforms of the 370s: recruiting soldiers and senators in the divided empire," *Revue des études byzantines* 56: 79–139
Zuckerman, C. (2004) "L'armée" in C. Morrison (ed.), *Le Monde byzantin*, vol. 1: *L'Empire romain d'Orient, 330–641* (Paris), 143–80

INDEX OF ANCIENT SOURCES

LITERARY SOURCES

Acts of Marcellus: 180
Acts of Marculus: 200
Acts of Maximian and Isaac: 200
Agathias **1**.17.5: 140; 1.18.1–2: 97; 1.19.3: 166; **2**.10.7: 129; **3**.23.13: 129; **4**.19: 225; **5**.13.2–3: 145; 5.13.7: 75, 77; 5.14.1: 119
Ambrose
  Letters 76 (20): 201
  On the Death of Valentinian II 22–7: 213
  On Elijah and Fasting 46–50, 62, 64: 170
Ammianus Marcellinus **14**.10.3–4: 97; 14.10.11–14: 61; 14.11.15: 166; **15**.5: 71; 15.6.3: 216; 15.7.2–5: 166; 15.8.4: 54; **16**.4.1: 166; 16.6.2: 128; 16.11.4: 218; 16.11.9: 140; 16.11.14: 152; 16.11.15: 228; 16.12.36–53: 125–6; 16.12.68–70: 38; **17**.8.1: 87; 17.8.2: 96; 17.9.2: 96; 17.10.6–7: 225; 17.10.10: 228; 17.13: 225, 228; **18**.2.3: 87; 18.2.4: 97; 18.2.10: 228; 18.6.10: 139; 18.7.3: 225; 18.8.13: 134; 18.9: 134, 165; **19**.2: 128, 224; 19.4: 135; 19.6.1: 134; 19.6.2: 136; 19.6.11–12: 223; 19.8.1–2: 136; 19.8.4: 135; 19.9.2: 225; 19.9.9: 135; 19.10.2–3: 166; **20**.4: 53, 68, 151; 20.4.6: 97; 20.6.6: 130; 20.6.7: 136; 20.7.15: 136; 20.8.13: 82; 20.8.20: 97; 20.11.5: 89; 20.11.6: 228; **21**.9: 166; 21.12: 125, 228; 21.13.16: 82; 21.16.15: 30, 66; **22**.12.6: 170; **23**.2.5: 4; 23.3.6: 95; **24**.1: 137, 225, 228; 24.3.9: 228; 24.4.2: 228; 24.4.24: 223; 24.4.28: 130; 24.6.15: 228; **25**.1.18: 228; 25.3.10: 228; 25.5: 54; 25.7.9–11: 118; 25.9.5–6: 137; 25.9.7–11: 118; **26**.2: 54; 26.6.12–14: 167; 26.7.17: 230; 26.8: 125, 228; 26.9: 15, 29, 228; **27**.6.1–5: 27, 54; 27.10.7: 225; **28**.2.1–8: 98; **29**.4.5: 225; 29.5.55: 228; 29.6.6: 139, 140; **30**.3.1: 225; 30.10.3: 70; **31**.4.4: 81; 31.5.8: 108; 31.6.4: 125; 31.7.15: 228; 31.7.16: 223; 31.8.8: 145; 31.13.18: 78; 31.15.4: 152
Anonymous Valesianus 9.39: 35
Athanasius
  Acephalous History 1.10: 203; 2.4: 200
  History of the Arians 8.81.6: 198, 200; 16.2: 38
Augustine
  City of God 18.18.10: 219; 18.54: 231
  Confessions 9.7: 201
  Letters 113: 227; 185: 155, 227; 189.4, 6: 187, 227; 220: 227
  Psalm against the Donatist faction: 203
Aurelius Victor *On the Caesars* 27.1: 53; 32.1: 53; 33.34: 24; 37.5: 53

INDEX OF ANCIENT SOURCES

Barsanuphius and John of Gaza
  Letters 831: 229
Basil of Caesarea
  Letters 99: 156, 227; 106: 226, 230; 116: 187; 148–9: 156, 227; 152–3: 156, 227; 155: 156, 187, 227; 165: 156, 227; 179: 156, 158–9, 227; 188: 187; 199.36: 142; 214: 156, 227
  On Virginity 15: 168
  Sermon against Drunkards 7: 170

Calendar of Polemius Silvius: 48
Candidus fr.1: 56, 166
Cassiodorus *Miscellanies (Variae)* 8.31, 33: 116
Cassius Dio 78.11.1: 213
Claudian
  Panegyric on the Fourth Consulate of Honorius: 32–3
  Panegyric on the Third Consulate of Honorius: 32
Clement of Alexandria *Exhortation to the Greeks* 10.100.2: 179
Constantine Porphyrogenitus *Book of Ceremonies* 1.86: 214; 1.91: 54–6, 62; 1.92: 56; 1.93: 57; 1.94: 56; 1.95: 57
Consular Lists of Constantinople, s.a. 379: 38
Corippus
  In Praise of Justin II 1.275–87: 42; 2.105–27: 41; 2.129–40: 57; 3.120–5: 42; 3.349–50: 120
  Iohannis 8.213–329: 189, 192
Cyril of Scythopolis *Life of St. Saba* 1: 81, 152; 9: 81, 191

Description of the Whole World (Expositio Totius Mundi) 36: 95; 50: 108
Dexippus fr.27: 222

Easter Chronicle p. 556: 54; pp. 562–3: 54; p. 568: 54; p. 590: 54; pp. 727–8: 39
Eugippius *Life of St. Severinus* 24, 27: 138
Eunapius fr.68: 47

Euphemia and the Goth: 150–1
Eusebius
  Church History 6.40.4–6: 194; 6.41, 16, 22: 196; 7.11.22: 194; 7.15: 180; 7.30: 199; **8.**1, 4: 181; 8.4: 196; 8.11.1: 194
  Life of Constantine **1.**22.1: 53; 1.28.2: 182; **3.**55–7: 195; 3.59.2: 203; **4.**9–13: 5; 4.18.3–21: 181; 4.56: 205–6
  Martyrs of Palestine 4.8: 194
Eutropius **9.**1, 11, 12, 19: 53; 9.24: 125; 9.25: 102; **10.**9: 68; 10.10.1: 30; 10.12: 73, 78
Evagrius *Church History* **1.**7: 201; **2.**1: 81; 2.5: 169, 201, 204; 2.18: 201; **3.**34: 201, 204; 3.43: 70; **5.**7: 5; 5.19: 137; **6.**10–13: 161; 6.12: 72

Firmus of Caesarea *Letters* 6: 219; 12: 171

George of Pisidia *On the Persian Campaign* 1.139–54, 2.86: 129, 209
Greek Anthology 4.3: 41; 9.656: 41; 9.802: 45; 15.9: 41; 16.65: 45
Gregory the Great *Letters* **1.**32: 227; 1.46: 162, 227; 1.59: 227; 1.72–3: 162, 227; **2.**4: 227; 2.7: 163; 2.27–8: 163, 227; 2.45: 217; **3.**31: 227; **4.**7: 162, 227; 4.25: 227; **5.**19: 227; 5.30: 217; 5.36: 139; 6.62: 227; 7.3: 227; 7.23: 138; **8.**24: 163; **9.**9: 162, 227; 9.16–17: 227; 9.53: 227; 9.65: 227; 9.71: 162, 227; 9.100: 163; 9.103: 163; 9.124: 227; 9.155: 162, 227; 9.156, 177: 163; 9.159, 162: 227; 9.207: 169; **10.**1, 5: 227; **13.**34: 162, 227; **14.**1: 227; 14.10: 169
Gregory of Nazianzus
  Letters 132: 156, 159, 227; 133–4: 156, 159, 227; 136–7: 156, 159, 162, 227; 181: 156, 159, 227; 225: 81, 156, 218, 227
  Orations 4.64: 182; 4.80: 42; 21.16: 219

INDEX OF ANCIENT SOURCES

Poems 11.1325–41: 201, 204
Gregory of Nyssa
   Homily on the Forty Martyrs: 80
   On the Divinity of the Son and the Holy Spirit: 203
Gregory Thaumaturgus *Canonical Letter* 1: 145; 5, 7: 138
Gregory of Tours *History of the Franks* 2.9: 34

Herodian 3.8.5: 148
Hippolytus *Apostolic Tradition* 16.17, 19: 179
Historia Augusta
   Life of Aurelian 7.4: 169; 7.5–8: 163–4
   Life of Severus Alexander 47.1: 96
History of the Monks in Egypt 1.64: 38

Isidore of Pelusium *Letters* 1.40: 173; 1.78: 173, 226; 1.390: 82; 2.203: 226

Jacob of Edessa *Chronicle* p. 240: 190
Jerome
   Chronicle s.a. 375: 80; *s.a.* 378: 222
   Commentary on Isaiah 12: 172
John of Antioch fr.187: 213
John of Biclaro *Chronicle* 578.3: 222
John Chrysostom
   Homily on Matthew 19.9: 38; 61.2: 228
   Letters 213, 218: 231
   Sermon on the words of Paul, "We do not want you to be ignorant": 47
   To a Young Widow 5: 143–4
John of Ephesus *Church History* 3.11: 216; 3.13: 150, 193; **6.6**: 136; 6.8: 103; 6.15: 137; 6.19: 136; 6.24: 125; 6.28: 72; 6.32: 224
John the Lydian
   On the Magistracies of the Roman State 2.11.3–4: 30; 2.28–9: 109; 3.28: 40; 3.41.3: 30; 3.43–4: 105, 217
   On the Months 1.27: 75
John of Nikiu 92.4–5: 201
Jordanes *History of the Goths* 138: 222

Josephus *Jewish Antiquities* 14.10.12: 229
Julian
   Beardhater (Misopogon) 369b: 95
   Letter to the Athenians 280a: 97; 286b: 95
   Letters (Bidez) 26: 183; 73: 222; 112: 203; 115: 89
   Orations 1.9a–13b: 30; 1.21b–d: 95

Lactantius
   Divine Institutes 6.16: 186
   On the Deaths of the Persecutors 7.2: 75; 7.8–10: 90; 8.1, 4: 181; 12.2–5: 193–4; 13.2: 38; 19.1–3: 53; 24.8: 53
Latin Panegyrics 2.31.2: 54; 6.22.4: 99; 8.14.1–3: 22
Leo *Letters* 12.8, 11: 145; 159: 138
Libanius
   Letters 2: 156, 227; 318: 158, 227; 350: 227; 369: 227; 426: 227; 436: 156, 158, 160, 227; 491: 158, 227; 520: 227; 556: 157, 227; 557: 227; 596: 227; 857: 227; 866: 158, 227; 867: 155, 160, 227; 868: 227; 884: 227; 897: 227; 898: 227; 925: 159, 227–8; 957: 227; 972: 153, 227; 1007: 227; 1024: 158, 227; 1054: 227; 1055: 159, 227; 1057: 155, 158–9, 168, 227; 1059–60: 158, 227; 1062: 227; 1104: 227; 1402: 4
   Orations **1**.166: 227; 1.219: 156, 157, 160; 1.220, 232: 160; **2**.9: 156; 2.26: 149; 2.39–40: 147; **18**.45: 223; 18.95: 151; 18.166–8: 183–4; 18.199: 228; 18.205–7: 30; 18.282: 104; **22**.4: 216; 24.5: 149; **30**.6: 195, 197; **47**.4: 167; 47.8: 174; **59**.83–6: 137; 59.157: 169
Liberatus *Breviary* 20, 23: 201
Life of St Eutychius: 141
Life of St Pachomius (Bohairic) 7–8: 80
Life of St Theodore of Sykeon 147: 171

INDEX OF ANCIENT SOURCES

Life of the Younger St Symeon the Stylite 62–3: 225
Livy 39.18: 195–6

Malalas *Chronicle* pp. 307–8: 90; pp. 308–9: 125; pp. 330–1: 228; p. 336: 228; pp. 337–8: 166; p. 463: 231; p. 467: 97; p. 479: 193
Malchus fr.2: 121, 134, 224; fr.18,1: 95; fr.18,3: 35, 121; fr.18,4: 140; fr.20: 104; fr.27: 72
Marcellinus *Chronicle s.a.* 393: 54; *s.a.* 500: 216
Mark the Deacon *Life of Porphyry* 63, 65: 195, 197–8
Martyrdom of Felix 31: 194
Martyrdom of Julius the Veteran 2.5: 216
Maximus of Turin *Sermons* 87.2: 230
Menander fr.1: 40; fr.6.1: 121; fr.18, 2–3: 121; fr.32,2: 36
Michael the Syrian *Chronicle* 9.9: 216; 9.16: 190–1
Miracles of St. Demetrius 200: 125

New Testament, Acts 10: 178; Luke 3.14, 6.27–38: 178; Matthew 5.38–48, 8.5–13, 26.52: 178; Romans 13.1–5: 178

Olympiodorus fr.7,1: 134; fr.9: 104; fr.10,1: 134
On Military Affairs (De Rebus Bellicis) 5.1: 88; 5.7–8: 79
On Strategy (Peri strategias) 2.4: 88; 4.9: 123; 6: 133
Optatus *Against the Donatists* 3.4: 200
Orientius *The Admonition* 2.165–84: 107
Origen *Against Celsus* 8.73: 179
Orosius 7.33.13: 222; 7.37: 103; 7.40.7: 68

Palladius *Dialogue on the Life of John Chrysostom* pp. 57–8: 202; pp. 71–2: 231
Paul of Aegina 6.88: 223
Paulinus of Nola *Letters* 25.1, 3: 186

Pelagius I *Letters* 31: 227; 60: 162, 227; 73, 90: 227
Philostorgius *Church History* 2.2: 203; 3.22: 67; 8.8: 54
Priscian *Panegyric* 63–5: 41
Priscus fr.2: 121; fr.6,2: 125; fr.9,3: 121; fr.11,2: 138, 223; fr.22,3: 47
Procopius of Caesarea
  Buildings 1.2: 47; 1.10.16–19: 45; 2.1.2–3: 98
  Secret History 19.7: 120; 24.12–14: 59; 24.27–9: 58, 216
  Wars **1**.7.30: 135; 1.7.34: 138; 1.9.4: 121; 1.14.35: 127; 1.14.52: 223; 1.15.25: 82; 1.18.15–16, 37: 189; 1.18.38–40: 78; 1.19.37: 198; 1.22.3: 121; 1.24.40–1: 167; **2**.5.29: 103, 136; 2.6.24: 103; 2.7.5–6: 103; 2.7.11: 136; 2.7.37: 72; 2.8.35: 145; 2.9: 102–3; 2.11.24: 103; 2.12: 103; 2.13: 103, 224; 2.14.1: 136; 2.19.25: 104; 2.19.32: 228; 2.21.3: 228; 2.27.35–6: 144, 224; 2.28.10: 121; 2.30.12: 228; **3**.2.25–6: 33; 3.10.1–18: 106; 3.12: 189, 228, 231; 3.15.13: 97; 3.17.10: 228; 3.19.11: 189; 3.21.10: 167, 228; **4**.1.21: 189; 4.3.24–7: 103; 4.4.15–19, 29: 228; 4.9: 69, 101, 103; 4.14: 64, 72, 152; 4.14.17: 82, 104; 4.18: 72; 4.20.28–9: 99; **5**.5.18–19: 69; 5.10.29, 36: 136; 5.20.5: 224; 5.25: 133–4, 153, 224; 5.29.26: 153; **6**.2.15–17, 25–7: 127–8, 141; 6.3.10–12: 224; 6.20.18–21: 134, 141; 6.21.29, 39: 135, 144; 6.23.9–10: 228; 6.29.18–28: 70; 6.29.37: 103; 6.30.1–2: 70; 7.1.1–3: 103; 7.1.3–6: 70; 7.1.8–10: 98, 223; 7.6.4: 145; 7.6.9: 97; 7.10: 135, 224; 7.11.13–16: 151; 7.12.4: 78; 7.12.7–8: 72; 7.16: 134, 224; 7.17: 134–5, 224; 7.20.29–31: 145; 7.21.26: 224; 7.23.1–2: 142, 151; 7.28.12: 228; 7.36.2: 134; **8**.11.27: 222; 8.11.35–8, 61–2:

130; 8.15.3–7: 121; 8.15.7: 120; 8.23.15–16: 95; 8.31.9: 223; 8.32.20: 223
Procopius of Gaza *Panegyric* 7–10: 41
Ps.-Joshua Stylites *Chronicle* 31: 88; 43: 173; 52: 139; 53: 135, 136; 54: 96, 97, 217; 62: 134; 65: 165–6; 70: 95, 97; 71: 223; 77: 97, 134, 224; 79: 140; 86: 165, 167, 168–9; 87: 99, 165; 90: 98; 96: 170, 172–3
Ps.-Maurice *Strategy* preface: 14; 2.9: 128; 2.18: 188, 192; 5.1–2: 153; 7.13: 153; 7B.6: 129; 7B.17: 128, 188; 10.2–3: 134; 10.3: 130, 134; 12B.7: 213, 221; 12B.20, 22: 228
Ps.-Zachariah *Church History* 3.5: 201; 7.1: 214; 7.4: 224; 7.5: 121, 134, 138, 224, 228; 7.6: 98; 7.8: 57, 216

Quodvultdeus *Book of Promises* 3.38.41: 231

Rufinus *Church History* 11.13: 30; 11.24: 231

Salvian *On the Government of God* 5.38–45: 229
Sebeos *Armenian History* 8: 103
Sermon on the Suffering of Donatus: 200
Severus *History of the Patriarchs of Alexandria* 1.13: 201, 204
Severus of Antioch *Letters* 1.8: 227; 1.40: 159, 227
Sidonius Apollinaris
Letters 3.3: 227; 4.17: 227; 6.12.5: 140–1, 225; 7.7.3: 134
Poems 5.38ff.: 34
Socrates *Church History* **1**.16: 45; **2**.13: 167, 200; 2.16: 200; 2.38: 200; **3**.21: 40; **4**.15: 200; 4.21: 200; **5**.16: 231; **6**.6.20: 228; 6.6.36: 40; 7.21.7–10: 40; 7.23: 38; 7.24: 213
Sozomen *Church History* **1**.8: 183; **2**.11: 200; **3**.6–7, 9: 200; **4**.9: 203; 4.21: 200; 4.30: 195, 197; **5**.17.8: 59; **6**.13: 200; 6.21.7: 209; 7.28: 201; **8**.21: 201; 8.23: 201, 231; 9.5.7: 129

Strabo *Geography* 4.200: 118
Suidas *s.v.* Christodorus: 40; *s.v.* Colluthus: 40
Sulpicius Severus *Life of Martin* 3.5–6: 231
Symmachus
Letters **1**.95.2: 38; **3**.54–69: 157–9, 161, 226; 3.70–3: 157–9, 226; 3.74–80: 157–9, 226; **4**.1–14: 157, 159, 161, 226; 4.15–16: 157–8, 226; **10**.1: 157–8, 226
Memoranda (Relationes) 47.2: 38
Orations 1.19: 61
Synesius
Constitutio: 161
Letters 6: 156, 227; 14: 156, 227; 24: 156, 227; 28: 156, 227; 59: 156, 159, 227; 62: 156, 158, 227; 77: 156, 227; 78: 74, 156, 158–9, 227; 94: 156, 158, 227; 101: 158; 130: 140, 156, 159, 168, 225, 227
On Kingship 13–14: 34

Tacitus
Annals 1.2: 1; 14.30: 195; 15.4–5, 10–13: 124
Histories 2.8: 152
Tertullian
Apology 42.2–3: 179
On Idolatry 19.1–3: 179–80
On the Wreath 1.4–5
"Testament of the piglet": 172
Theodoret
Church History **2**.13: 89; **3**.3.7: 231; **4**.1.6: 183; 4.17–18: 201; 4.19, 21: 200; 4.24.4: 200; **5**.6.4: 228
Letters II: 191; VI: 156, 227; XI: 156, 159, 227; XVIII: 156, 159, 227; 23: 156, 159, 227; 45: 156, 227; 65: 156, 158, 227; 71: 156, 190, 227; 73: 190, 227; 79: 156, 227; 92: 156, 159–60, 227; 97: 158, 227; 103: 227; 111: 156, 227; 119: 156, 159, 227; 121: 156, 227; 139: 156, 159, 227; 140: 156, 159, 227; 145: 188, 226; IV.25: 159, 227–8

INDEX OF ANCIENT SOURCES

Theophanes *Chronicle* p. 101: 201;
  p. 118: 224; p. 121: 56; p. 251: 65;
  p. 293: 136; pp. 310–11: 129, 209;
  pp. 313–14: 39; pp. 321–2: 222
Theophylact Simocatta **1**.3.7: 121;
  1.4.5: 121; 1.7.2: 36; 1.13.8–12:
  225; **2**.2.6: 129; 2.2.7: 189; 2.3:
  189, 209; 2.4: 128; 2.5.5–6: 128;
  2.6.10–11: 129, 223; 2.8.6: 228;
  2.10.8–9: 78; **3**.1–2: 72; 3.1.9:
  228; 3.2.1: 228; 3.5.10: 161; 3.6.5:
  38; 3.15.13–15: 137; **5**.16.1–6.3.8:
  36–7; 7.10.1: 228; 7.15.7: 36;
  7.15.14: 121

Urbicius *Invention* 13: 228

Vegetius *Epitome of Military Science* 2.5:
  52, 184; 2.7: 167, 228; 3.6: 153;
  4.7: 134; 4.8: 130; 4.25: 144, 224
Victor of Vita *History of the Vandal
  Persecution* 1.25: 138
Virgil *Aeneid* 7.604: 222; 8.671–713:
  206

Zonaras 12.23: 136
Zosimus **1**.33.3: 138; 1.36.1: 171;
  1.43.1: 222; 1.43.2: 139; 1.69:
  134, 226; **2**.15.1–2: 75; 2.29.5:
  182; 2.34: 10, 166; 2.43.2: 67;
  3.10.2: 96; 3.24.1: 152; **4**.10.4: 95,
  97; 4.11: 153; 4.22: 223; 4.33, 50:
  30; 4.35: 68; 4.53: 213; **5**.26.5:
  103; 5.29.9: 119, 121; 5.39.2–3:
  135; 5.41.4–7: 121; 5.49: 189

LEGAL AND ADMINISTRATIVE SOURCES

Justinian *Edict* 13.18: 64
Justinian *Novels* 22: 142; 41: 109; 50:
  109; 85: 220; 105: 69; 109: 231;
  117: 142; 130: 62, 228; 134: 97;
  163: 114
Justinianic Code **1**.4.20: 190;
  1.5.12.17: 193; 1.17.1: 62; 1.27.1:
  62, 205; 1.27.2.4, 11: 62; 1.27.2.8:
  87; **4**.40.4: 62; 4.54.1: 161;
  4.65.31: 62; **5**.4.21: 150; 5.17.7:
  142; **6**.21.3: 62; 7.64.9: 62;
  8.50.12: 62; **10**.26.2: 62;
  10.27.2.10: 109; **11**.52.1: 108;
  12.8.2.4: 97; 12.35.18.1, 3–4, 6:
  62–3; 12.37.17.1: 62–3; 12.46.1:
  60, 229; 12.50.22: 63

Majorian *Novels* 1.1: 63

Notitia Dignitatum
  East 5.57: 192; 7.49: 185; 11.18–39:
    90, 92; 13: 94; 28: 84; 28.19:
    167; 31: 84
  West 9.16–38: 90, 92, 220; 11: 94;
    42.33–44: 82

Severus *Novels* 2: 82

Theodosian Code **1**.32.5: 108; **3**.5.5:
  150; **5**.6.3: 218; 7.1.3: 150, 151,
  152; 7.1.5, 8: 81; 7.1.13: 228;
  7.1.14: 81; 7.1.18: 62; 7.4.1, 6, 22:
  62; 7.4.4, 6, 25: 169; 7.4.17: 63;
  7.5.2: 62; 7.6.4: 62; 7.6.5: 63; 7.8.4:
  167; 7.8.5: 168; 7.8.13: 62; 7.8.15:
  215; 7.9: 168; 7.13.16: 152; 7.20.2:
  60, 183, 229; 7.20.4: 11; 7.20.6, 9:
  60; 7.20.12: 81; **10**.22.4: 80;
  11.7.3: 62; 11.24.1, 3–5: 174;
  11.28.7, 12: 116; **12**.1.56: 11;
  12.1.96: 108; 12.1.124: 108;
  16.8.24: 190, 229; 16.10.18: 231;
  16.10.19: 62, 89; 16.10.21: 190
Theodosius II *Novels* 4.1.2: 215; 4.3:
  62; 6.1: 62; 24.4: 87

Valentinian III *Novels* 1.2: 116; 15.1:
  215

INSCRIPTIONS AND PAPYRI

AE 1937.232: 59–60, 62; 1976.631: 143; 1981.777: 229; 1993.1231: 116, 139; 1994.1552: 171

BGU 140: 148

CIL 3.405: 11; 3.12336: 171; 3.14191: 171; 5.8742: 89; 5.8764: 229; 8.9248: 64; 13.3256: 230
CPL 199: 169
CPR 6.76: 226; 24.15: 192

IGR 1287: 99
ILS 551: 173; 798: 45; 2810: 64; 9841: 231

P. Abinnaeus 1, 18, 28, 43, 48: 174–5
P. Beatty Panopolis 1.213–16, 314–46: 220; 1.221–4: 85; 2.109–13: 169; 2.161–4: 58–9
P. Cairo 67321: 64
P. Columbia 7.188: 150
P. Dura 30, 32: 150; 54: 176
P. Edfu 9: 225
P. Euphrates 9: 182
P. Freer 08.45 c–d: 64
P. Hermopolis 7: 218
P. Italy 13: 141
P. London 3.982: 52, 83; 5.1655: 218; 1914: 167, 170, 203
P. Munich 9: 128
P. Nessana 35: 192; 36: 128
P. Oxyrhynchus 60: 167; 561: 59; 1103: 72; 1214: 150; 1449: 197; 3581: 172; 4367: 58; 4373: 218; 4598–603: 221
P. Rylands 609: 14, 79
PSI 7.820: 169
P. Strasbourg 480: 40

SEG 9.356: 63; 34.1271: 141–2

GENERAL INDEX

Abinnaeus (officer) 174–5
accession ceremonies 26–7, 53–7
Achilles 41, 45
acorns, as source of sustenance 134, 141
Adraha 99
Adrianople 29, 35, 78, 108, 143–4, 149, 166, 222
Aetius (general) 7, 33, 35, 70, 210
Agathias (historian and poet) 15, 41, 75, 77
Agri Decumates 114–15, 118
agricultural destruction 140
Alamanni (Germanic people) 23, 38–9, 84, 97, 139–40, 151
Alans (Asiatic people) 115
Alaric (Gothic leader) 119–21
Aldio (general) 163
Alexander the Great 5, 32, 212
Alexandria 38, 70, 124–5, 152, 166–7, 169–70, 191, 195, 198
Amaseia 141
Amida 15, 134–5, 139, 165, 223–4
Amiens 27, 54, 93
Ammianus Marcellinus (historian) 14–15, 38, 71, 126–7
Anastasius (emperor) 49, 58, 70, 79, 109
  background and accession 13, 36, 56, 214
  civil war with Vitalian 70, 108
  financial management 88, 106, 120
  Isaurian war 9, 40–1,
  Persian war 40, 96, 99
Anatha 137
Anatolius (general) 156, 159–60, 162
Anchialus 11

Anemurium 185
Anthemiolus (general) 36
Anthemius (emperor) 36
Antioch 72, 90, 95, 135, 137, 153, 156, 166–7, 170, 174, 199
  attacked by Persians 111, 113–14, 136, 145
  as imperial capital 25, 27, 183
Antoninus Pius (emperor) 22, 25
Anysius (general) 156, 161
Apamea 113, 136
Aper (praetorian prefect) 24
Apollonius (general) 156, 190
Aquileia 125, 138
Aquitaine 86
Arabia (province) 99
Arabs 1, 6, 9, 27, 73, 119, 138, 209–10
Aragua 171
Arbogast (general) 30, 161, 213, 217
Arcadius (emperor) 32–3, 45–6, 48, 54, 65
Areobindus (general) 156, 159
Ariadne 36, 68, 71
Arian Christians/Arianism 72, 155, 160, 192–3, 199, 202–6
Arinthaeus (general) 156, 158–9, 162
Armenia 12, 72, 102, 113, 156, 164, 219
army, Roman
  "barbarization" 12, 83–5,
  bucellarii 13
  centralized command in west 33
  chaplains 183, 191–2, 231–2
  Christianization of 181–93
  cost 88–9
  demographic parameters 77–8

270

donatives 55–60, 83, 87–8
evolution of in late antiquity 9–14
federates 13
food supplies 85–9, 95–8
hereditary service 81, 94
imperial strategies for retaining loyalty of 51–66
Latin, role of 13–14, 213
manpower needs 74–9
military oath 52–3, 57, 177, 184
military standards 55–6, 60, 176–7
mutiny in 9, 66, 72–3,
pay shortages 72, 217
presence in urban centers 164–7
privileges 60
recruitment
   methods 79–85
   non-Romans 12, 81–2, 83–5
   Romans 79–81
role in
   appointment of emperors 53–7
   doctrinal controversies 198–205
   religious persecution 193–8
size 74–9
size of campaign armies 76, 96
training 12, 78–9
unit size 76
units named after emperors 64–5
veterans 60
weapons and clothing supply 89–94
see also soldiers
arsenals 89–94, 220–1
Arsinoe 174
Artemius (general) 197
Arzanene 84, 117, 137
Asclepiodotus (praetorian prefect) 22
Aspar (general) 35, 38, 70, 156, 160, 193
assassination of generals seen as threats 70–1
Athanasius (bishop) 198, 203
Athens 224
atrocities *see* brutality
Attila (Hunnic ruler) 7, 47, 120–1, 135, 138, 210, 214
Augsburg 116, 139
Augustine (bishop) 155, 161, 187
Augustus (emperor) 147–8, 206

Aurelian (emperor) 24, 116, 164, 199
aurum
   coronarium 88
   oblaticium 88
   tironicum 80
Autun 99, 125
Auxonius (praetorian prefect) 97
Avars (Asiatic people) 120, 212
   besiege Constantinople (626) 37, 108
   besiege Thessalonica 135, 210
   hostile presence on lower Danube (sixth/seventh century) 8, 78, 108
Avitus (general) 35

Bacaudae (Gallic rebels) 9, 212
Bacchus 195–6
Bahan (general) 163
Balkans 68
   as source of emperors 24, 28
   as source of recruits 24, 178
baptism of soldiers 185, 202, 231
Barbatio (general) 154–5
Barberini ivory 42, 44
Basil of Caesarea (bishop) 154–62, 186–7, 208
Basiliscus (usurper) 56, 68
battle in late antiquity
   experience of soldiers 125–33
   methodological issues in understanding 126–8
   see also Adrianople; Callinicum; Solachon; Strasbourg; Taginae
Bauto (general) 157, 161
Belisarius (general) 15, 41, 43, 69–70, 78, 98, 101, 103, 106, 189, 218, 223, 224, 228, 231
Berbers (north African people) 8, 73, 99, 104, 212
Beroea 72, 136
Bezabde 136
billeting *see hospitalitas*
Bishapur 136
bishops
   ransoming prisoners 138
   relationships with generals 154–62
   relieving famine 140

Bithynia 129
booty
  as motivation for soldiers to fight 129, 197–8, 202
  as motivation for war 5, 6
  pays for fortifications 99
  as result of war 69, 101–4, 221–2
  see also prisoners of war; slaves
Boppard 185
Borani 137
Bostra 99
Britain 9, 86, 118, 122
brutality
  Germanic 135, 139
  Persian 135–6
  Roman 129, 135–6, 140, 223–5
bucellarii 13
Bulgars (Asiatic people) 108
Burgundians (Germanic people) 144
bureaucracy, Roman 2, 88–98
  see also praetorian prefecture

Callinicum 78, 189
Campania 116–17, 162
cannibalism 134–5, 224
capitals, imperial 25, 27, 30–1, 183
  see also Antioch; Constantinople; Milan; Rome; Serdica; Sirmium; Trier
Cappadocia 81, 152
Caracalla (emperor) 64–5
Caria 109
Carinus (emperor) 28
Carthage 138
Carus (emperor) 4, 24, 27, 53
causes of war in late antiquity
  between Roman empire and Germanic peoples/kingdoms 6–8
  between Roman and Persian empires 3–6
cavalry
  Hunnic 7
  Persian 4
  Roman 10, 12–13, 85, 175
Cerealis (officer) 159
Chalcis 137
chaplains, military 183, 191–2, 231–2
Christianity
  debate about role in fall of western empire 207–10
  influence on
    accession ceremonial 56–7
    art 44–5, 48–9
    literature 42
    morale 129, 135, 209
    Roman army 53, 177–93
    Roman foreign policy 5, 205–7
    warfare 39, 129, 135
Christians
  differing attitudes to military service and war 177–81, 186–8
  doctrinal controversies 198–205
  persecution of 38, 181, 193–4, 196
  in Persia, as *casus belli* 5, 205–7
  see also Arian Christians; Monophysite Christians
Christodorus (poet) 40
chrysargyron 88
church councils 208–9
  Arles 187
  Chalcedon 160, 190, 203–4, 209, 213
  Ephesus 159–60
  Rome 186
  Toledo 186–7
churches
  constructed by army officers 230
  destruction of 193–4
  in military forts 185, 192
circus factions 199
civil war
  in Persia 5–6, 119
  in Roman empire 8–9, 28, 51, 66–73, 78, 108, 182–3
civilians
  impact of war on 133–46
  relations with soldiers
    negative 167–73, 174–5
    positive 173–5
classicizing historians 14–15
  use of *topoi* in battle descriptions 126–8
Claudian (poet) 32–3
Claudius II (emperor) 24, 27
Clement of Alexandria (theologian) 179
Clermont 134

272

GENERAL INDEX

coins, Roman
   as source for imperial ideology 18
   theme of victory on 48–50
collatio lustralis 8
Colluthus (poet) 40
Cologne 115
columns, victory 45–6, 215
comitatenses (field army troops) 10–12, 109, 150, 164–5, 185, 192, 213
conscription *see* army, Roman, recruitment
Constans (emperor) 66, 68, 151, 169
Constantina (empress) 67
Constantine I (emperor) 28, 30, 45, 60, 64–5, 99, 215
   accession 53, 67
   army reforms 10, 166
   Christianizing measures in army 181–3
   civil wars with Maxentius and Licinius 8, 66, 75, 132, 182
   discrimination against pagans 195, 197
   planned invasion of Persia (337) 5, 205–7
   supports Christianity 5, 182, 208
Constantine II (emperor) 66
Constantine III (usurper) 68
Constantinople 59, 70, 86, 89, 97, 116, 156–7, 193, 197, 202–4
   attacks on 6, 37, 69, 108, 119, 125, 135
   Bronze Gate 43
   Hagia Sophia 39, 56
   Hebdomon 54–7, 216
   hippodrome 56–7, 101
   imperial palace 43, 56–7, 214
   limited use as imperial base (fourth century) 30–1
   military units based near 165–7, 192
   victory celebrations in 38, 69
   victory monuments in 43, 45–7
Constantius I (emperor) 22, 25, 67, 106, 180
Constantius II (emperor) 29, 30, 37–8, 42, 47, 61, 71, 95, 134, 151, 169, 186

civil wars with Magnentius and Julian 8–9, 66, 68, 73, 78, 166, 183
Persian wars 97, 137
religious policies 198–9, 208–9
Constantius III (emperor) 213
consulship 25
   as reward for successful generals 69
Coptic 213
Corippus (poet/panegyrist) 13, 41
count of the sacred largesses 88
Cremna 134, 224, 225–6
Croton 138
Ctesiphon (Persian capital) 4, 6, 221–2
curiales (town councilors) 86, 88, 108,
Cyclades 109
Cynegius Maternus (praetorian prefect) 195, 197
Cyprus 109, 137
Cyrenaica 154, 157, 168
Cyrrhus 156
Cyrus of Panopolis (praetorian prefect/poet) 41
Cyzicus 125

Dacia 108, 118
Damascus 90, 165
Danube frontier
   lower 87, 90, 95, 108–11, 138
   middle 139
   upper 138
   see also Avars; Goths; Huns; Quadi; Slavs
Dara 98, 127, 129, 136, 224
decapitation of captured enemy 129, 223
Decius (emperor) 24, 194, 196, 232
Demetrius (saint) 135, 210
deserters 80, 82–3, 151
Dichin 87
Diocletian (emperor) 27, 53, 64, 85, 90, 104, 125, 180, 220
   arch of 45, 214
   army reforms 10, 75, 81
   background and accession 24, 53
   develops Tetrarchy 25–8, 213, 214–15
   persecution of Christians 38, 181, 193–4, 196
   taxation system 86, 94

273

GENERAL INDEX

Diogenianus (general) 71
Dionysias 165, 174
diplomatic subsidies, as alternative to war 119–22
discipline, military 11, 12, 137, 148–9,
disease
  Antonine plague 77, 148
  in besieged cities 135
  pandemic (sixth century) 8, 78, 107, 114,
Donatists/Donatism (Christian sect) 155, 203–4
donatives 55–60, 83, 87–8
Druids 195
Dura-Europos 130–1, 133, 176–8, 222, 224, 228

Edessa 90, 99, 138–9, 144, 151, 168, 170, 172, 175, 224
Egypt 17, 81, 124, 164, 174
  economic value 7, 119
  military units 84, 165
  Monophysite sympathies 191
  source of grain 86, 95, 116
Ellebichus (general) 156, 158, 160
Emilia 141
emperors, Roman
  accession ceremonial 53–7
  identification with troops, language of 61–4
  legitimation of rule 21, 53–7
  loyalty of troops, strategies for retaining 51–66
  mobility in third and fourth century 25–30
  naming of army units after 64–5
  (non-)involvement in warfare 21–37
  qualifications
    heredity 21, 27–30
    military experience 21, 24–5, 28, 30
  social background 23–5
  victory titles 39–40
  visual representations of 42–50
epitaphs 11, 17, 143, 149–50, 166, 173, 180–1, 192
equestrians 23–5
Eudocia (empress) 40

Eugenius (usurper) 9, 29, 38, 161, 212, 217
Euphemia 150–1
Eutropius (court eunuch) 34

fabricae see arsenals
failure, military, financial costs of 105–6
families
  impact of war on 138
  of soldiers 142–4, 147–53
Faustina (empress) 67
federates (Roman army, sixth century) 13
field armies *see comitatenses*
Firmus (rebel) 157
Flavius Zeno (general) 35, 69, 156, 190
Florentius (praetorian prefect) 97
food, sources of
  during sieges 133–5
  for army
    on campaign 95–8, 171, 221
    peacetime 85–7, 219
  from bishop 140–1
  see also cannibalism
fortifications 98–100, 114, 116, 221
Franks (Germanic people) 82, 84

Gainas (general and rebel) 9, 33, 40, 45–6,
Galerius (emperor) 4, 11, 45, 102, 104, 180
Gallienus (emperor) 10, 24, 27, 53, 99, 115
Gallus (Caesar) 156
Gaul
  economic impact of war 114–15, 140–1
  Gallic empire 114
  laeti in 82
  unsettled conditions (fifth century) 9, 106–7
Gaza 195, 197
Gelimer (Vandal king) 69, 101,
generals, Roman
  delegated military responsibility 21
  non-Romans as 84–5, 157, 162, 219
  relationships with elite civilians and bishops 153–62

274

GENERAL INDEX

religious allegiances of 70–1, 186, 190
threats from
  containment of 68–70
  elimination of 70–1
ties to imperial family (sixth century) 71–2
George of Cappadocia (bishop) 199, 219
George of Pisidia (poet) 41–2
Germanic peoples
  increasing strength in third and fourth century 6, 23
  military capability, siege warfare 125
  see also Alamanni; Franks; Goths; Juthungi; Lombards; Quadi; Vandals
Germanus (general) 66, 70–1,
"Ghurka syndrome" 83, 219
Gibbon, Edward 207–10
Gildo (rebel) 161
Gordian III (emperor) 4, 24, 53, 171
Goths (Germanic people) 23, 35, 38–9, 45, 73, 78, 95, 108, 116, 125, 141
  adherence to Arian Christianity 192–3, 202
  allowed to enter Roman empire (376) 7, 80, 108,
  conquered by Justinian 43, 70, 104, 129
  service in Roman army 80–1, 192–3
  war with the empire 97, 108, 133, 135–6, 145, 151
  see also Adrianople
Gradishte 87
granaries 87, 219–20
Gratian (father of Valentinian) 29
Gratian (Roman emperor) 27, 29–30, 54, 68, 215
Gregory of Antioch (bishop) 72, 161
Gregory the Great (bishop) 124, 154–5, 161–3
Gregory of Nazianzus (bishop) 154–62

Hadrian (emperor) 25, 148
Hagia Sophia (church) 39, 56
Harran 138–9
Hebdomon 54–7, 216

Heliopolis 165
Heraclius (emperor) 32, 37
  defeats Persians 6, 39, 41–2, 119, 129, 208, 219
Heraclius (father of emperor) 38
Hermopolis 79, 165, 175
Hippolytus (bishop) 179
Homer 41, 153, 161
Honorius (emperor) 32–3, 45, 46, 54, 65, 89, 216
horses, supply of 85
hospitalitas (billeting) 163–4, 167–9, 171–2, 174
Housesteads 185
Huns (Asiatic people) 7, 35, 41, 47, 69, 129
  cause destruction in Balkans 108–9, 111, 138, 145, 151, 213
  invade Gaul 7, 135, 210
  military capability, horsemanship and archery 7, 13
Hypatius (general) 71

Iatrus 87
Illus (rebel) 9, 41, 71, 212
Illyricum 151, 165
Ioannes (general) 71
Isauria 9, 40–1, 68, 83, 219
  see also Zeno
Isis 195–6, 198
Italy
  economic impact of war 115–17, 141
  war in 78, 116, 124, 139, 151, 166
ivory, as artistic medium 42, 44

Jerusalem 195
Jews, Roman
  and military service 177, 190
  revolts by 23, 222
John (usurper) 38
John the Cappadocian (praetorian prefect) 97, 106
John Chrysostom (bishop) 202–4
John Gibbus (general) 69
John the Lydian (bureaucrat) 40, 75
John the Scythian (general) 69
John Troglyta (general) 228

GENERAL INDEX

Joshua the Stylite (Ps.-) (chronicler) 15–16, 124
Jovian (emperor) 28–9, 54, 118, 208
Julian (emperor) 11, 29, 35, 89, 129, 203, 216
    conflict with Alamanni 38, 125–6, 140
    in Gaul 54, 166
    Persian expedition (363) 4, 14, 28–9, 78, 95–6, 104, 106, 118, 130, 137, 183–4
    religious policies 5, 183–4
    usurpation 8, 53, 67–8, 125, 151, 166, 183
Julius Nepos (emperor) 36
Jupiter Dolichenus, cult of 177
"just war" 187, 206, 230
Justin (general) 70–1
Justin I (emperor) 13, 36, 56, 70–1, 84, 190–1, 193
Justin II (emperor) 5, 36, 41, 57, 70, 215
Justinian (emperor) 16, 71, 142
    abolition of donatives? 58–9
    and army size 75
    army units named after 64
    background and accession 13, 36, 57
    building program 98
    celebrates victories 39–40, 42–7, 69
    conquest of Goths 43, 70, 104, 129
    conquest of Vandals 42–3, 69, 101, 103–4
    creates additional field army for Armenia 12
    depiction on various artistic media 42–7
    diplomatic use of subsidies 119
    elimination of Vitalian? 70
    equestrian statue of 45, 47
    Nika riot 8–9, 167
    peace treaties with Persia 5, 119–20
    Persian wars 5, 40, 102–3, 113, 130, 136, 189
    religious policies of 193, 198
    western campaigns 1, 8, 14, 97, 104, 106, 189, 205–6
Justinian (general) 71

Juthungi (Germanic people) 84, 116, 139

Kaiseraugst 185
Kavad (Persian king) 5, 15, 95–6, 138
Khusro I (Persian king) 5, 102–3, 136
Khusro II (Persian king) 6, 39, 119
Koblenz 185

labarum 55, 216
Lactantius (Christian writer) 75, 186
laeti 81–2, 84, 218
Laguatan (north African people) 189
Latin, as language of Roman army 13–14, 213
Lejjun 165, 230
Leo I (emperor) 35–6, 68, 215
    accession 54–6, 216
    Vandal expedition (468) 96, 105–6, 217
Leo II (emperor) 56
Leontia (imperial princess) 68
letters, as evidence for military–civilian relations 153–63, 172–5
Libanius (rhetorician)
    as landlord 174
    relations with generals 153–60
    on the Roman army in fourth century 147–9, 153
Libya 76
Licinius (emperor) 8, 11, 59–60, 66
limitanei (troops in frontier provinces) 10–12, 59, 77, 87, 109, 150, 164–5, 175, 212–13, 229
Litorius (general) 190
logistics 85–98
Lombards (Germanic people) 8, 104, 116, 124–5, 138–9, 163, 166, 212, 222
Longinus (rebel) 9
Lucania 116
Lucillianus (general) 166
Lyons 73, 140

Macrinus (emperor) 24, 213
Magnentius (usurper) 8, 40, 67–8, 73, 78, 115, 222

GENERAL INDEX

Magnus Maximus (usurper) 9, 29, 68–9, 73, 157–8, 160
Maionia 143
Majorian (emperor) 35
manpower
  major losses 78
  numbers 74–9
  shortages 29
  sources for army 74, 79–85
Marcellinus (general, early fifth century) 156, 161
Marcellinus (general, mid fifth century) 36, 71, 190
Marcian (emperor) 35, 45, 54–5, 68, 81, 160, 204, 213–14, 215
Marcian (general) 71
Marcian (usurper) 68
Marcus Aurelius (emperor) 23, 46, 216
Martin of Tours (bishop) 197, 231
martyrdom
  death of Heraclius' troops against Persians as 129
  of Christians 194
  of Christians in Roman army 180
master of the offices (*magister officiorum*) 93–4,
Maurice (emperor) 38, 71
  army pay reduction 72
  background and accession 36, 57, 216
  involvement in expeditions 36
  military treatise attributed to 16
  overthrow (602) 5–6, 9, 37, 72–3
Maxentius (usurper) 8, 28, 75, 132, 182, 216
Maximian (emperor) 27, 53, 180, 193
Maximinus (emperor) 23–4, 53
Maximinus Daia (emperor) 66
Maximus of Turin (bishop) 197
medical treatment in war 128
Meletians (Christian sect) 203
Menander (historian) 15, 40
Merobaudes (general) 70
Mesopotamia, northern
  economic impact of war 111–14, 138–40
  war in 95, 135–6, 139, 165–6, 168–9
metalware, as medium for imperial propaganda 42–3

Milan 25, 27, 47, 54, 117, 144
military treatises 16
Mithraism 177, 185
Modares (general) 156, 162
Moderatus (general) 155
Moesia 109
monks 80, 207–8, 233
Monocarton 72
Monophysite Christians 191, 204, 209
Montanism 179
morale, maintenance of
  Christianity's role 129, 135, 209
  civilians 135, 209
  soldiers 129
mosaics
  as propaganda medium 43, 45
  by Roman prisoners in Persia 137
Mundelsheim 139
Mursa 73, 78
mutiny, in Roman army 9, 66, 72–3, 161, 193, 217

Naissus 125, 138, 183
Naples 117, 136, 169
Narseh (Persian king) 102
Narses (general) 166
navy, Roman 212
Nepotianus (usurper) 67
Nessana 165, 192, 230
Neupotz 102, 225
Nicaea 54
Nicomedia 38, 90, 194
Nicopolis 109, 111, 167
Nika riot (532) 8, 9, 167
Nisibis 4, 117–18, 135, 137, 139, 210
North Africa 157
  economic value 12, 86, 104–6, 118
  reconquest of by Romans 42–3, 69, 101, 103–4, 152
  Roman attempts to recapture from Vandals 8, 14, 96, 105–6
  Roman troops mutiny 9, 72
  Vandal occupation of 7, 116, 118, 145
Notitia Dignitatum (administrative document) 17, 74
  on army distribution 164–5
  on army size 76
  on arsenals 90–4

277

GENERAL INDEX

Nu'man (Arab leader) 138–9
Numerian (emperor) 24, 28

oaths 52–3, 57, 142, 177, 179, 184, 190–1
Origen (theologian) 179
Orleans 135, 210
orphans 144
Orsino 163
Osrhoene 113–14
Oxyrhynchus 72

Pachomius (monk) 80, 233
Paeonius (general) 156
pagans
  exclusion from army 189–91
  sacrifice 176–7, 179, 183–5, 188
  temples, destruction of 194–8, 202, 204–5
  see also generals, Roman, religious allegiances of
Palmyra 165
pandemic (sixth century) 8
panegyric 41, 157, 160, 221
Panium 166, 192
Panopolis 85
Paphlagonia 142, 145
Patiens (bishop) 140–1
patronage 158, 173–5
Paul of Samosata (bishop) 199
Paul of Tinnis (bishop) 204
Paulinus of Nola (bishop) 186
Pelagius I (bishop) 155
Persepolis 136
Persia 41
  military capability
    cavalry 4
    siege warfare 4, 98, 124–5
  political and economic organization 3–4
  Sasanian dynasty
    as self-proclaimed heirs of Achaemenid dynasty 4
    overthrown by Arabs (seventh century) 6
    replace Parthian Arsacids 1, 23
  treasury in Ctesiphon 221–2
  wars with Roman empire

    third century 1, 4, 97, 111, 130–1, 133, 171
    fourth century 1, 4, 95–6, 104, 130, 134, 136, 151, 167
    fifth century 40, 156, 206
    sixth century 1, 5, 15–16, 40, 84, 95–6, 99, 102–3, 113, 124, 130, 135–6, 141, 165–6, 189
    seventh century 1, 5–6, 37, 119, 124, 129, 136, 208, 219
Peter (general) 71
Peter the Patrician (bureaucrat) 215–16
petitions 171, 174
Petra (Caucasus) 130
Petrus (general) 84
Philae 198
Philip (emperor) 24, 171
Philippicus (general) 71, 189
Philippopolis 222
Phocas (usurper and emperor) 9, 37, 72–3, 111, 215–16
Phrygia 194
Picenum 116, 141
Pisidia 95
Placentia 224
"Plains of Cato" 189, 192
poetry, as medium for celebration of victory 40–2
Pompeius (general) 70
Pontus 141, 145
Postumus (emperor) 115
praetorian prefecture
  deputies and campaign logistics 97
  quaestura exercitus 109–11
  responsible for taxes (late third century onward) 86
  stepping stone to imperial office (third century) 24
Priscian (grammarian) 13
Priscus (historian) 138
prisoners of war
  foreign, in Roman empire 103–4
    depictions of 43, 49
    settlement on Roman land 129, 137
    use in army 104, 129
    ransoming of 138
    return home 138

GENERAL INDEX

Roman, in hands of Germanic/Asiatic
   peoples 116, 125, 137–9, 144–5
Roman, in Persia 5, 102, 111, 113,
   135–7, 225
slaughter of
   after battle 129
   after sieges 135–6
Proba, Faltonia Betitia (poet) 40
Probus (emperor) 24
Probus diptych 42
Procopius (historian) 223
   as classicizing historian 14–15, 126–7
   hostility to Justinian 58–9
   on Justinian's building program 98
Procopius (usurper) 9, 29, 35, 67, 125, 167, 228
Promotus (general) 69, 157, 160
Proterius (bishop) 204
Pulcheria (empress) 160

Quadi (Germanic people) 84, 139, 215
quaestura exercitus 109–11
Quintillus (emperor) 27, 53

Radagaisus 103
rape 141–2, 144–6, 169
Ravenna 41, 103, 163
   capture by Justinian's forces 70, 103
   imperial capital 33
   papyrus documents from 17
Regensburg-Harting 139
Resafa 165
Rhine frontier 86, 98, 151
Richomer (general) 153, 155, 157–8, 160–1
Ricimer (general) 35
ripenses, precursors of *limitanei* 11
Rhone 140–1
Roman empire
   fall of in west 3, 7, 12
   wars with Asiatic nomads 7, 107–11
   wars with Germanic peoples 1, 6–7, 42–3, 45, 103–4, 116, 135–6
   wars with Persia
      third century 4, 97, 111, 130–1, 133, 171
      fourth century 4–5, 95–6, 104, 111–13, 130, 134, 136, 151

fifth century 5, 40, 156, 206
sixth century 5, 40, 95–6, 99, 102–3, 113–14, 130, 135–6, 141, 165–6, 173, 189
seventh century 5–6, 114, 119, 129, 136, 208, 219
see also army, Roman; bureaucracy, Roman; emperors, Roman
Rome, city of 59, 86, 89, 117, 157, 159, 161, 163, 166, 195
   declining role as imperial base 25–6, 30–1
   Gothic sack (410) 33
   sieges of 127–8, 133–5, 139, 145, 151
   Vandal sack of (455) 101, 138
   victory celebrations in 26, 31, 47–8
   victory monuments in 45, 132, 212

sacrifice (pagan) 176–7, 179, 183–5, 188
Saldum 185
salgamum 168–9
Salona 163
Samaritans 9, 38
Sapores (general) 156
Saracens 41
   see also Arabs
Sardinia 162
Sarmatians (Asiatic people) 82, 84
Sasanians *see* Persia
Saturninus (general) 156
Scaptopara 171
Scythia 109, 143
Sebastianus (general) 69, 154
self-mutilation 82–3
Selymbria 166
senate, role in appointment of emperors 53
senatorial aristocracy 43
   lack of military training 23
   liability for gold tax 88
   loss of military commands 2, 24–5
   source of emperors until mid third century 23
Septimius Severus (emperor) 10, 23, 148–9, 152
Serapis/Serapeum 195–7, 232

GENERAL INDEX

Serdica 25, 38
Severus Alexander (emperor) 23–4, 176–7
Severus of Antioch (bishop) 155
Shapur I (Persian king) 102, 111, 136
Shapur II (Persian king) 4, 102, 135–6, 206
Sicily 116
Sidonius Apollinaris (aristocrat and bishop) 34
sieges 223–4
   Germanic lack of competence 124, 222
   hazards of equipment and techniques 130, 133
   impact on civilians 133–8
   Persian competence 98, 124–5
   prominence of in late antiquity 126
Silvanus (usurper) 71
Simplicius (general) 156
Singara 118, 136–7
Sirmium 138, 166, 224
   as imperial base/capital 25, 27
Sittas (general) 71
slaves
   as booty 43, 102, 104, 111, 113, 135–8
   flight of during war 141
   owned by soldiers 87, 152–3
   release of 138
   see also prisoners of war
Slavs (Danubian people) 8, 108, 135, 210, 212
Solachon 128–9, 189
soldiers
   and alcohol 86, 137, 169–70, 175
   land ownership 87, 229
   relations with civilians 163–75
   religious allegiances 176–93, 202–5
   requisitioning 171, 174
   wills 148, 150
   wives and families of 59, 142–4, 147–53, 170, 193
   see also army, Roman
solidi (gold coinage) 48–50, 57–8, 89, 102–3
South Shields 185
Spain 118–19

Sporacius (officer) 156
statues
   equestrian, of emperors 45
   honoring deceased soldiers 129
Stilicho (general) 32–3, 70, 84, 119, 157, 159, 161
Strasbourg 38, 125–7, 223
Sueves 82, 115
suicide 135
Sura 136, 165
Symmachus (aristocrat) 154, 157–62
Synesius (philosopher and bishop) 33–4, 154–62
Syria 95, 136, 165
   economic impact of war 111–14, 137
Syriac (Aramaic dialect) 15, 151, 213

Taginae 129
taxation
   burden 88–9
   clothing (*vestis militaris*) 94
   commutation (*adaeratio*) 87
   conscription as component of 80
   foodstuffs (*annona*) 85–7
   precious metals 87–8
   remission of 108, 113, 116
   supplementary levies 97–8
temples, destruction of 194–8, 202, 204–5
Terentius (general) 156
Tertullian (theologian) 179–81
Tervingi (Gothic tribe) 7
Tetrarchy 28, 64–5, 75
Theodora (empress) 43, 71
Theodoret (bishop) 154–62, 188, 191
Theodoric (Gothic leader) 121
Theodosius (general) 71, 157
Theodosius I (emperor) 16, 31–2, 38, 45–6, 48, 64, 68, 108, 153
   background and accession 29, 54
   civil war with Magnus Maximus and Eugenius 9, 12, 29, 38, 69, 73
   first emperor to use Constantinople as base 30–1
   religious policies 184–5, 188, 204
Theodosius II (emperor) 16, 32, 38, 172
   background and accession 5, 33, 54, 215

GENERAL INDEX

wars with Persia 5, 206
Theophylact Simocatta (historian) 15
Thessalonica 45, 125, 135, 210, 213, 222
Thrace 36, 59, 145, 165, 167
   economic impact of war 107–11, 137
Thyatira 11
Tiberius II (emperor) 36, 57, 71, 78, 114, 193, 216
Tibur 224
Timasius (general) 69, 157
Timesitheus (praetorian prefect) 24
Titus (officer) 156
Totila (Gothic king) 145
Trabzon 137
Traianus (general) 156
Trajan (emperor) 22–3, 32, 41, 46, 216, 222
Trier 25, 99, 115, 157, 215
triumph ceremonies 25, 26, 47, 68–9, 101
triumphal arches 45, 132, 214
Tuscany 116, 141

Udruh 165
Umbria 163
usurpation *see* civil war

Valens (emperor) 16, 80–1
   allows Goths to enter empire 80, 108
   background and accession 29–30, 54
   civil war with Procopius 9, 29, 67
   death at Adrianople 29, 143
   war with Goths 95, 97
Valentinian I (emperor) 27–9, 42–3, 54, 61, 64, 70, 98, 209
Valentinian II (emperor) 29–30, 42–3, 68, 70, 214–15, 217
Valentinian III (emperor) 33–5, 49, 213
Valerian (emperor) 24, 97, 194
Vandals (Germanic people) 35–6, 42, 73, 84
   defeat of in Africa 69, 72, 101, 103–4, 152
   invade Gaul 115

   Leo's expedition against (468) 96, 105–6
   occupation of north Africa 7, 116, 118, 145
Varronian (father of Jovian) 28
Varronian (son of Jovian) 28
Velox (general) 163
Verina (empress) 68
Verona 132
vestis militaris 94
veterans 60
Vetranio (usurper) 67
Victor (general) 156
victory
   altar of 157
   as imperial ideal 37–50, 55–6
   celebrated in architecture and art 42–8
   celebrated in poetry 40–2
   celebrated on coinage 48–50
   ceremonial 47–8, 69–70
   columns 45–6
   imperial victory titles 39–40
   official reports of 38, 214
   personifications of 43–4, 47–9
Vienne 34
villas, economic impact of war on 108–9, 114–17
Viminacium 138
Virgin Mary, cult of 135
Visigoths (Germanic people) 35–6
Vitalian (general) 36, 70–1, 108, 212
Vulcacius Rufus (praetorian prefect) 97

weapons *see* arsenals
wills 148, 150
women
   enslavement 140, 144
   involvement in fighting 144
   problems of remarriage 138, 142
   rape of 141–2, 144–6, 169
   Vandal 72, 152
   wives of soldiers 59, 142–4, 147–53

York 67

Zeno (emperor) 35–6, 71, 83, 95, 209
   accession 56
   and civil war 9, 41, 68
   hostility toward 68

Zoroastrianism 206
Zosimus (historian) 10–11, 75, 166
Zurzach 185